THE NEWEL POST

BOOK ONE

For Illy, of course.

Published by Friendly Monster Press LLC - Portland, Oregon, USA
friendlymonsterpress.com
ISBN: 978-1-967814-00-8

THE NEWEL POST

BOOK ONE
NONREPRESENTATIONAL
CARD PANELS

THE ART OF
SCOTT CANNON

FRIENDLY MONSTER PRESS - PORTLAND, OR, USA

First, an essay in four parts
DAILY

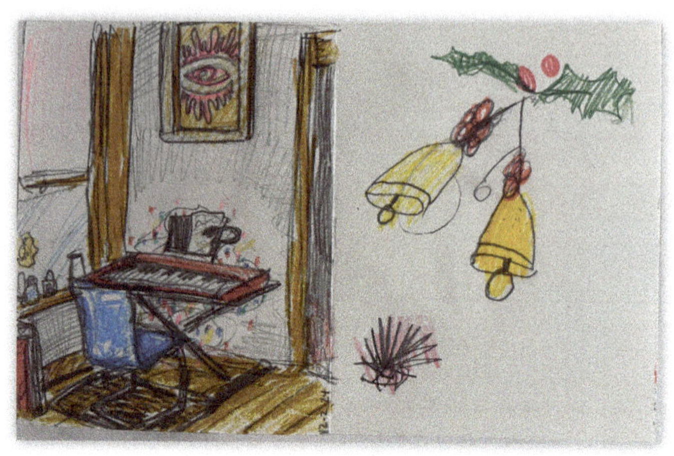

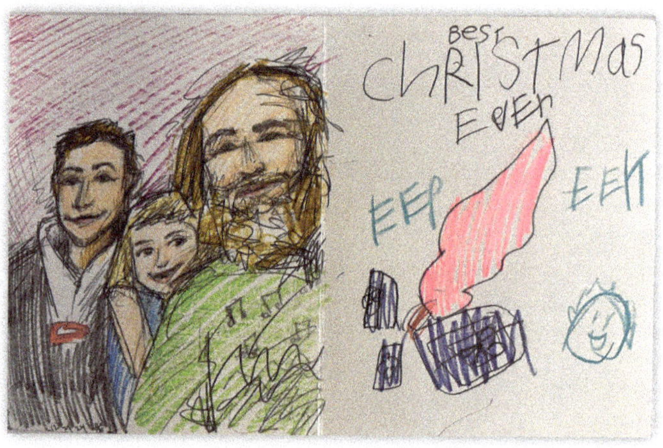

best
CHRISTMAS
EVER
EEP
EEK

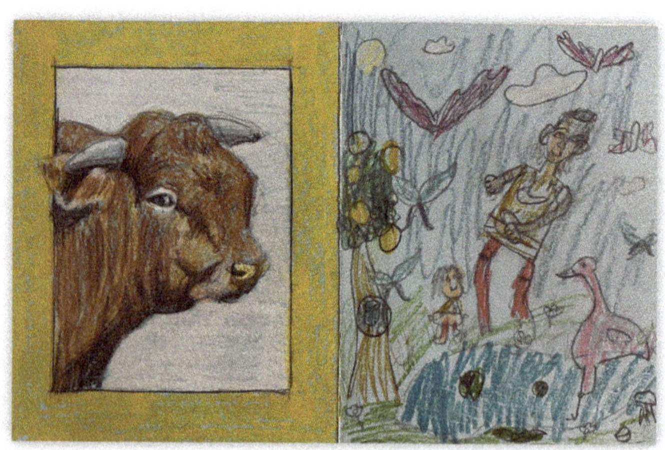

DAILY

Part One: The song of our family's day

8pm Pacific Standard Time. The transom window is hinged open, and cool evening air pours into our living room. We've just read to Illy, said our goodnights, and now it's time for me and Leana to have an hour together before she also goes to bed. We chat a bit, then put on some show or movie in the background. She unwinds from her demanding work day, follows her own hobbies, and I do what I've done most evenings for the last three and a half years: draw two panels of a four panel card for an audience of one.*

I begin by deciding what to draw. Often, something has so sparkled in the day, that's easy to choose that as the subject. As an avid journaler for years I can't help but want to capture the big and small moments in our lives. This might include an achievement like Illy passing her swim test, a beautiful flower we saw, a science or nature fact we discussed, a new interest she's found... a million things that fill her days and mine. I value this kind of drawing because it allows me to highlight her achievements and interests and to honor her unique experience in the world.

Other days I might choose to draw something that inspires me personally, some fine art or street art or product packaging. I copy a lot of Picasso because his heavily stylized lines and fields of color are often instructive to me. I like to draw Simpsons characters or

---

* *The cards are sold in a variety of colors and textures by the Paper Accents Company under the label 'Super Value Pack''. They come creased along the center and are 4.25″ × 5.5″ when folded. At the time of this printing, a pack of 300 costs $13.49 at my local art store. The collection of finished card panels following this essay are printed at actual size.*

Lego builds or sports-related things because they're things I like, and Illy likes them too.*

By far, the artist I use the most for inspiration is Illy. I love to use something she drew as a jumping off point for my art. She has her own style and makes endlessly interesting decisions. She teaches me so much about freedom and staying loose. Besides, she feels validated when I like her card enough to recreate it. Also, when I recreate anyone's art I see details I didn't notice at first. The close inspection I make when recreating her art shows me things in her process that I would have missed otherwise.

Other days, I might work on my portrait skills, an urban landscape, the inside of a room (a subject I'm increasingly attracted to) or I might let my mind and pencil wander to an imaginary place.

Finally, some days I make nonrepresentational art, or what many people call 'abstract'† art. These pieces investigate line and color and the illusion of space without focusing on a 'subject'. This final group of card panels, these nonrepresentational ones, are the only ones featured in this collection.‡

No matter what subject I choose for Illy's card, my goals remain relatively consistent.

To teach Illy about art: To show her that her choice of subject and style is boundless, to teach her the tools and archetypes of visual communication, the basics of line and form, and to encourage her to keep creating fearlessly.

To connect with Illy: I never forget my audience, and who I am to my audience. The card practice already feels so much like giving and receiving a handmade gift, that it's not much of a stretch to say it's an act of love. I think about it poetically as 'a note in the song of

---

* *Illy, you can be anything you want in this world, but I prefer you be a Cowboys fan.*

† *A master painter and YouTuber named James Gurney, to whom I owe a lot in my studies of urban landscapes, comments that all painting is abstract. The point of painting is to take the limitless detail of nature and represent it by deciding what will be simplified and what will be omitted. 'Non-representational' is perhaps a better word for what is usually called 'abstract'. In this essay, both words are used interchangeably for readability.*

‡ *In spite of having subjects, card panels in the collage-style are also included in this collection. Part Two of this essay will explain their inclusion.*

our family's day'. It's certainly an avenue of communication that I find worthy of working to maintain.

To grow as an artist myself: Portraits and figure drawing have always been areas of weakness for me, and I've seen great improvement in those areas as I've challenged myself over the past few years of this practice. I've also seen significant growth in my ability to recreate others' art, make comic strips, and more realistically capture real-life objects and places. Though I have mostly made abstract art in my life, I'm more comfortable sitting down and making abstract art today than ever before.

> *It's around 5am the next day, still two hours before I wake up. The girls are up, though. Leana feeds demanding cats, and gets breakfast going for Illy. Illy practices piano, and then moves on to find the card I've made for her on the table.* She begins on her part of the card, draws one or two panels, either in response to what I've drawn or something else entirely. She's engaging in artistic practice, working out her creative muscles first thing in the morning. She's communicating and connecting with me, making me a gift that I'll find when I wake up.*

The card practice is color-play and shape-play. It's staying loose and emotive, not too locked in or losing the fun. It's about taking chances, working on weaknesses, learning the wisdom that can only come from time and habit. It's about considering yesterday's work and asking how to improve upon it, considering the other's work and how to respond to it. It's a chance to teach and learn together, to encourage, guide, reinforce, and introduce new ideas.

There are 201 card panels in this book, but notice how much is missing. As those readers with a knack for quick calculations might have already realized, my production of two panels a day for three and a half years results in around 2,500 panels I've drawn for this practice.

------

* *For the first 2 years or so, I left the card on the newel post at the top of the stairs for Illy to find in the morning. That's where the title of this series comes from. I also enjoy the duel-meaning of 'post' in this context.*

Though this collection of abstract work is exactly the collection I want to show you, it's a small subset of what I've been working on.

Also, notice how much more is missing. Other than the occasional (and welcome) scribble on my panels and the few cards shown alongside this essay, Illy's work isn't represented in this book. She's made about 1,600 card panels in this time, almost none of which are included here. This book is like listening to part of a stranger's conversation on the phone next to you, wondering, *What's the person on the other end of the line saying?*

This is only Book One in The Newel Post series, and in future books we will highlight Illy's work.

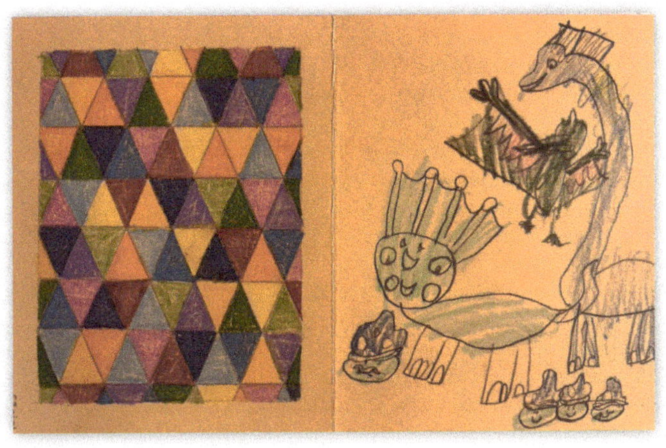

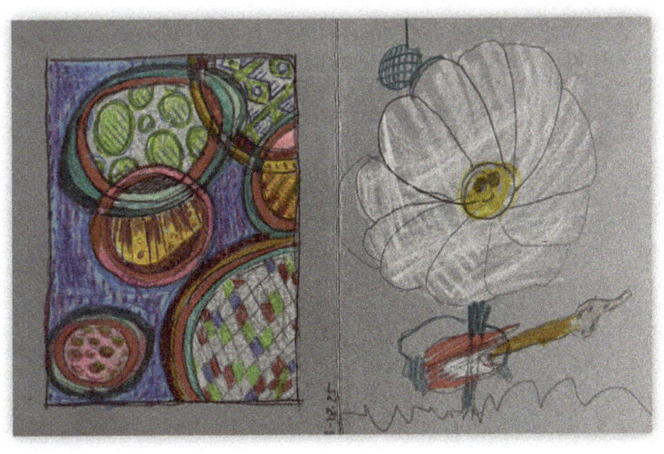

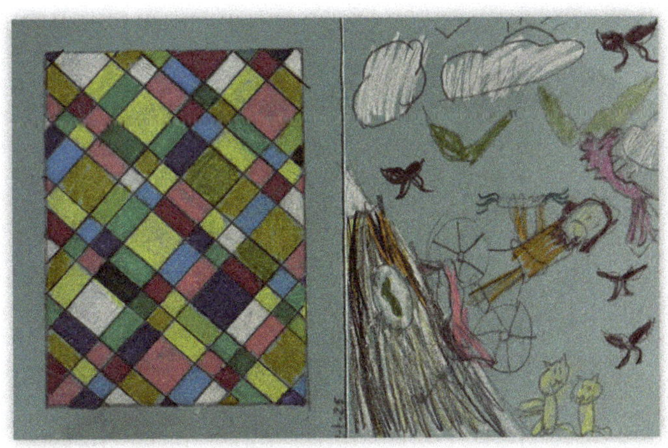

Part Two: A brief catalogue, 21 years of learning to art

Time machine, 2004 in Arlington, Texas. On my breaks working as the overnight supervisor at a 24-hour Starbucks, I began experimenting with intricate collage drawings using ultra-fine point Sharpie markers. First, I filled a small 4″ × 6″ Moleskine notebook with a sort of relentless doodling inspired by street art, tattoo flash, ornament, and organic life. Every page was a borderless, seething mass of intertwining patterns, objects and animals.

The style demanded a slow pace, and the result was impressive in its way. This was the first time since childhood that I was excited about my drawing. While this sort of doodling collage is not technically abstract, it is centerless enough to have a similar viewing experience, and is the origin of my appreciation for ornament.[*]

I switched to working on larger scale pieces in this style on fine paper or mat board. My largest was 3' × 3' and the details continued to get tighter and tighter as I delved deeper into the form. While a small Moleskine page took me a couple hours to fill up, these pieces took up to six weeks to finish. I would come home from work at dawn to the tiny[†] apartment I shared with a friend just off of UTA campus. I'd draw for hours just to finish a few square inches before passing out as the rest of the city went to work.

I held my first art show in 2004 at a local coffee shop across from City Hall in Arlington. I couldn't afford high-quality prints at this time, so I went to a local blueprint shop and hired them to make prints on their large format printers. It was a cost-effective, if not professional solution. To this day, my friends and family still send me pictures of the large prints from this show framed and hung up in their homes.

I stepped away from visual art for a long time to pursue alcoholism and woodworking. In a stroke of cosmic luck, I would end up coming back to this style of art nearly a decade later, now an adult student

---

* *There's a book called <u>The Grammar of Ornament</u> by Owen Jones that was an invaluable reference and source of inspiration for me when I was starting out. I recommend it for anyone interested in learning more about the evolution of graphic patterns throughout the world.*

† *...and filthy*

stylized paintings of Cafe Bustelo cans and nostalgic baseball scenes. I showed them at the East Austin Studio Tour in 2019.

More and more, woodworking overtook painting as my main artistic practice, I made spoons, picture frames, and even a few outdoor structures. Steady business allowed me to buy equipment for a hobby woodshop in my home in Austin, and to this day woodworking remains one of my favorite pasttimes.

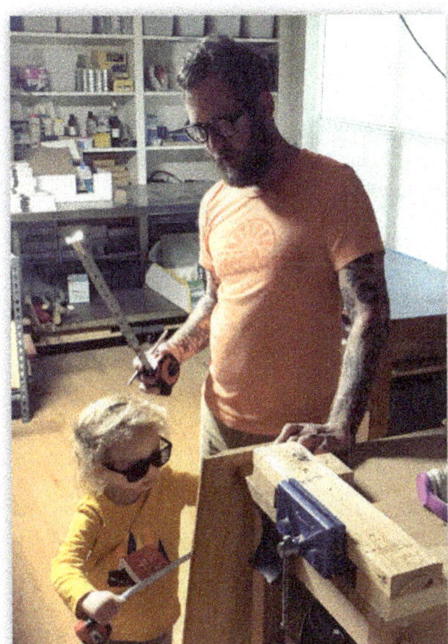

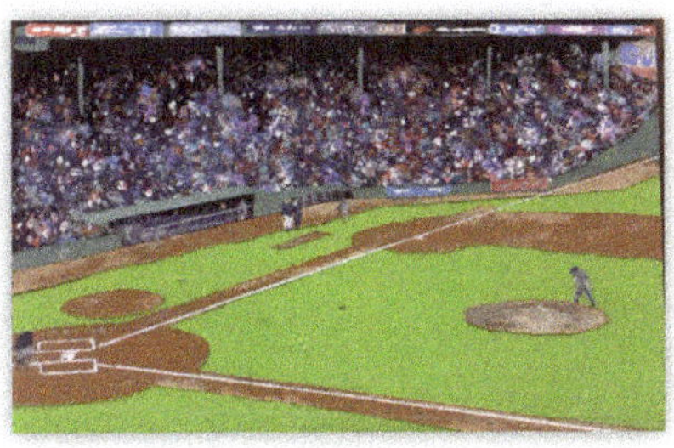

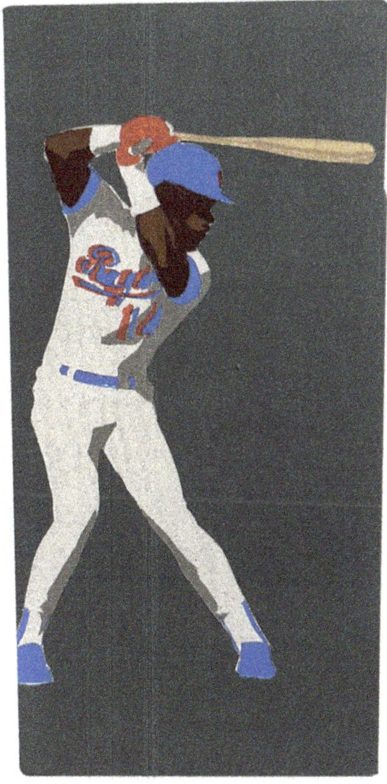

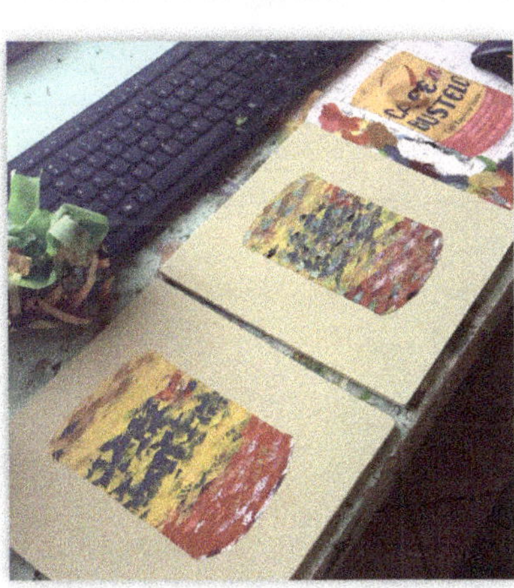

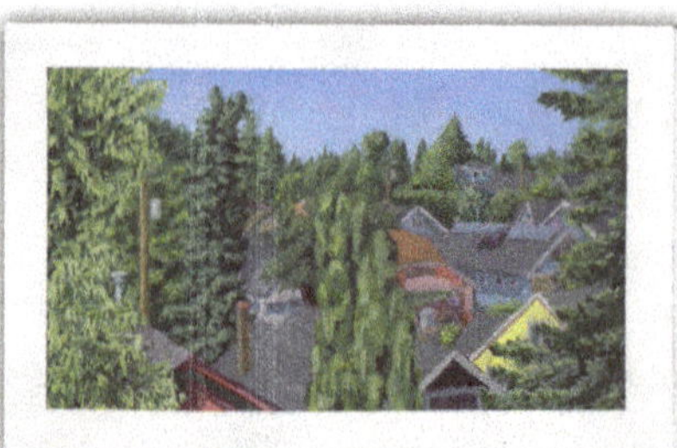

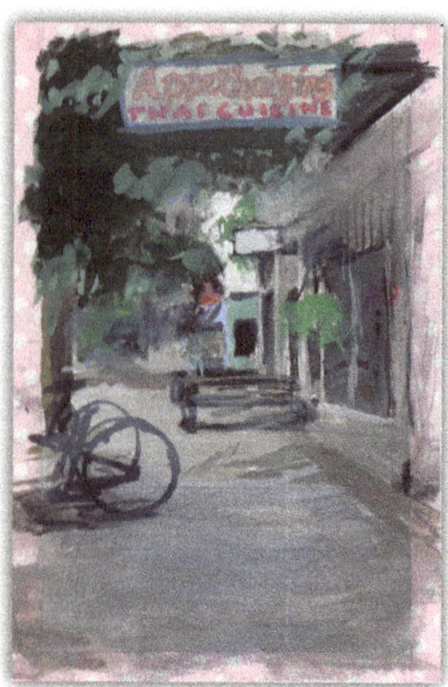

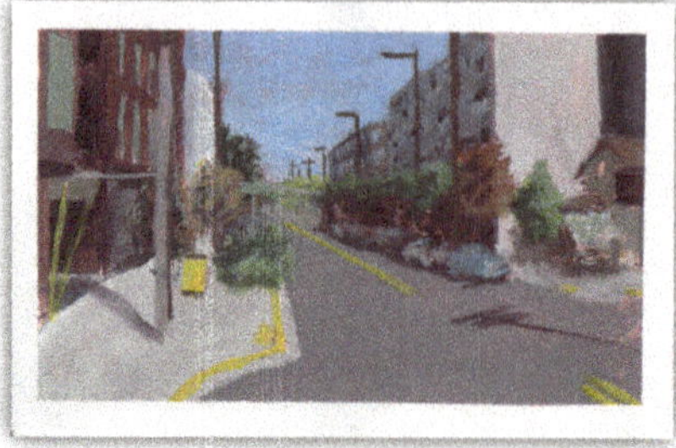

I continued to make art sporadically as we prepared to move, but mostly had to put it down until we landed and got settled again in Portland, Oregon. Here, in this beautiful city, I took up urban landscape painting in gouache, and had an art show in that style called "Attempts" at the Fresh Pot on Hawthorne in the fall of 2021.[*]

The collaborative card practice described in Part One, from which the following collection is taken, began in July 2022 and continues through the time of this printing in early 2026. Though I'd dabbled in colored pencils before, this was the first time I'd used the medium on a regular basis since childhood. The application of the colored pencil medium to the style I worked on with acrylic paints and masking showed a surprising benefit: the setup was so much faster. No masking! No waiting for paint to dry or washing brushes! This allowed me to go from producing a piece in four to six hours to producing a piece in an hour or less. I could experiment more and

---

[*]   *There were around 40 pieces in this show, but 34 of the pieces were of the same subject: the view out our window from our apartment overlooking the Richmond neighborhood. The show was called "Attempts" because I attempted to paint the same scene every day to see how much I could improve. The answer was, I improved a lot at it. I could go on and on about this time in my life, but that's for another book.*

ask myself more complicated questions of what's possible in the space and time allowed.

Previously, when working with the acrylic paints, the practice could feel exacting, demanding sharp lines and clear intentions. But with this practice and the limited time constraints, I accept the looseness of it. I'm happy to see the sketchy guide-lines and something less than perfect color coverage. That's also for Illy, to tell her that art doesn't need to seek perfection to be perfect.

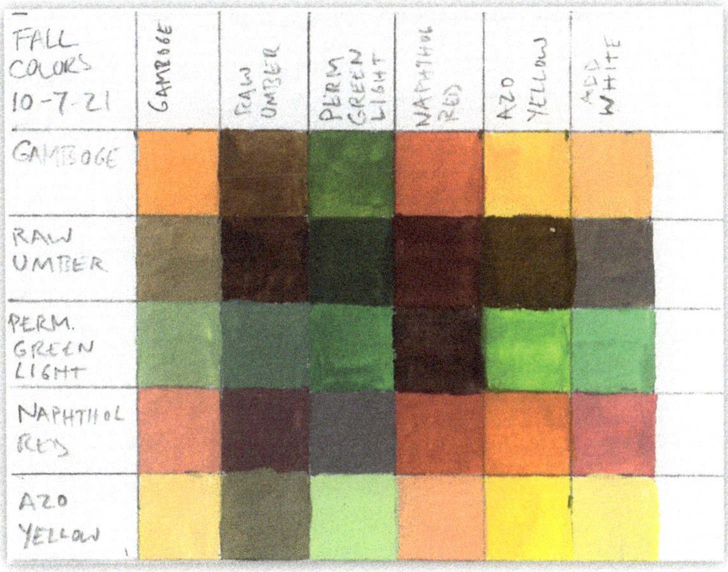

FALL COLORS 10-7-21	GAMBOGE	RAW UMBER	PERM GREEN LIGHT	NAPHTHOL RED	AZO YELLOW	ADD WHITE
GAMBOGE						
RAW UMBER						
PERM. GREEN LIGHT						
NAPHTHOL RED						
AZO YELLOW						

Part Three: Study is the second most authentic form of flattery

I make centerless art because I want people to stop and look at it for longer than a glance. I want people to spend time inspecting the bare fields of color that ask clear questions. I want people to spend time with competing static that only reveals itself as intentional upon closer inspection. I hope that in employing this centerless strategy, I reward the viewer's attention, that they drift along the map I made as they wish, and discover more the longer they look.

As to the format of this book, it seems to me to be both the perfect way to show this art and also an ineffective way to show this art considering my stated goal of prolonged viewer engagement.

It's perfect because these panels are not for sale, nor are they easy to display as a collection in a show, but they are easy to organize and display in the book format.* Even if the pieces were for sale, I would still value this format for its accessibility. For a small sum, you can enjoy all of this art in any way you'd like, on the comfort of your own toilet, perhaps. In this format, there's no limit to how many people might get the chance to engage with this art. As the artist, this seems perfect.

At the same time, this format seems a terrible fit for encouraging the kind of interaction I hope for. Each of these panels was created to be considered alone, to reward attention. I hoped that each of them would hold in it the voice I heard inside my head when I drew; that you would hear the questions I asked myself when I made each panel, and see the answers for yourself.

I worry that flipping through this collection as one might enjoy a magazine in a waiting room feels a bit overwhelming. I personally get

---

The collection would be even easier to display on a website or social media, and probably even more people could be reached, but something about that idea doesn't work for me. Perhaps it's that we now spend so much time looking at screens, they work like numbing filters, graying out the details in the hurry and flood of content. Maybe it's thinking about all the ads you'd see, all the clicks you'd need to get through the collection, the way every app on your phone competes with every other app... At least this book is only this book. Single-ingredient reality, dude.

dizzy with the spin of it. To paraphrase one of my favorite bands, The Elected, it's like eating too much butter, or drinking too much rum.

To that end, I wonder if I might ask that sometimes you cover one side of the book and consider a panel all by itself. Spend time with it, the way I did, like we're both watching the same thing being built.

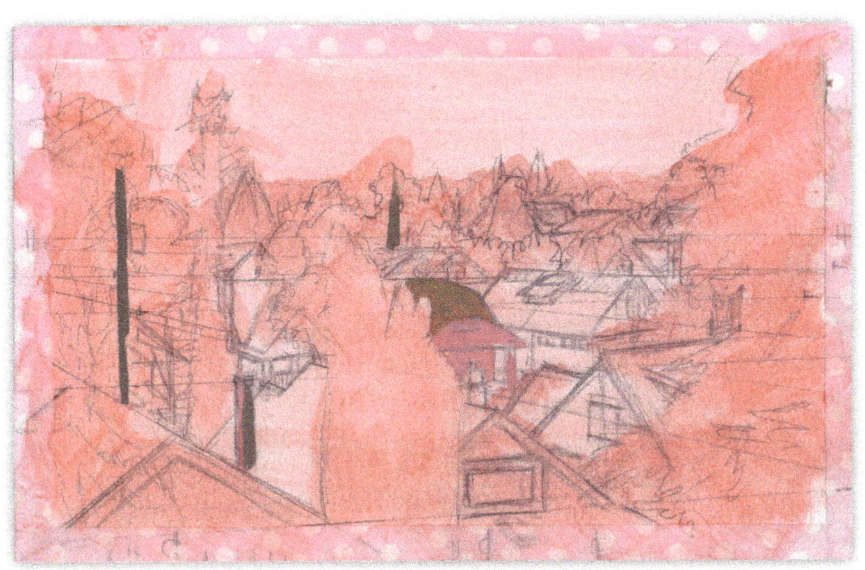

Part Four: Grandma makes art like the sun makes shine

Susie Moore is Illy's Grandma, my mom. It would be impossible to tell the story of my artistic journey without her. My earliest childhood memories of art and craft are of my mom tamping almost dry brushes dusted with pink chalk paint through stencils onto farmhouse-style furniture. I remember the kiln in the garage, surrounded by porcelain figures in various stages of glaze, and doing the craft show circuit for a while.

Twenty years ago and more, after I'd moved out of the house, she found scrapbooking. In spite of working long hours at a local radio station, she dove into her new hobby headfirst. Night after night, and year after year, she honed her skills and filled countless books with ever-improving pages of our family's now memorialized memories.

In the end, I think it's fair to say she mastered scrapbooking. If she'd had a mind to, she probably could have been nationally famous in those circles, but that never seemed to interest her. Instead, she was content to run a scrapbooking retreat space with her handy husband, Randall, in a beautifully restored farmhouse in Maypearl, TX. They created the space that she had always wanted for her and her crafty friends, and over the years, hundreds of women enjoyed spending time there connecting and creating together.

Susie shifted from scrapbooking to cardmaking somewhere along the way, and for a decade she made a new card every day. Unlike me, who hoards their cards like a dragon, she freely mails hers away to loved ones. I have quite a collection of her work myself, and I assume there's a large circle of people who are also blessed to receive her art in the mail.

She still makes papercraft often, but has also delved into restoring furniture. Always a keen eye for diamonds in the rough, and never one to shy away from a tedious task, she's brought a lot of beautiful pieces back to life.

Even when she's not making art or making sawdust, she's playing art-focused games on her phone or learning about new methods or tools. This woman is addicted to color and craft, an artist through and through. To this day, you'll still most likely find her in her magazine-worthy papercraft room creating magic.

I learned from her to find the beauty in old things, that art requires work, and that a skill is most rewarding when done often. Her example of daily practice resonates through my art and throughout my life. Her work ethic is something I don't even bother aspiring to, but I learned from her how to show up every day and practice my art.

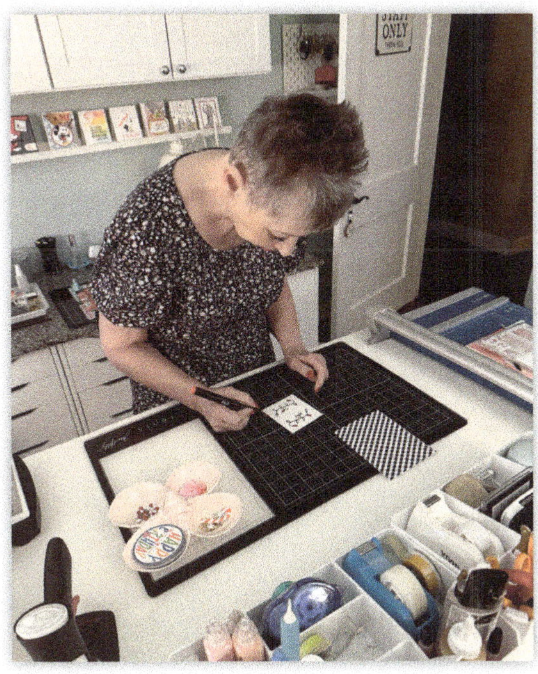

We are different. Where I am loose, she is exacting. She would never suffer the smudges and off-kilter alignment of my art. The love and care she feels when she creates remains in the perfection of the finished product. That is to say, I hear the question she asked herself when she made the art, and I see the answers clearly for myself.

Where she is exacting, I am loose. There's something in leaving the process visible that I like. There's something in leaving in the mistakes, or the sketch lines, or the first try that seems to me to mirror the hectic edges of reality. Maybe it's just that I'm lazier than my mom, and my gen-x[*] ethos chooses the path of least resistance to success. Whatever the reason for the divergence in our styles, I'm proud to present this collection to you, something wholly different from what my artist mother would make, but impossible to make without her.

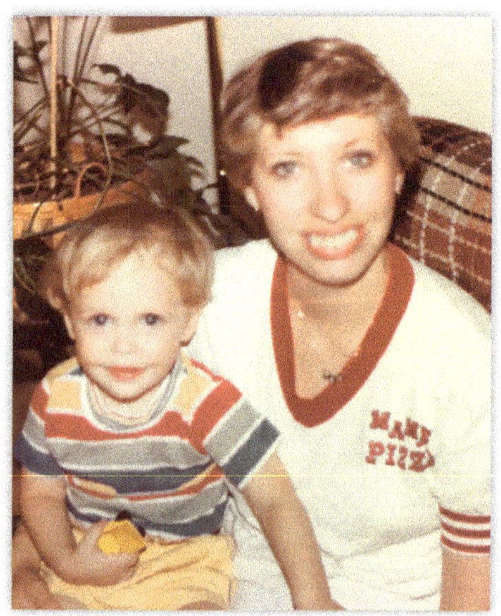

** Technically I'm an elder-millennial, but considering I only learned that term in the editing process for this book, I don't feel like I'm part of anything but happily lost in the crack between generations; and I can't think of a more gen-x sentiment than that.*

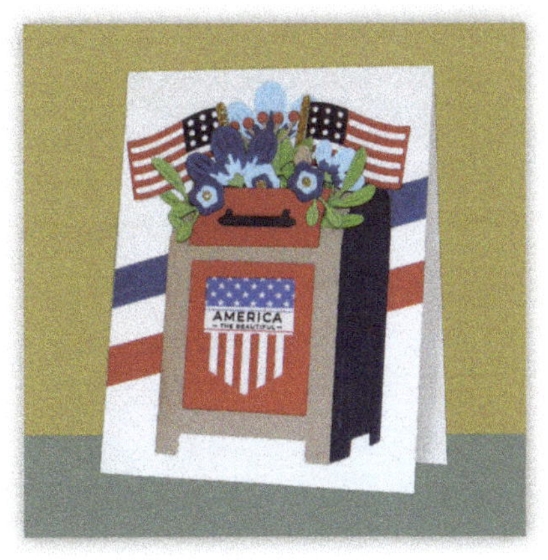
AMERICA
THE BEAUTIFUL

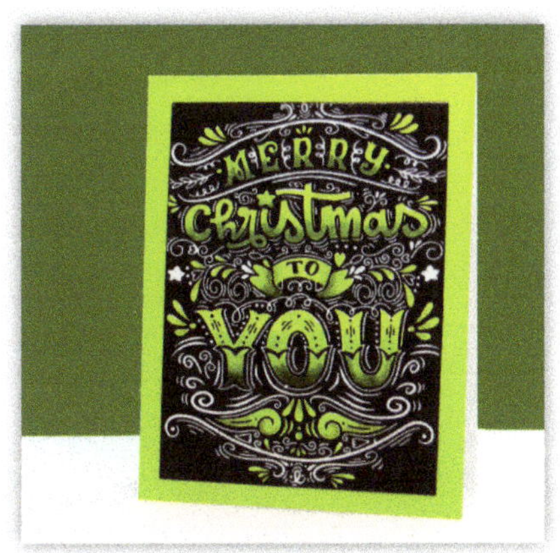
MERRY
Christmas
TO
YOU

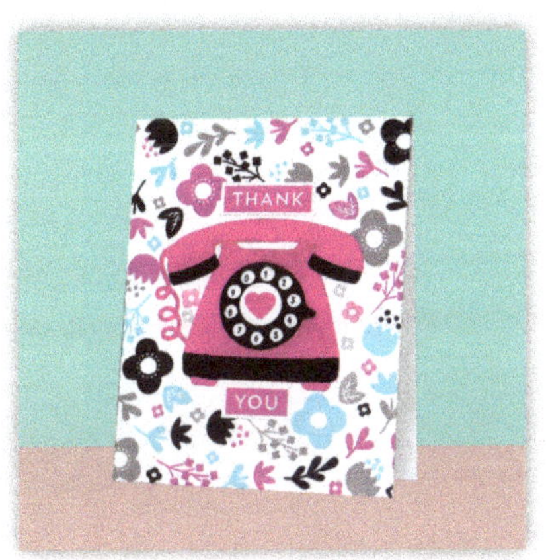
THANK
YOU

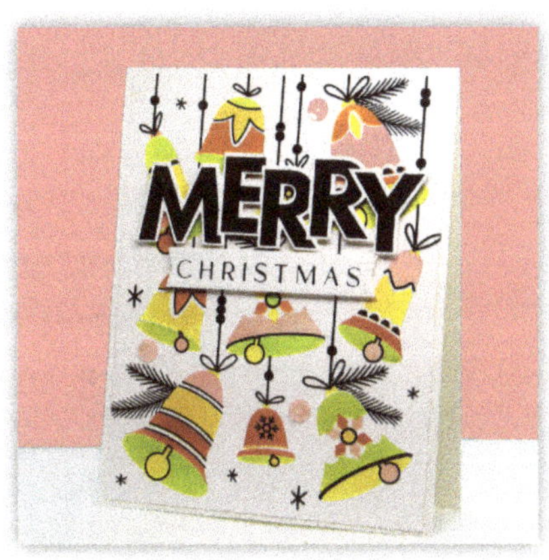
MERRY
CHRISTMAS

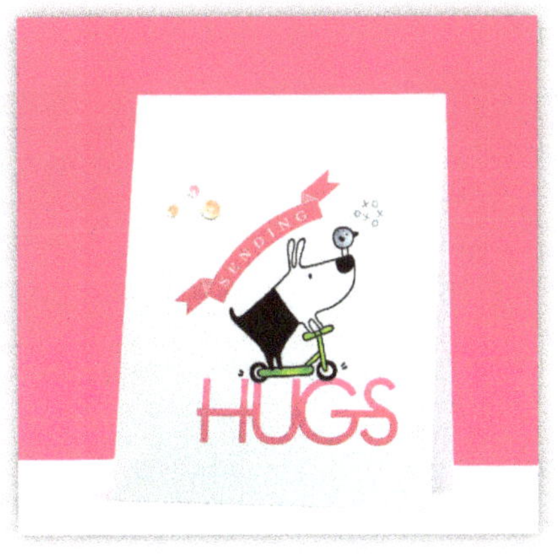
SENDING
HUGS

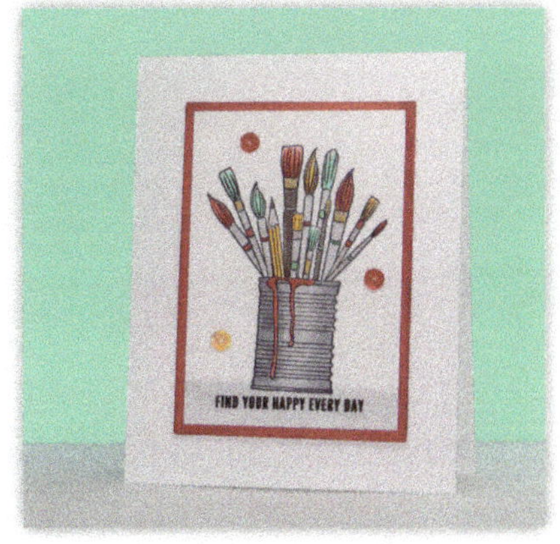
FIND YOUR HAPPY EVERY DAY

Now,
201 Nonrepresentational Card Panels

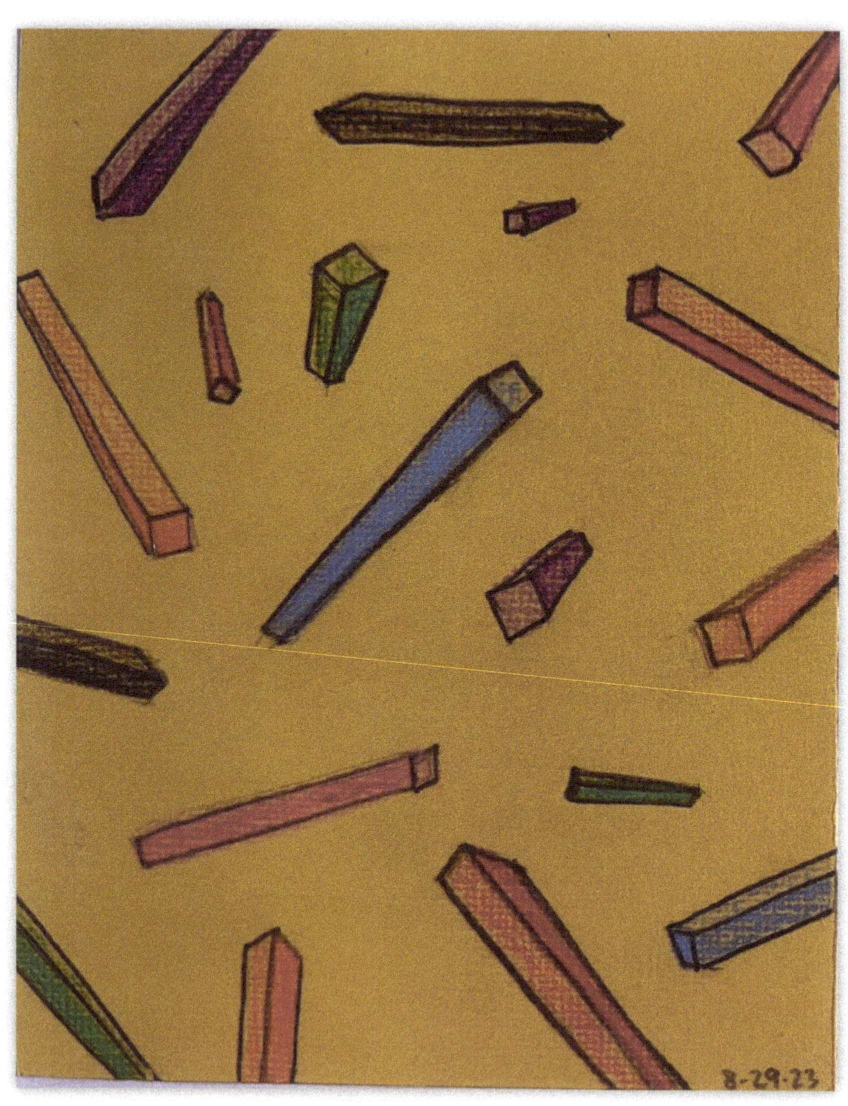

8-29-23

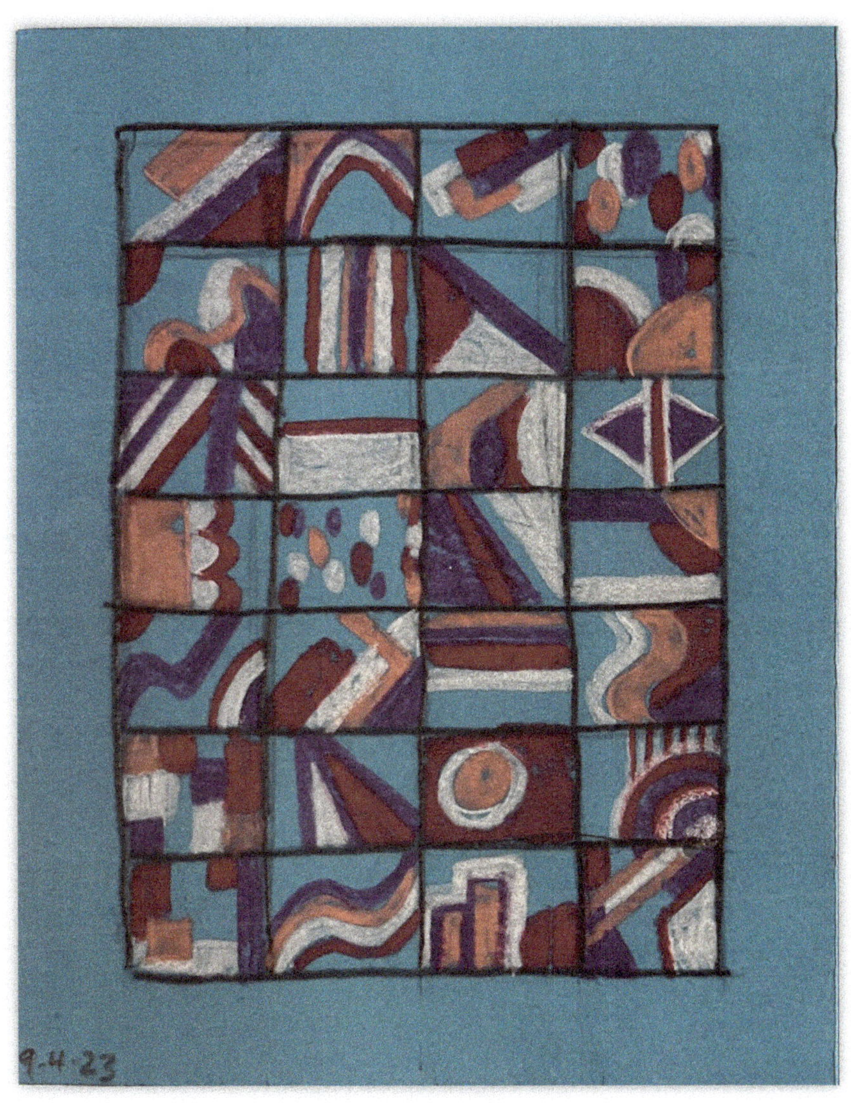

9·4·23

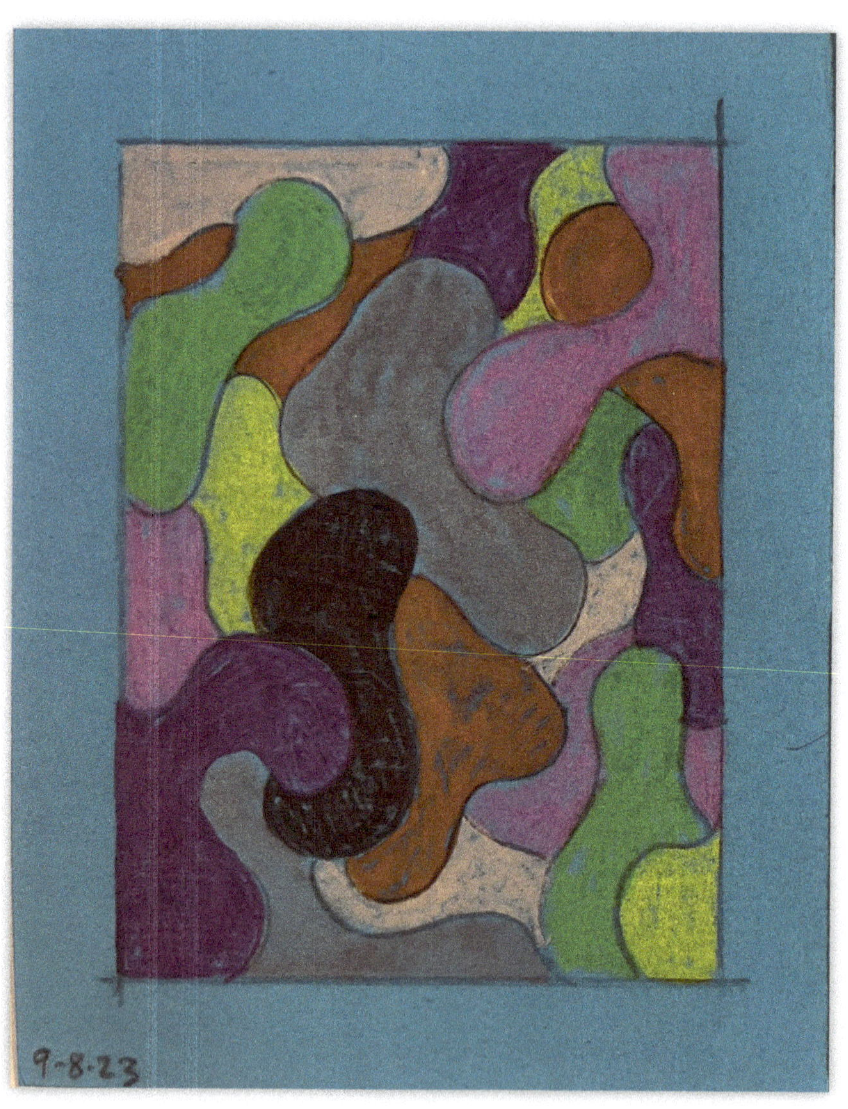

9-8-23

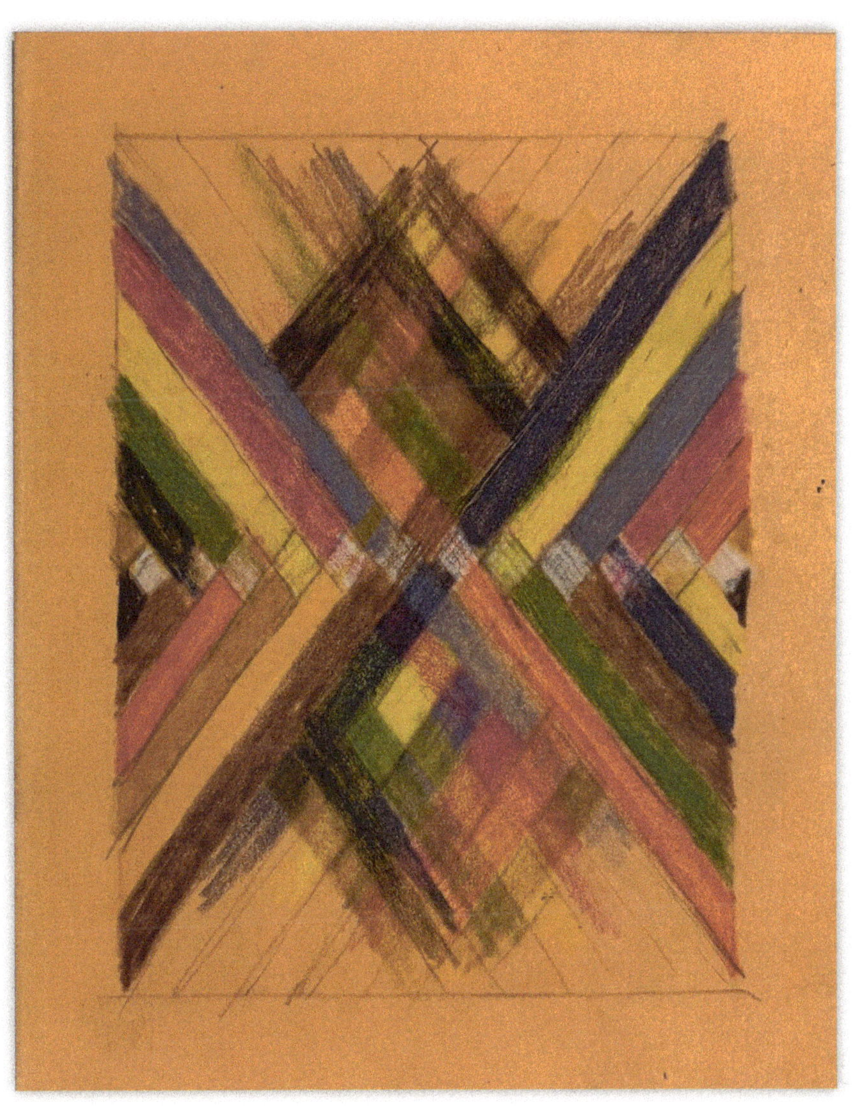

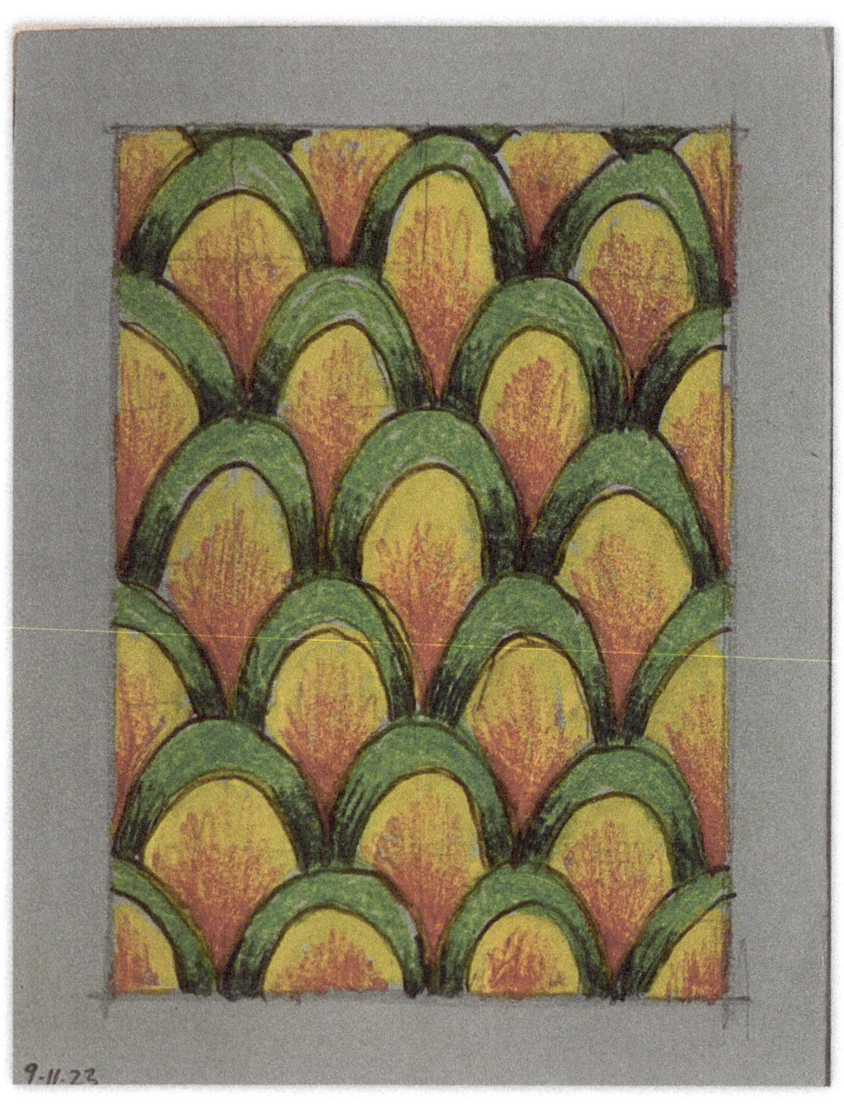
9-11-23

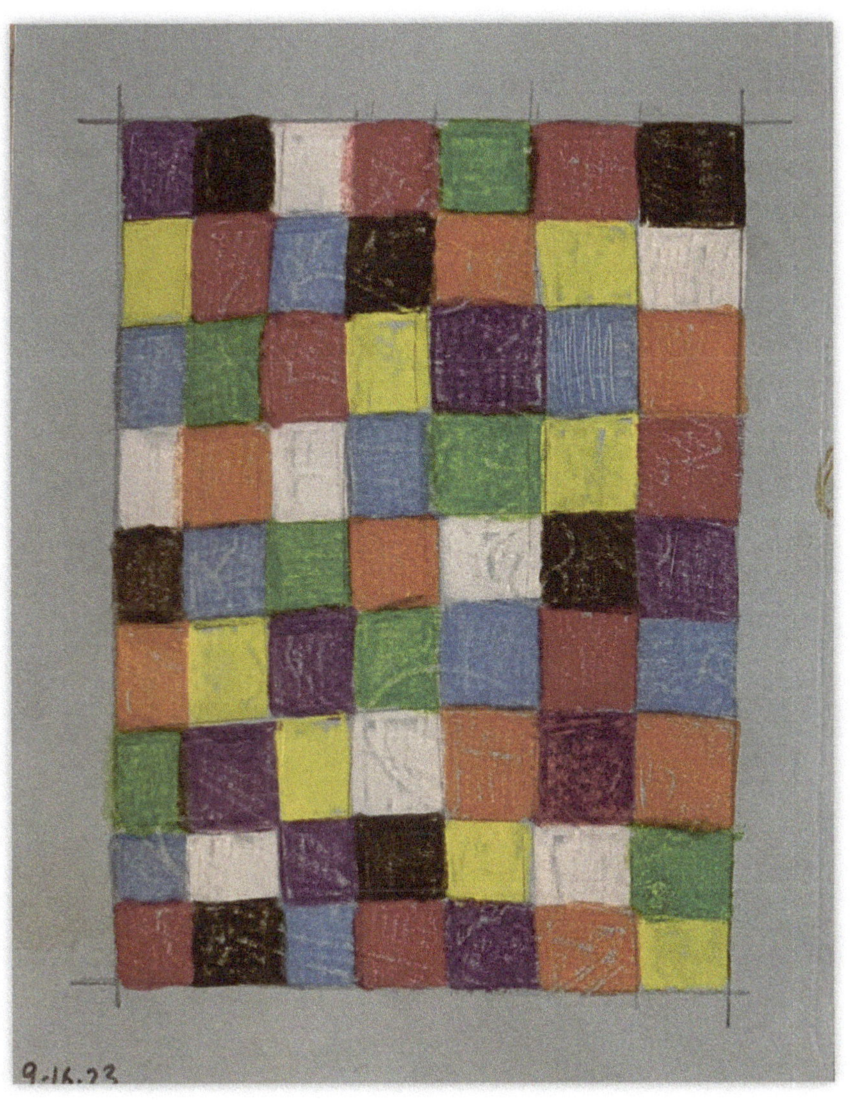

9.16.23

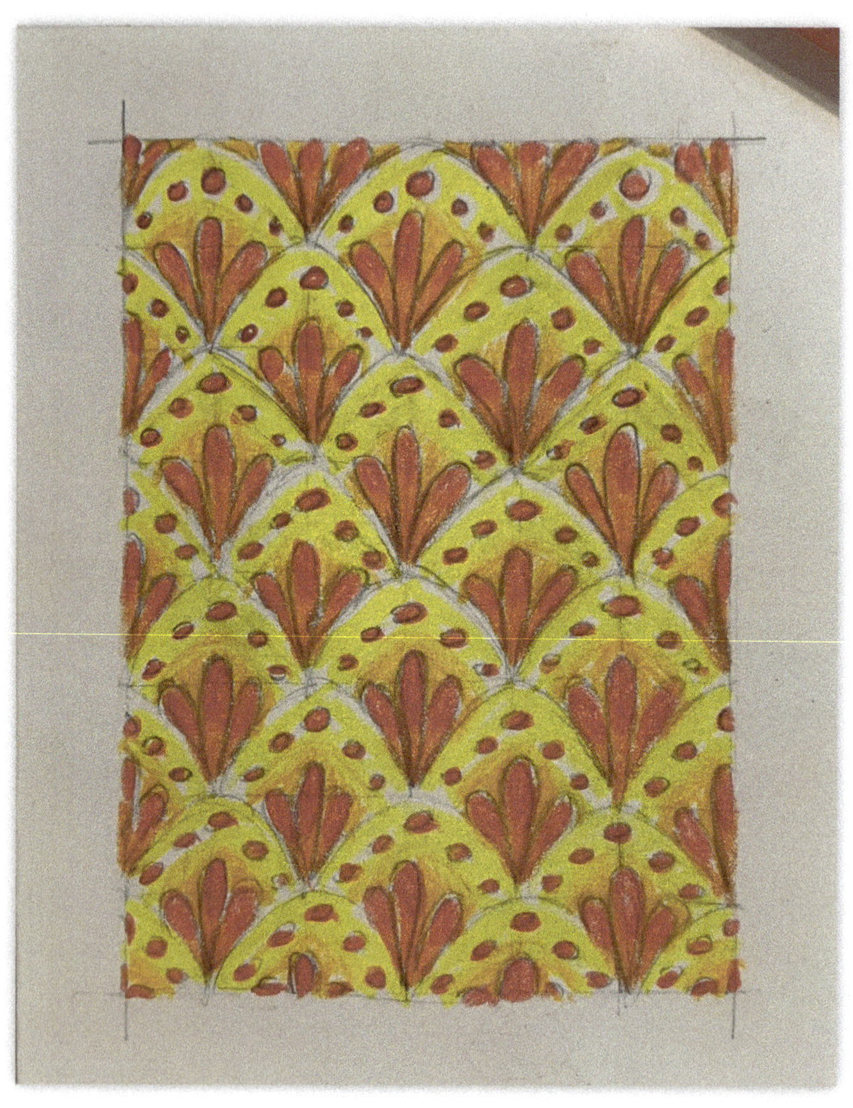

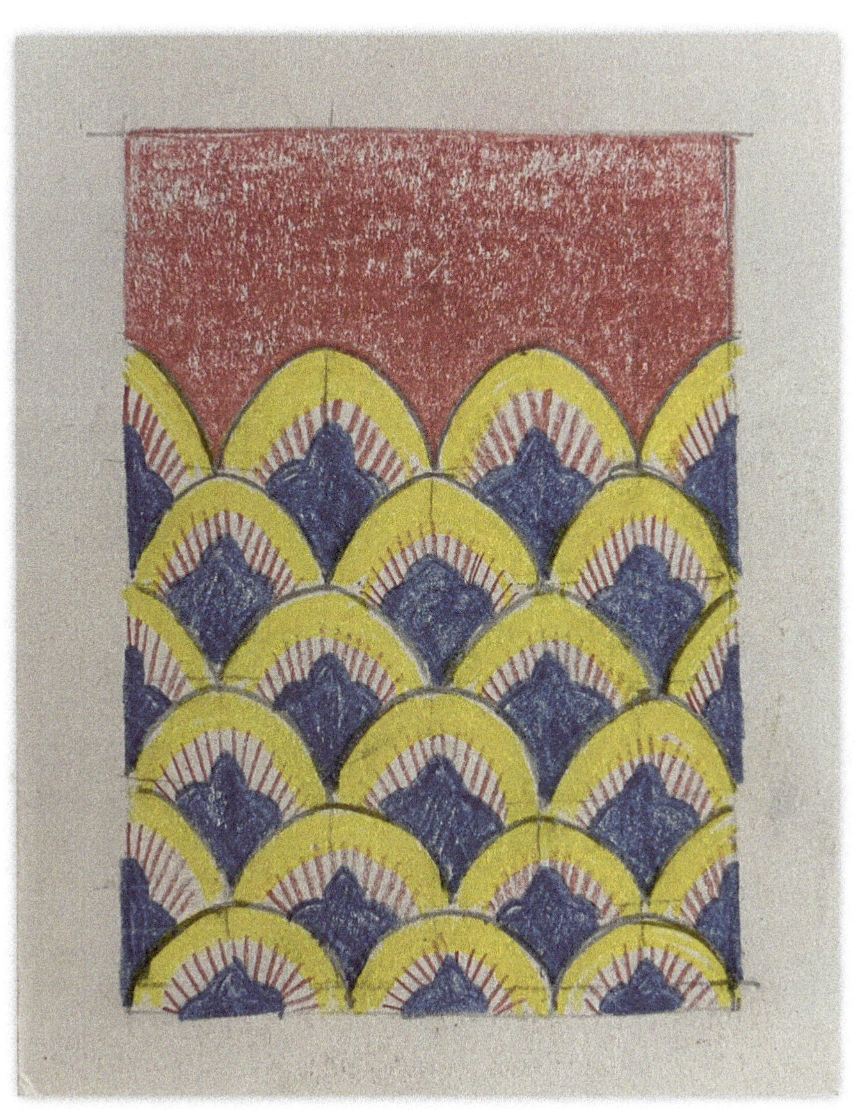

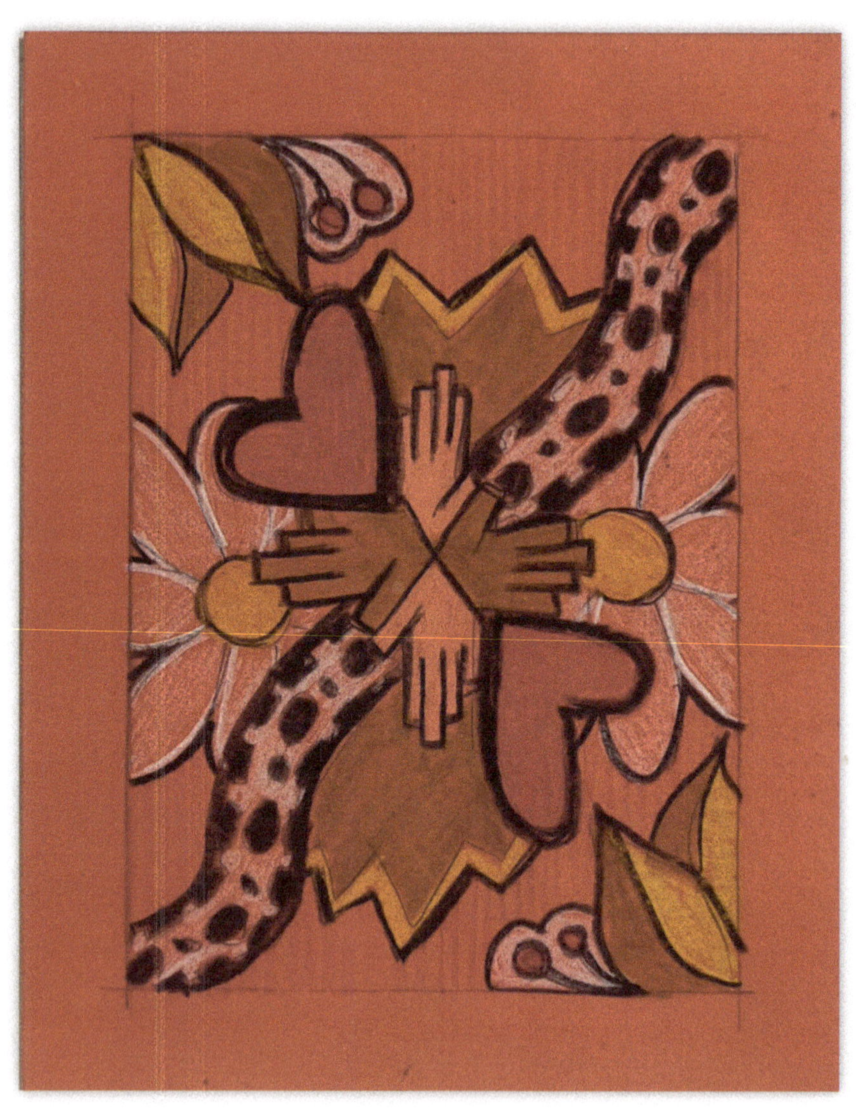

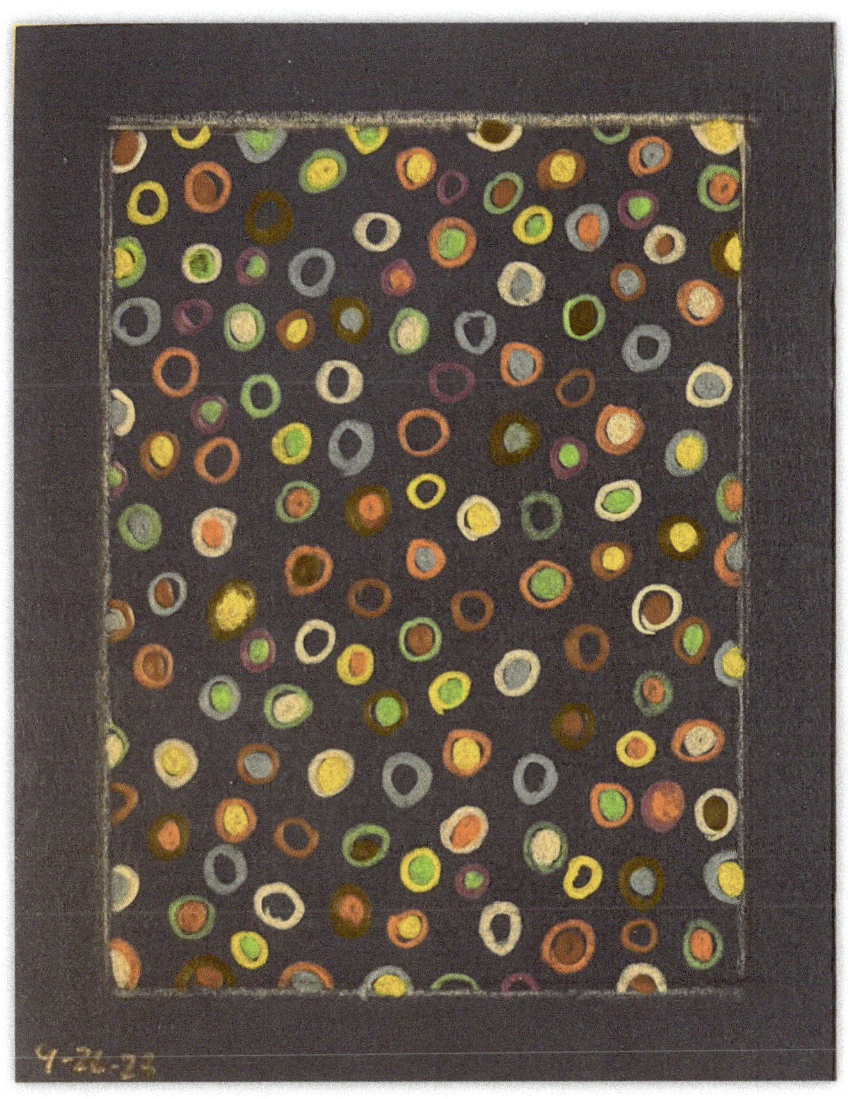

4-26-29

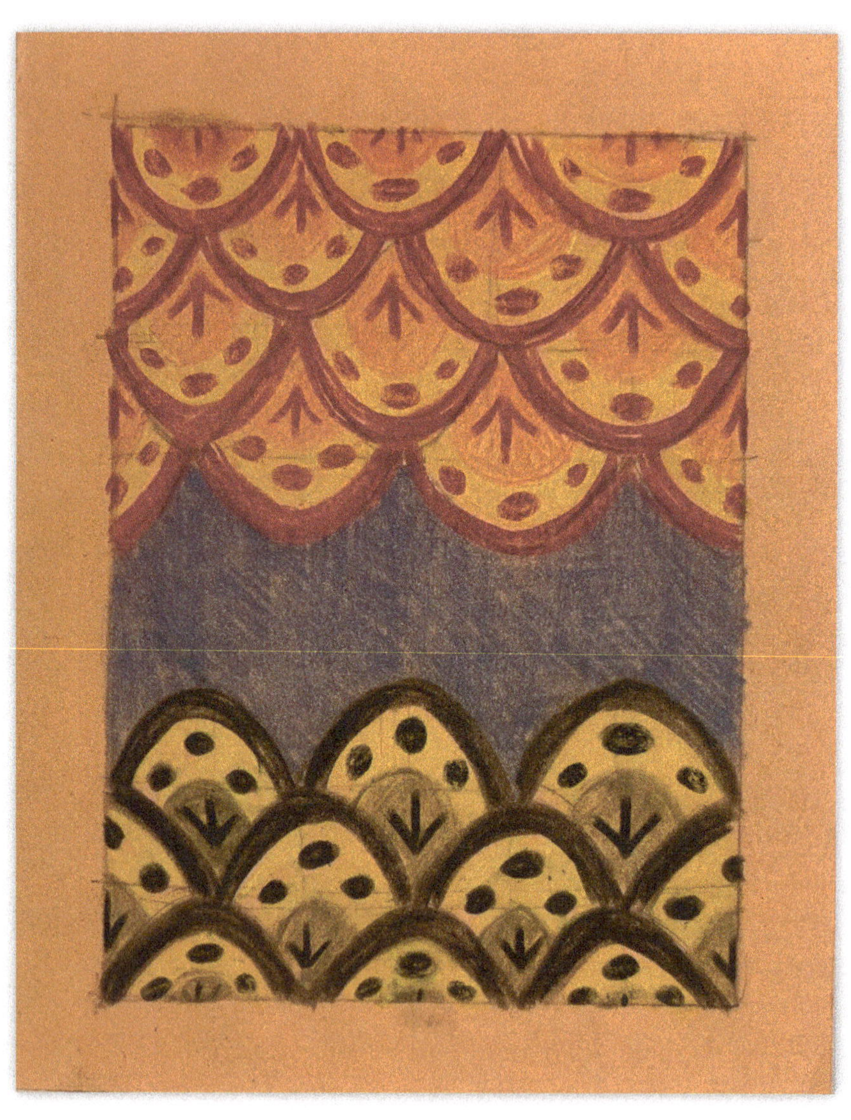

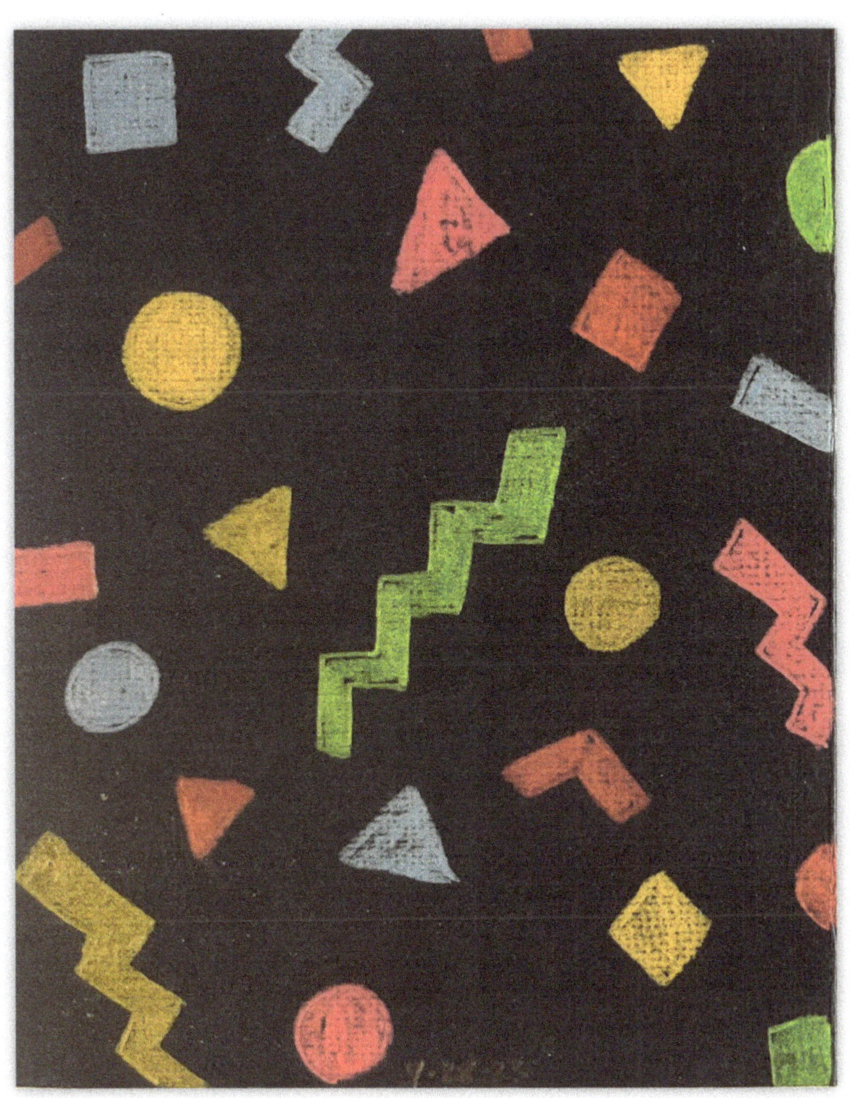

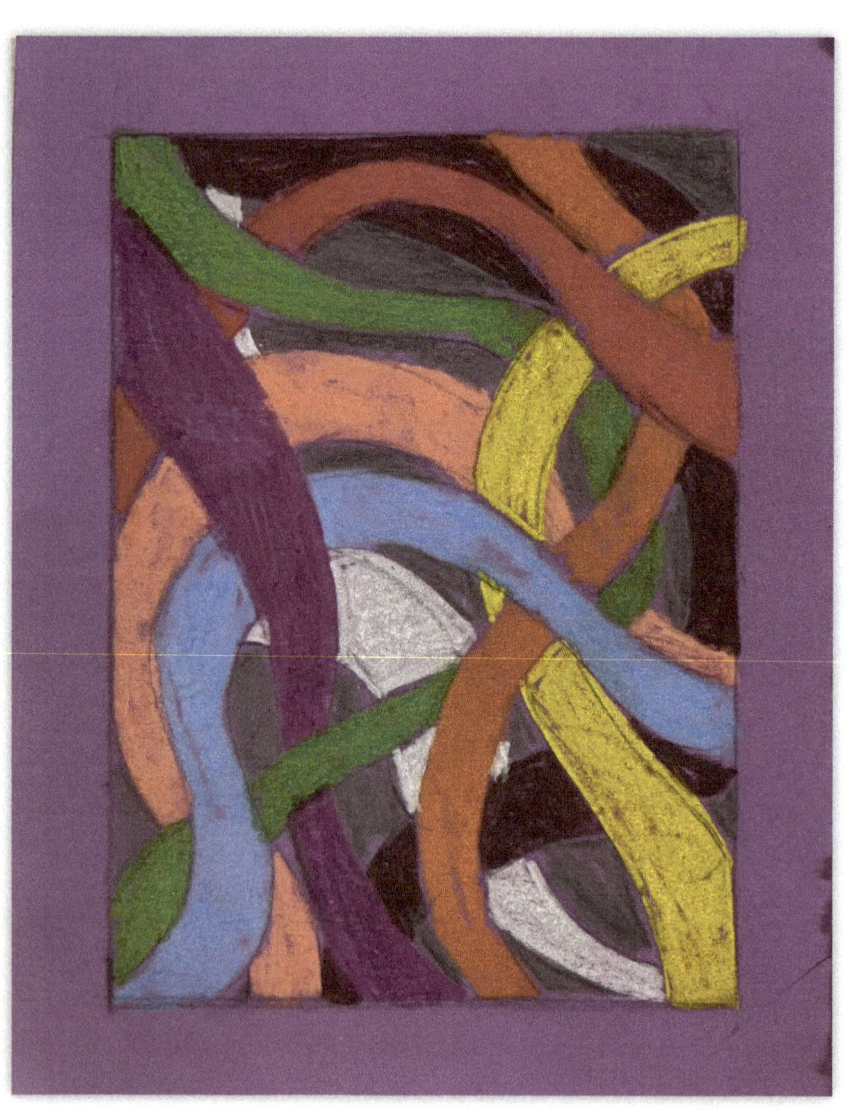

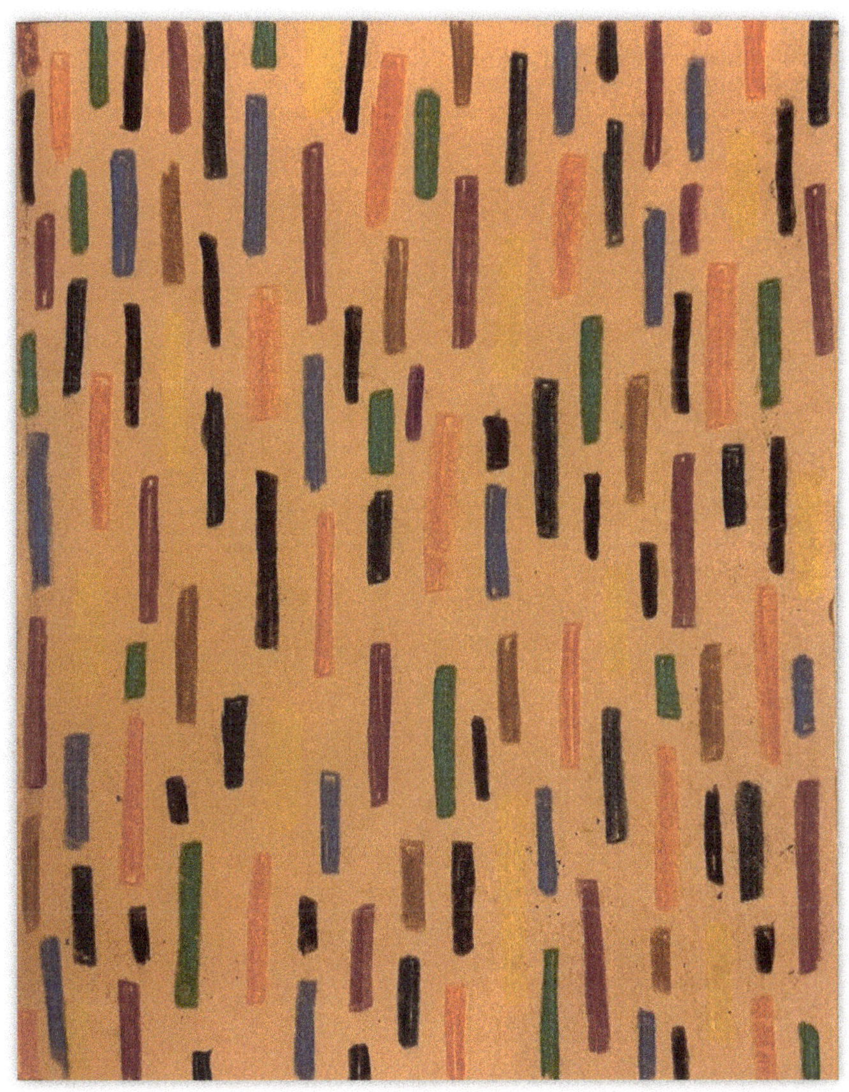

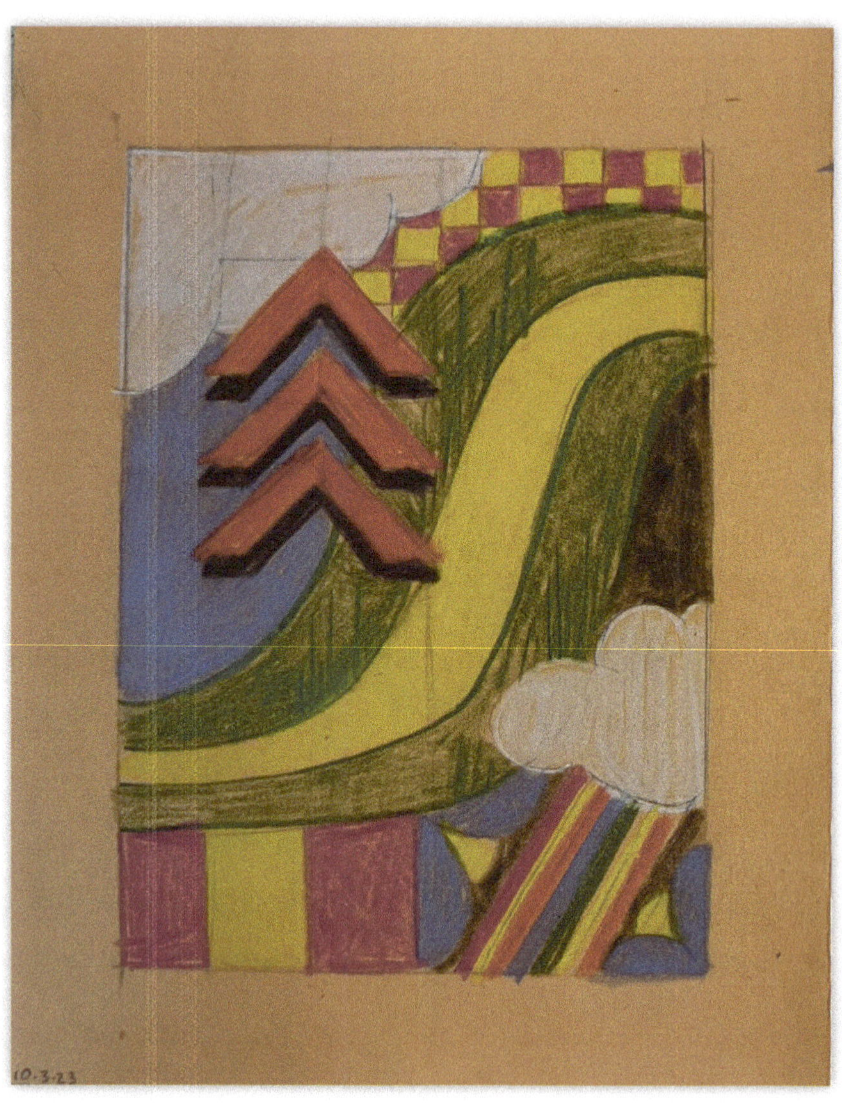

10·3·23

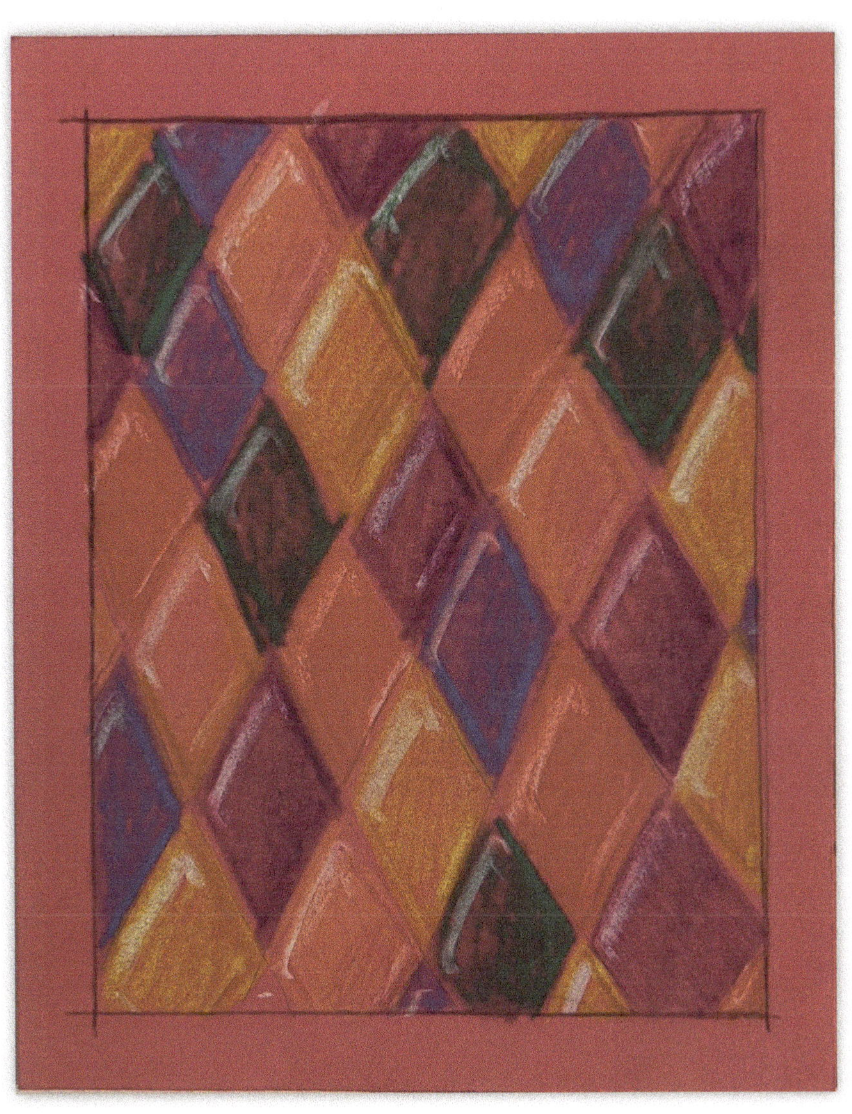

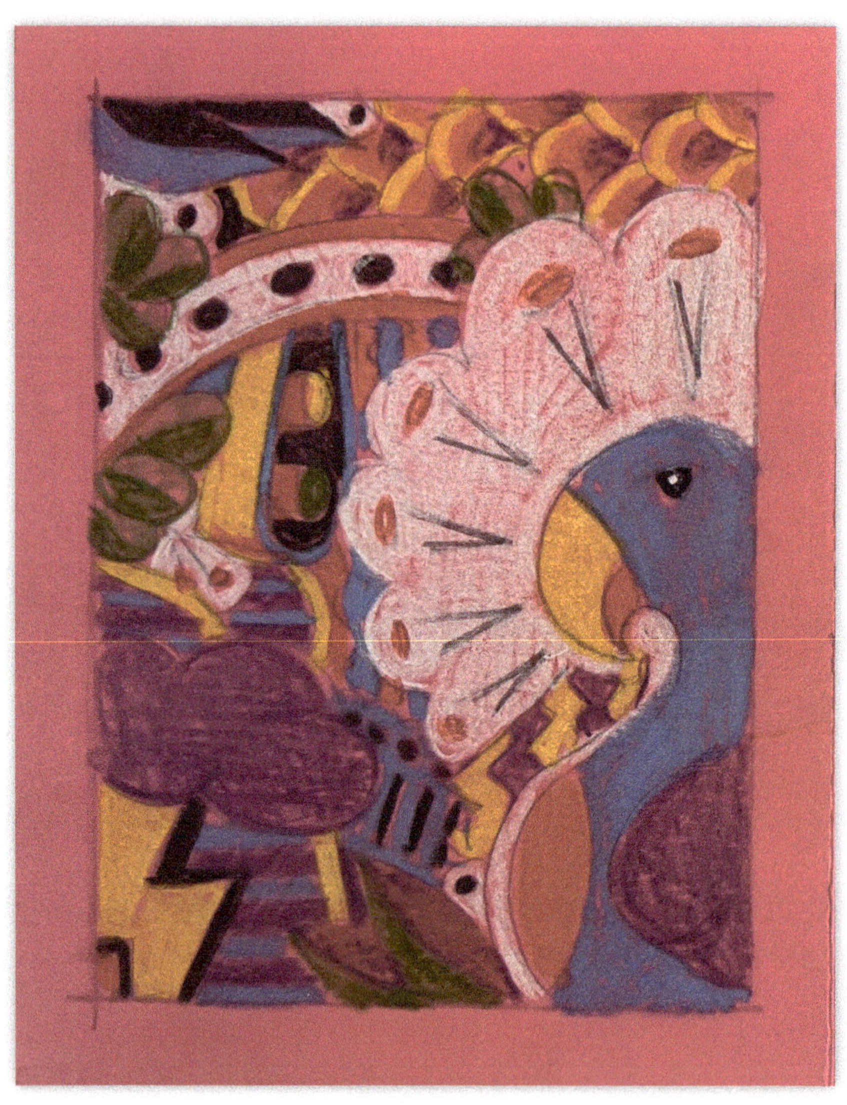

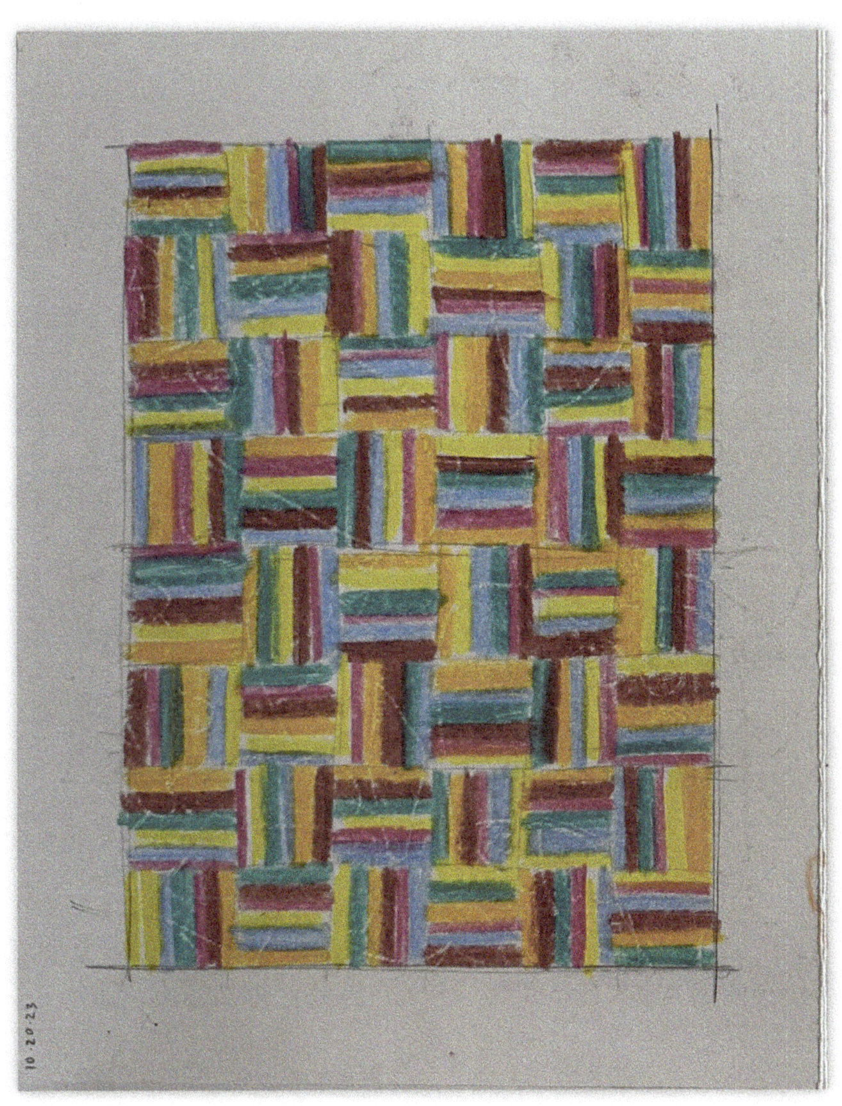

45

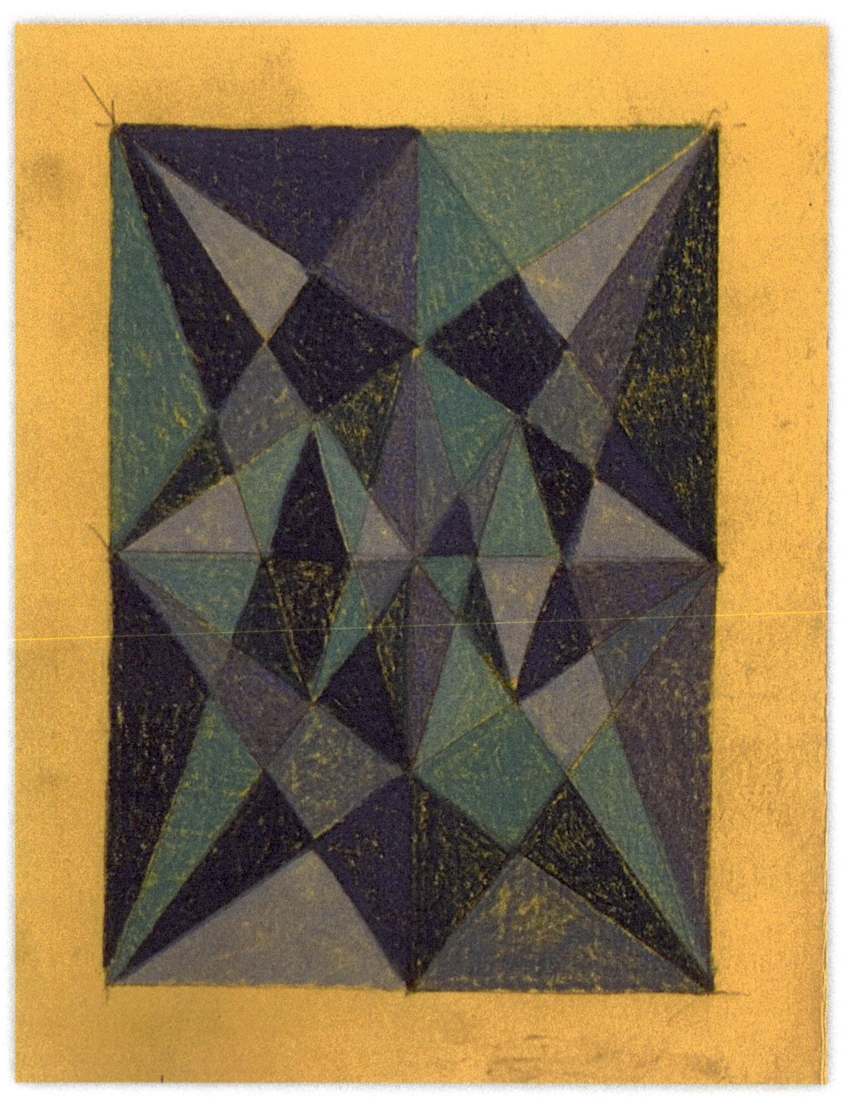

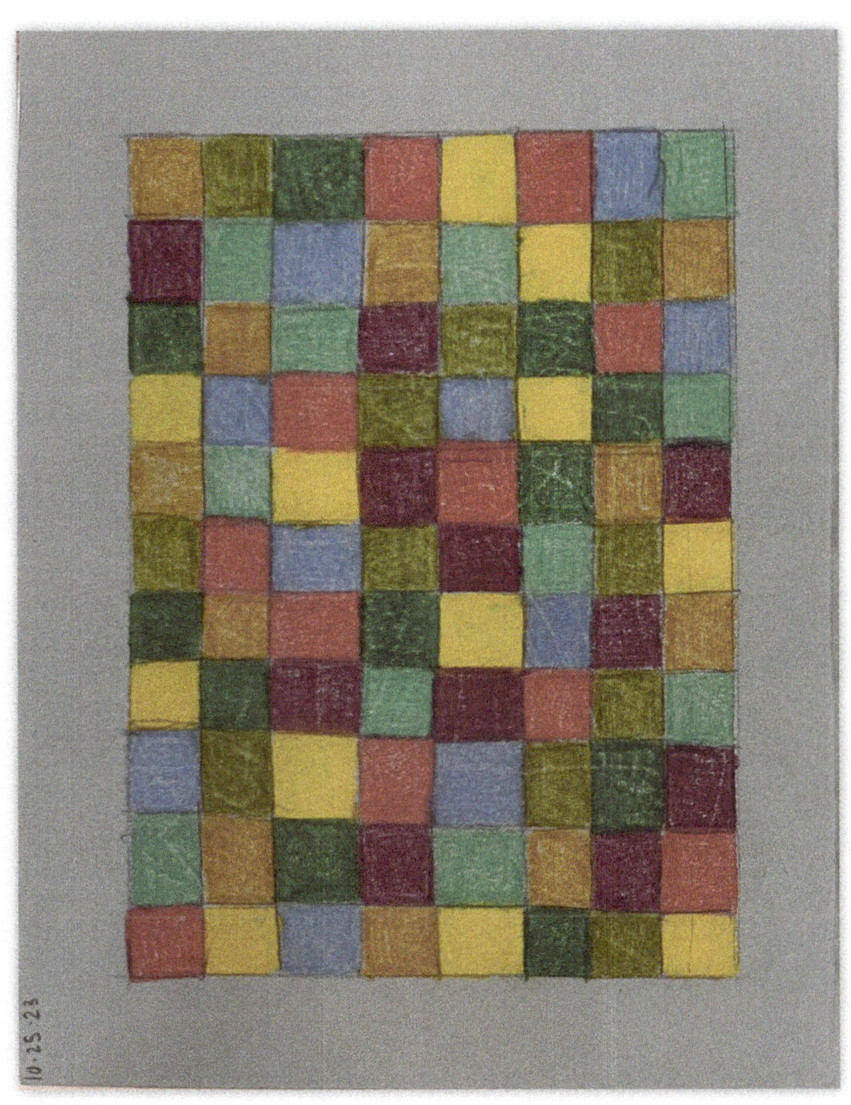

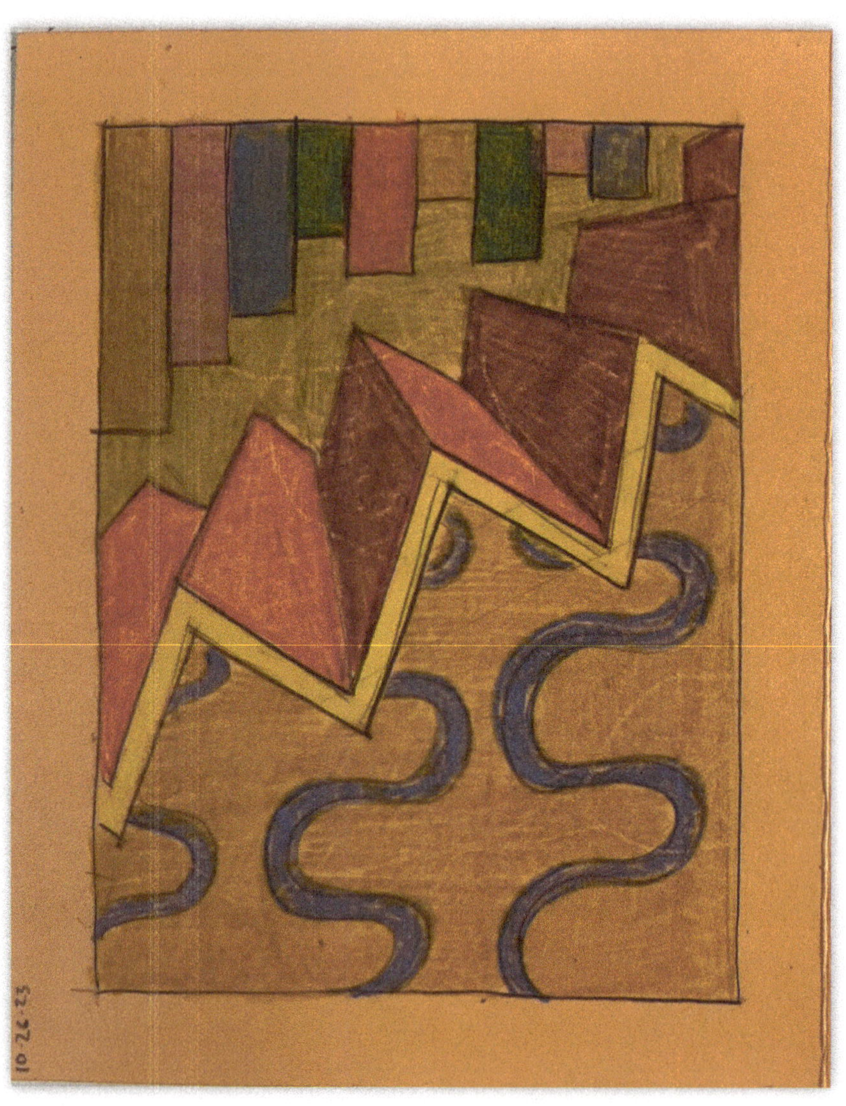

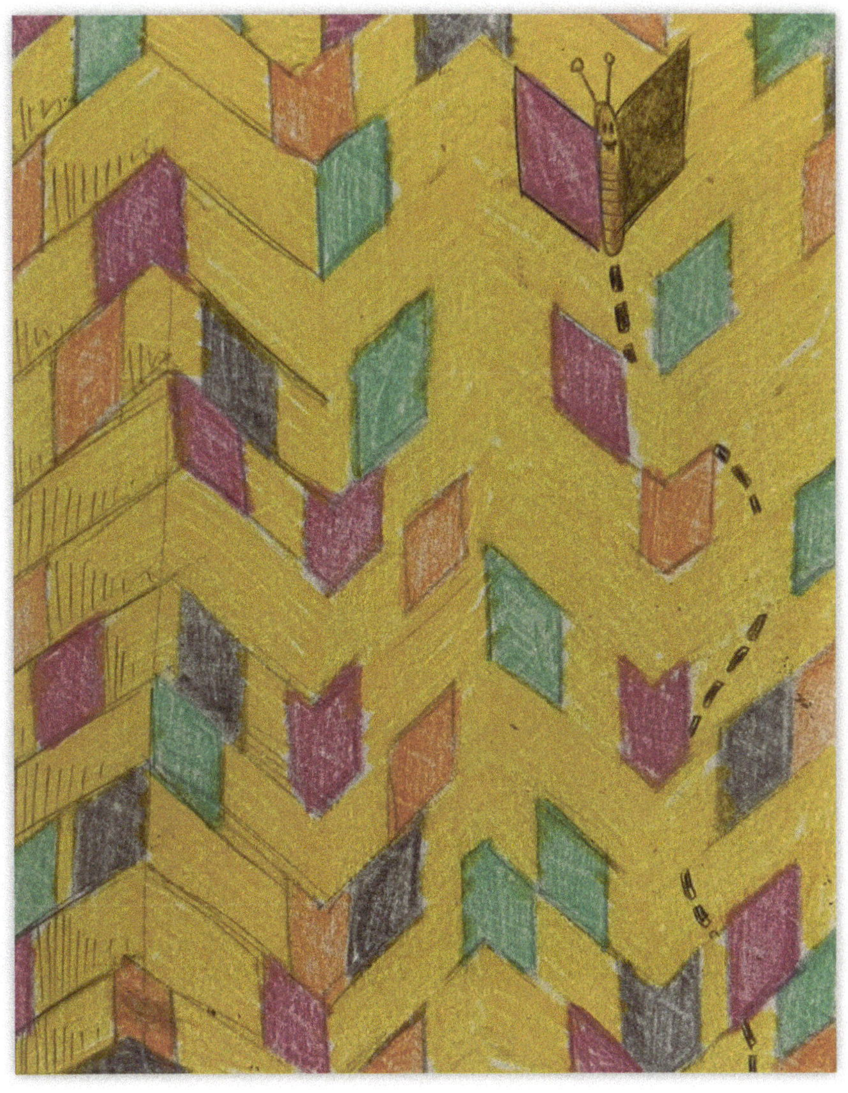

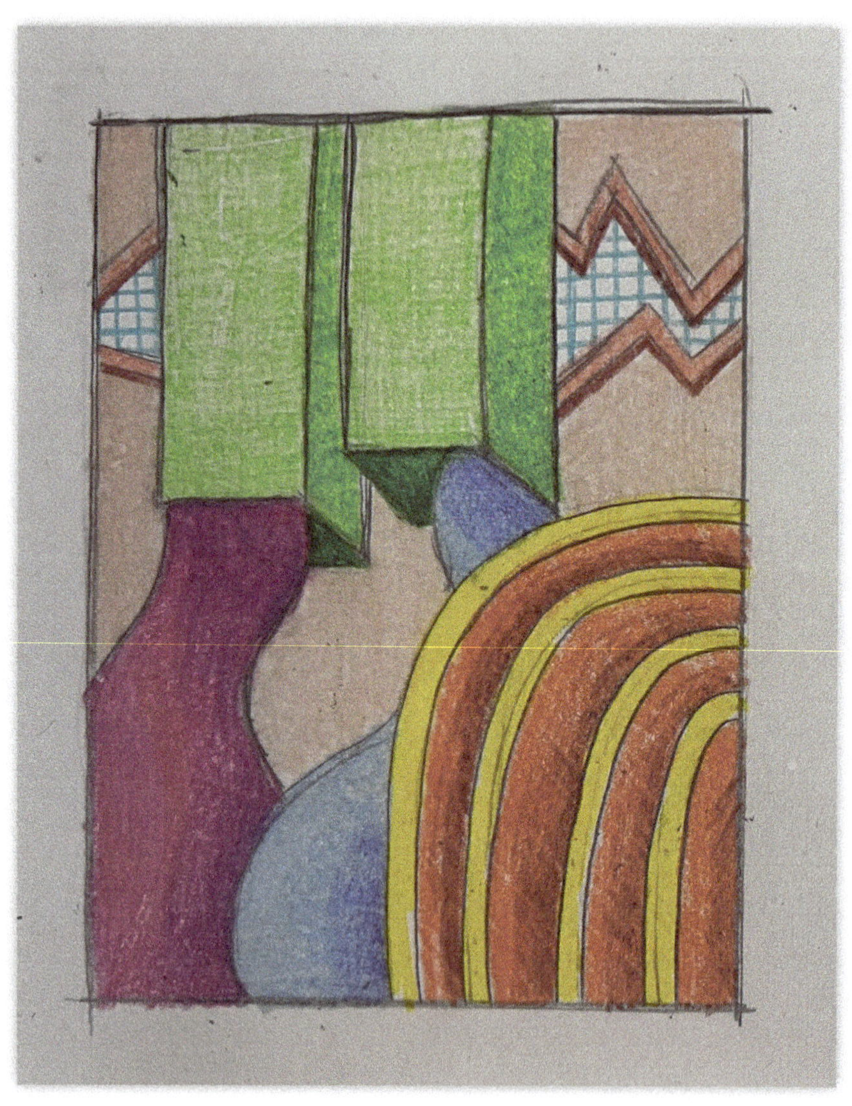

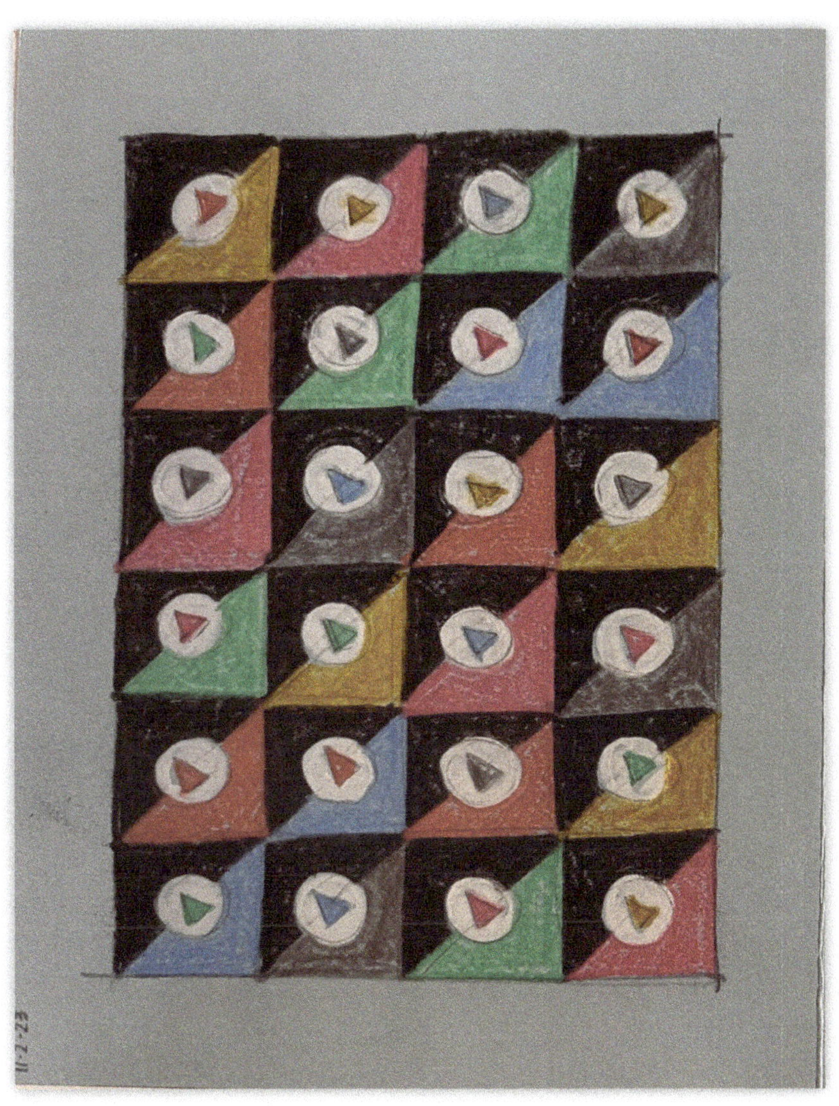

11·2·23

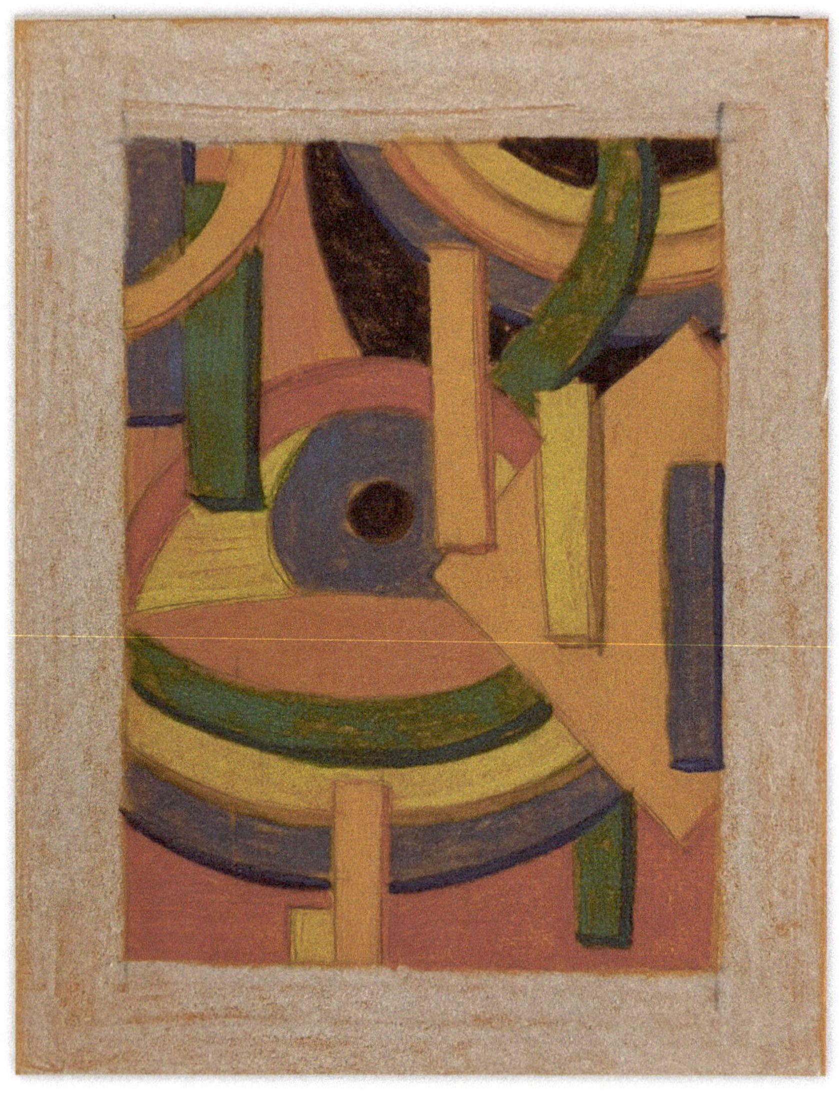

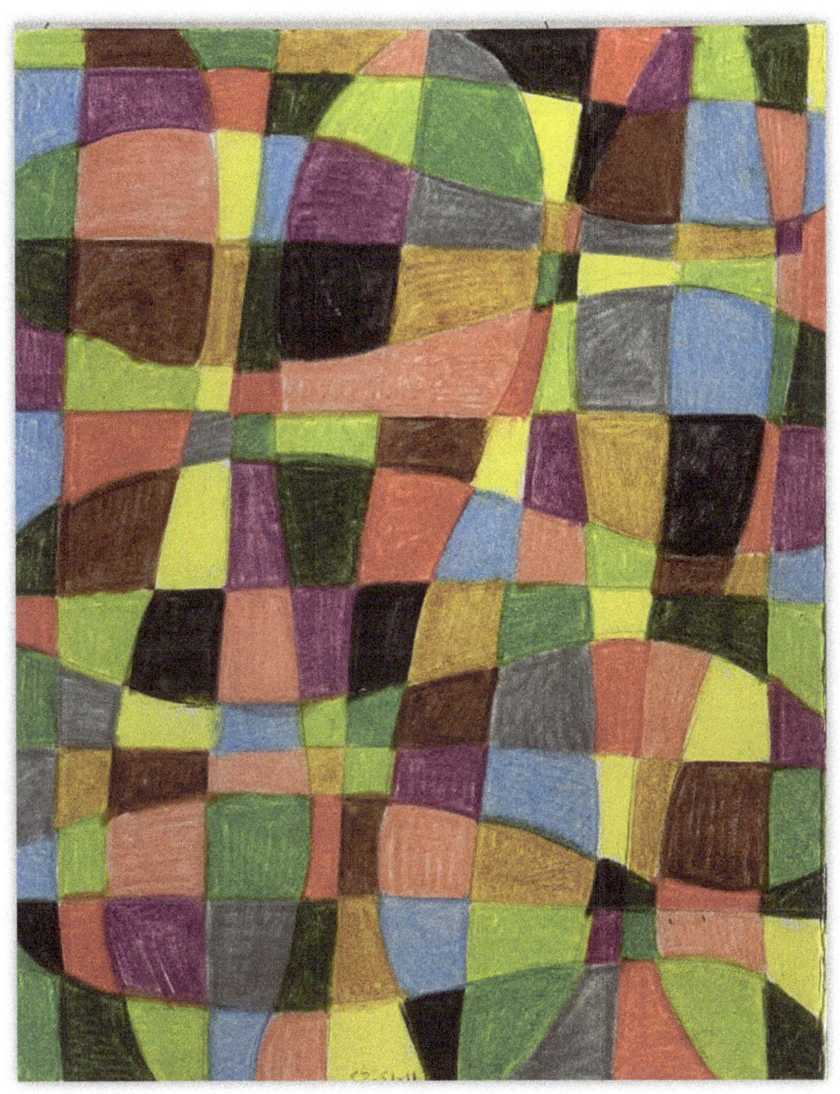

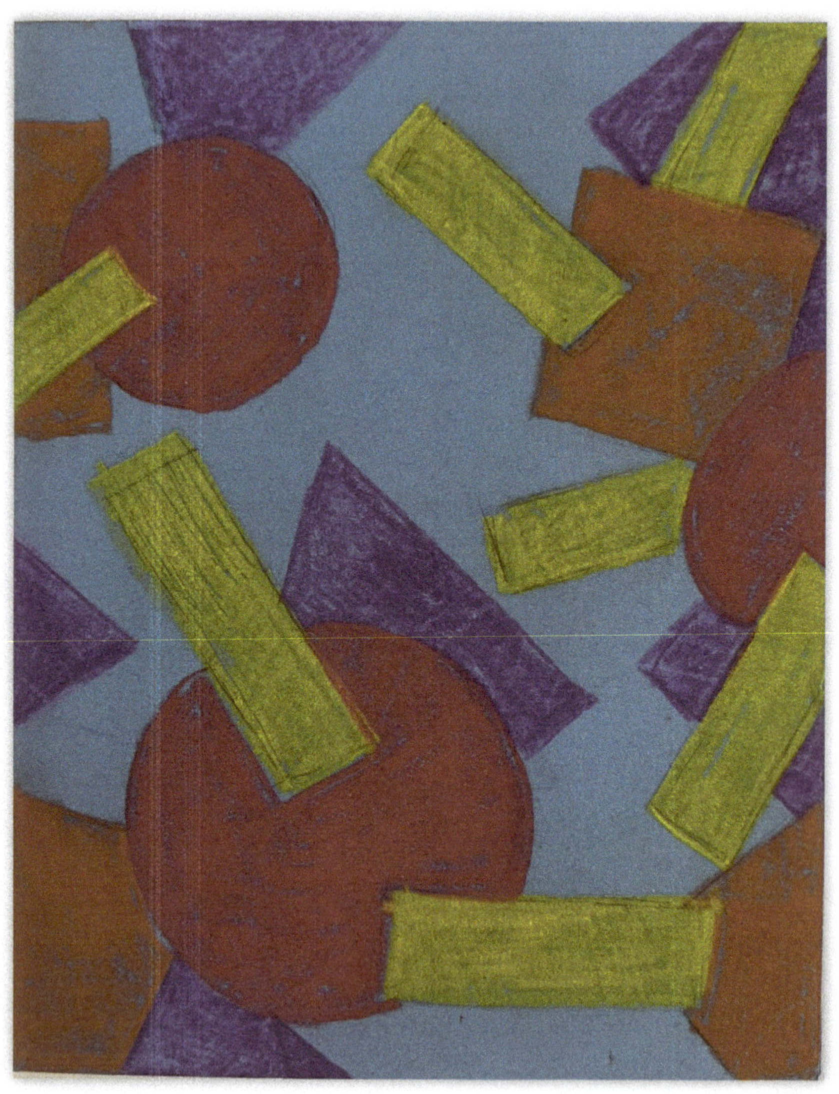

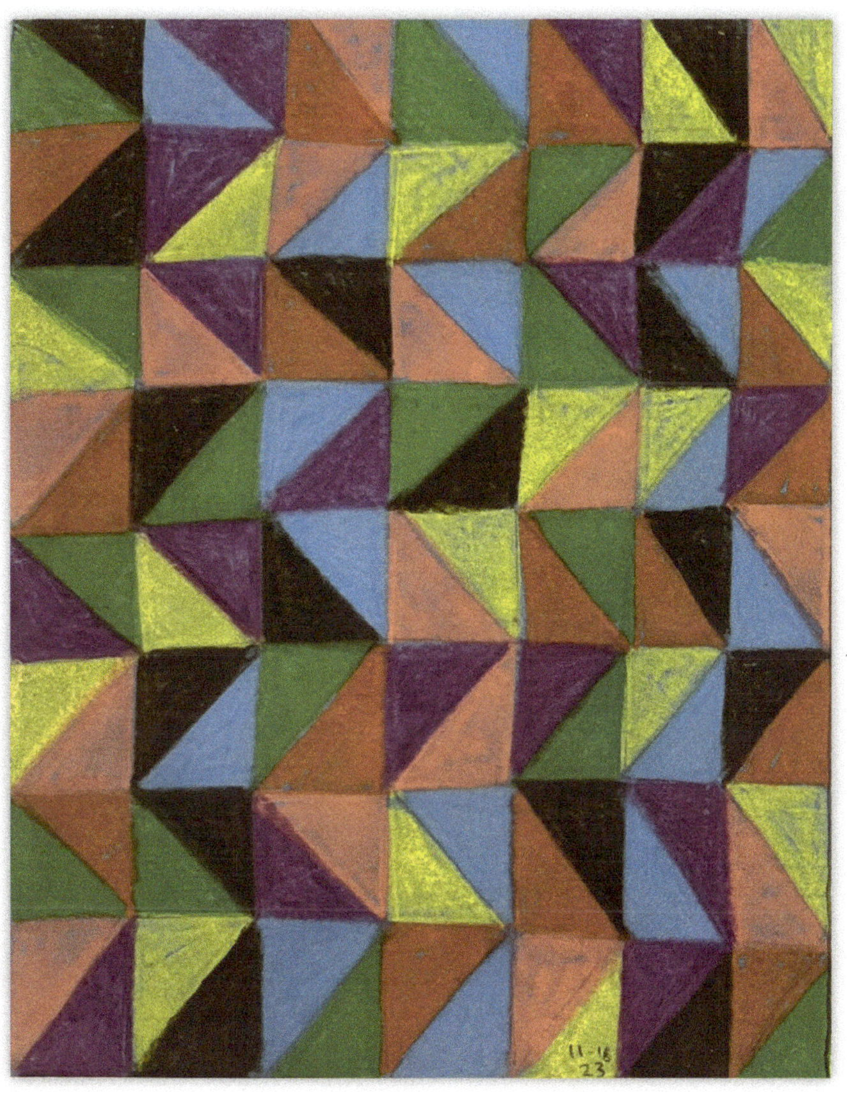

11-18
23

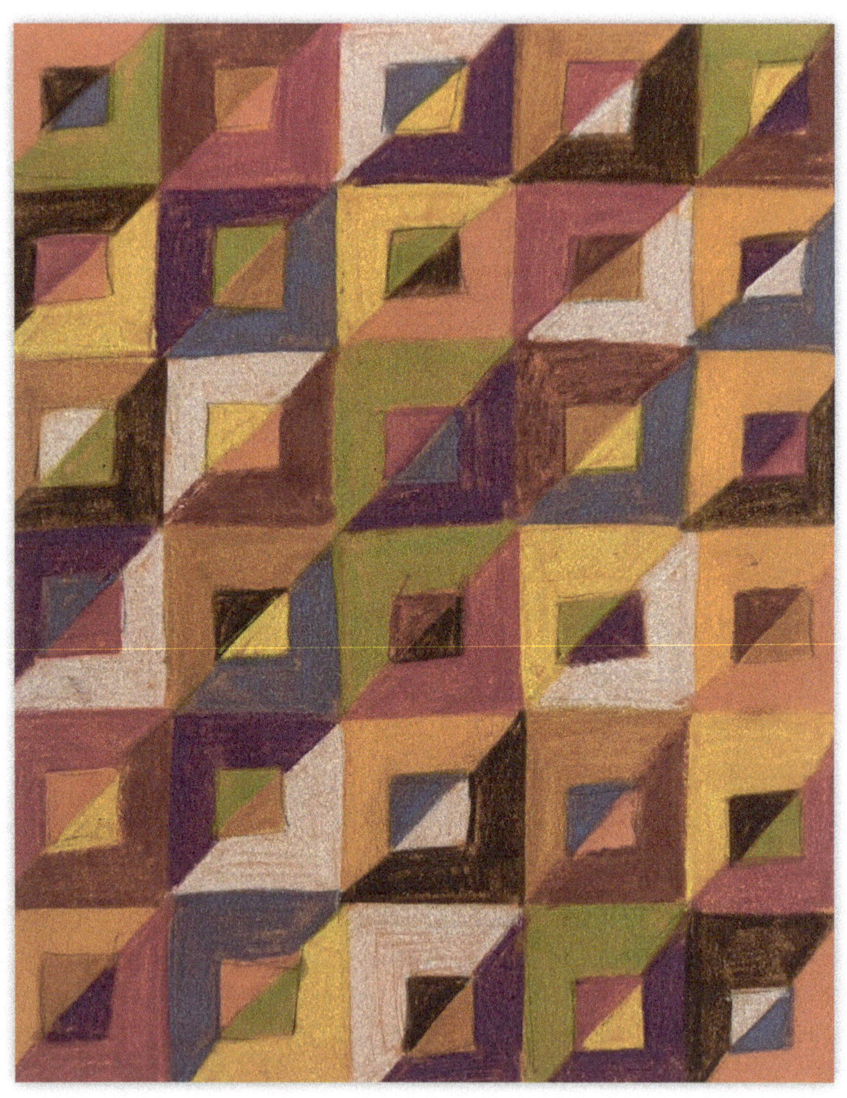

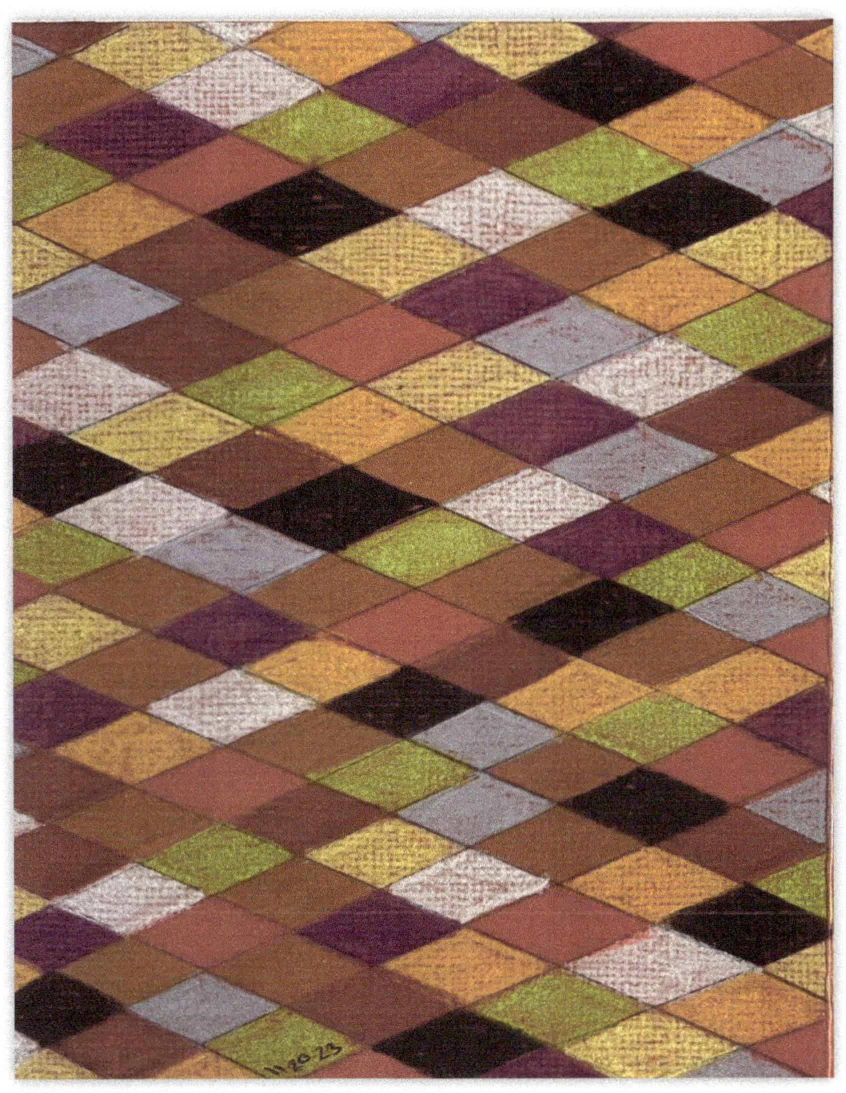

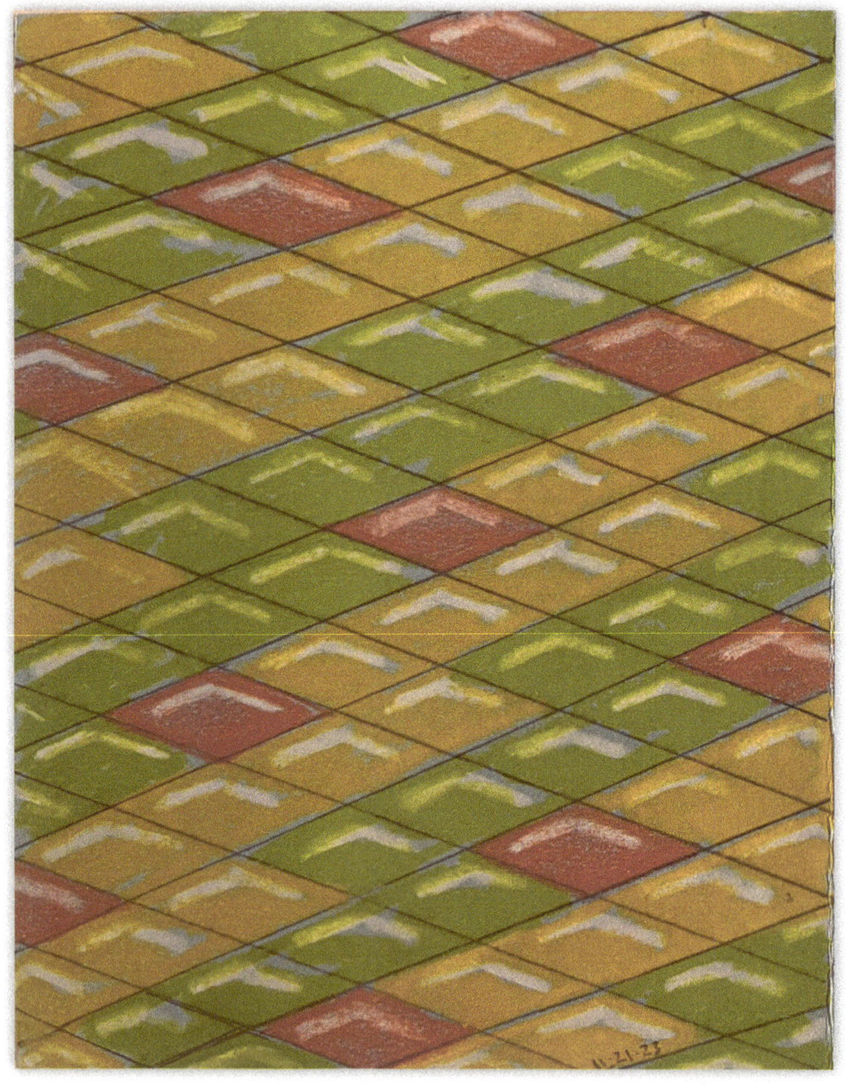

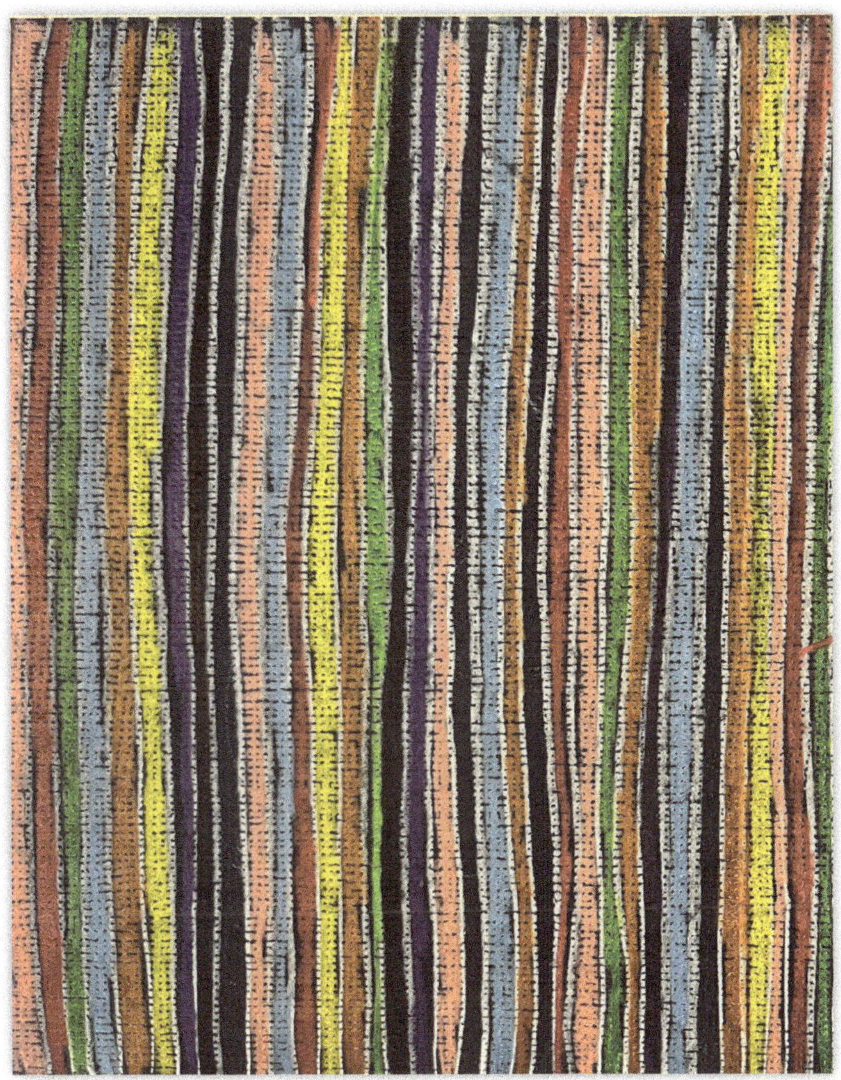

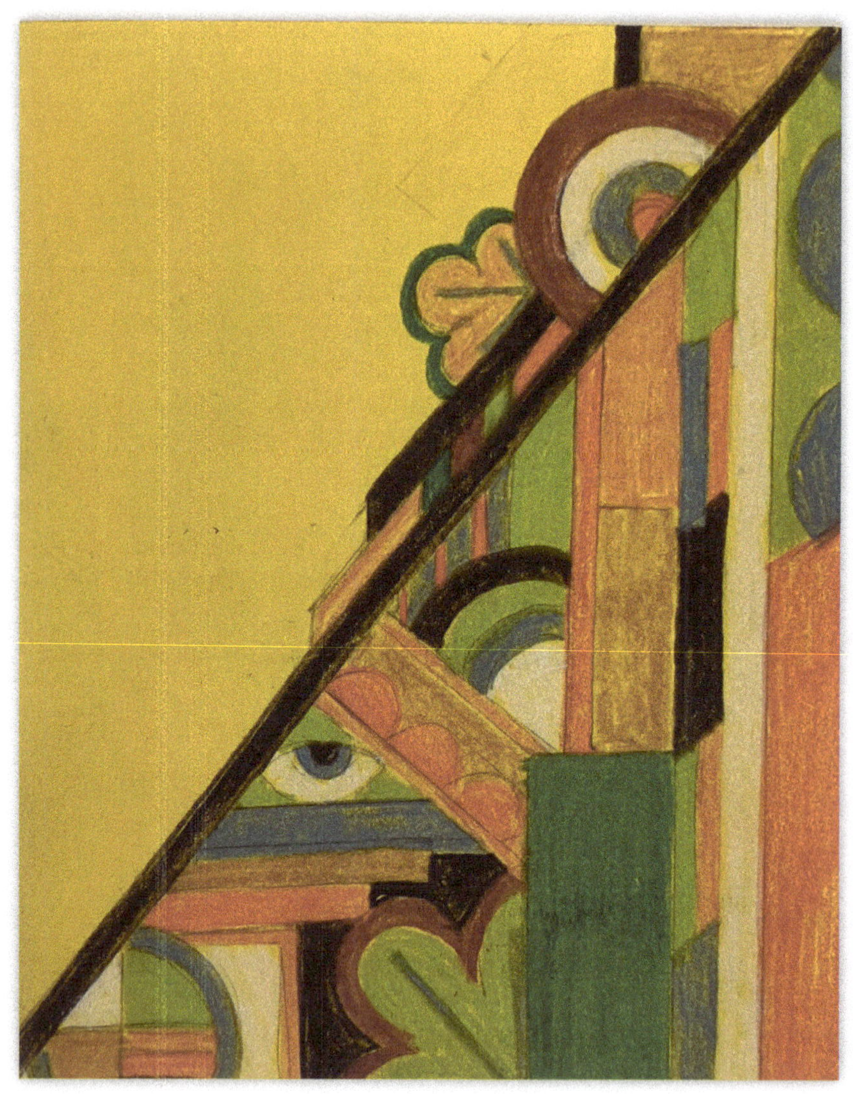

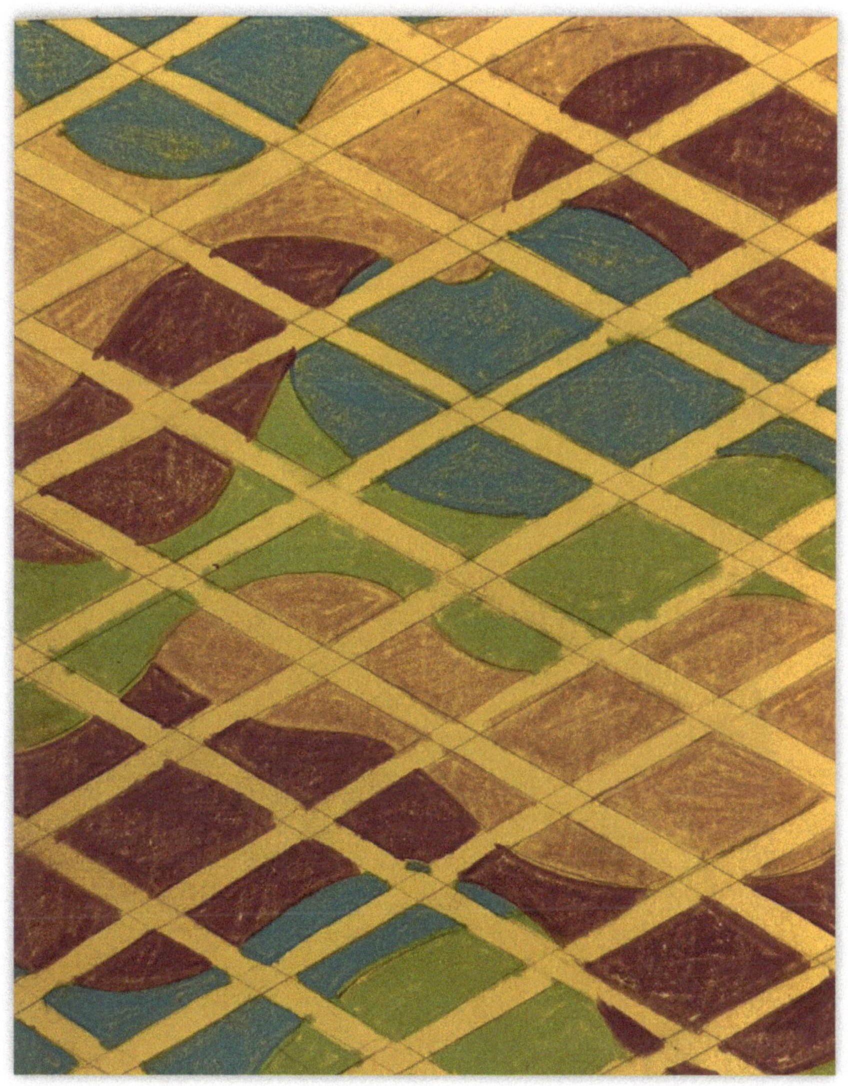

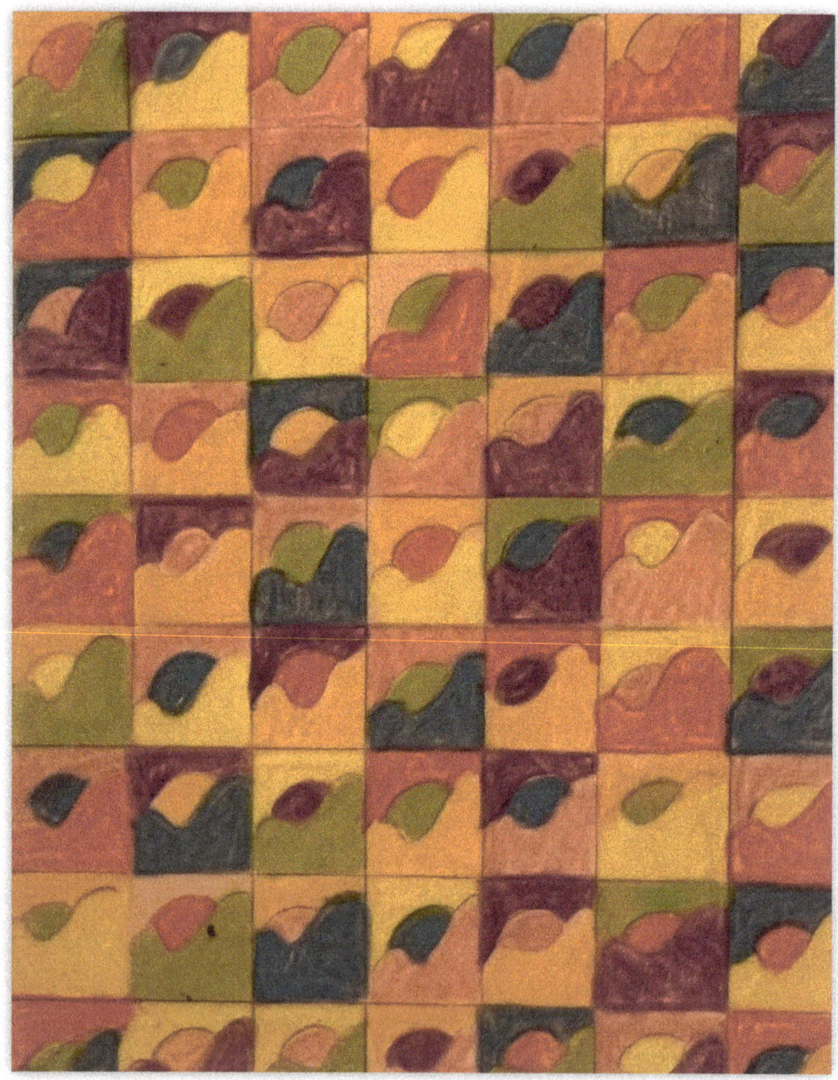

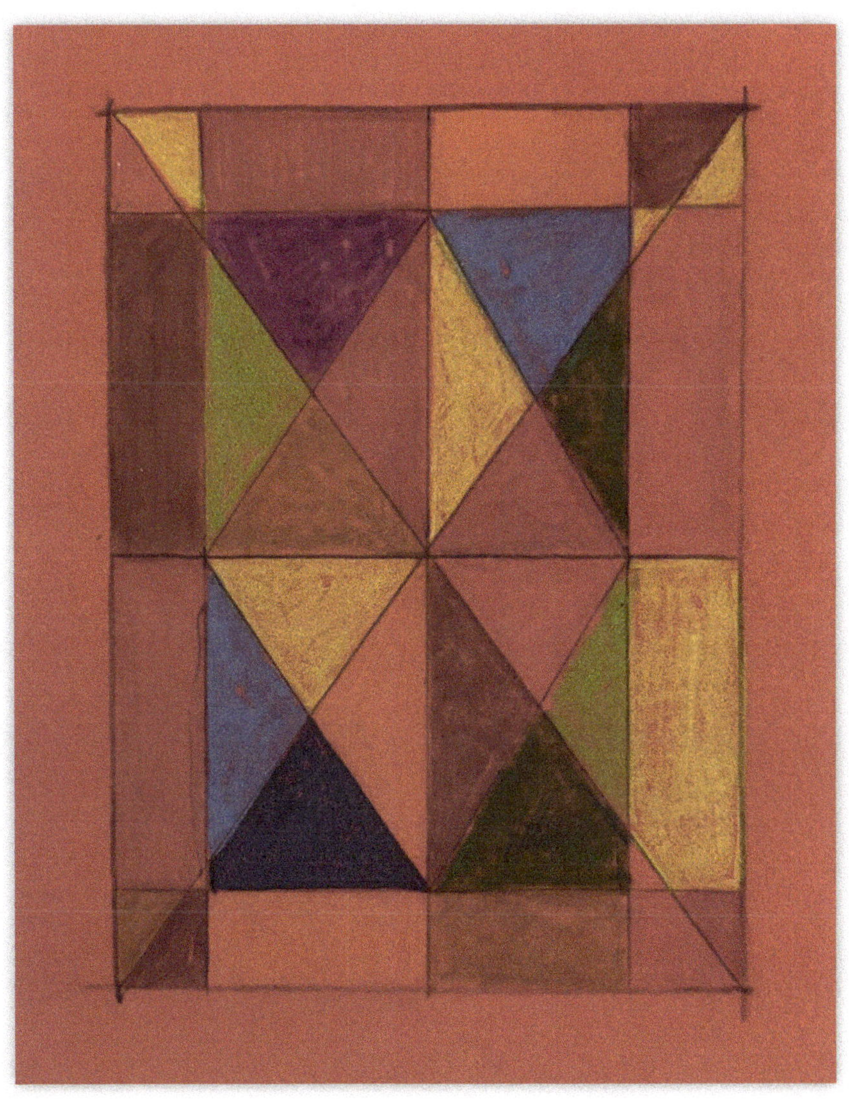

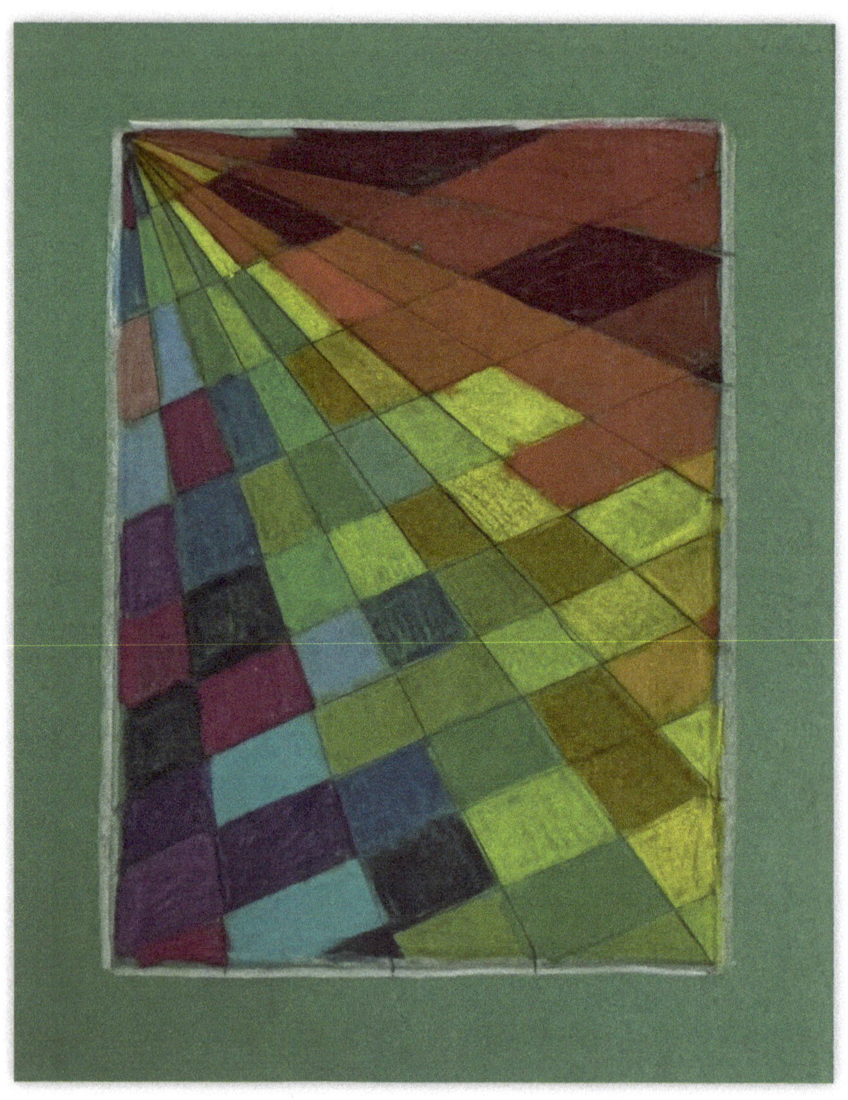

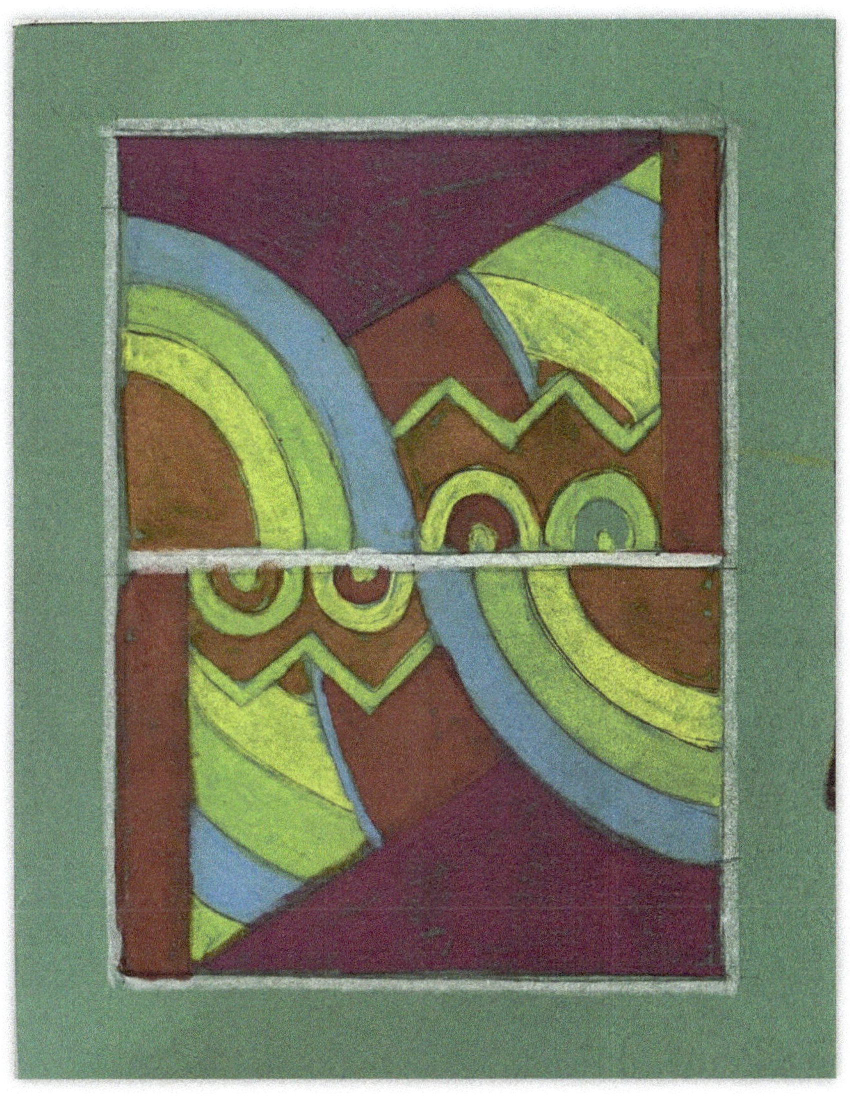

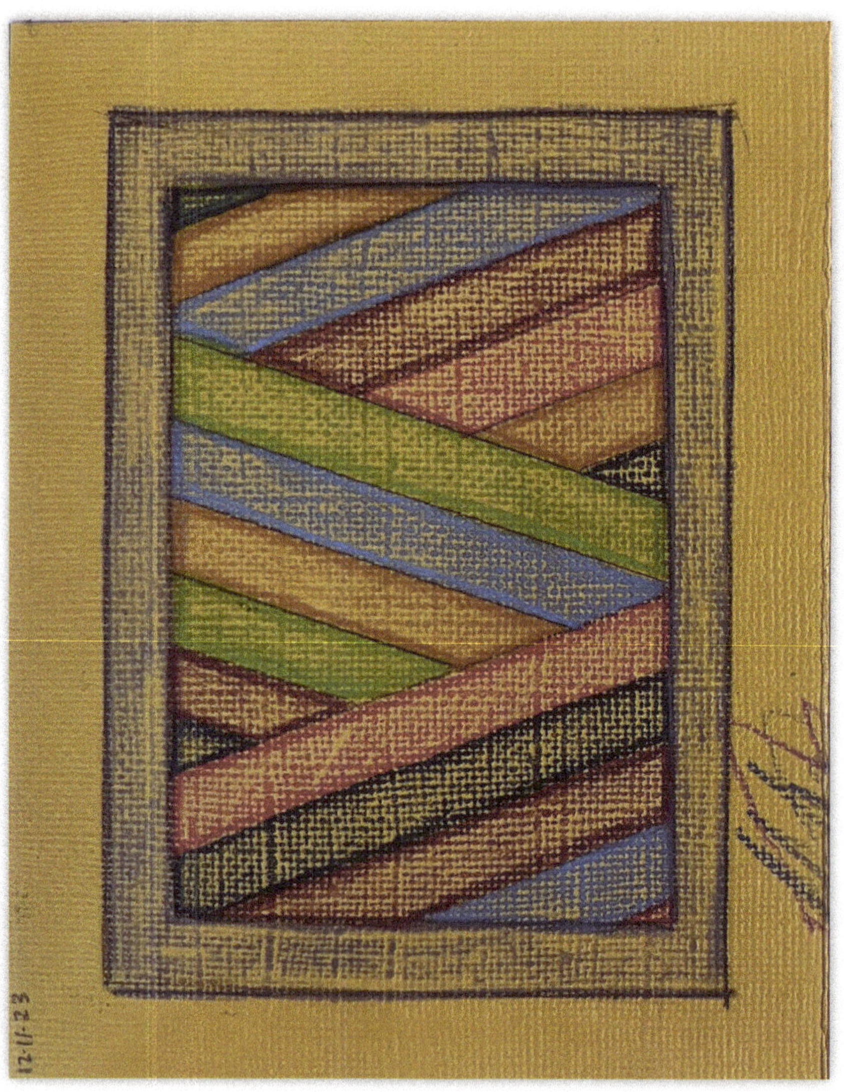

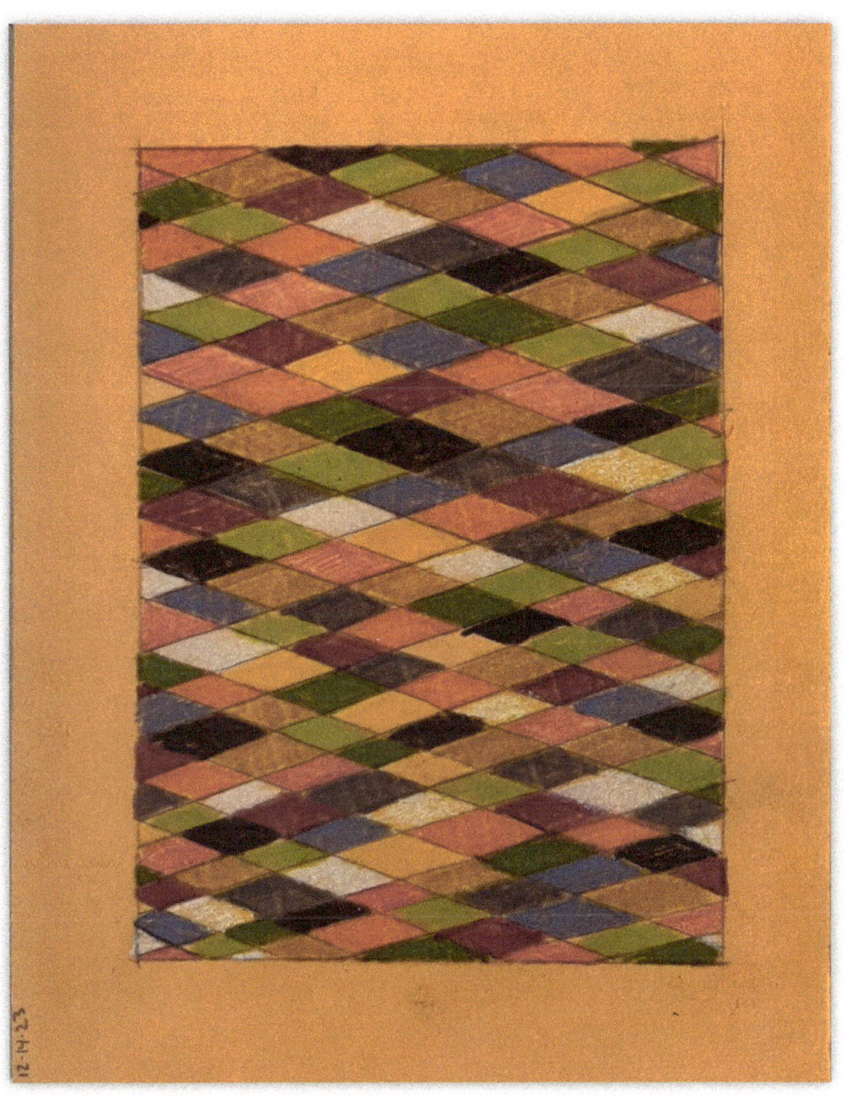

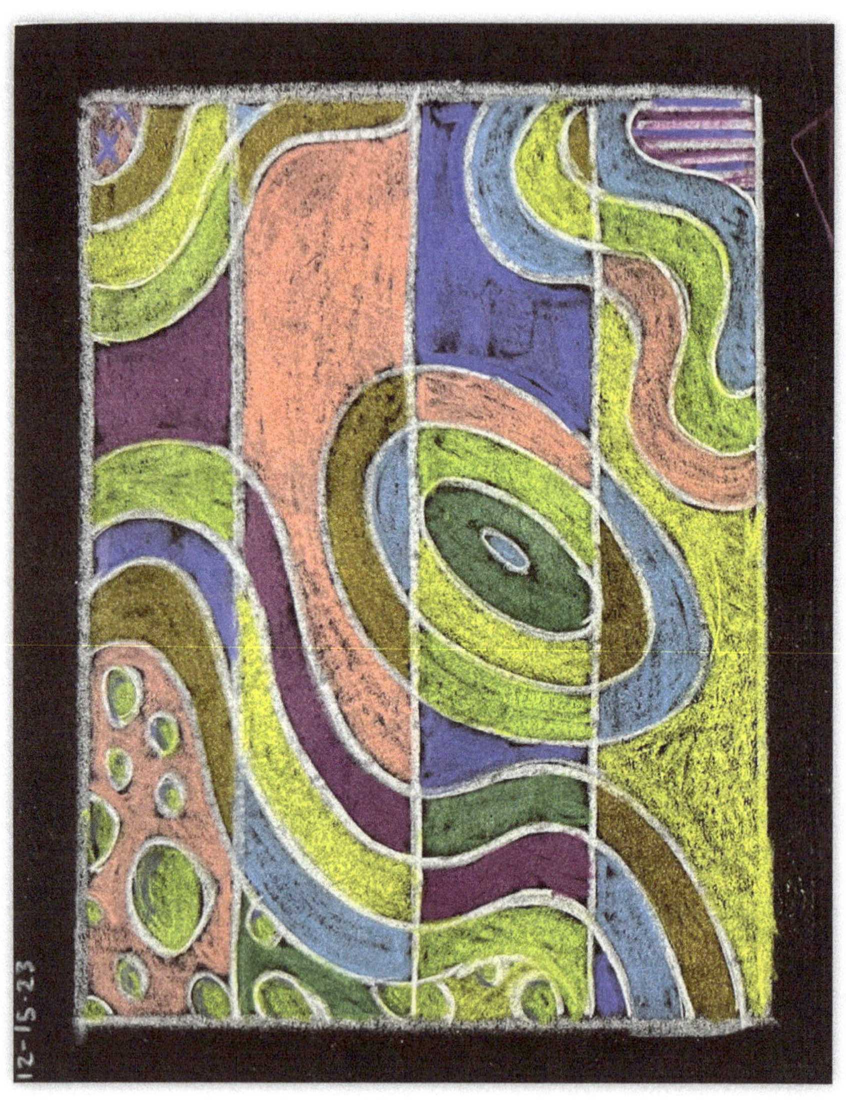
12-15-23

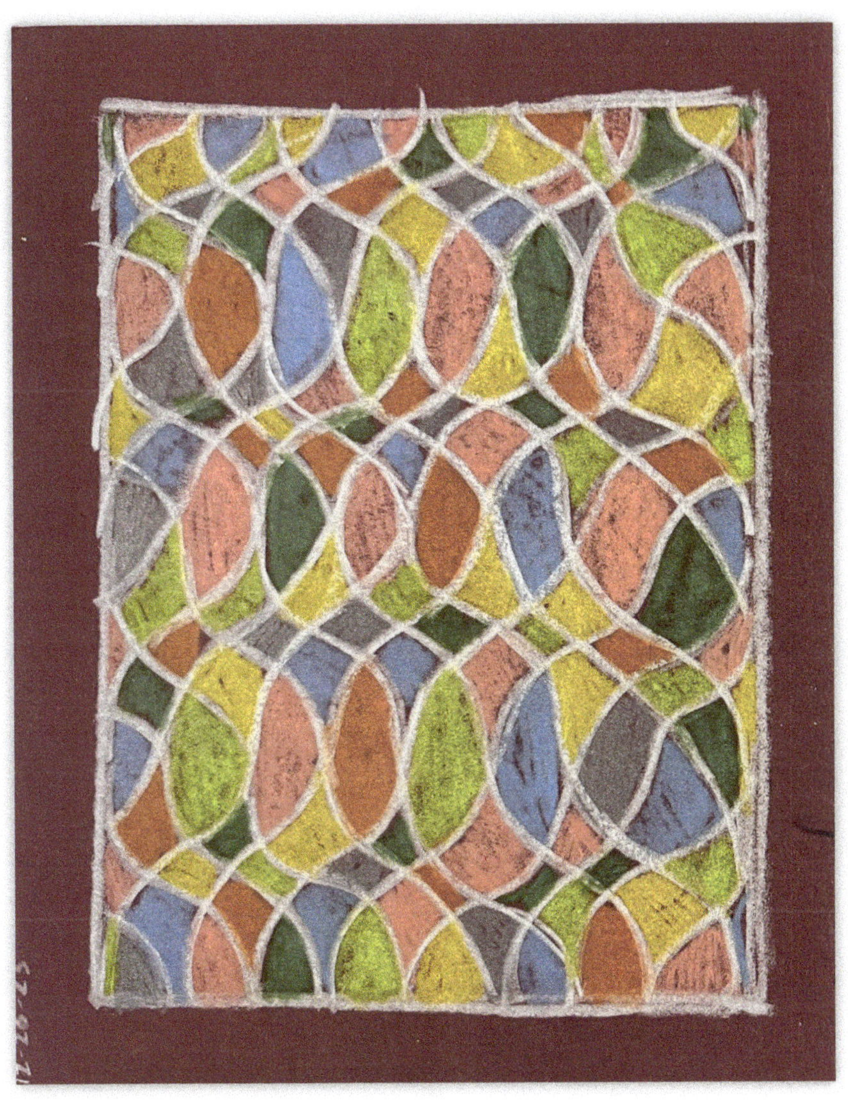

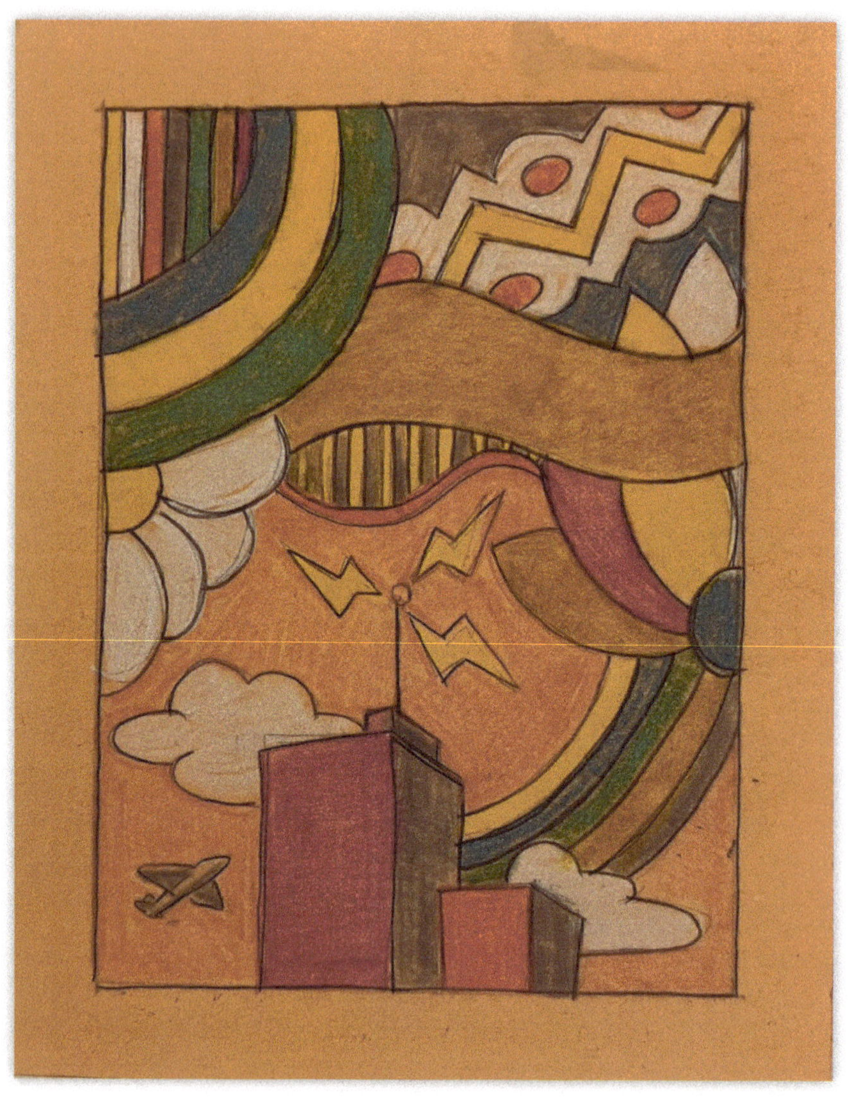

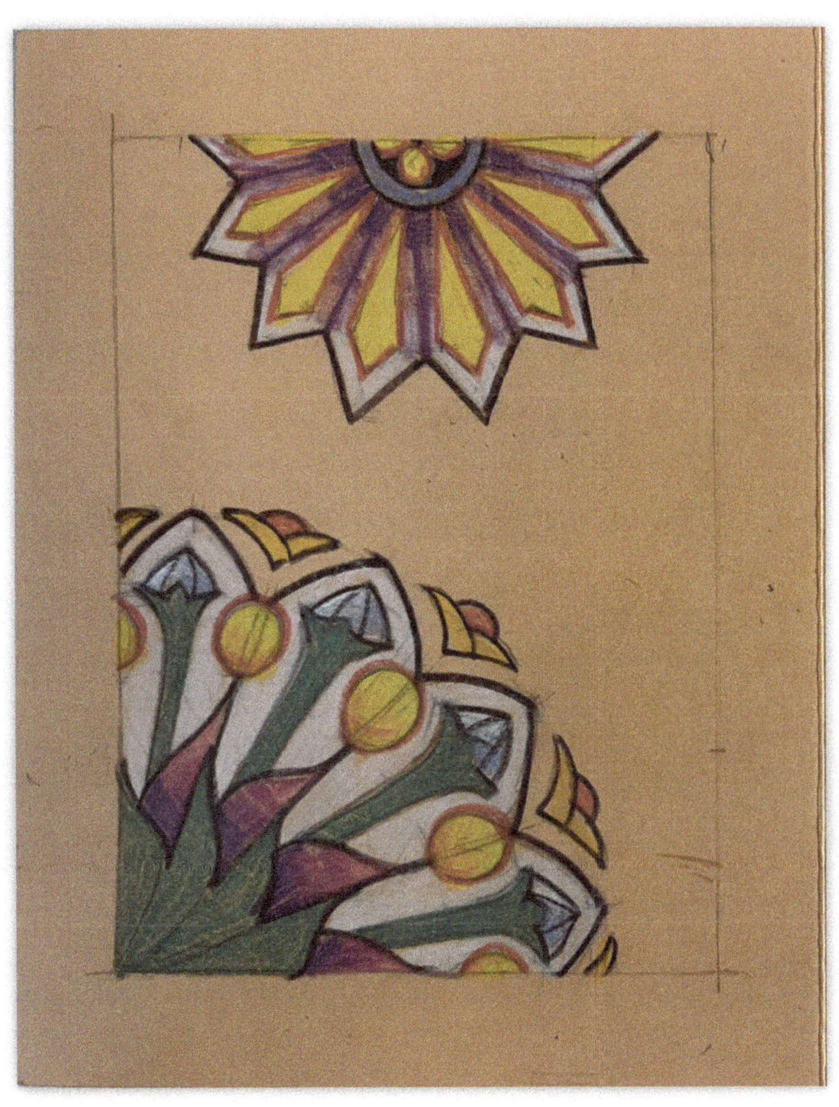

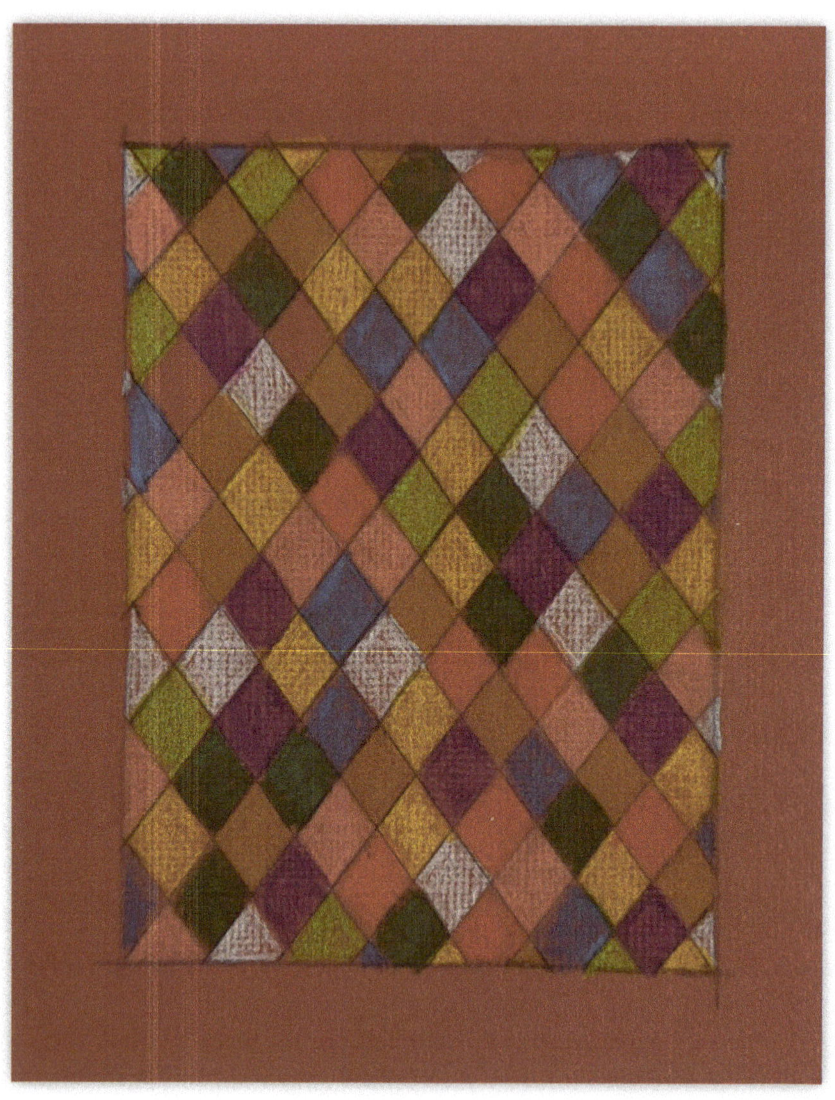

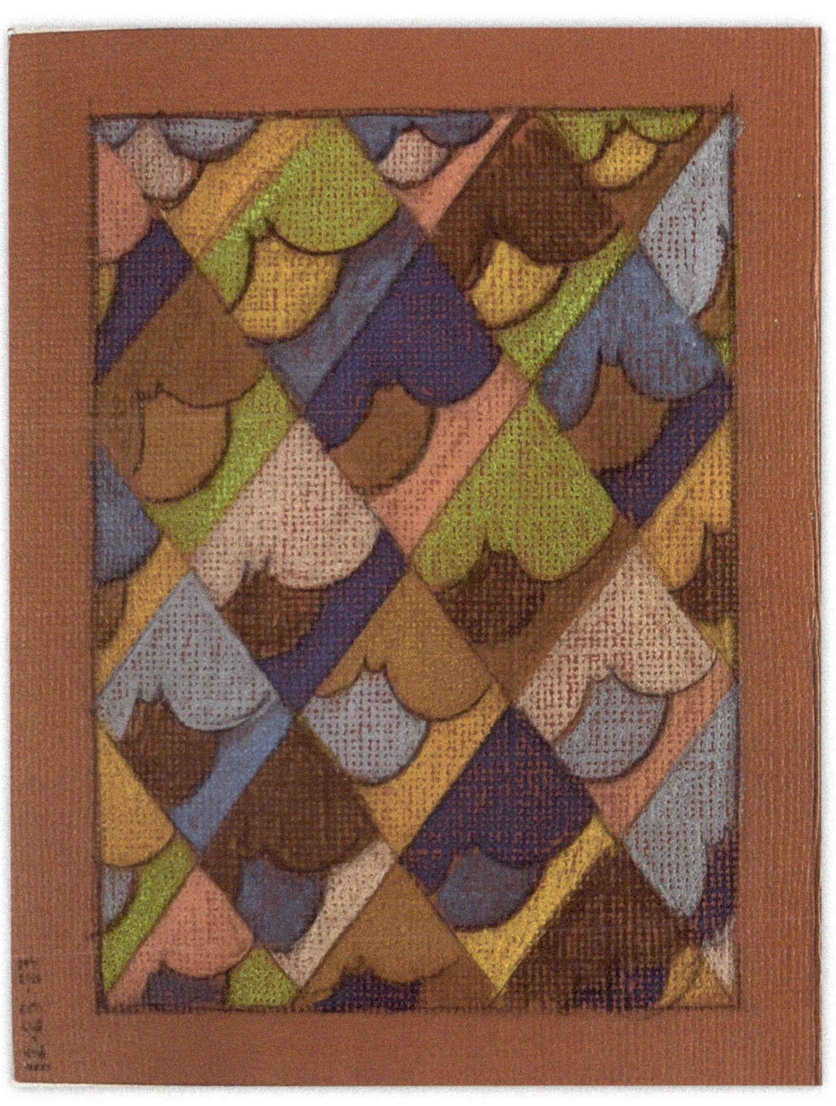

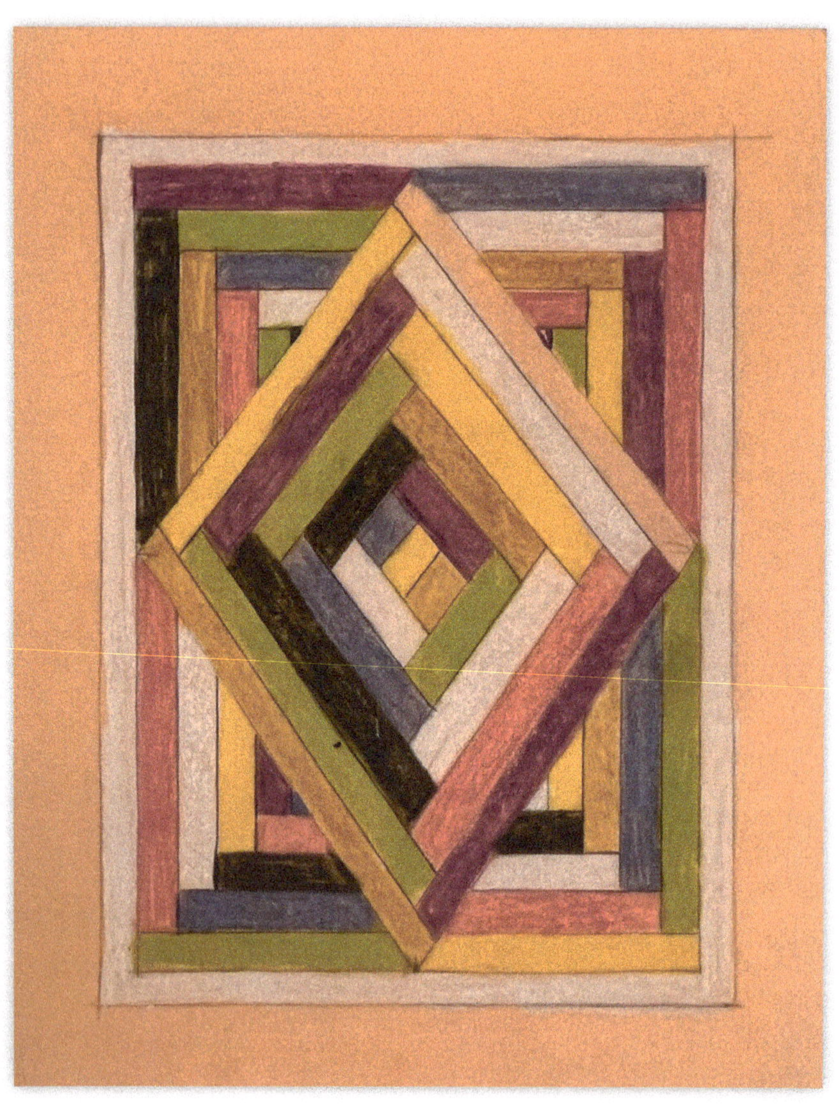

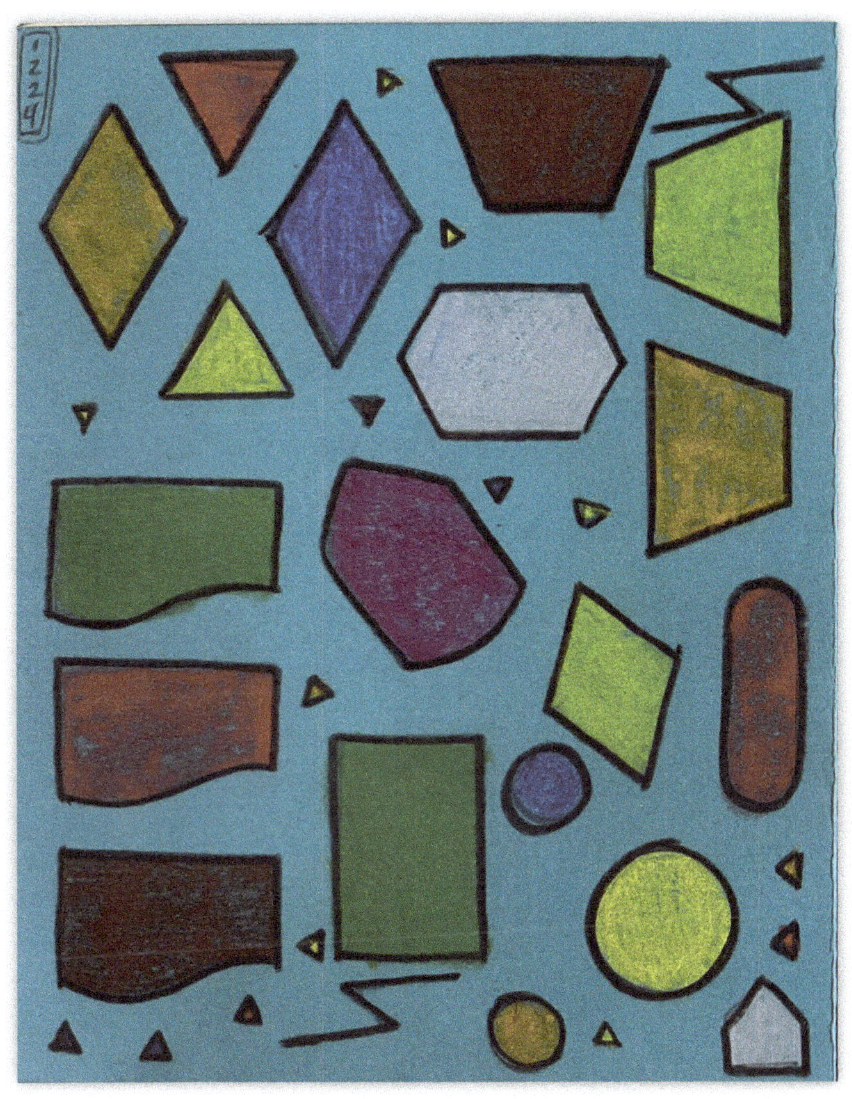

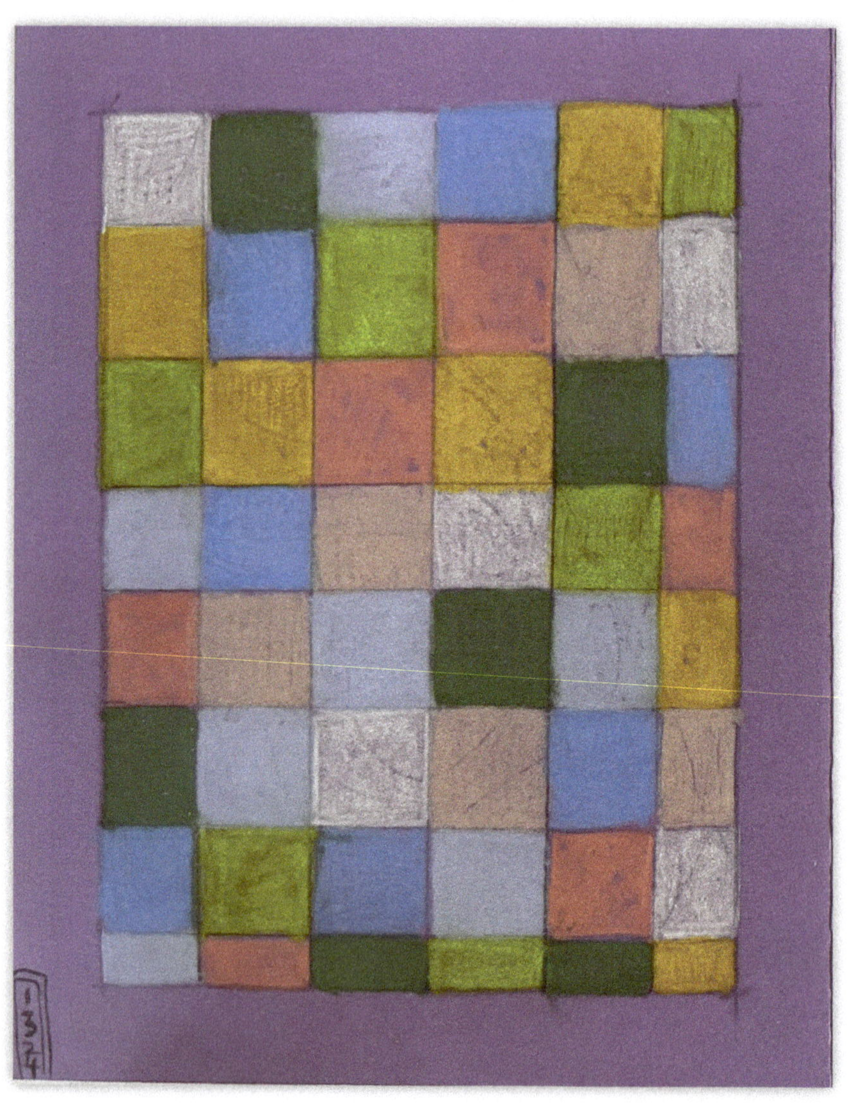

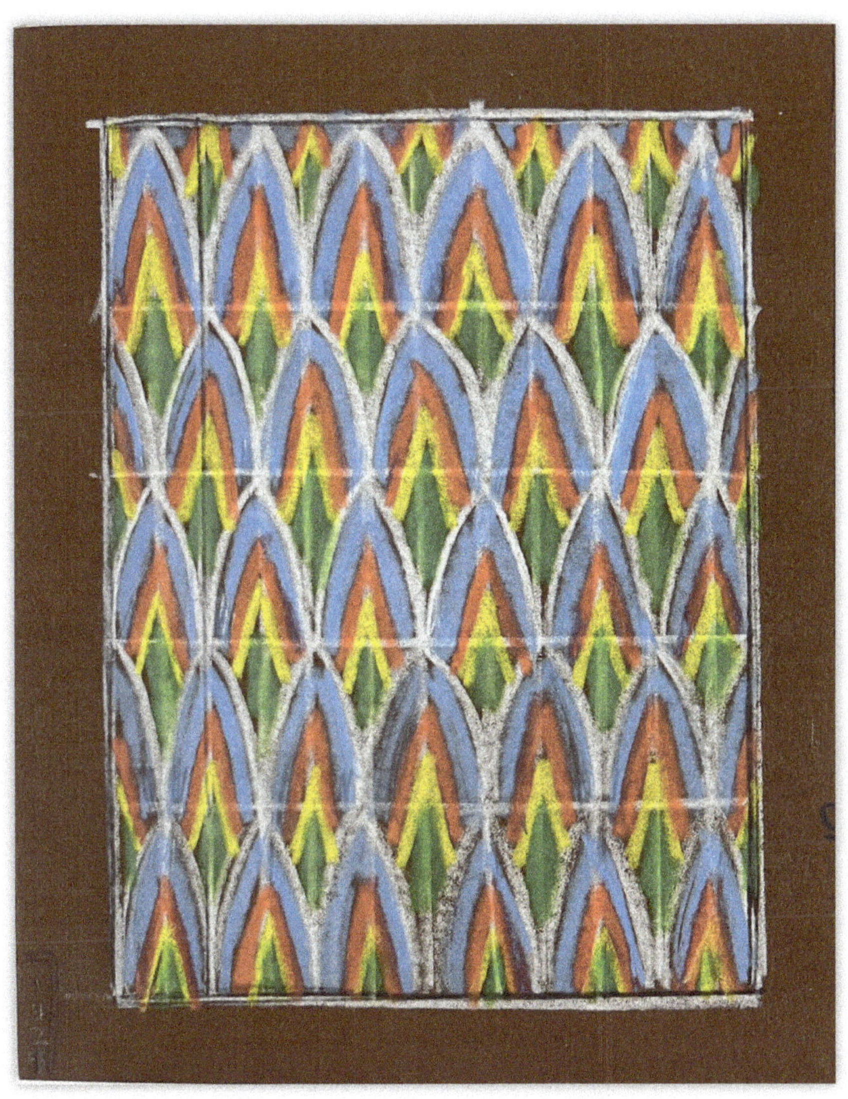

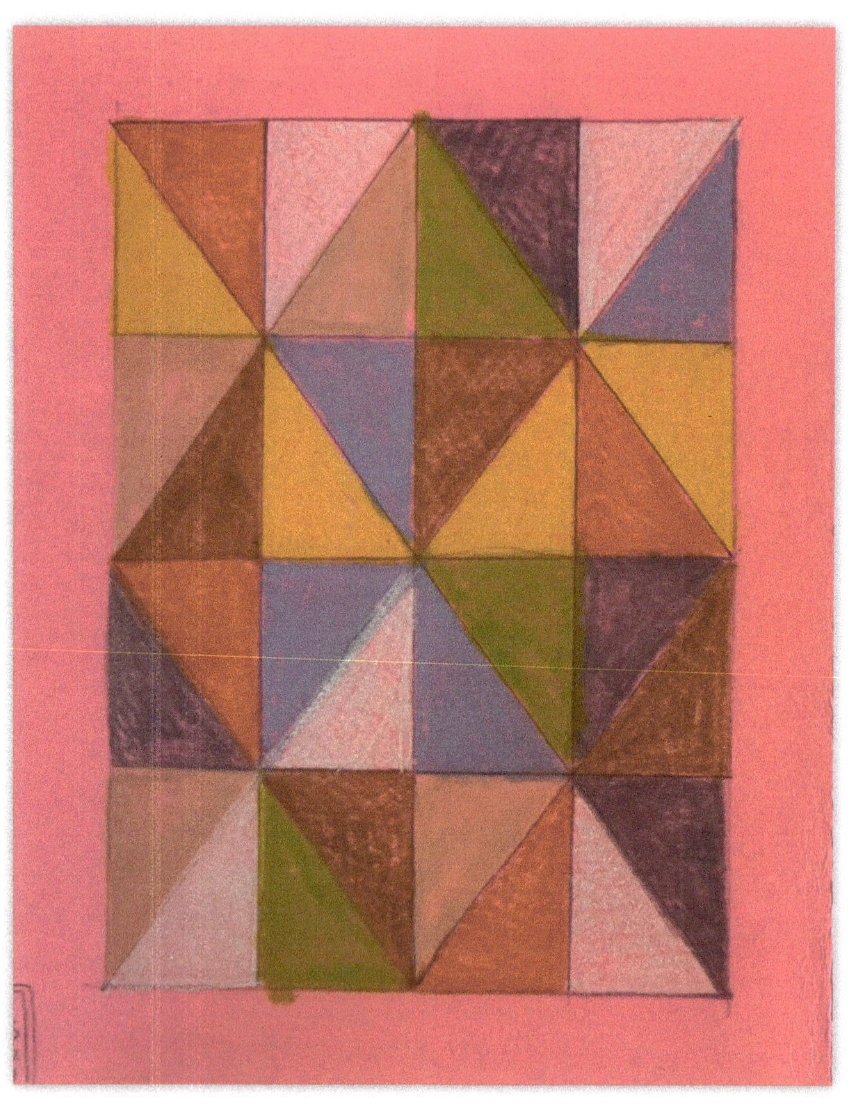

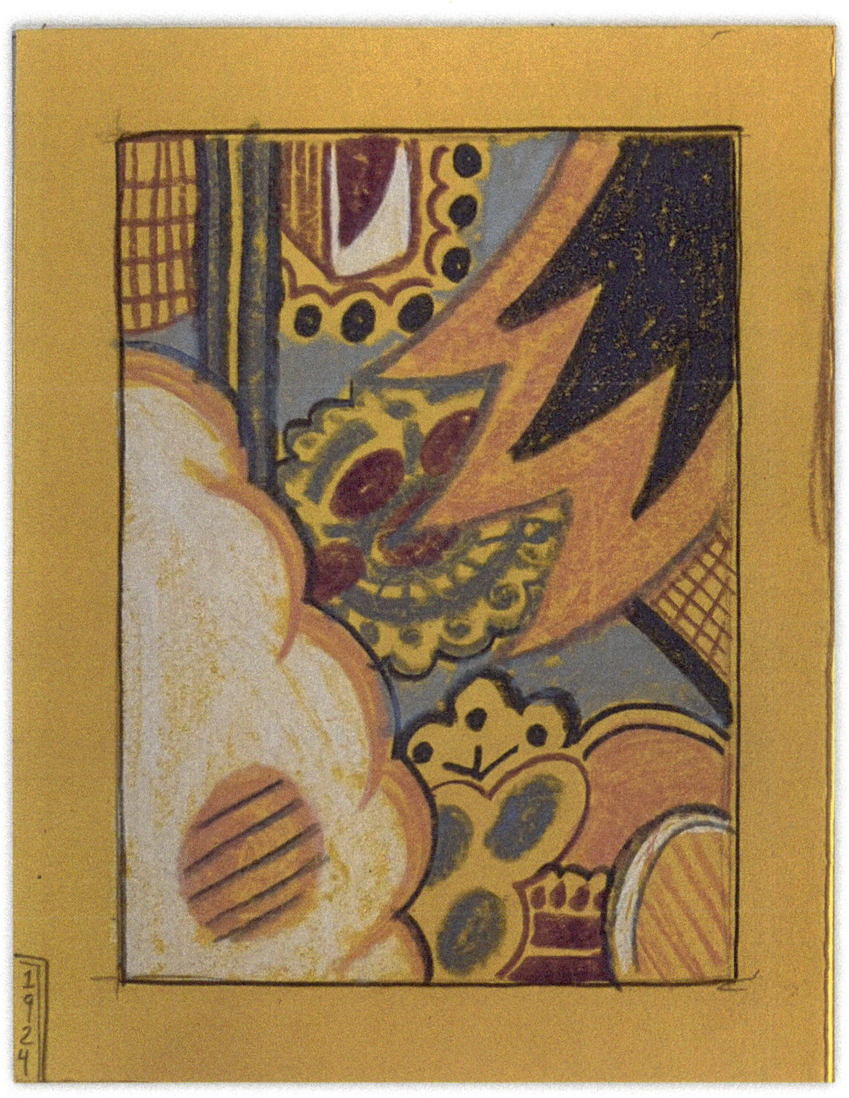

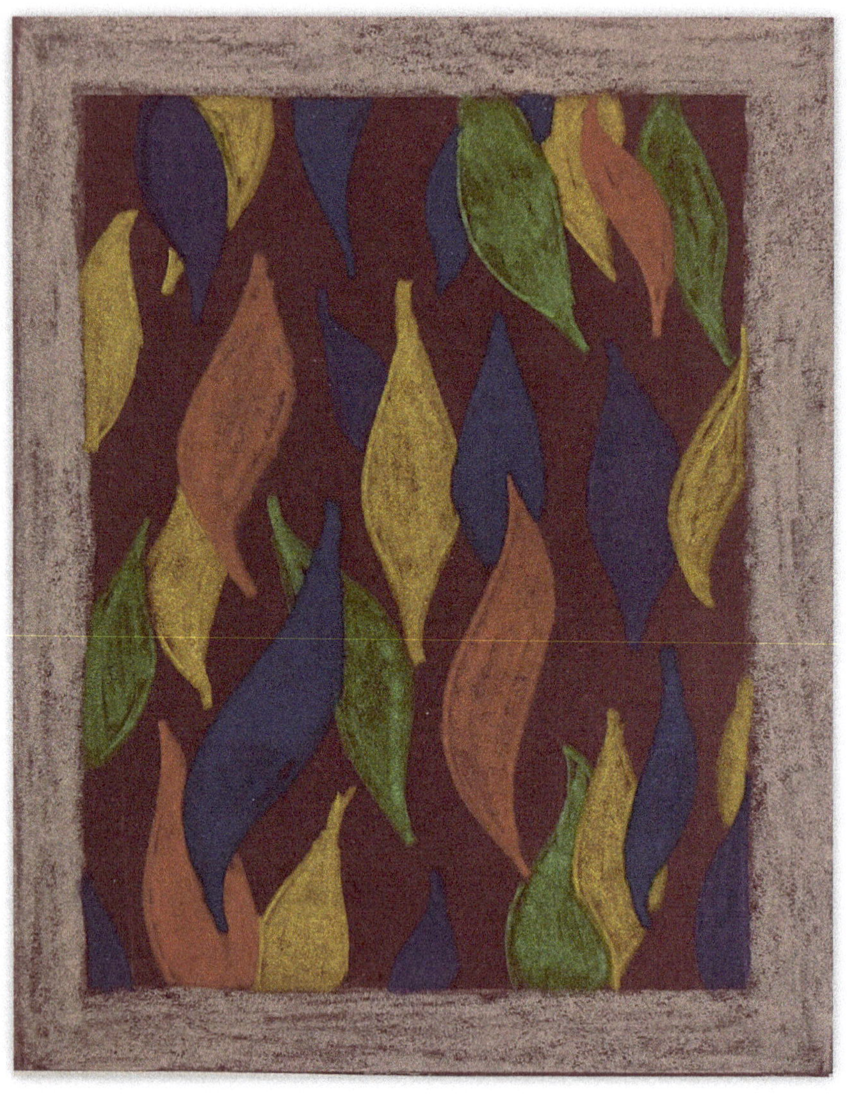

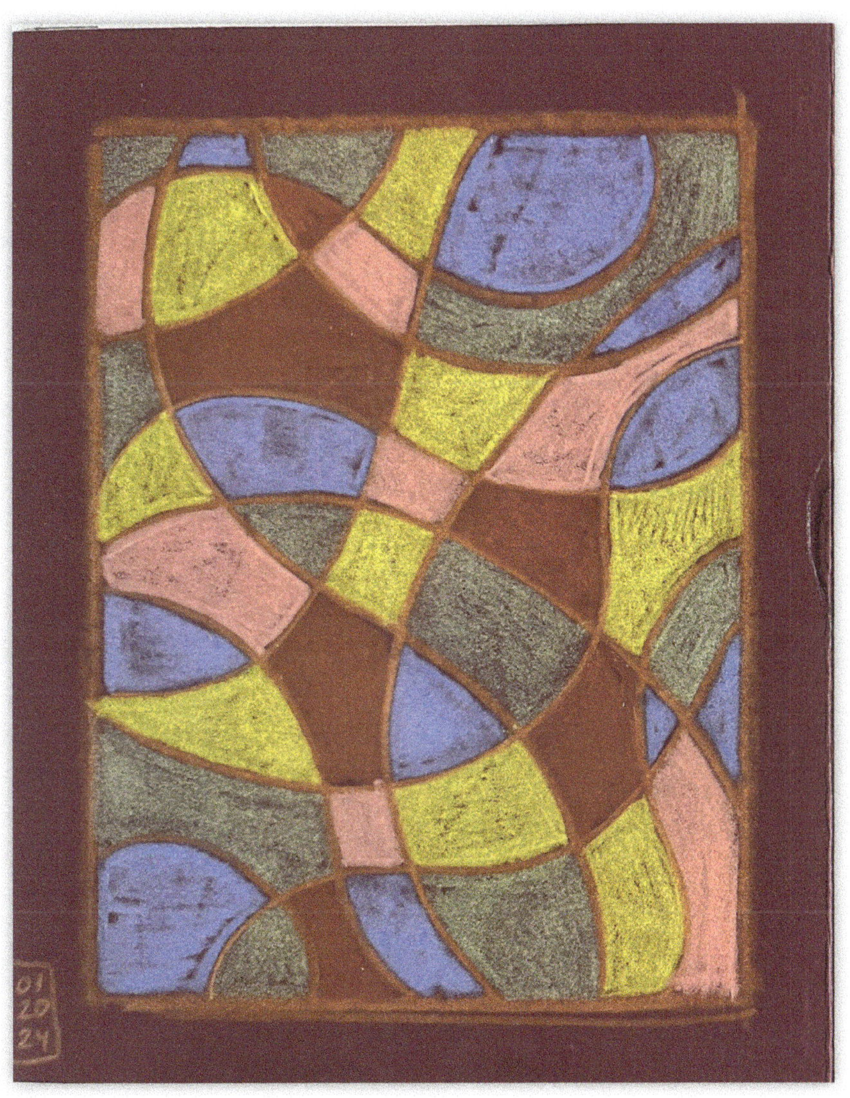

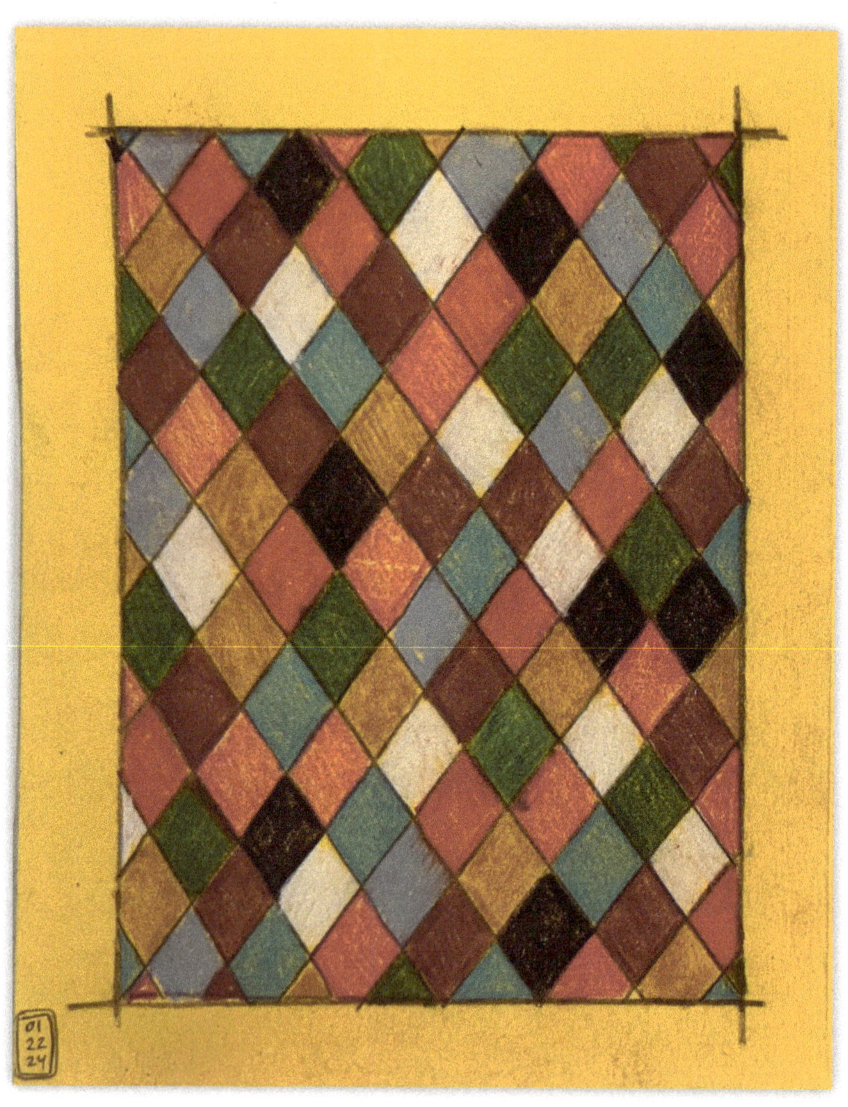

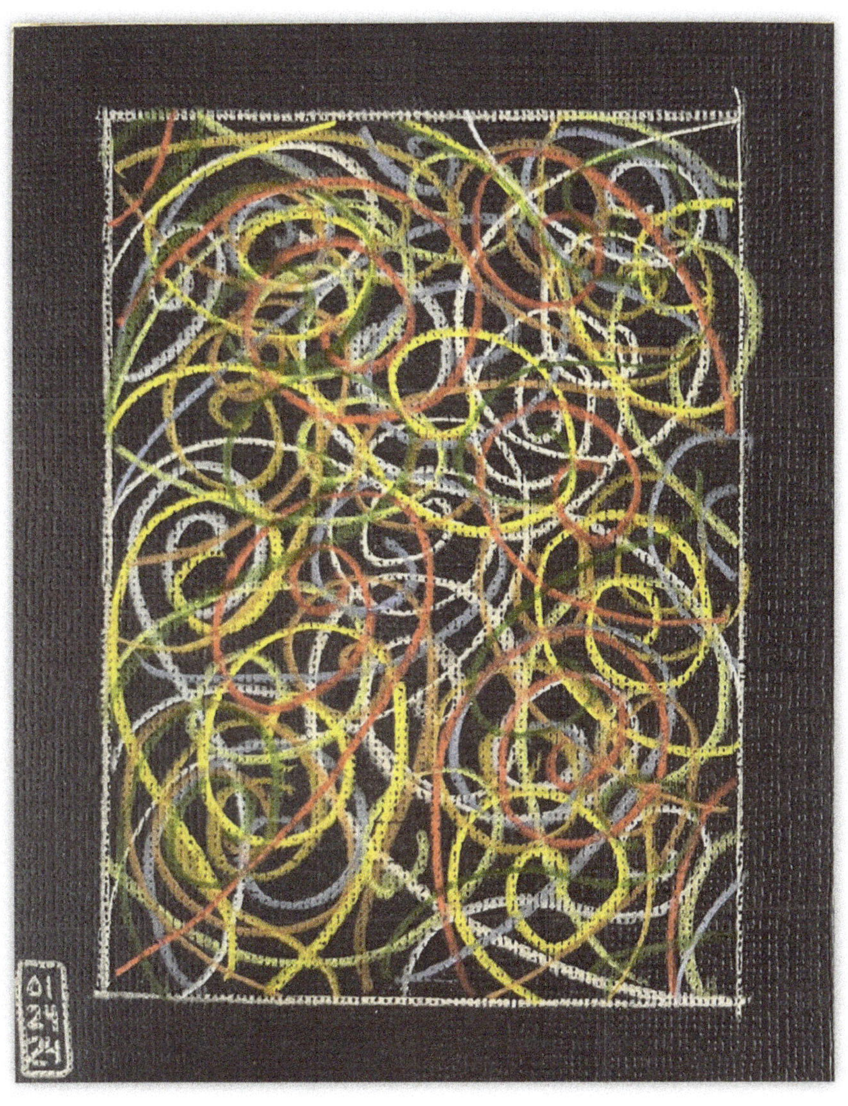

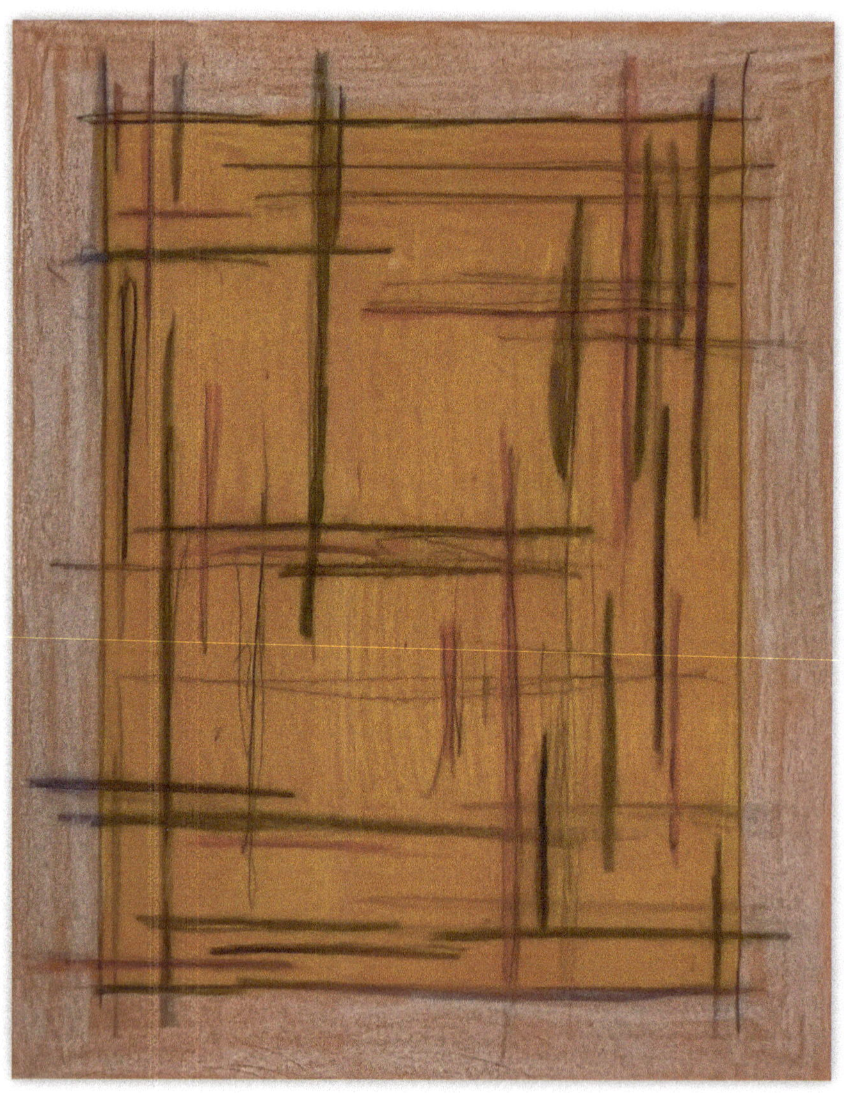

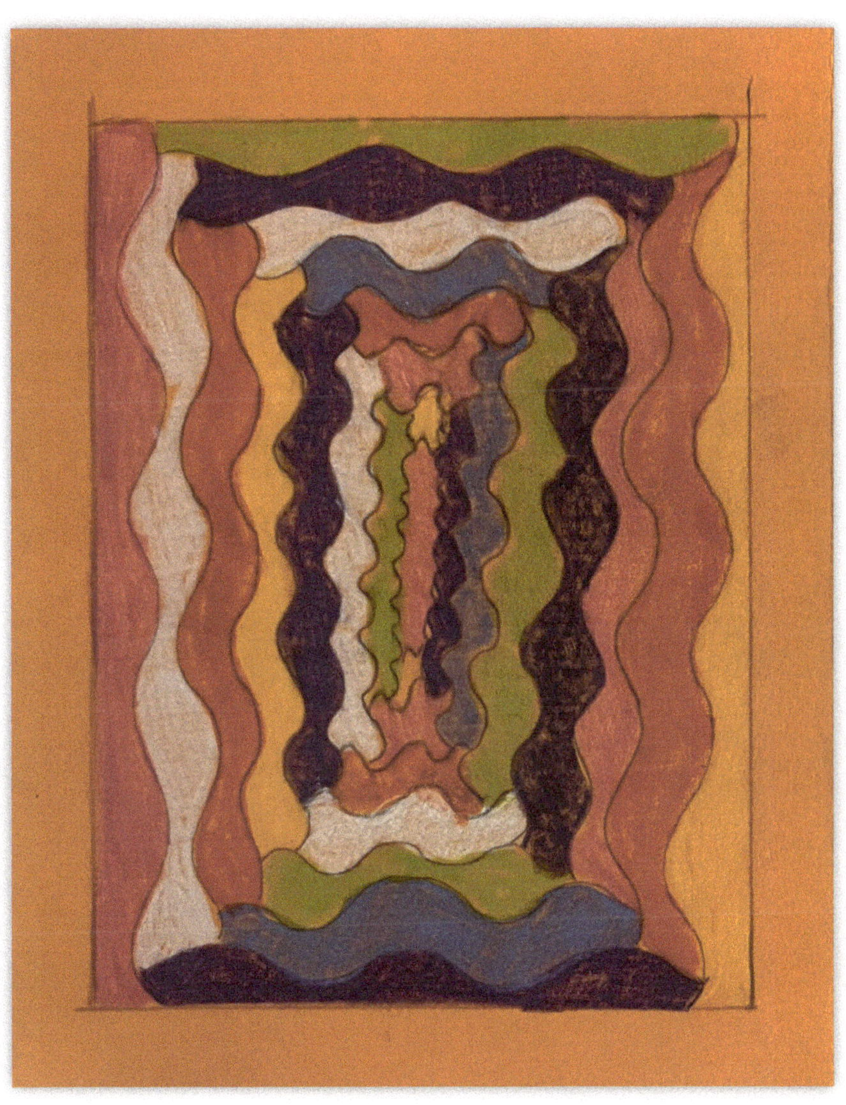

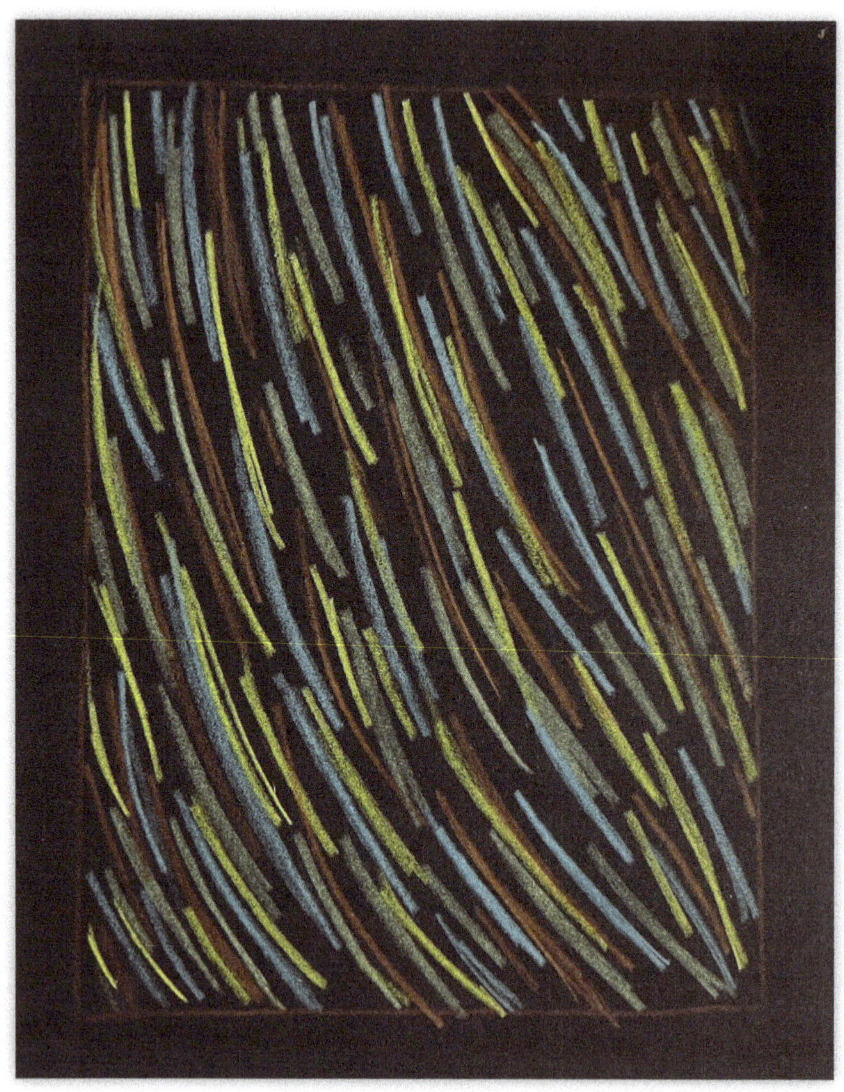

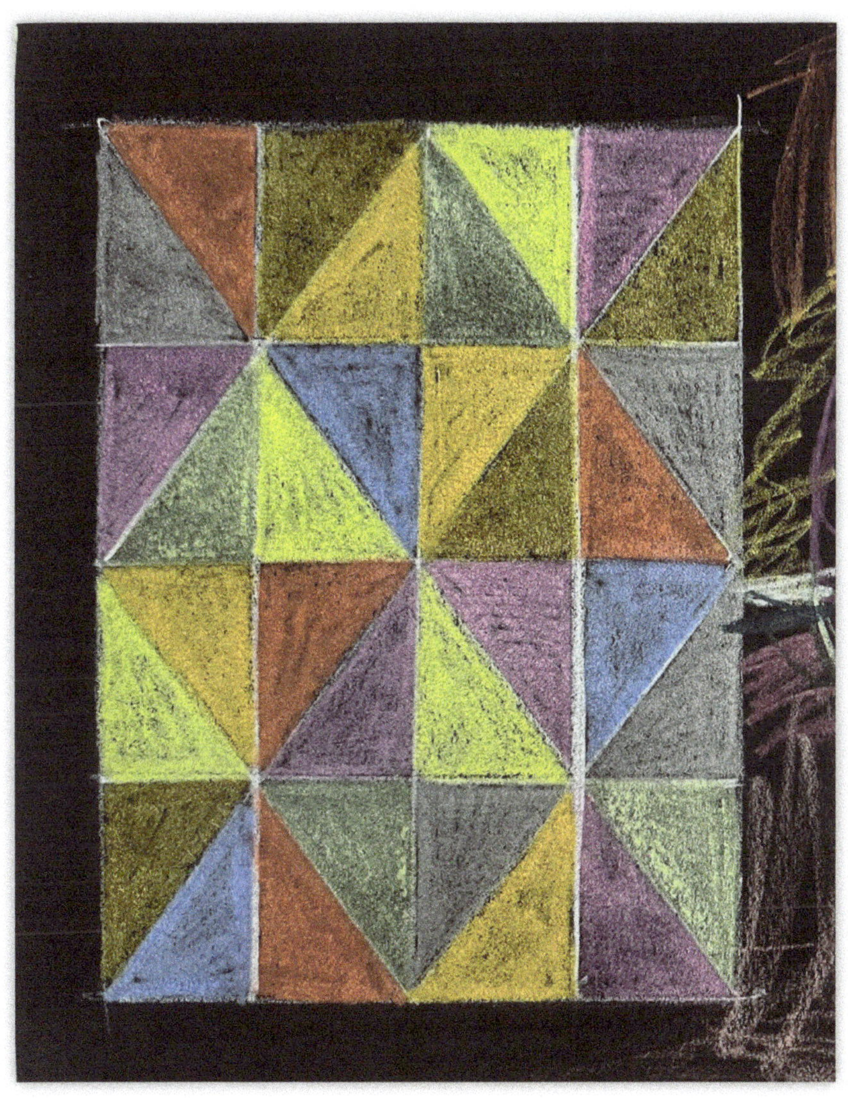

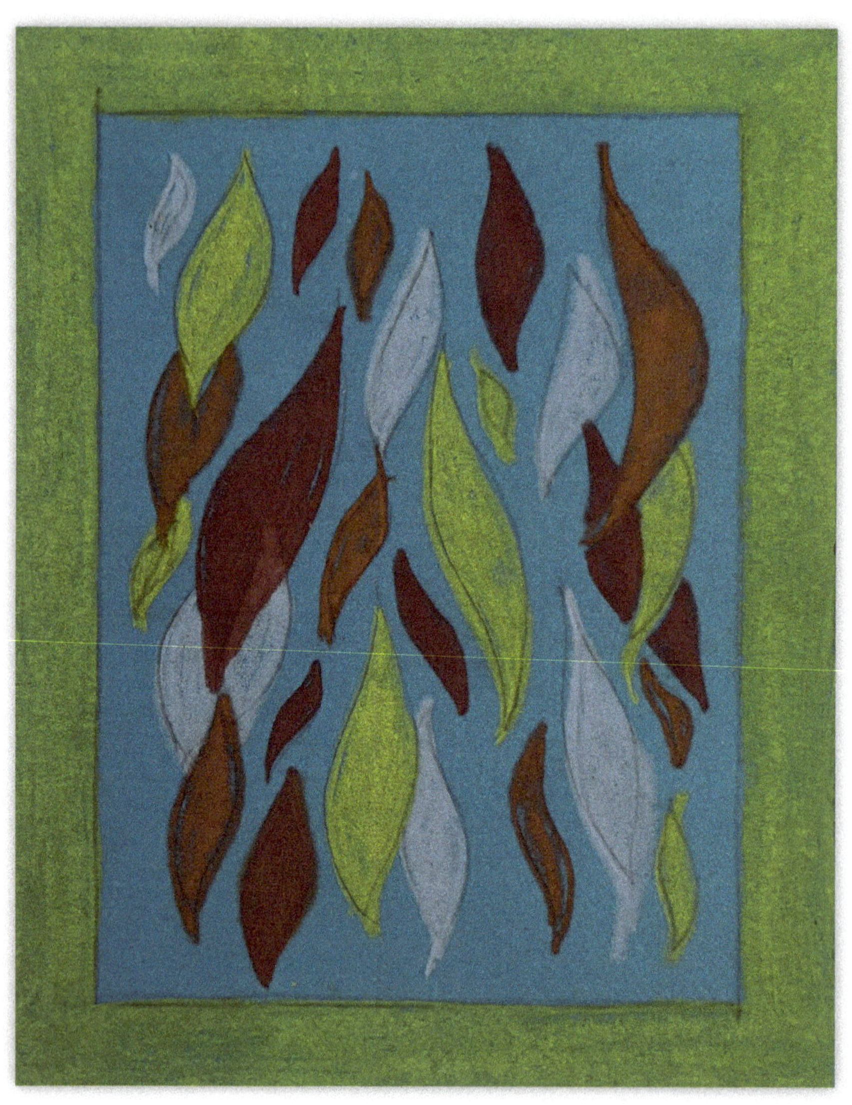

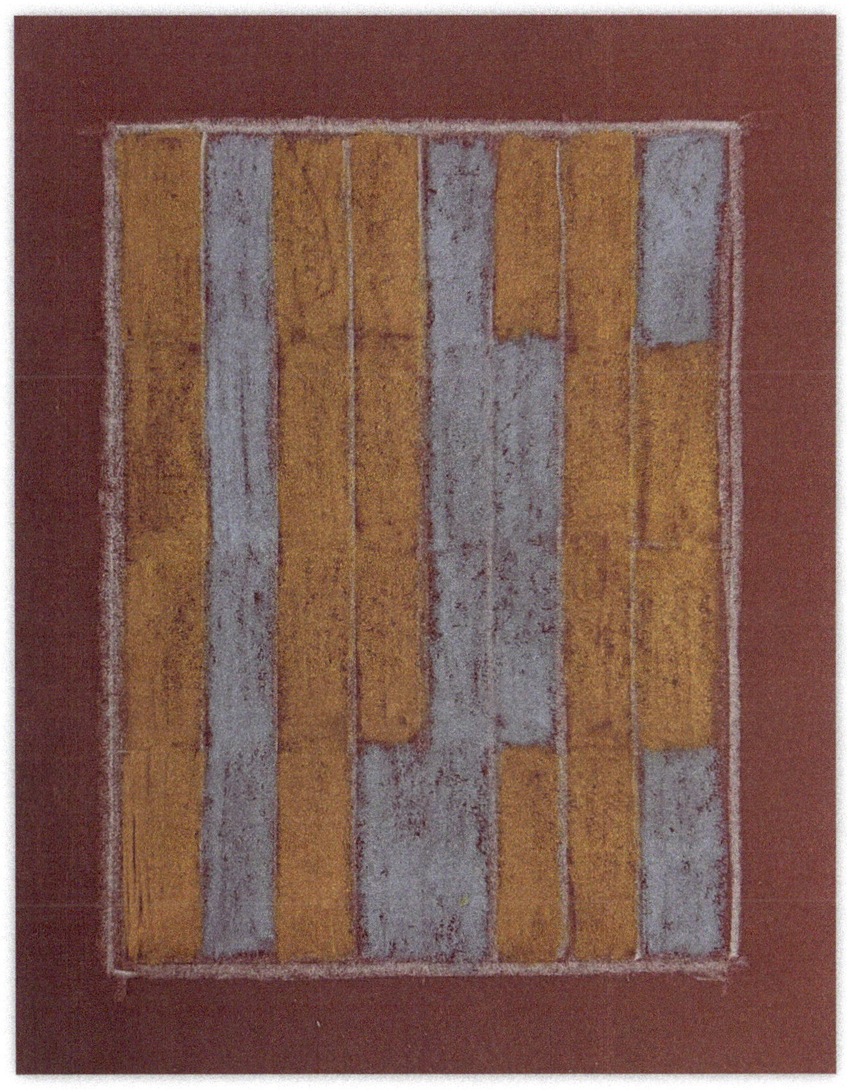

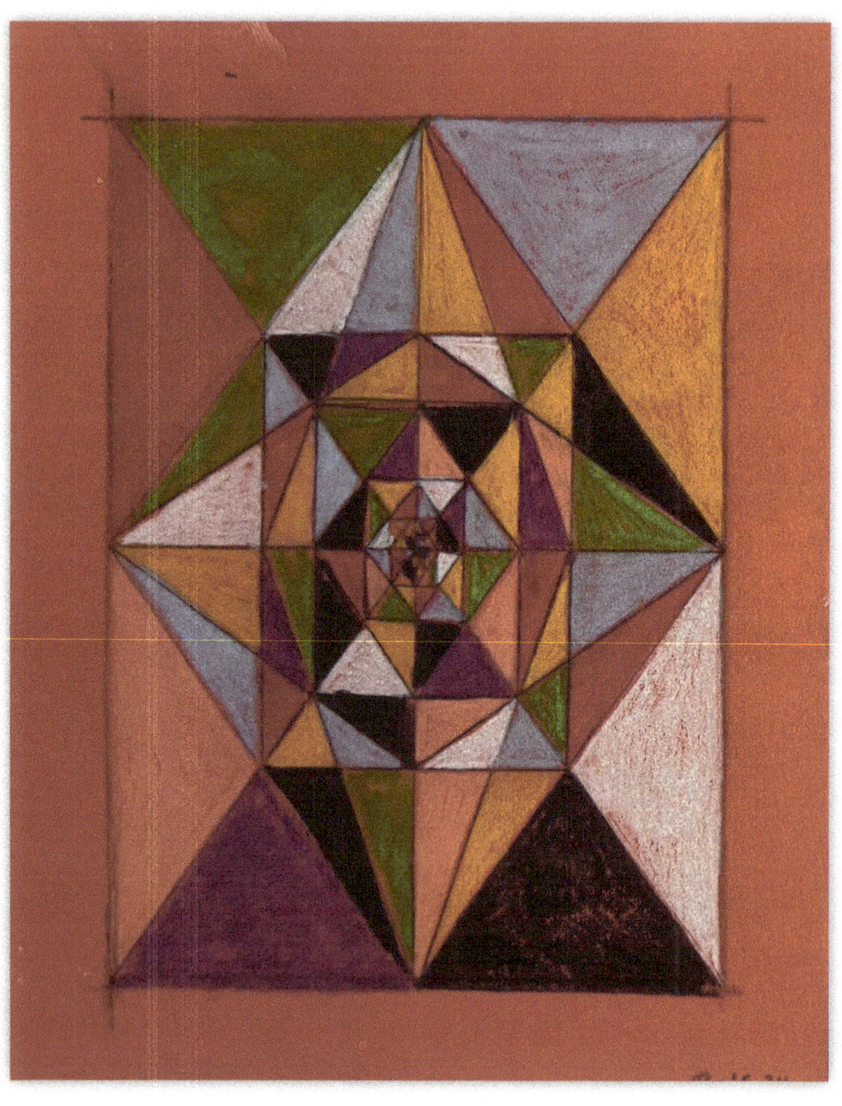

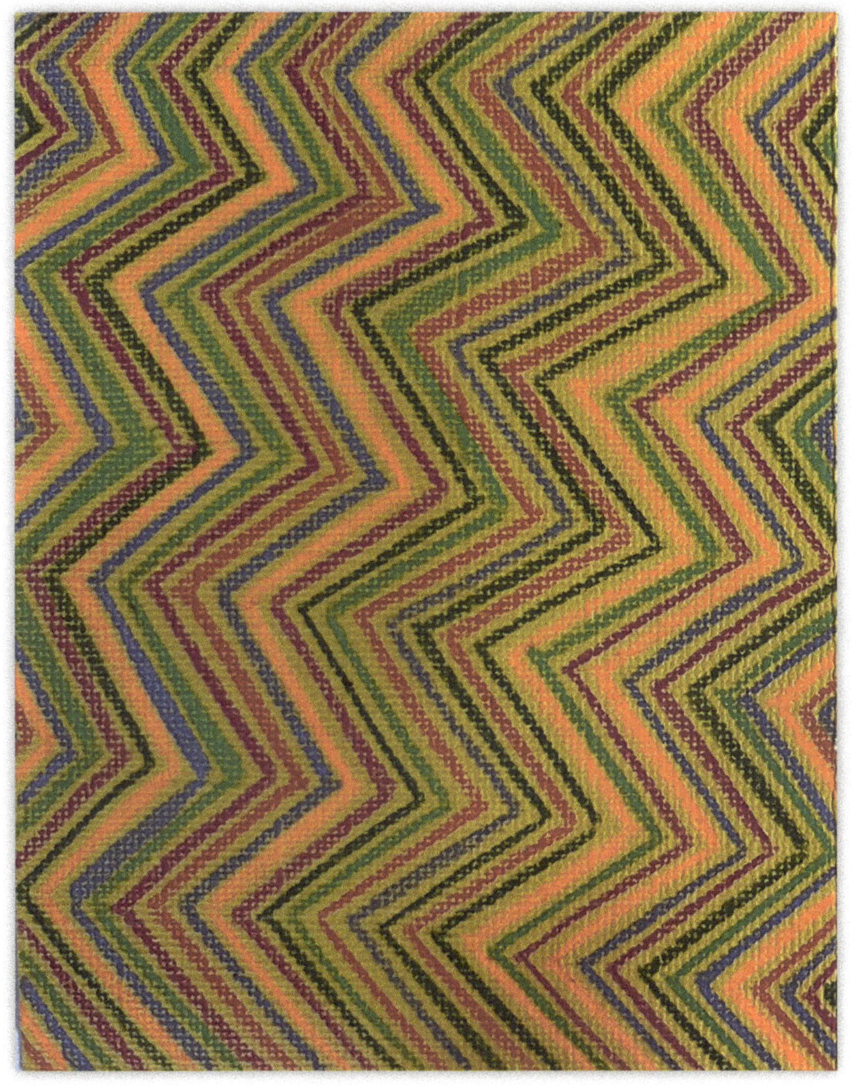

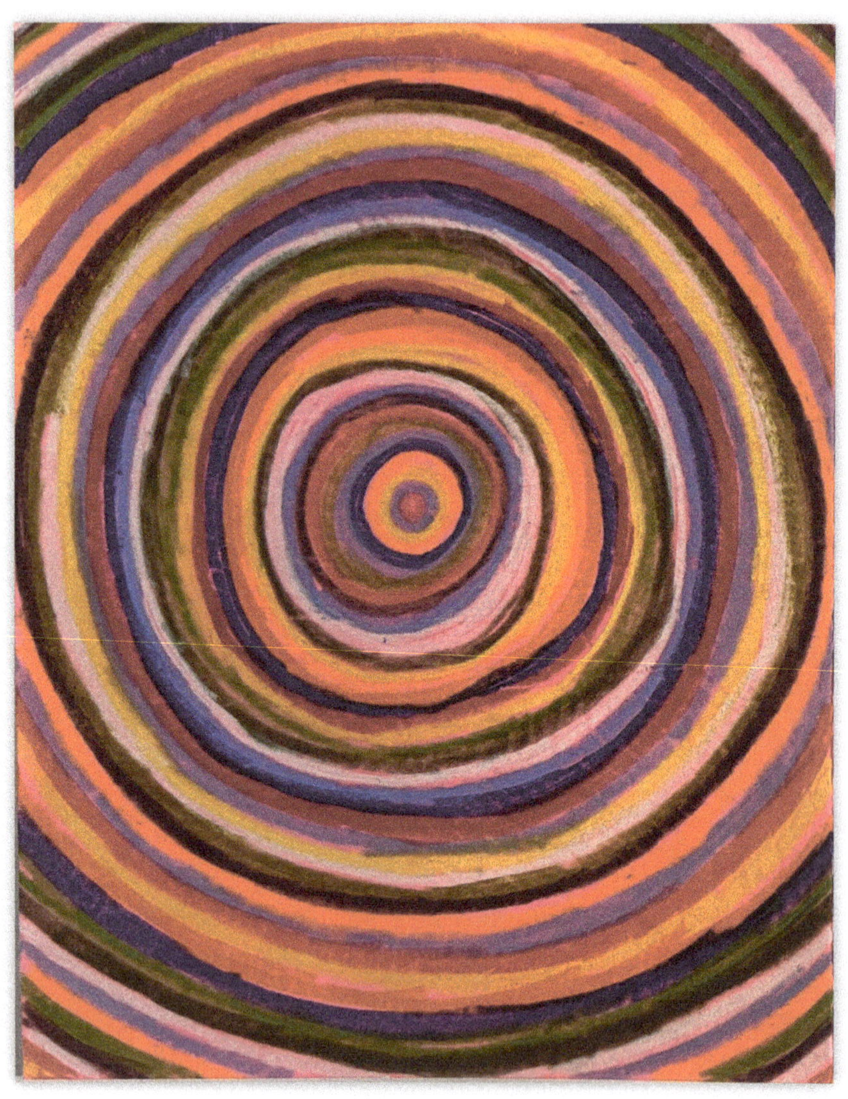

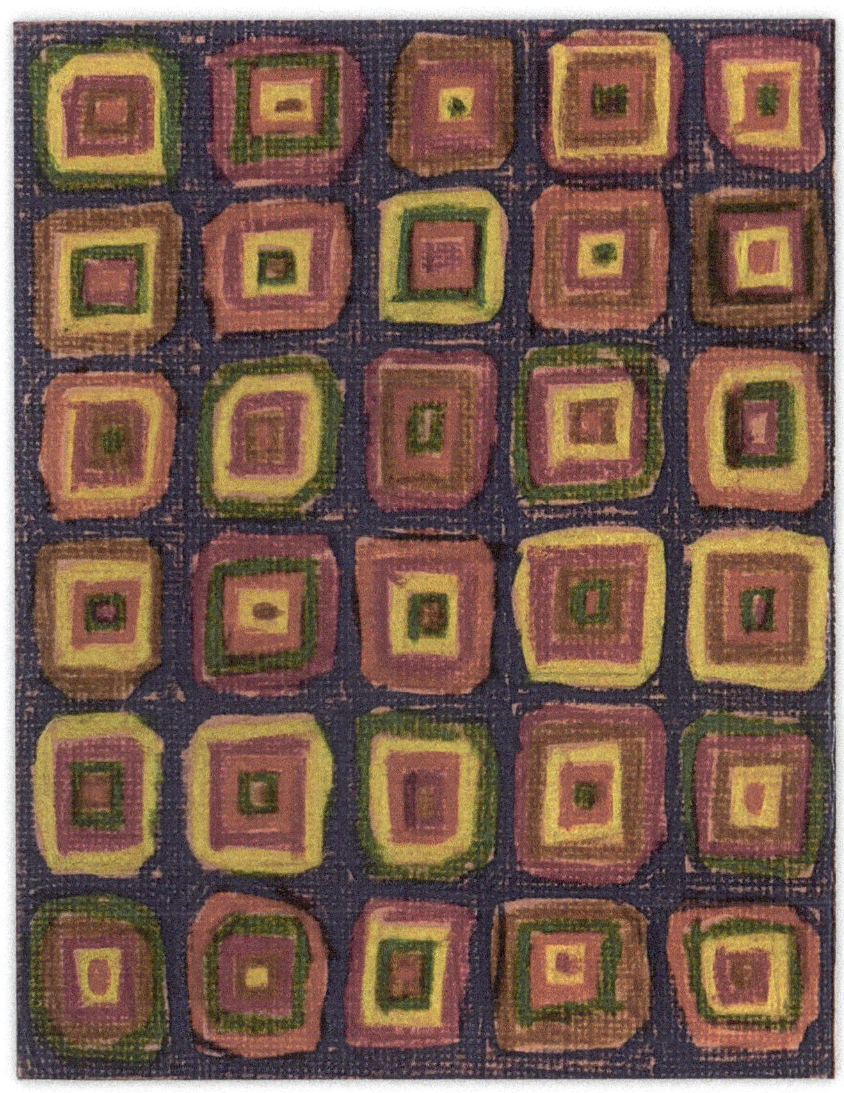

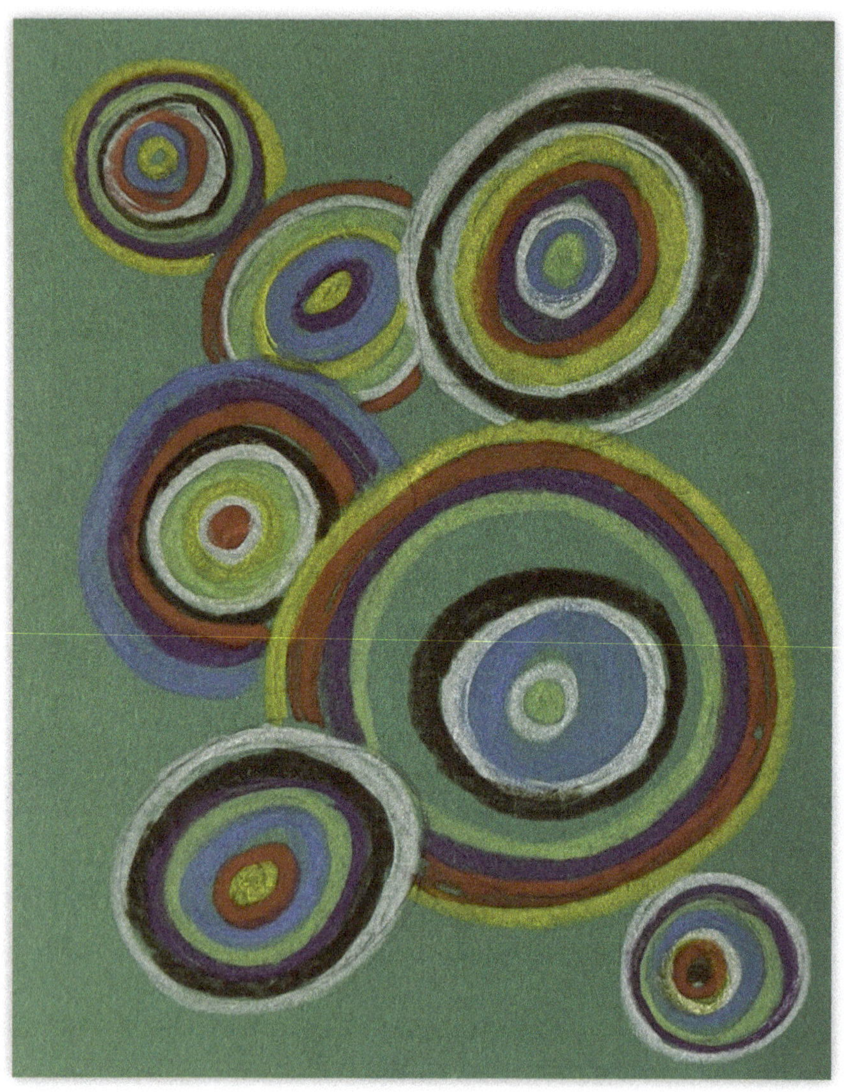

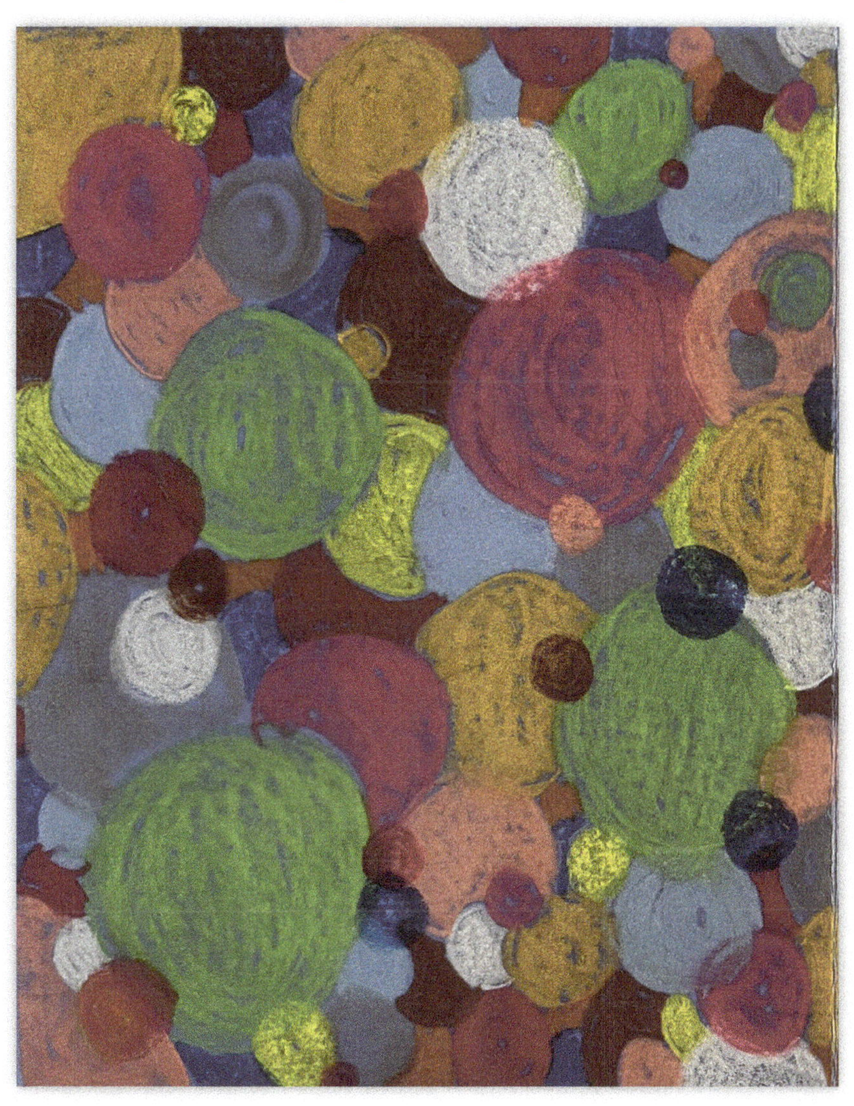

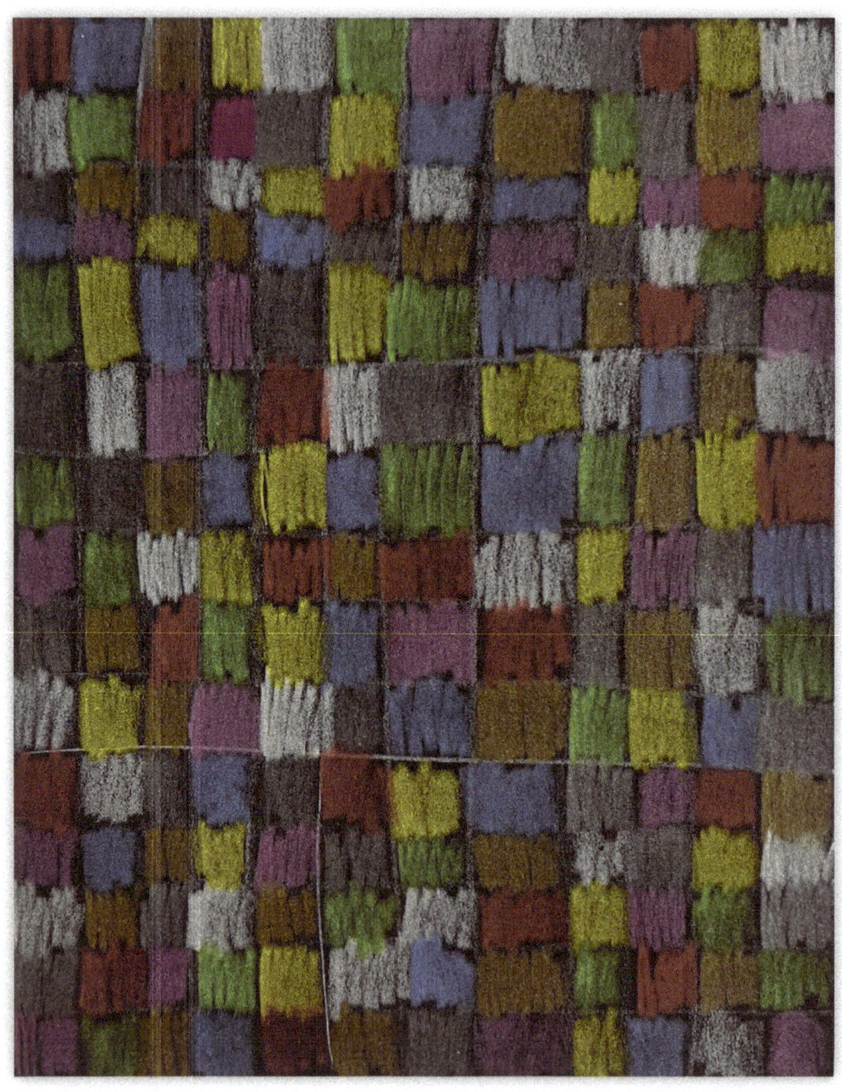

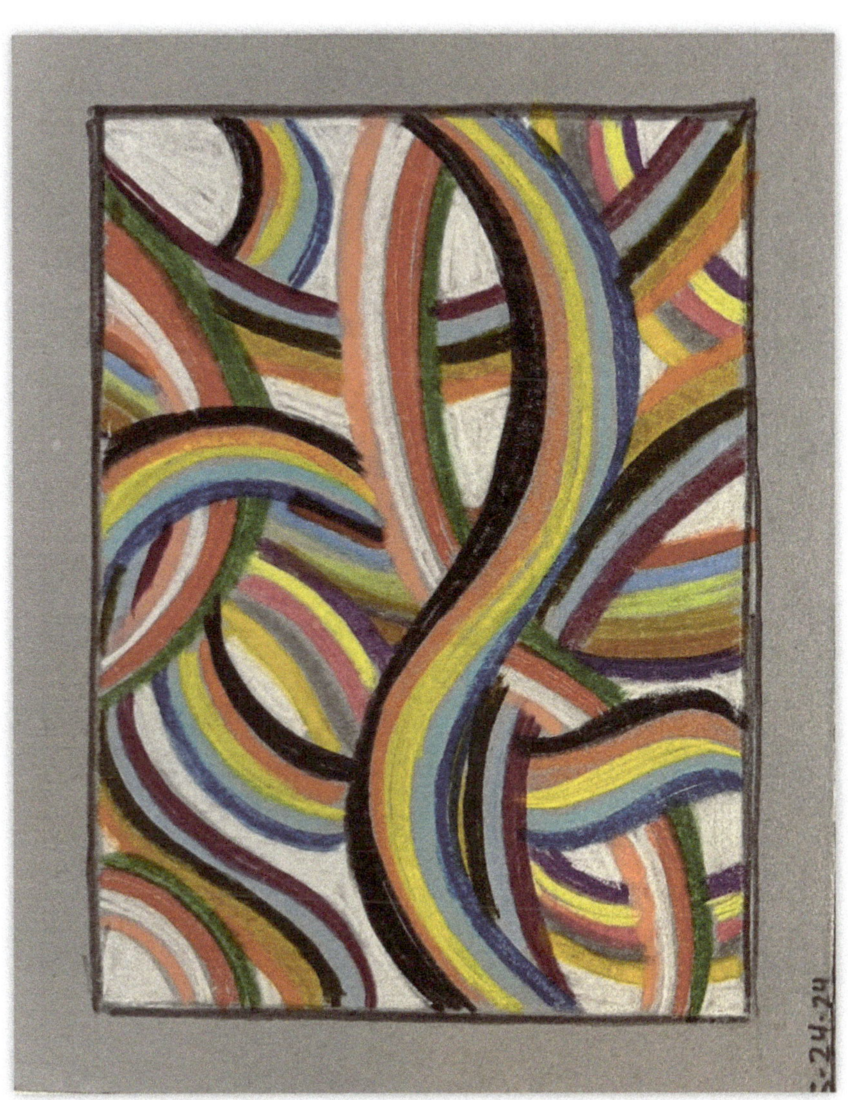

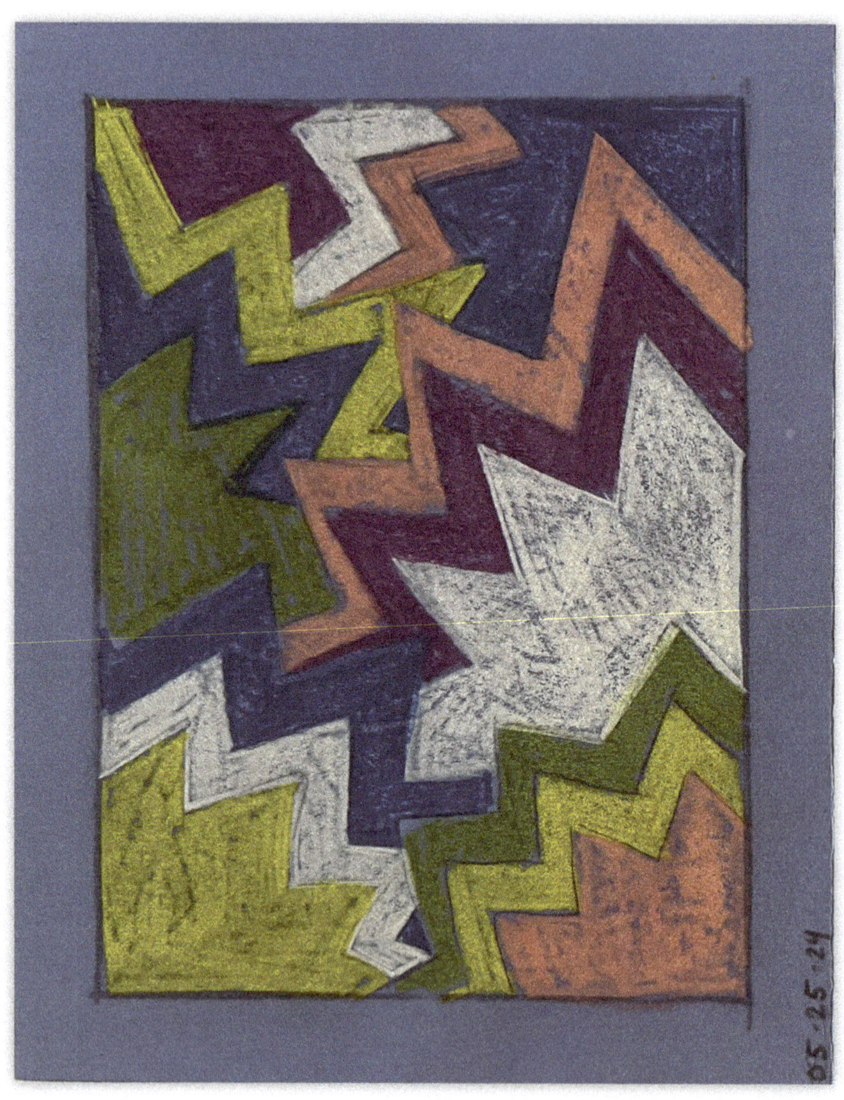

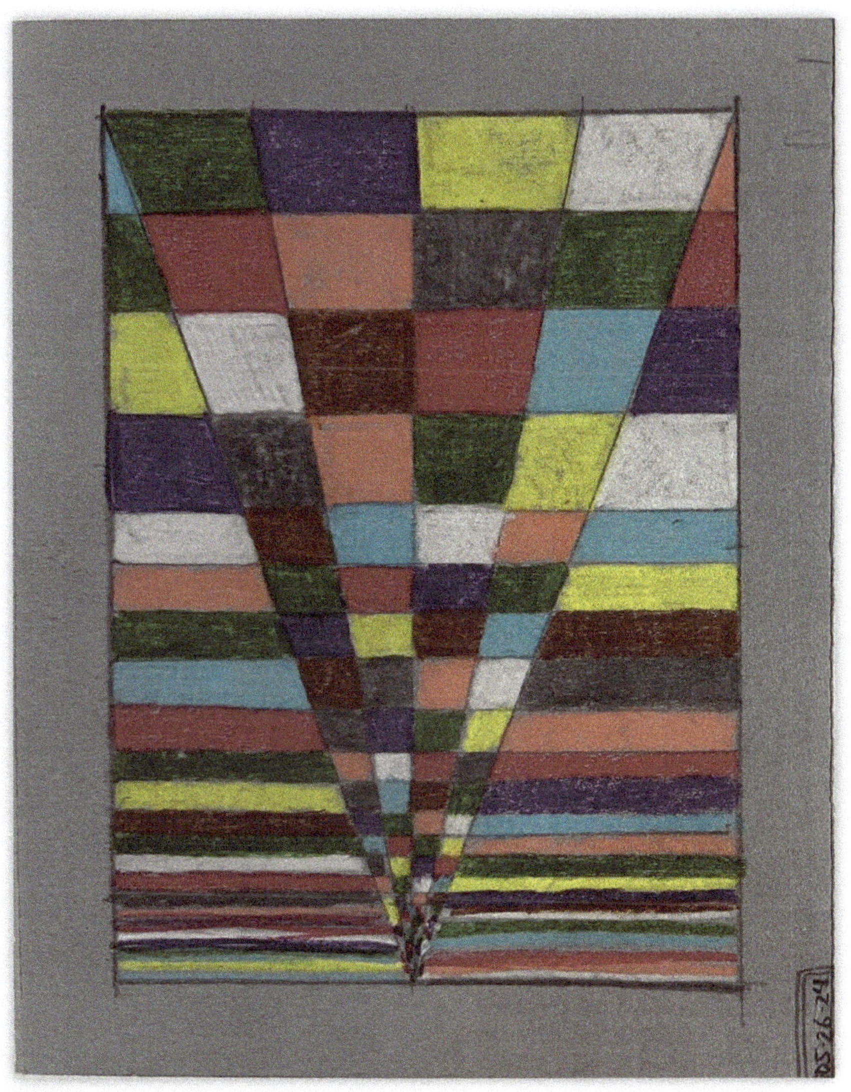

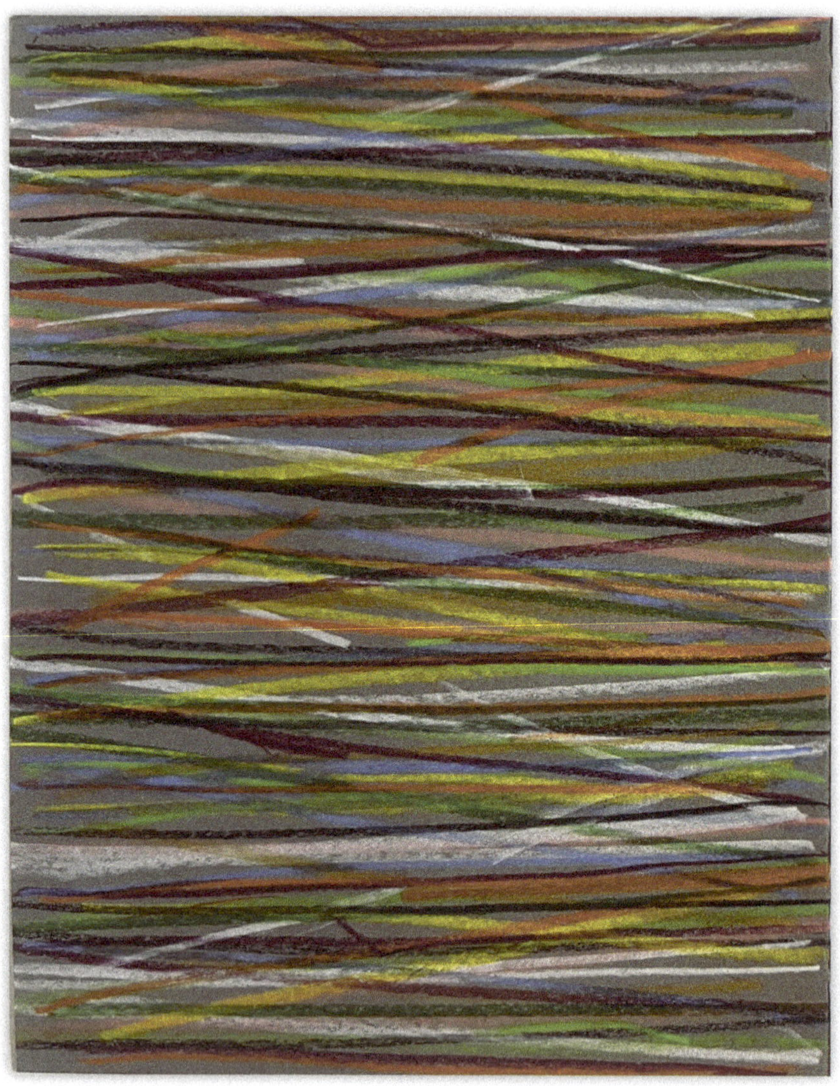

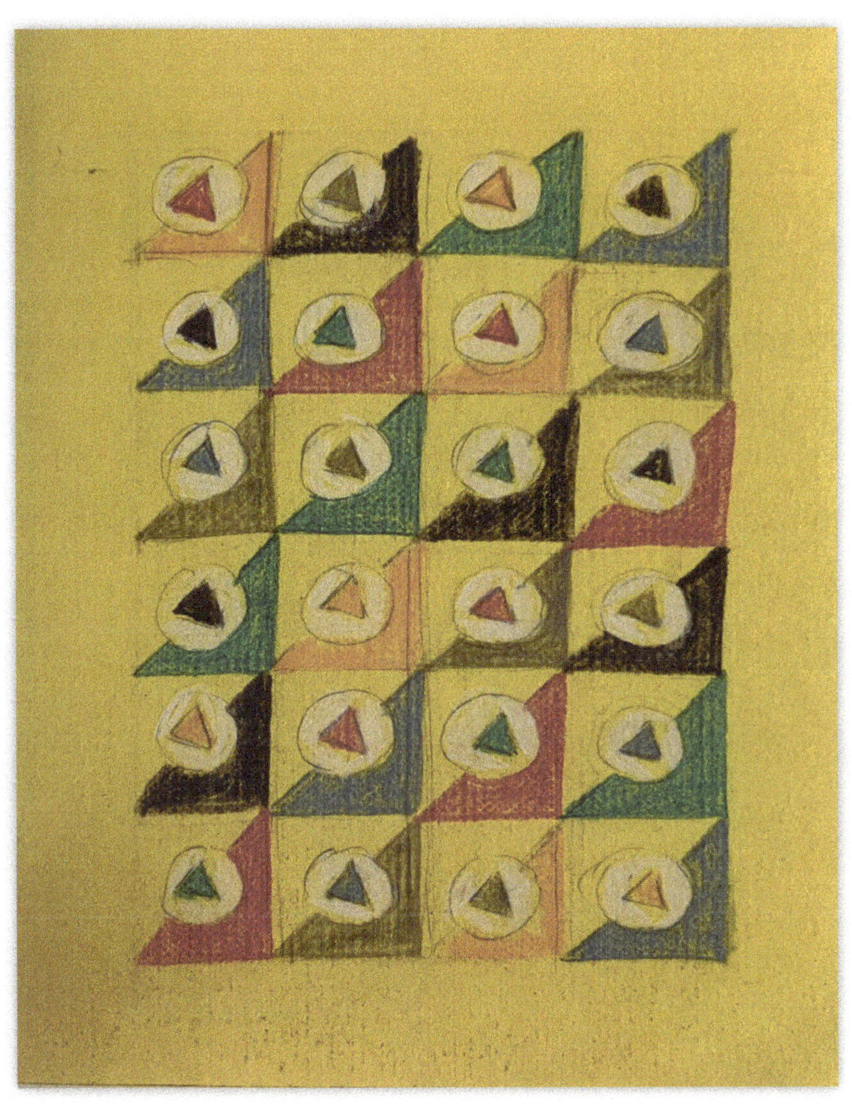

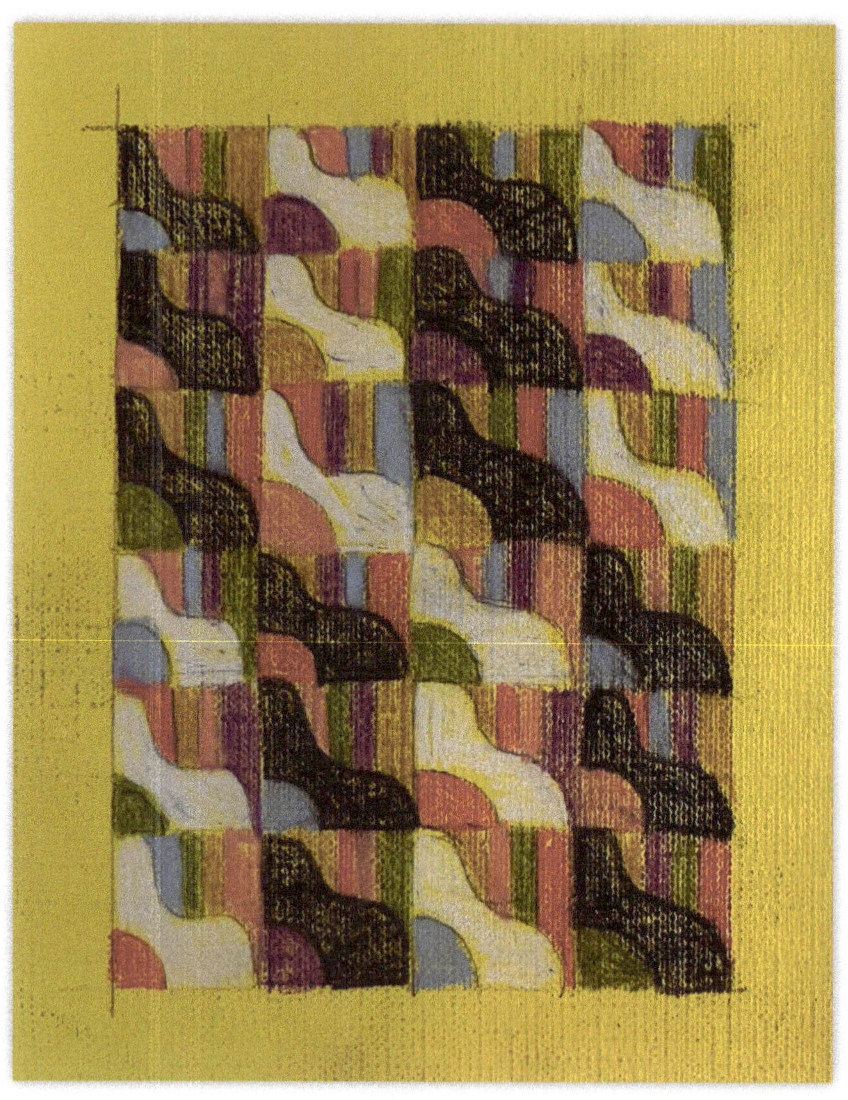

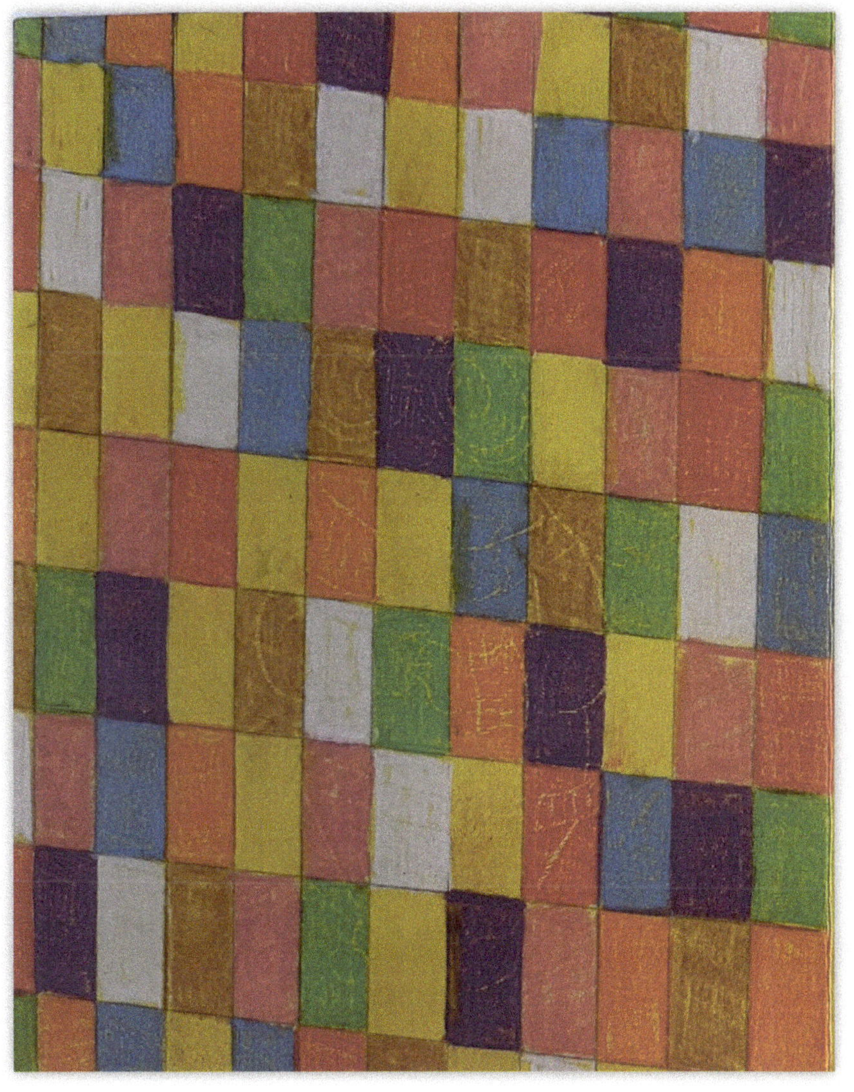

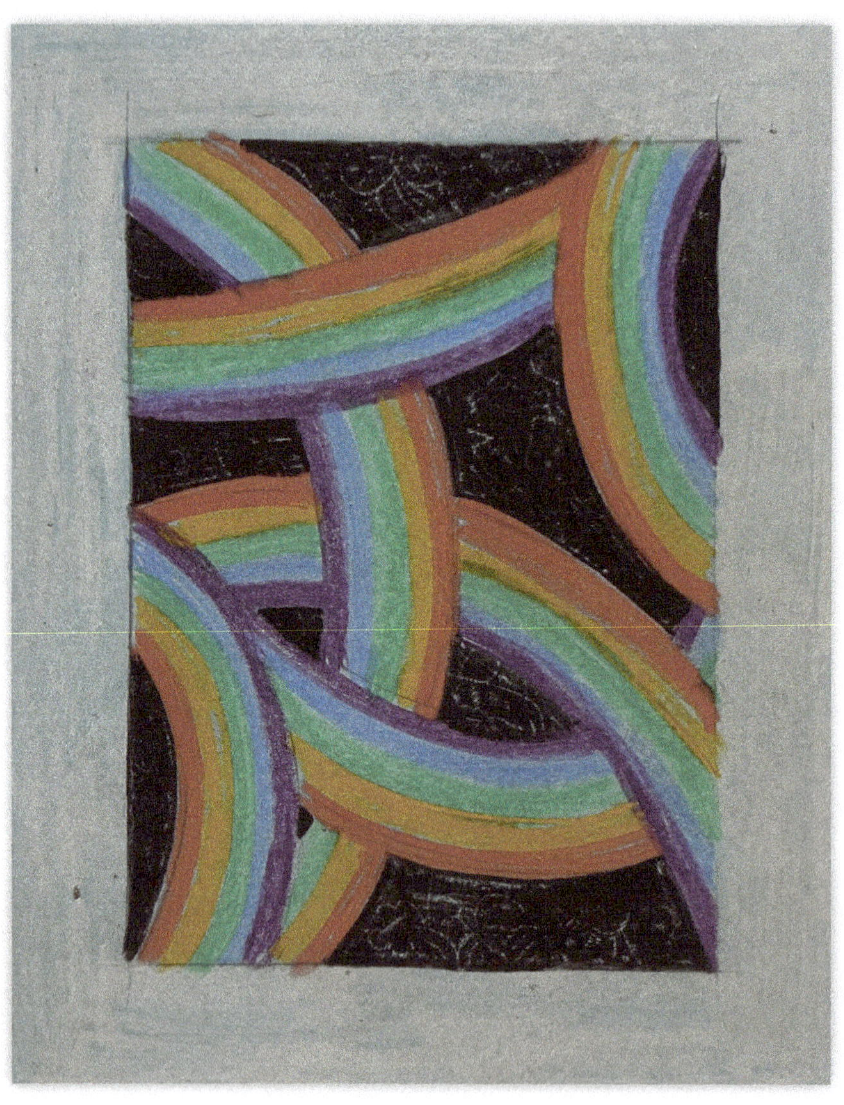

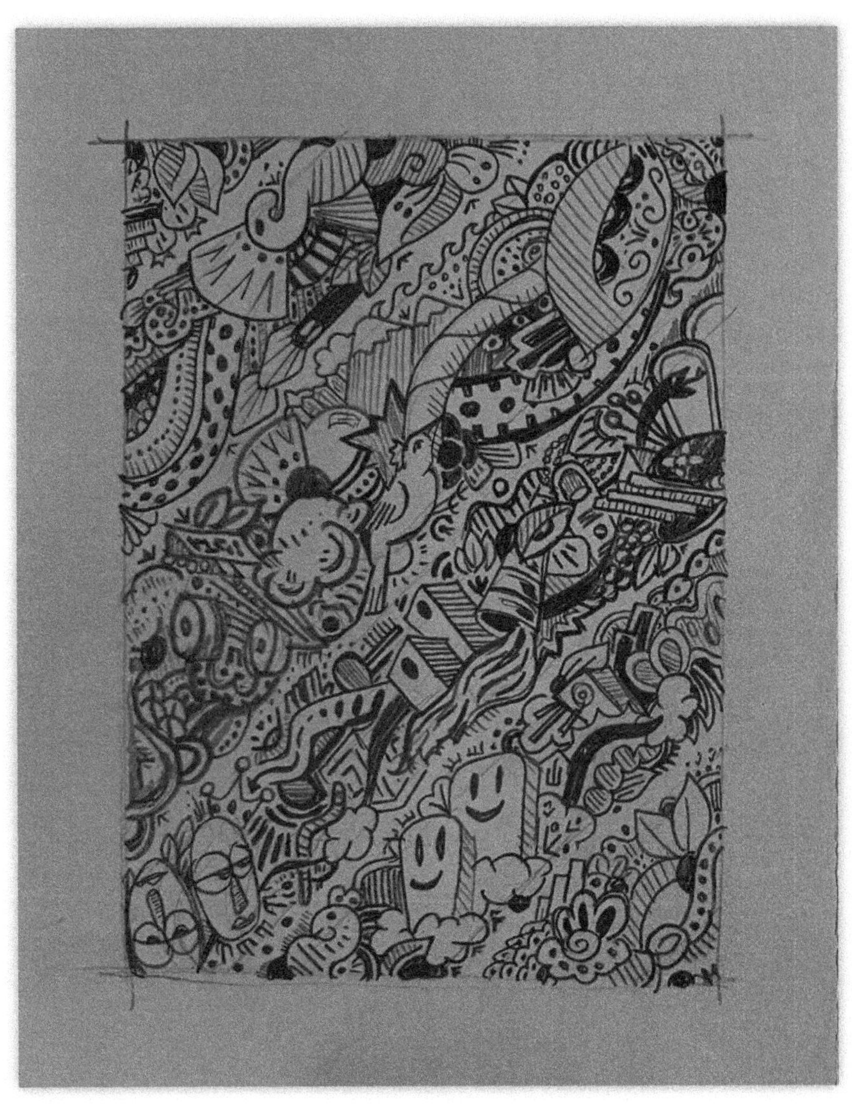

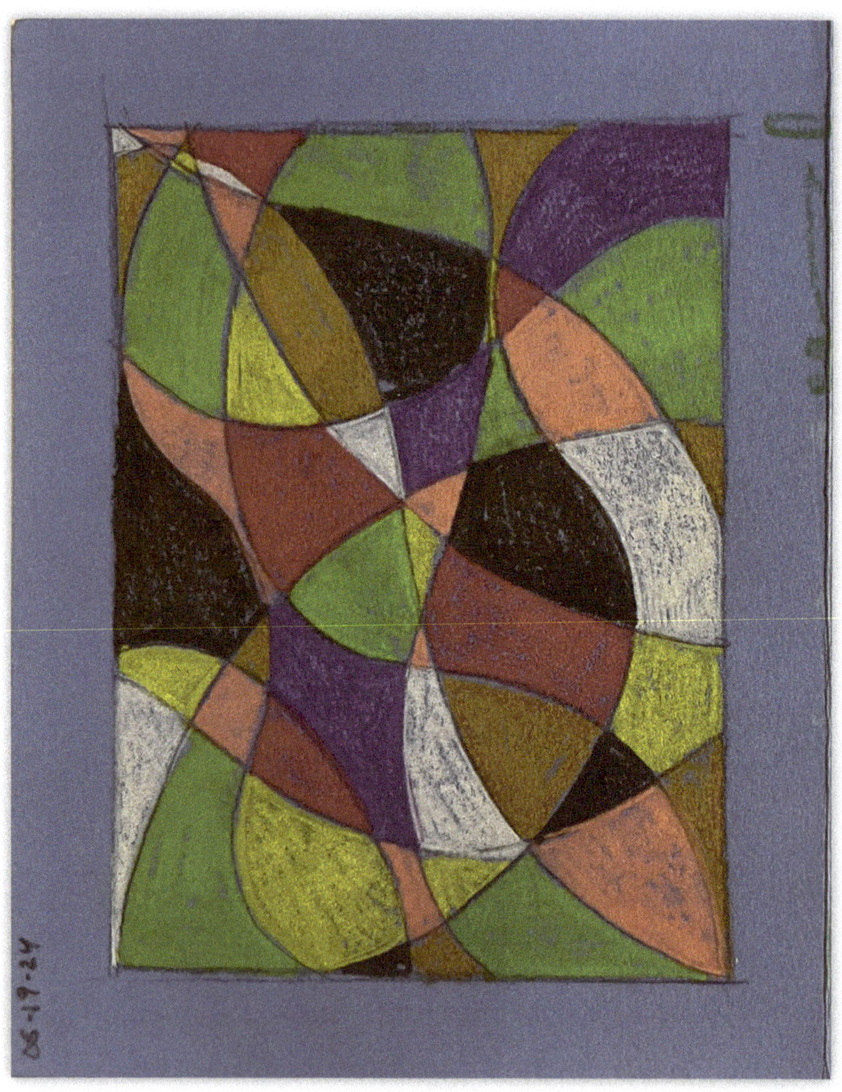

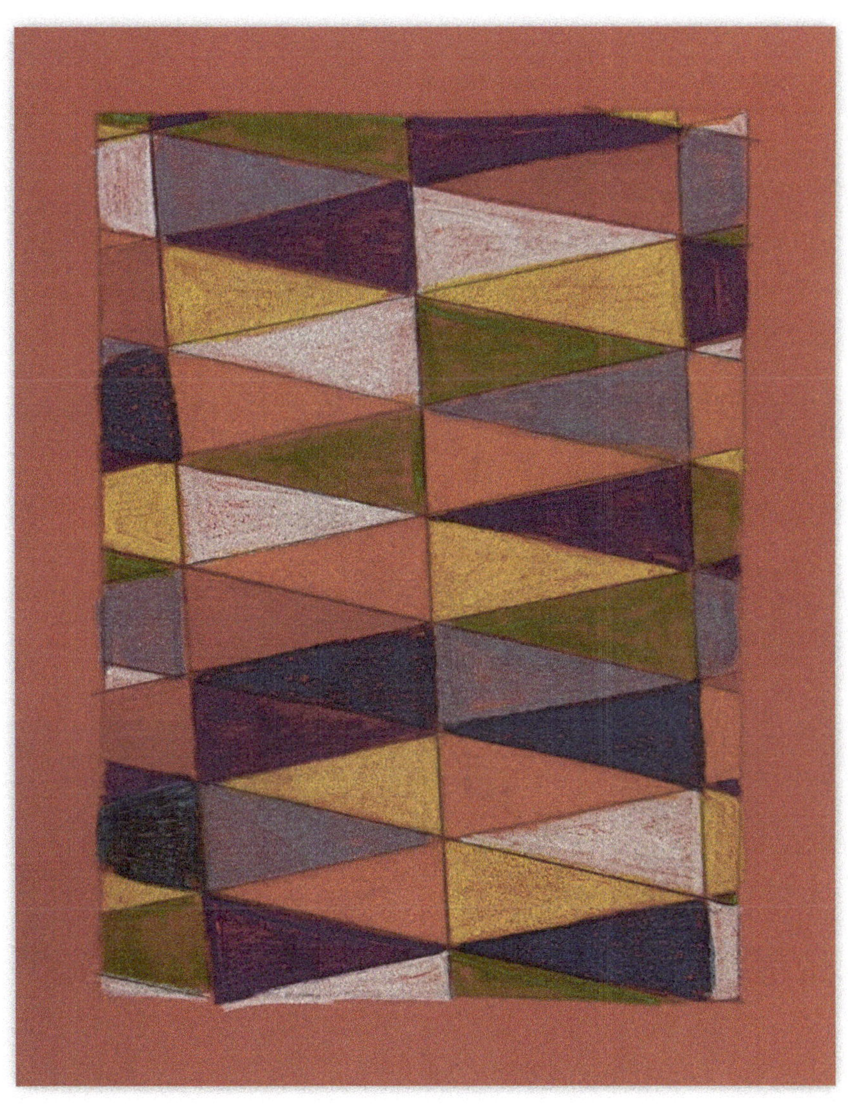

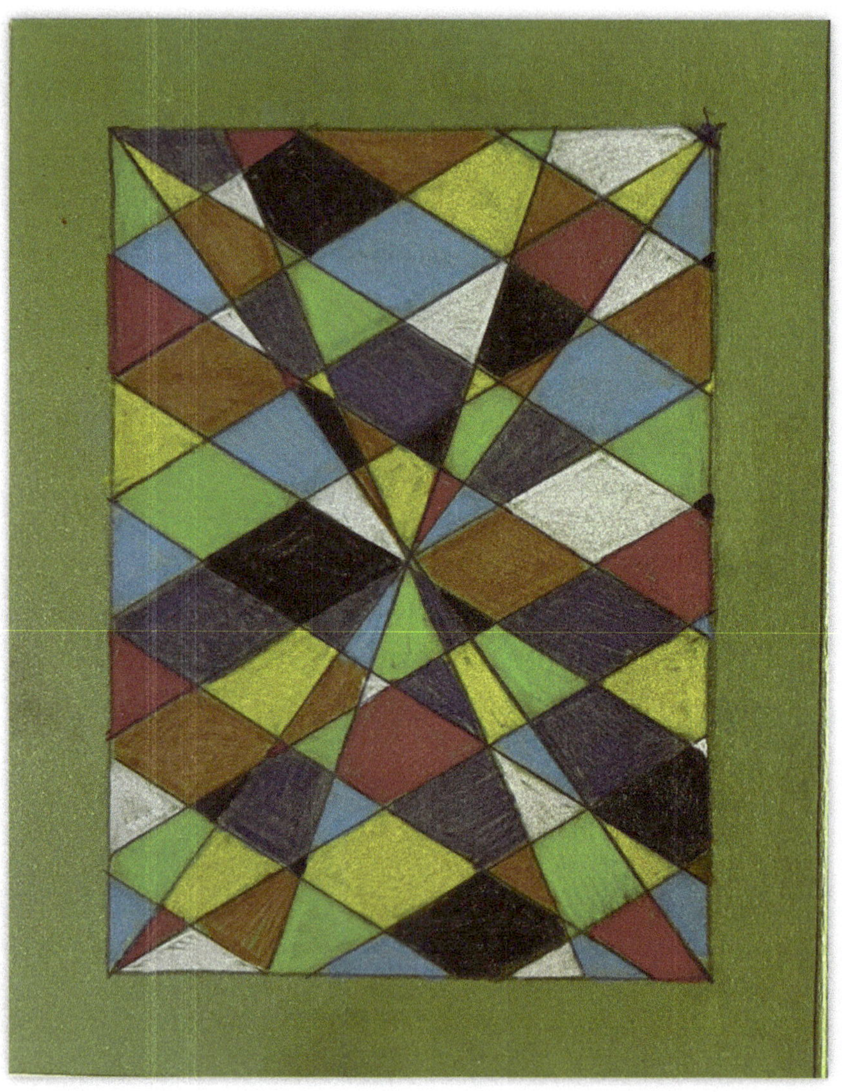

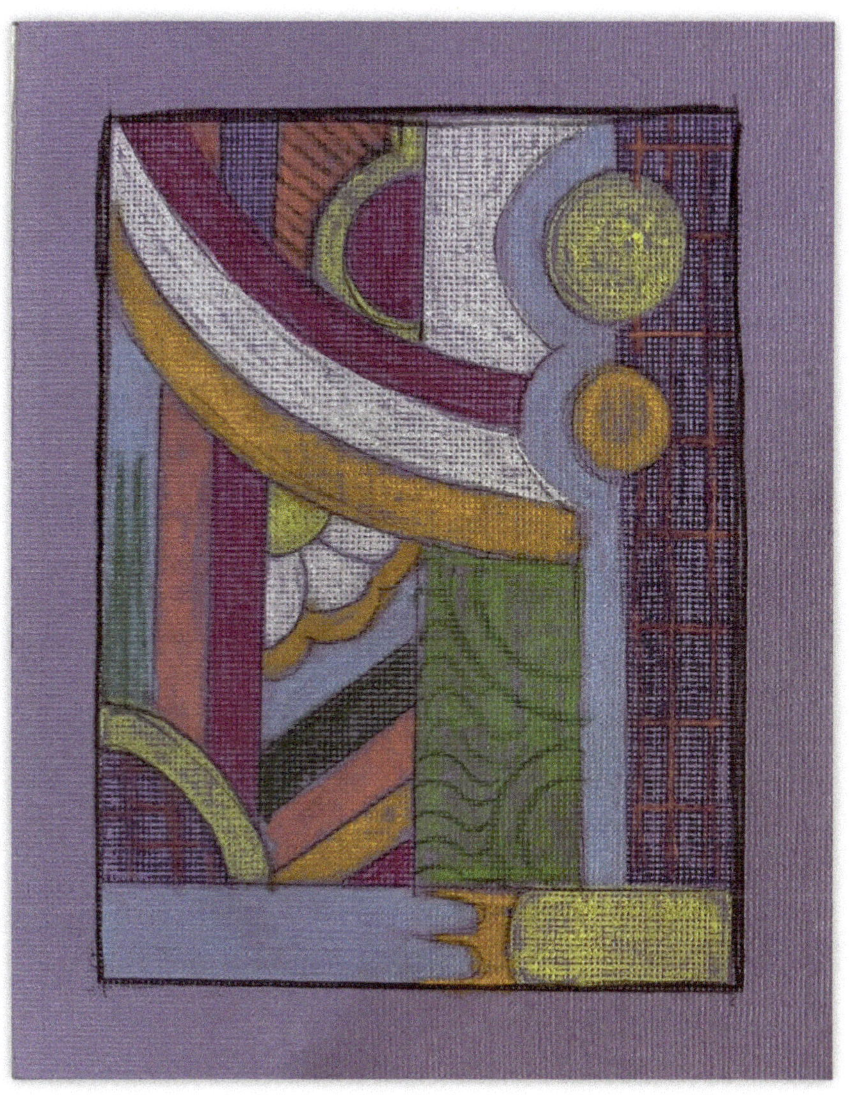

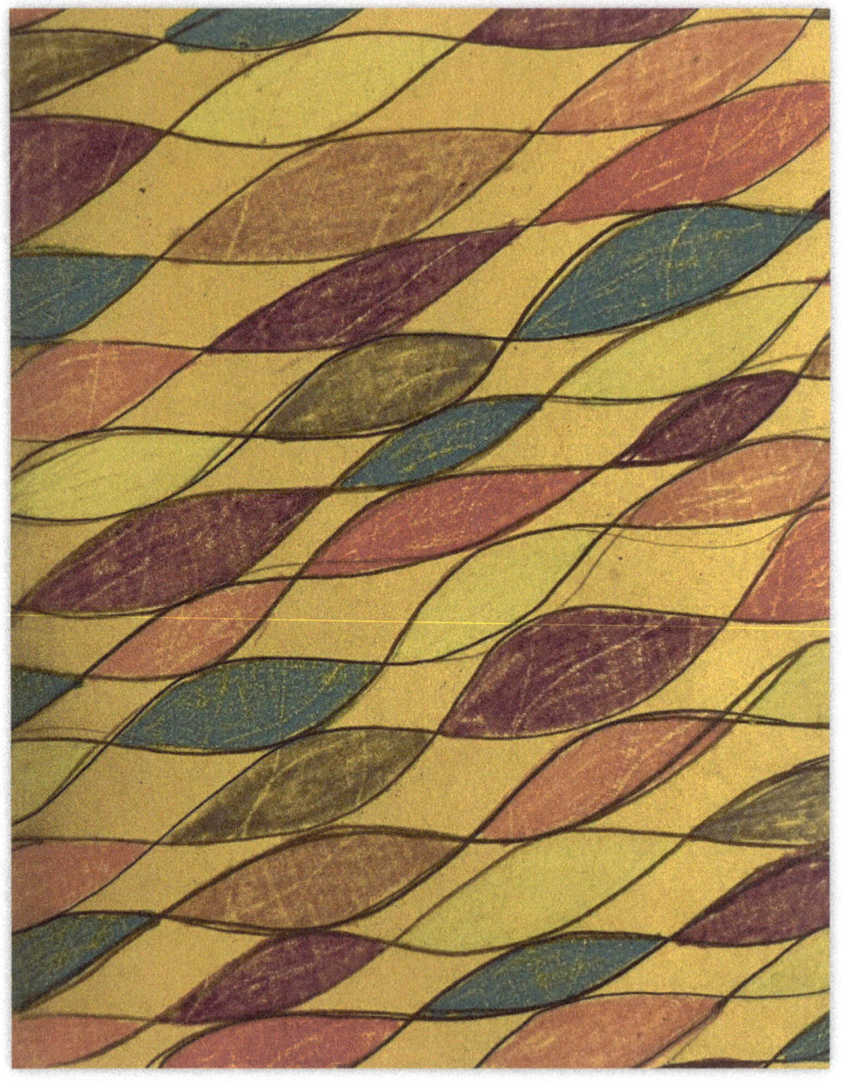

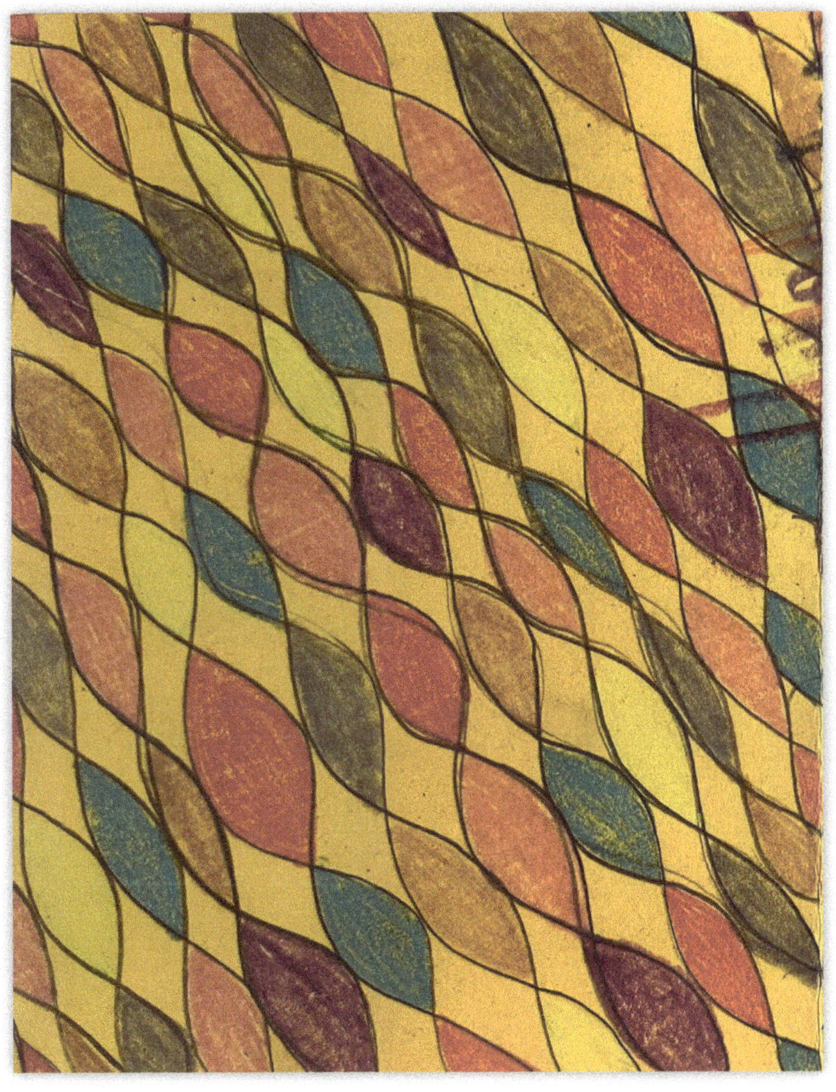

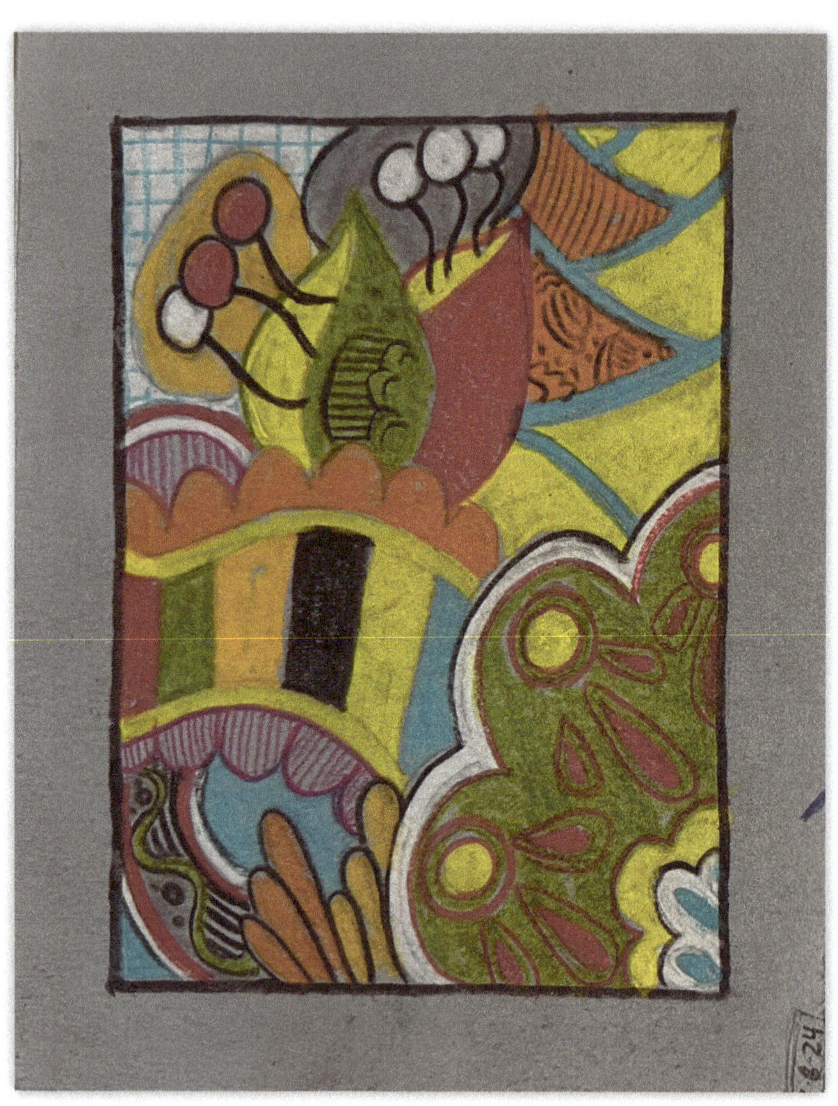

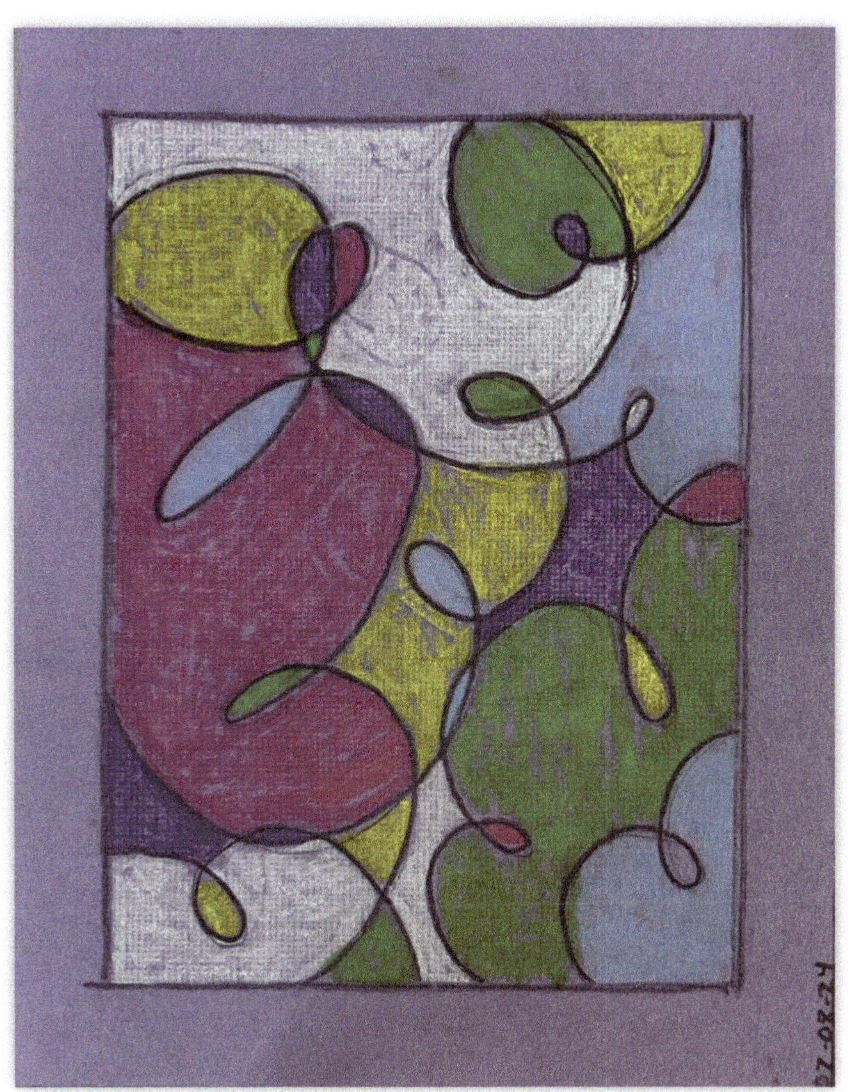

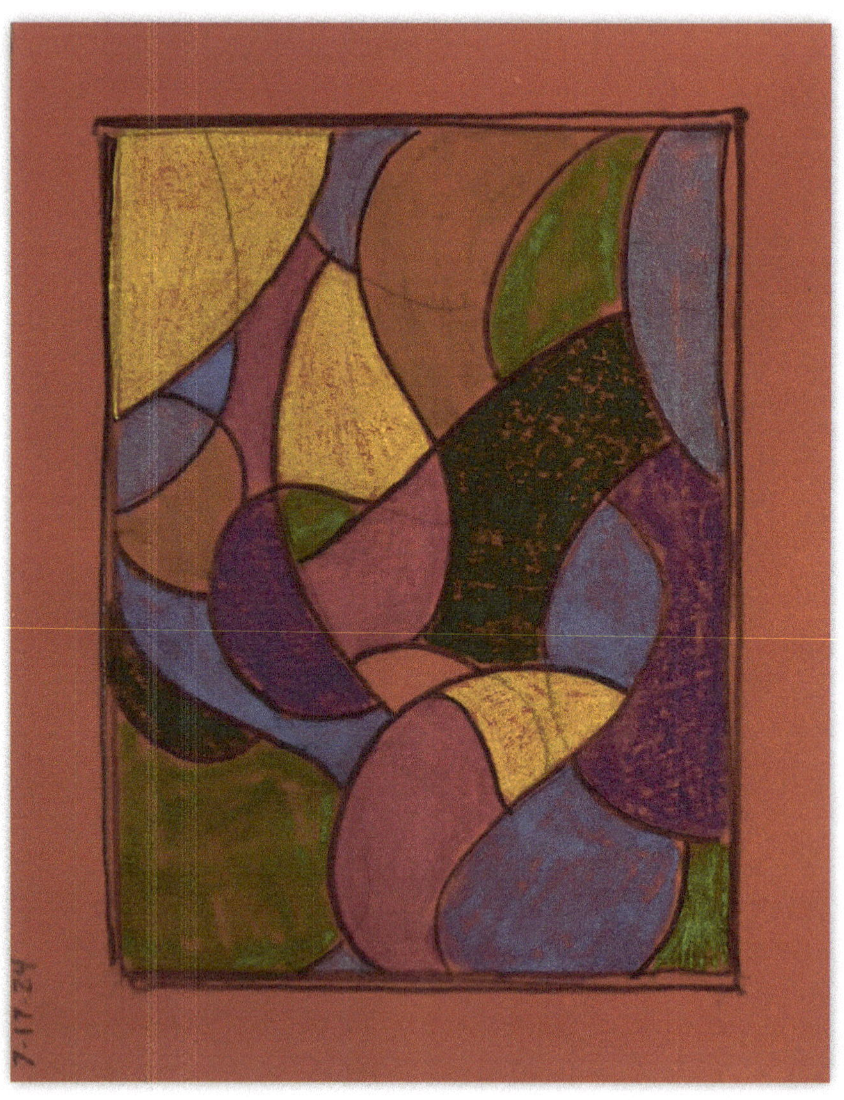

7-17-24

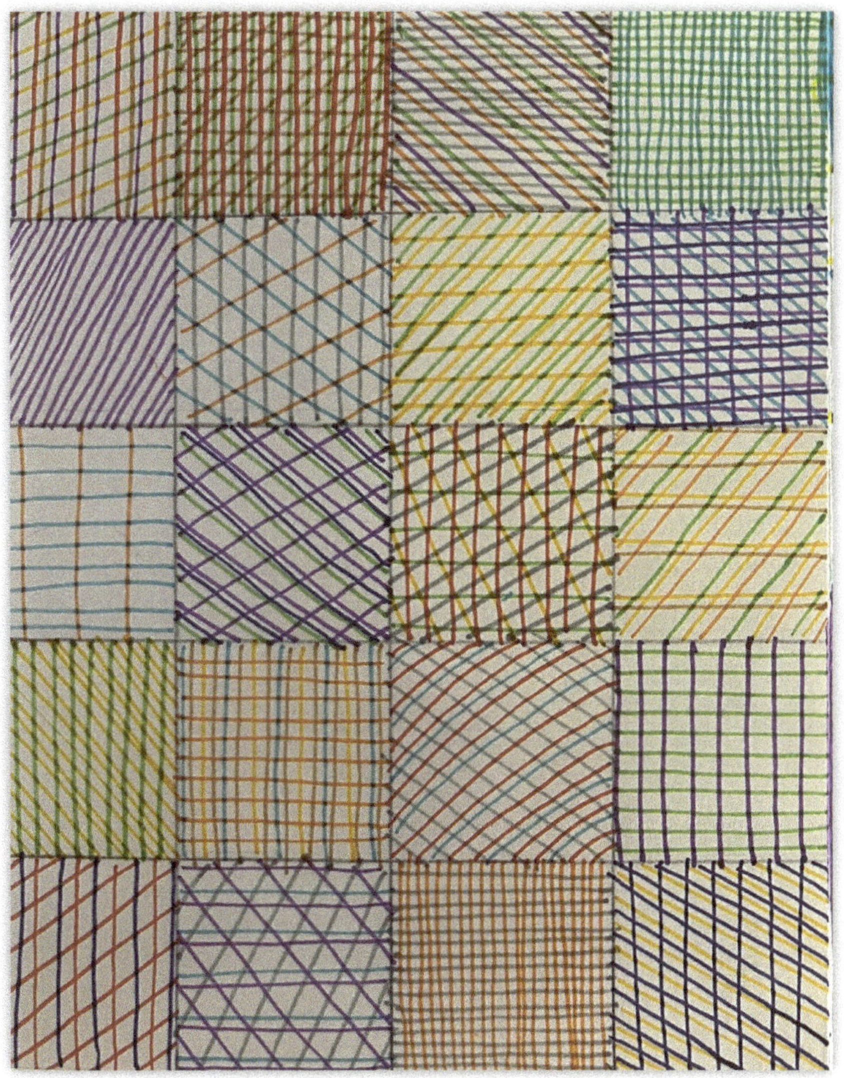

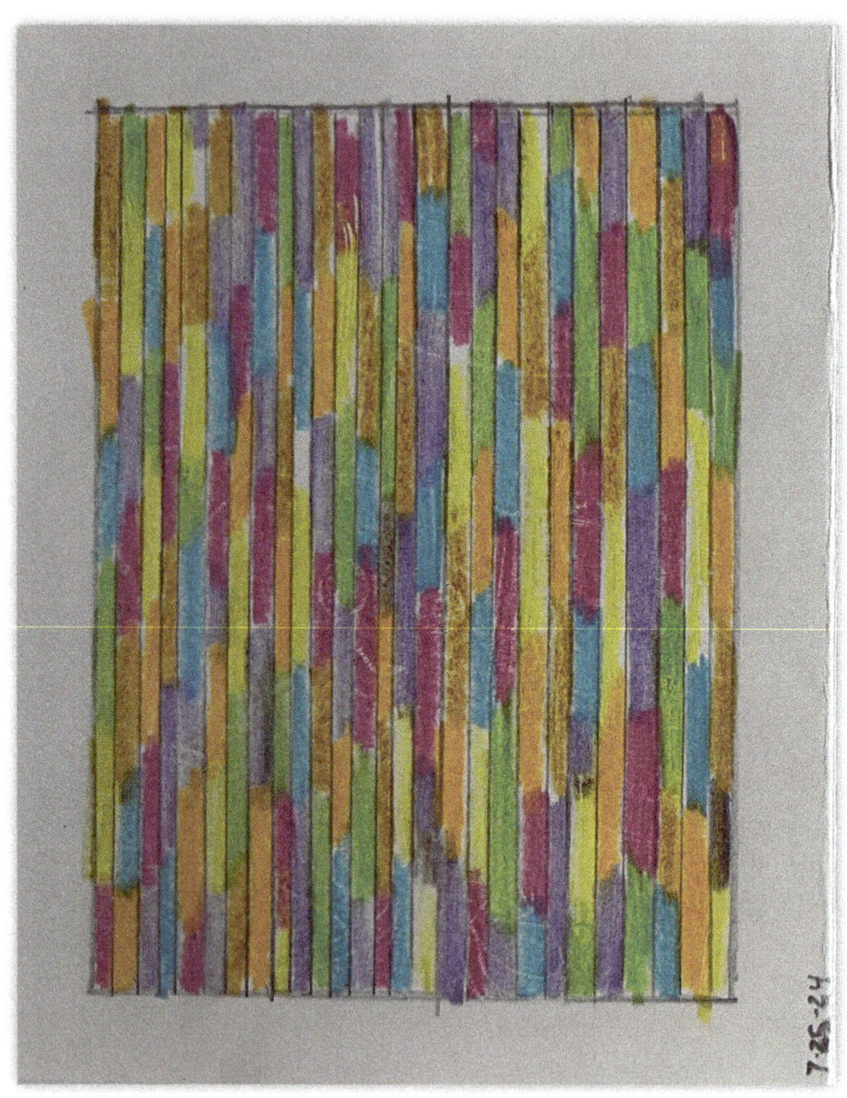

7.25-24

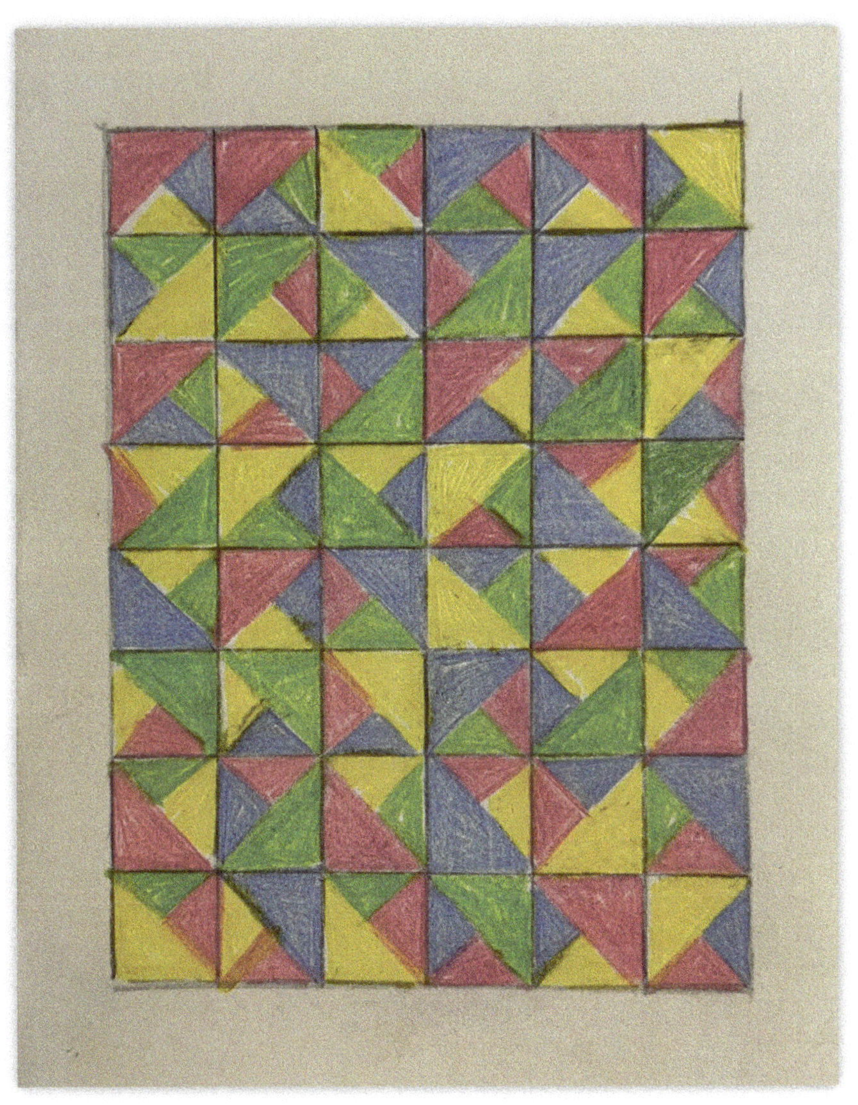

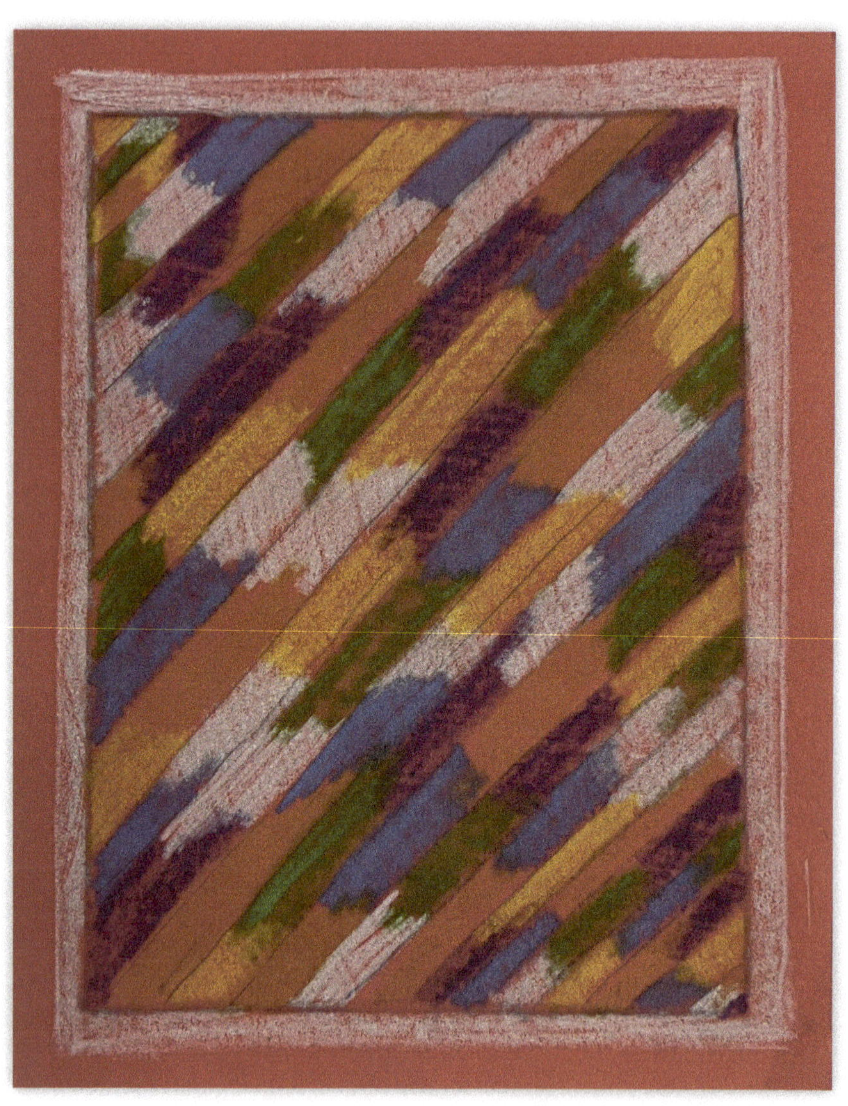

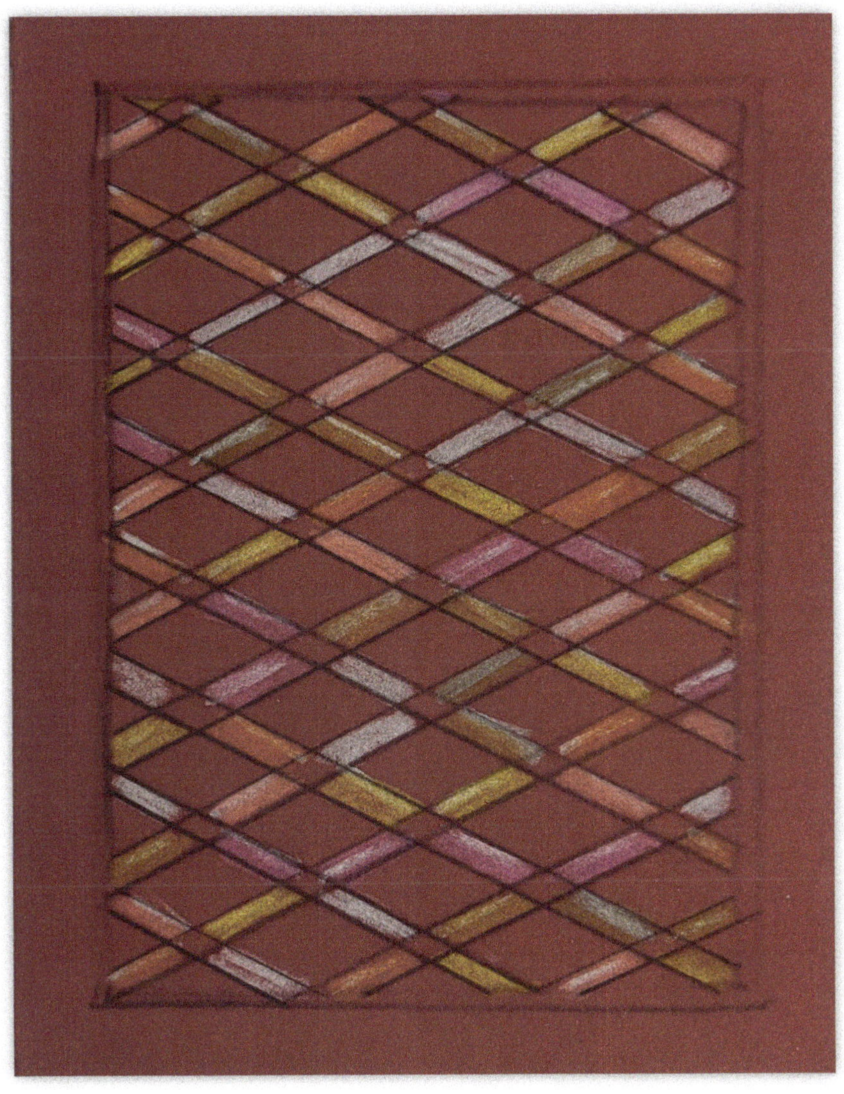

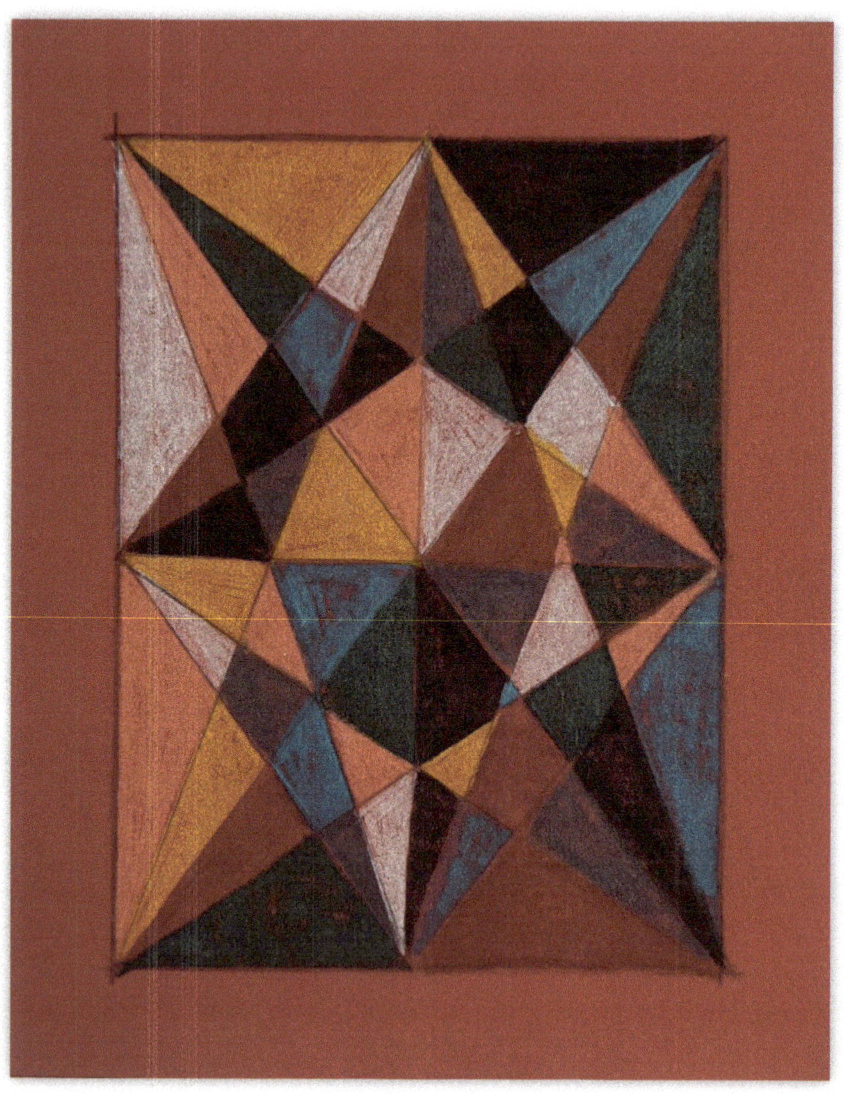

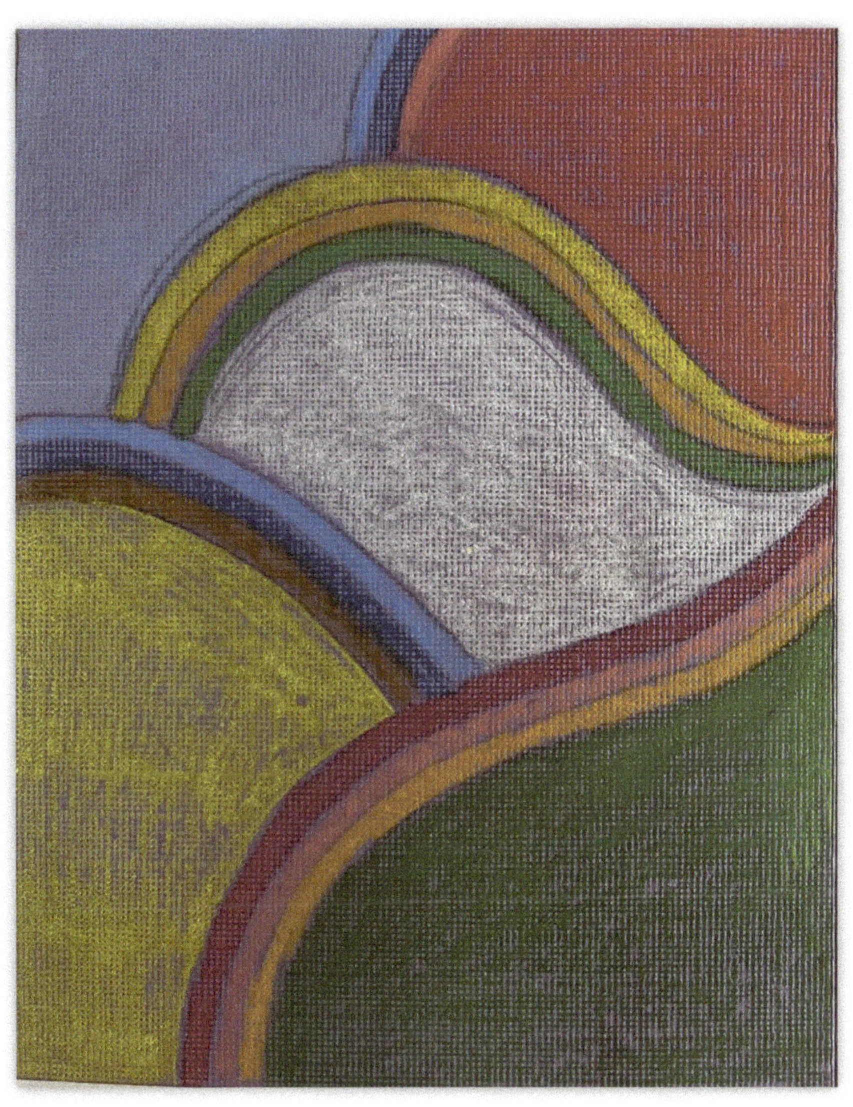

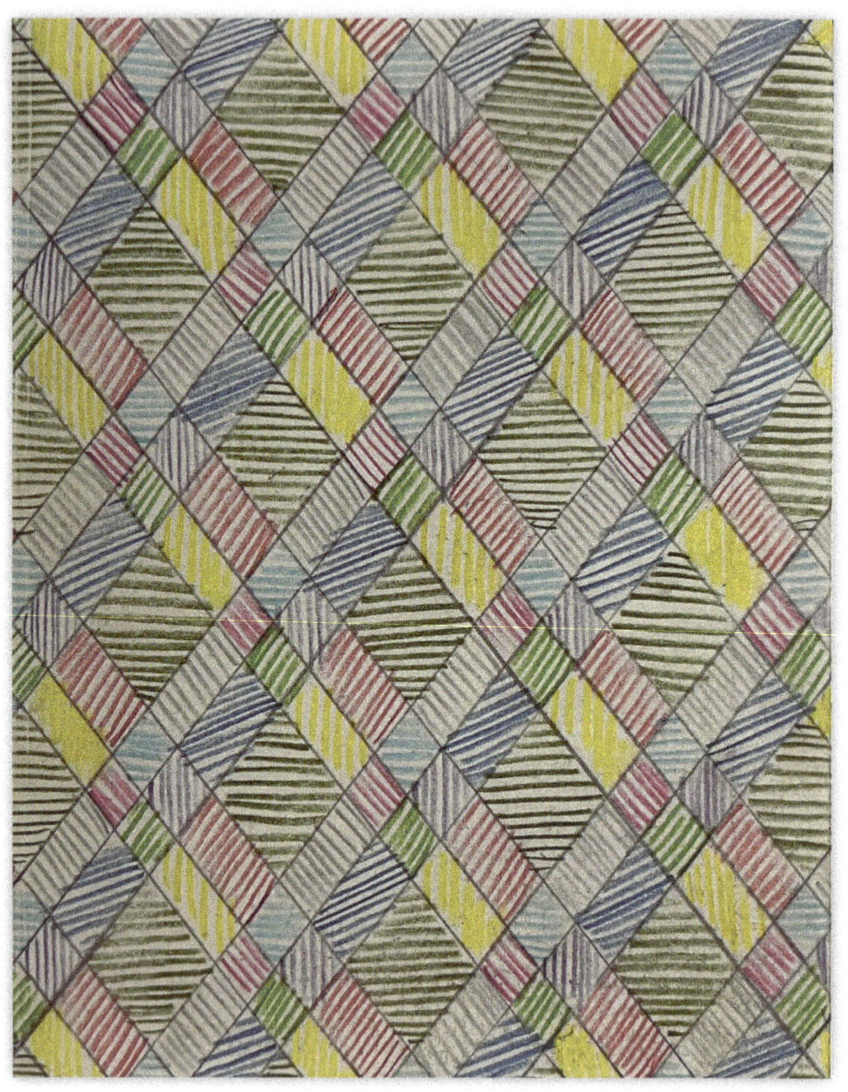

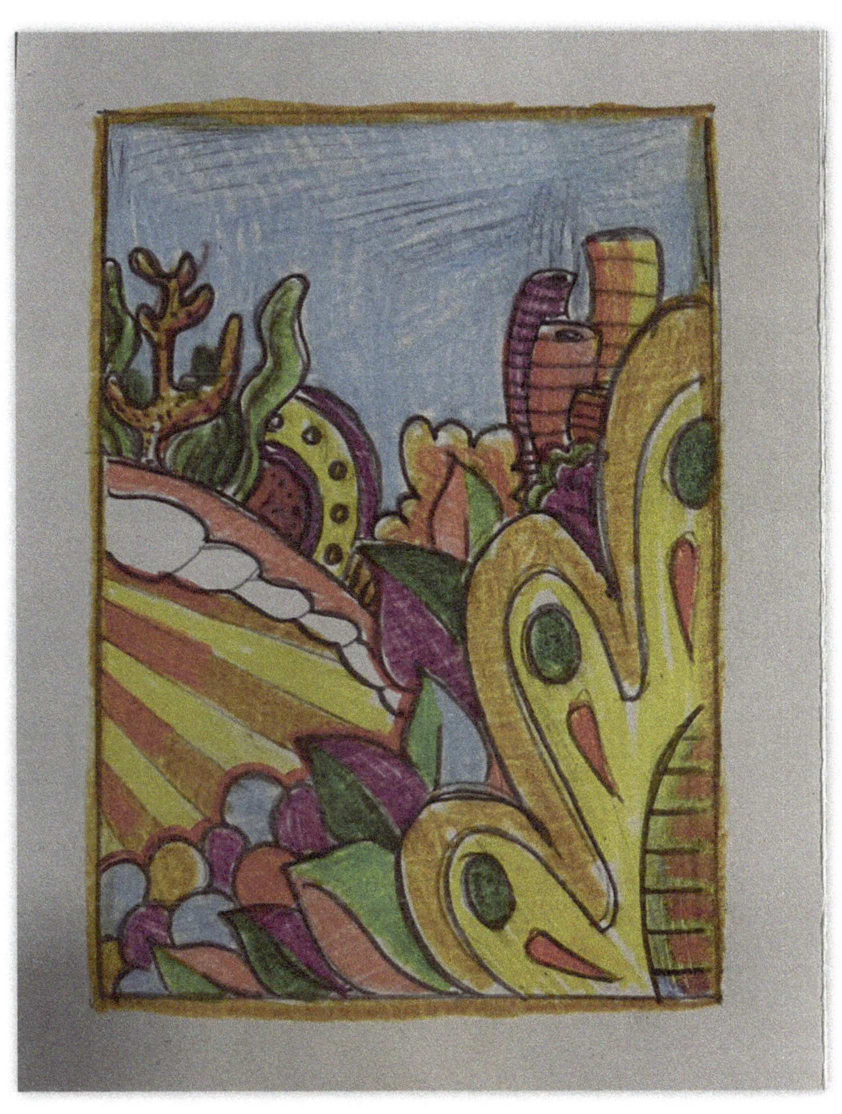

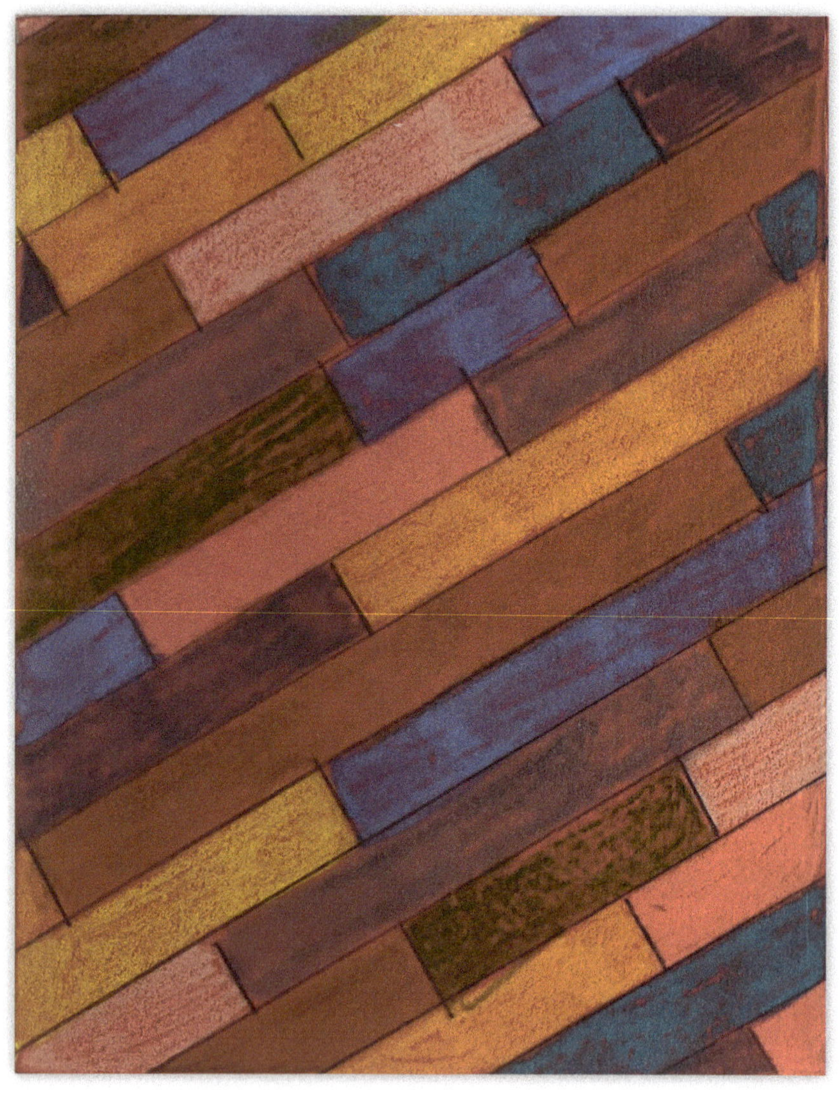

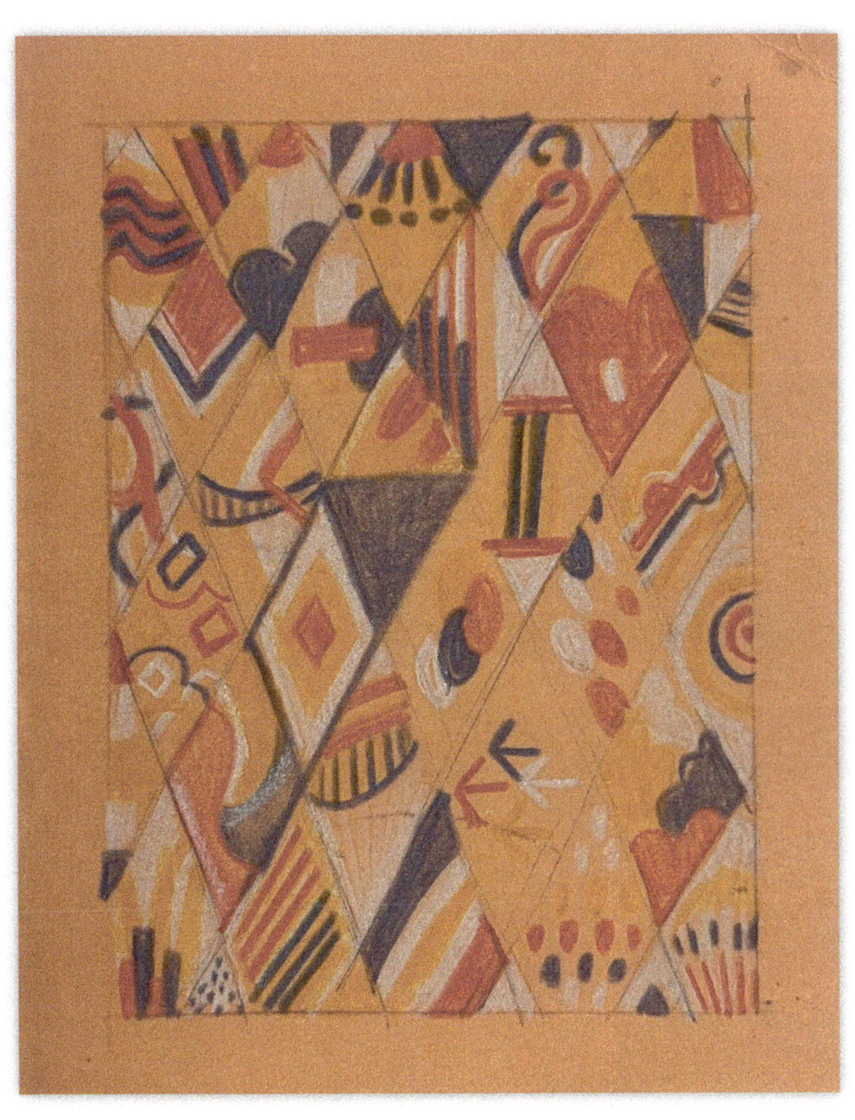

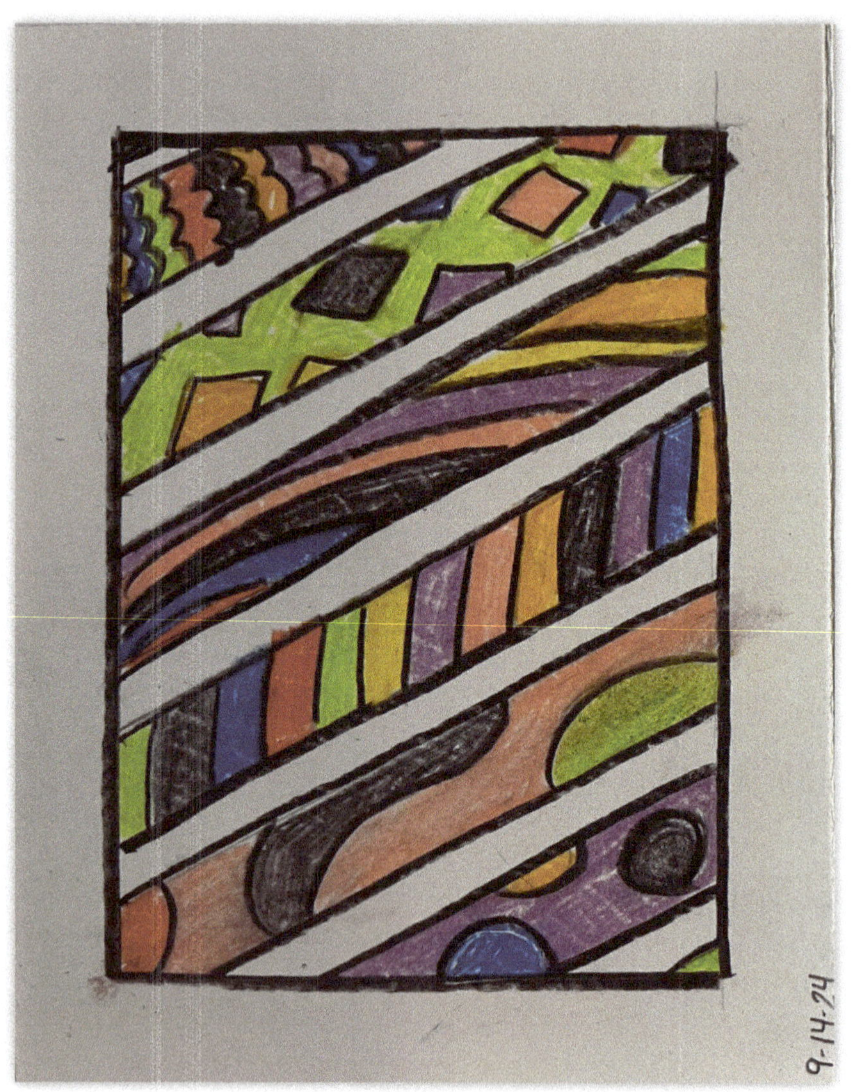
9-14-74

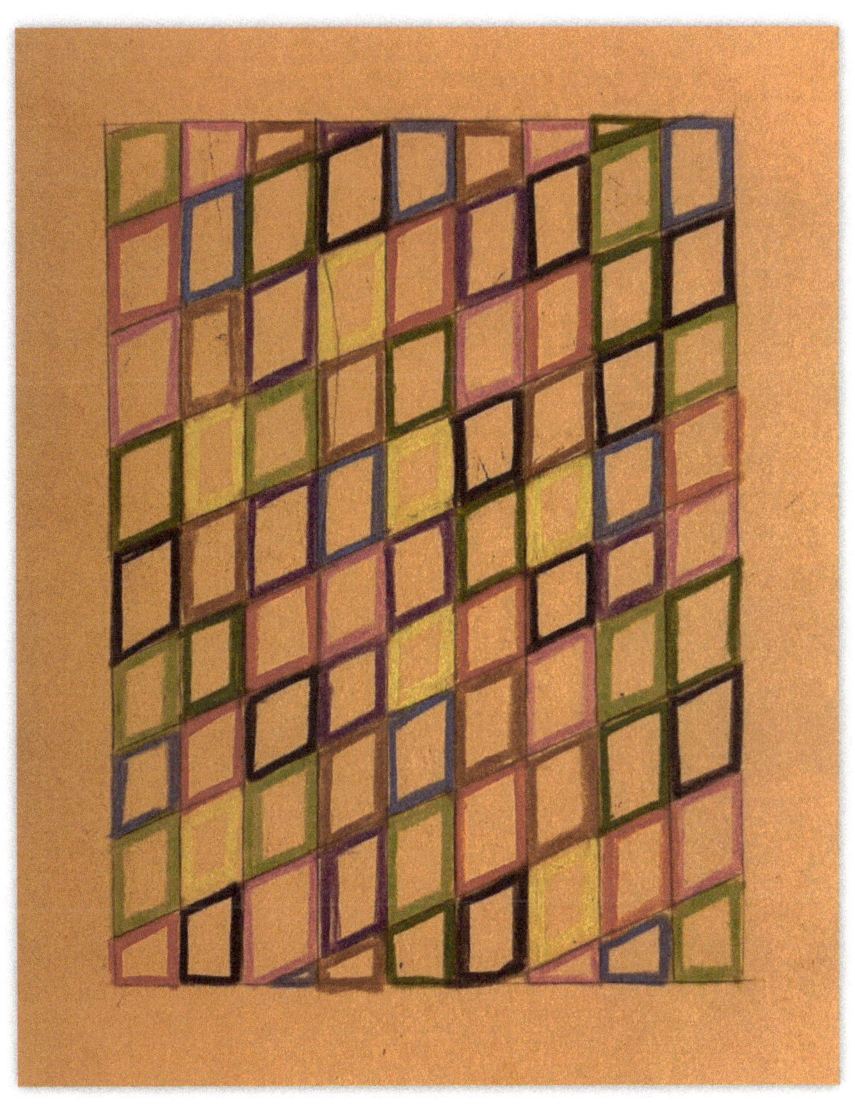

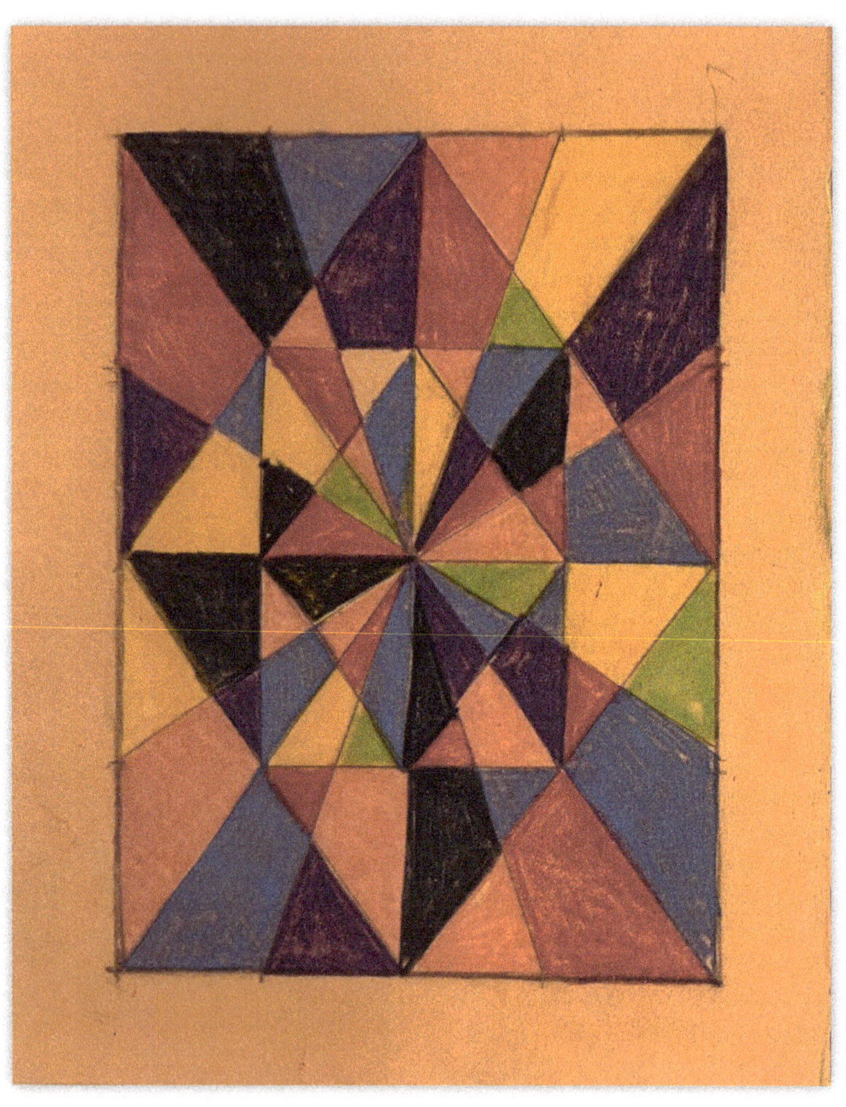

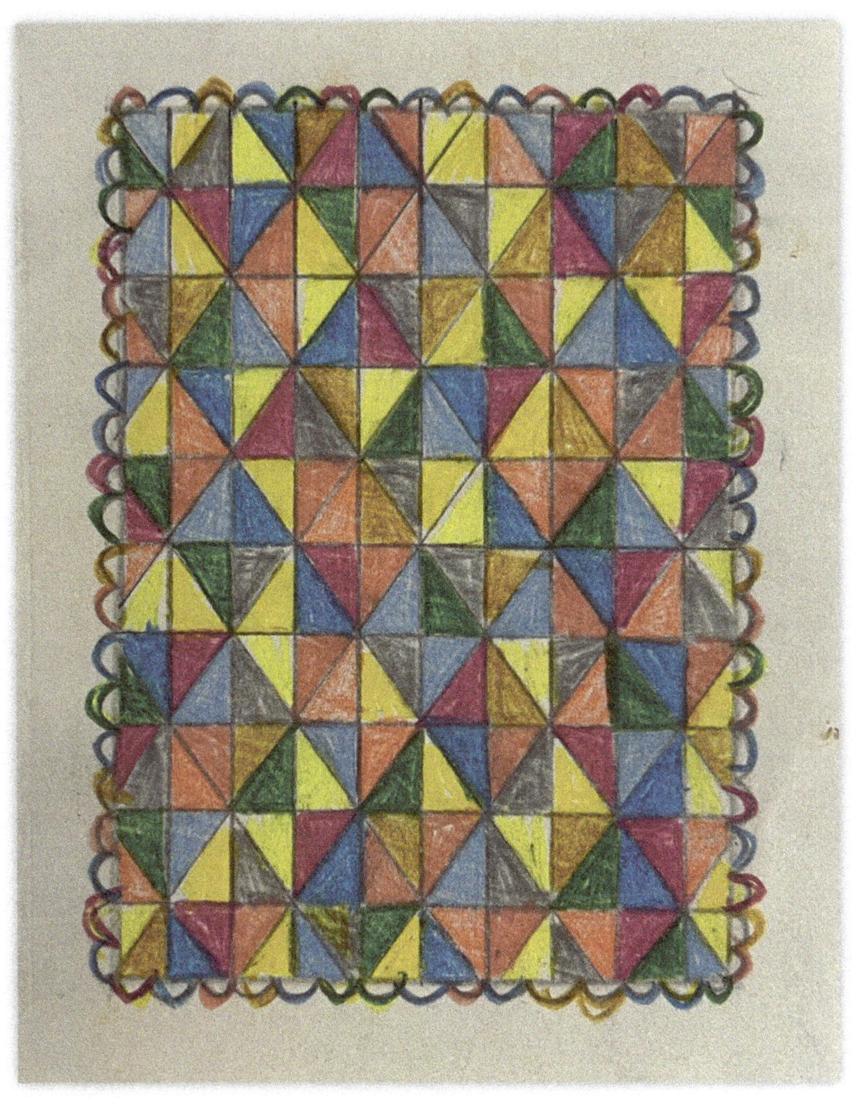

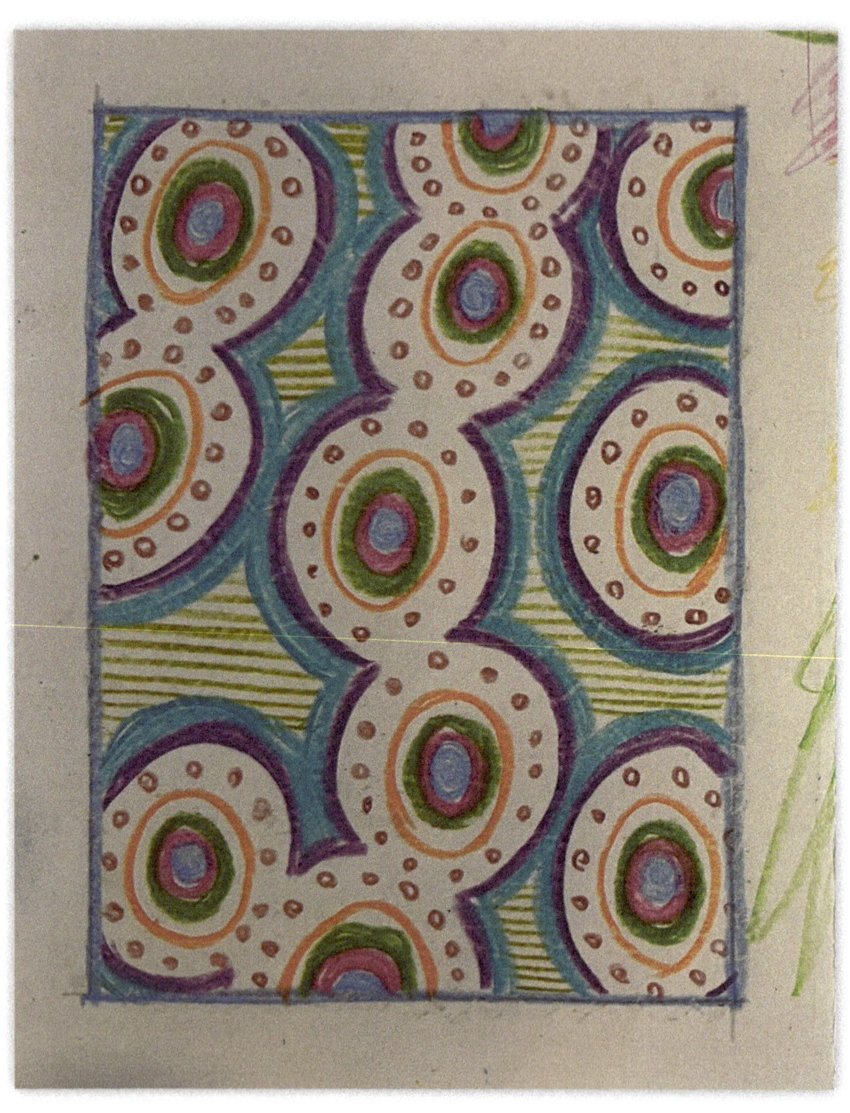

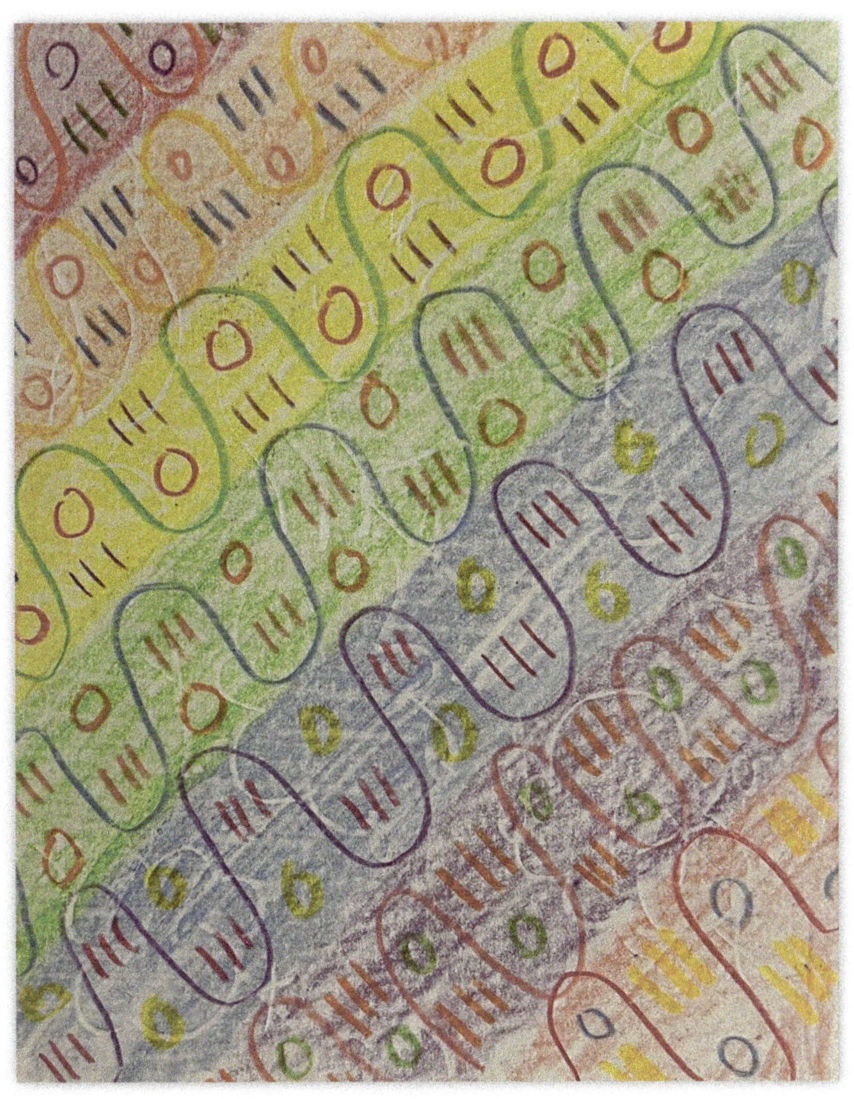

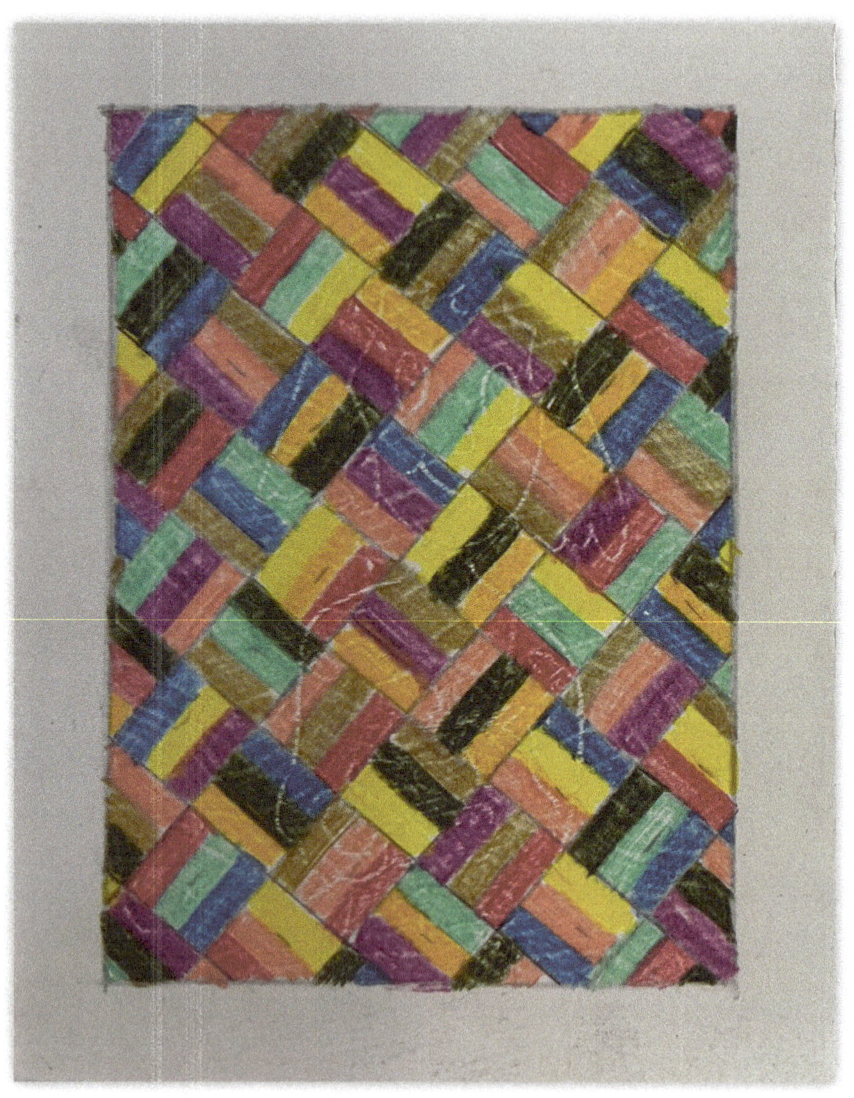

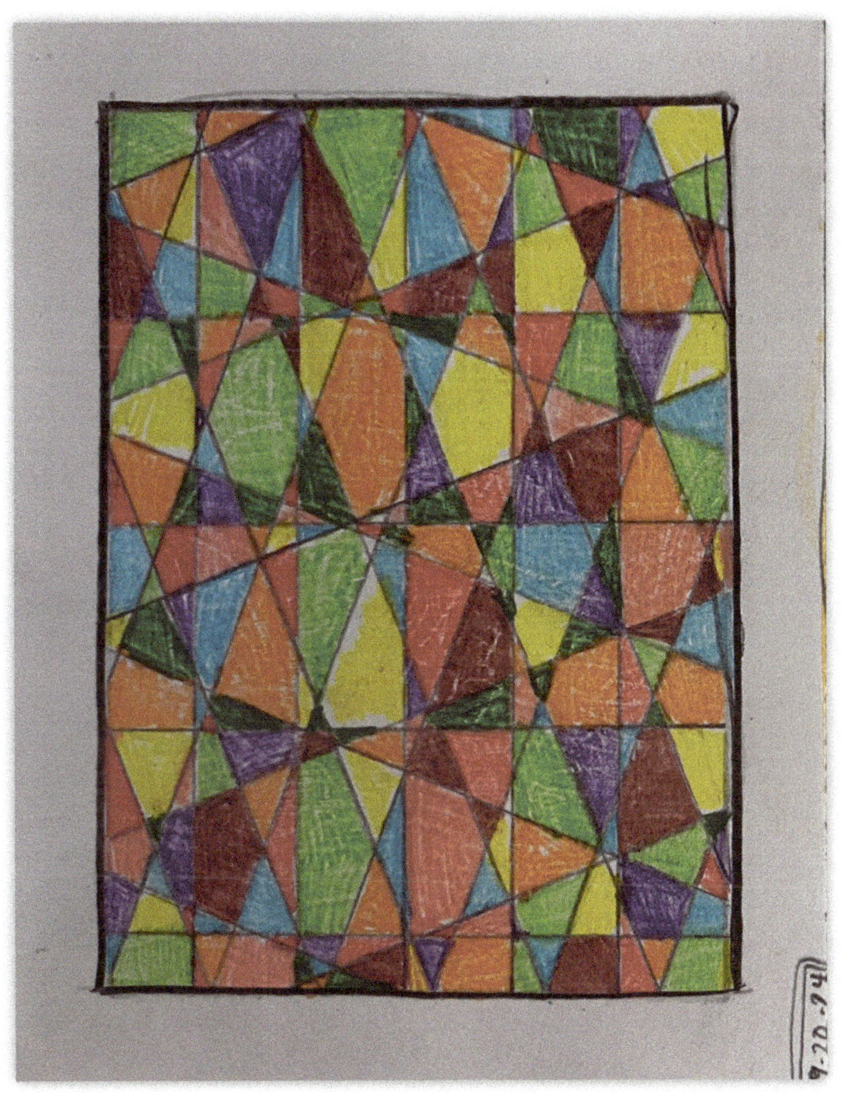

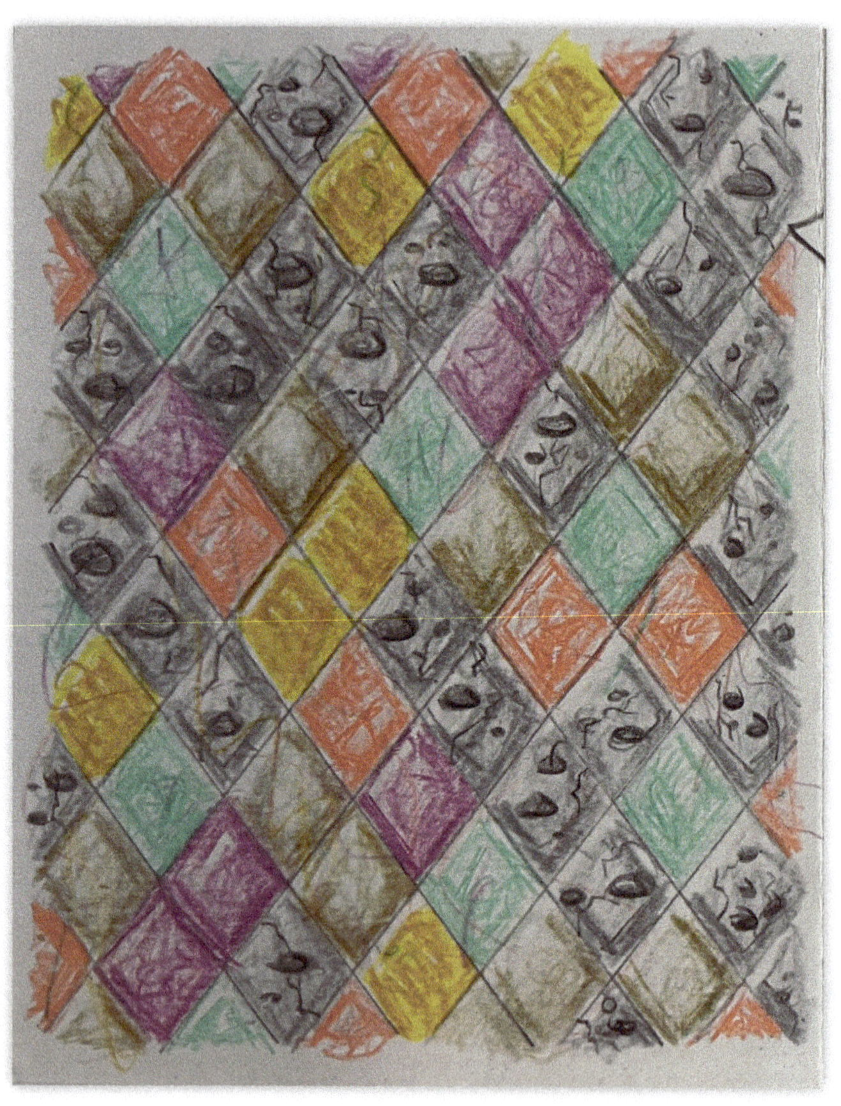

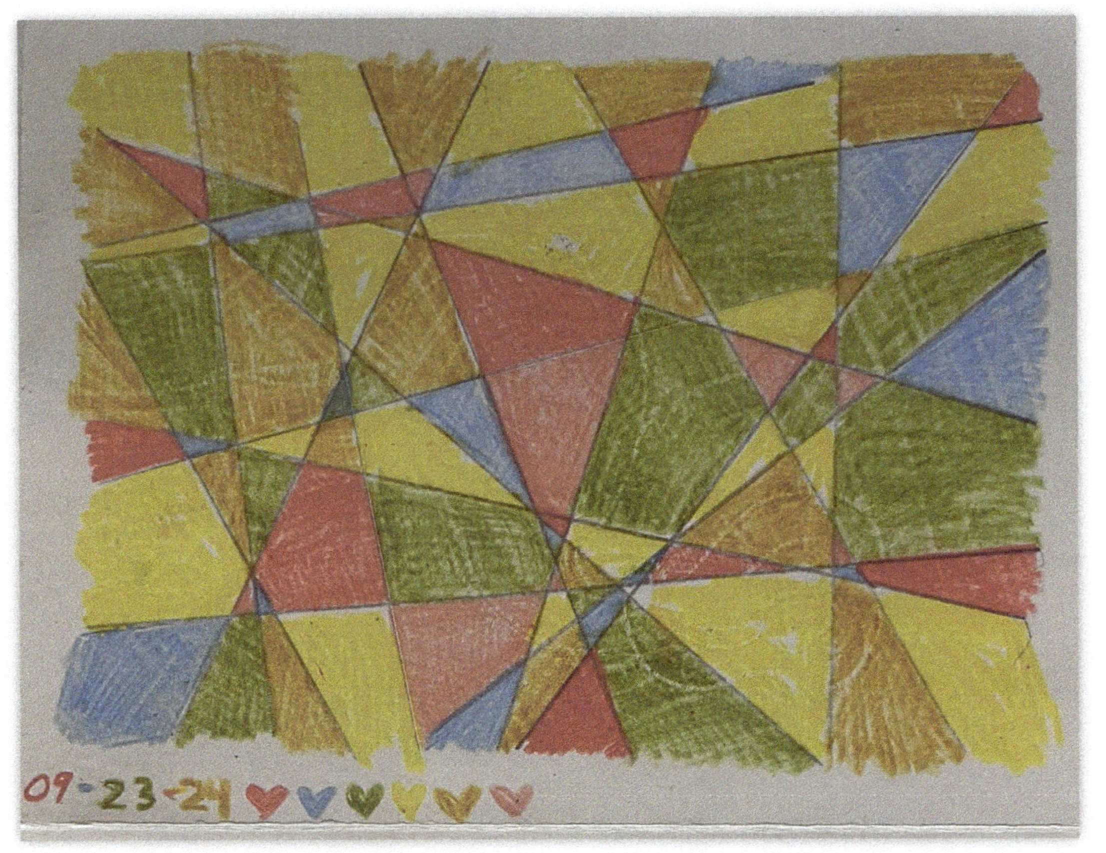

09-23-24 ♥ ♥ ♥ ♥ ♥ ♥

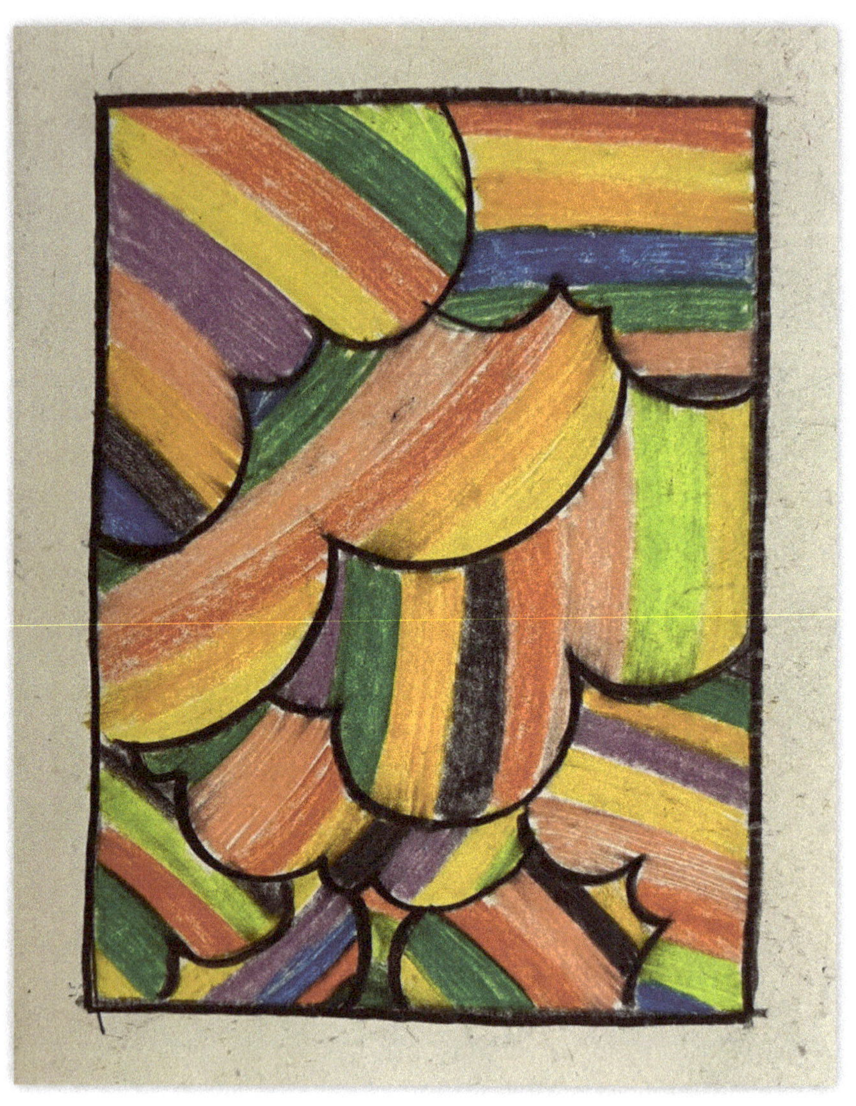

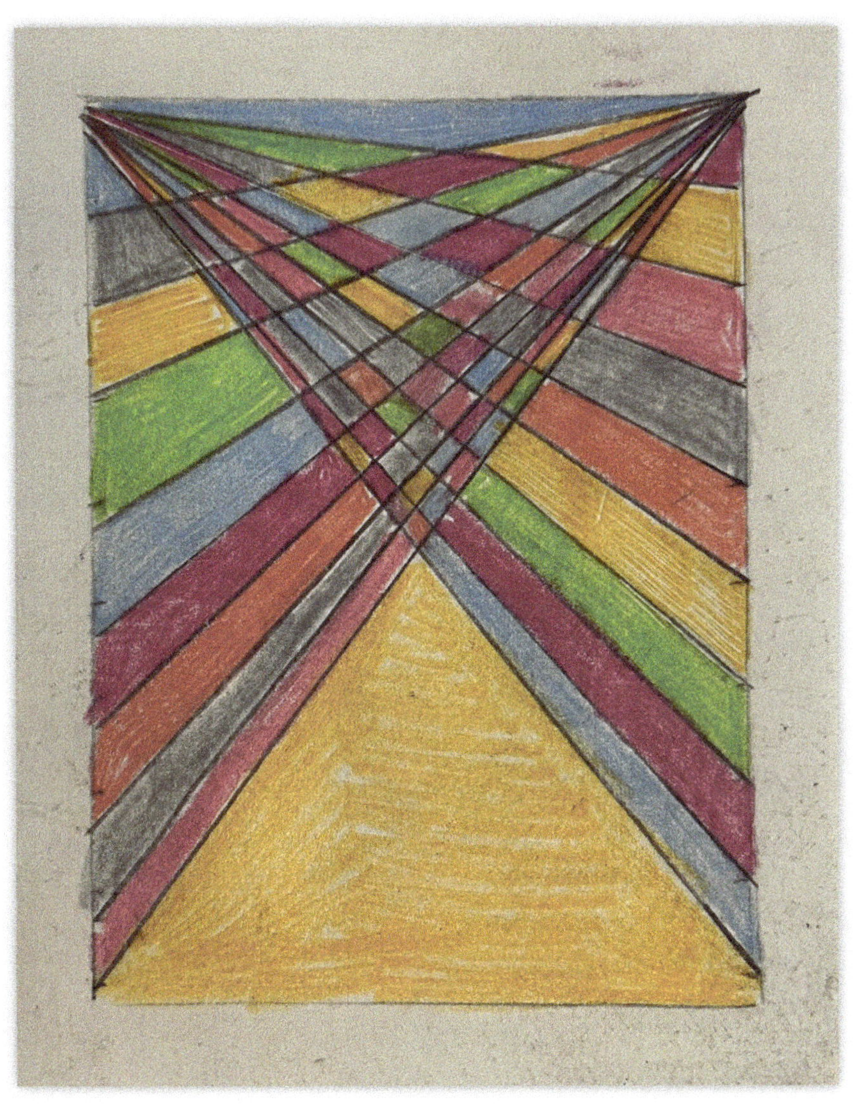

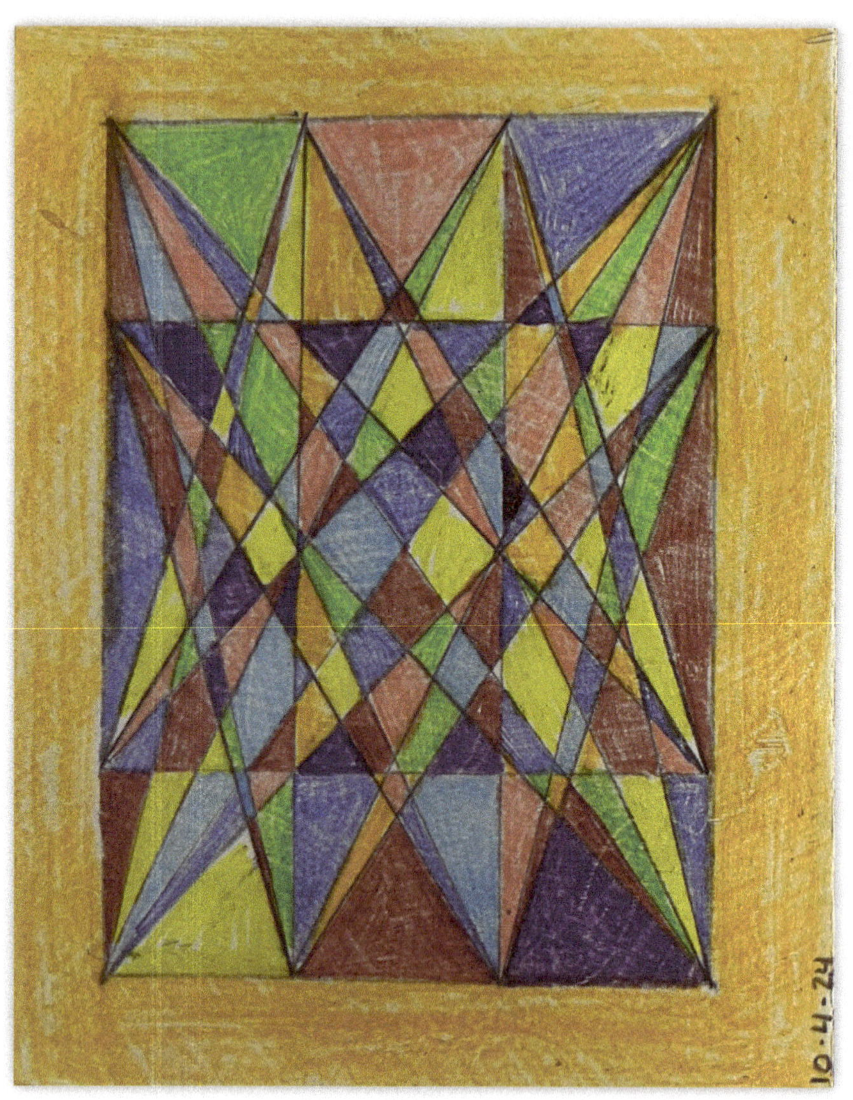

10-4-24

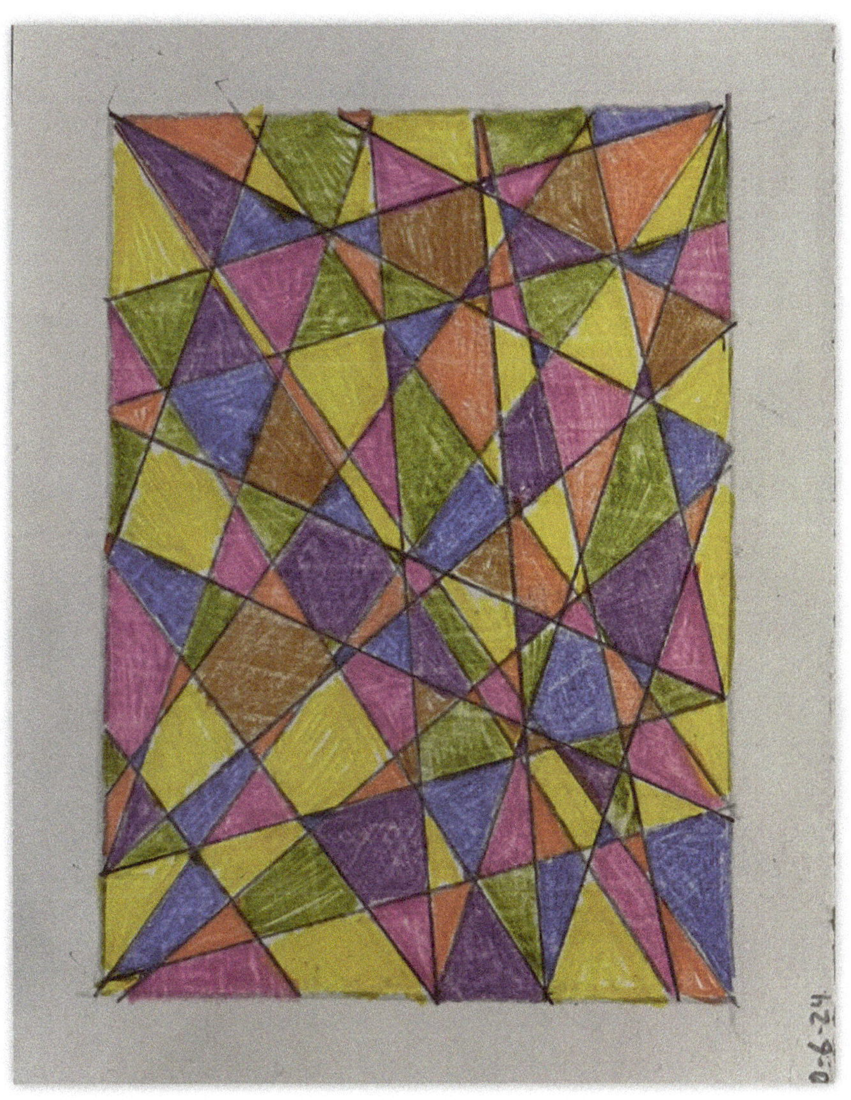

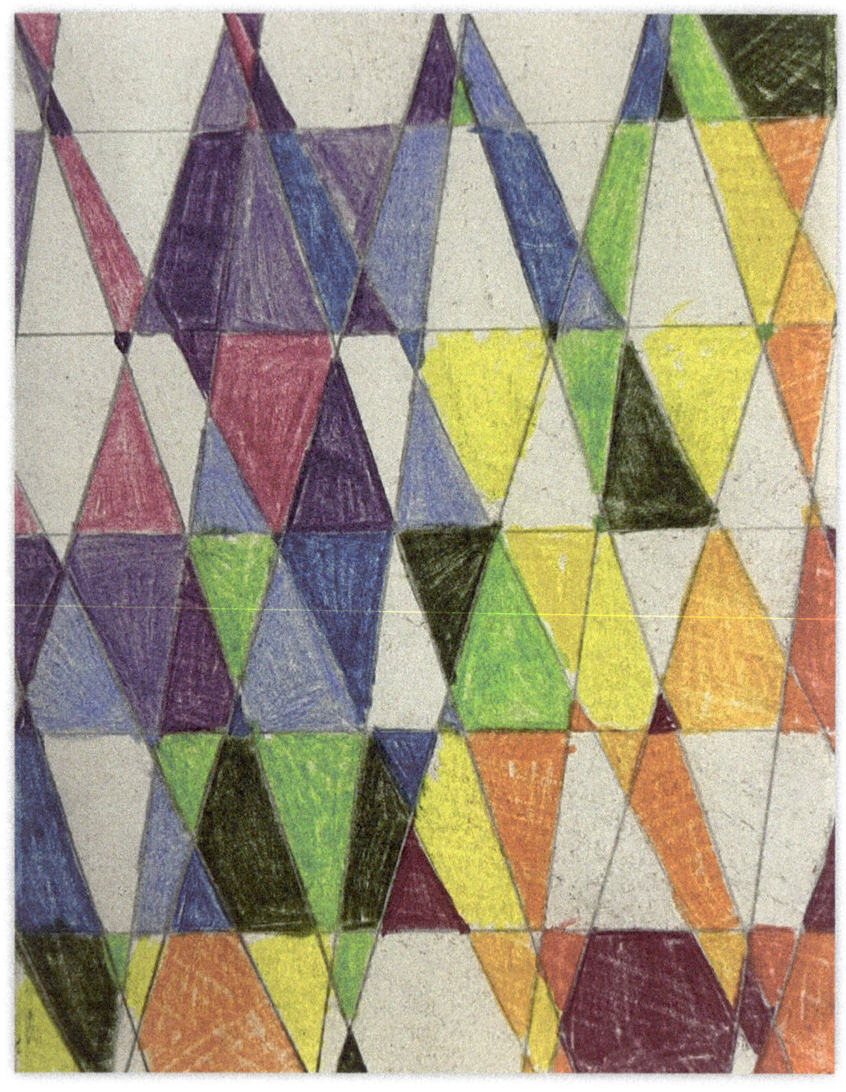

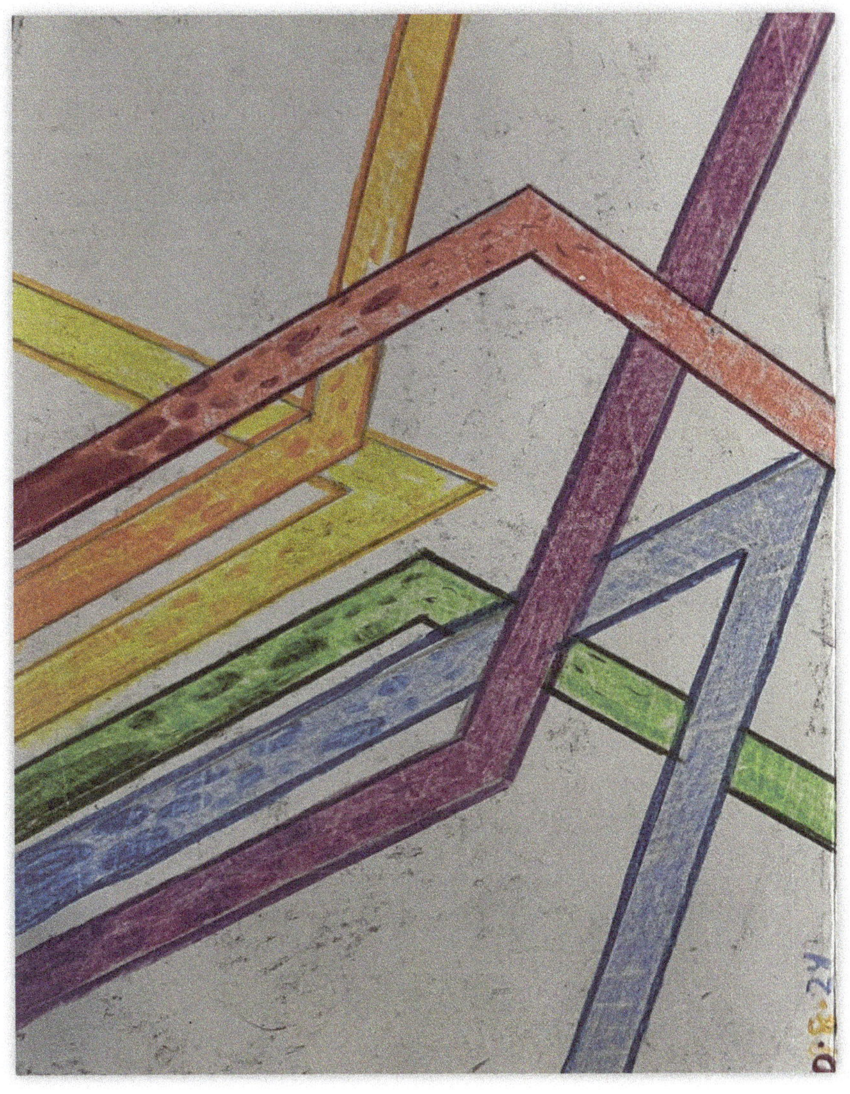

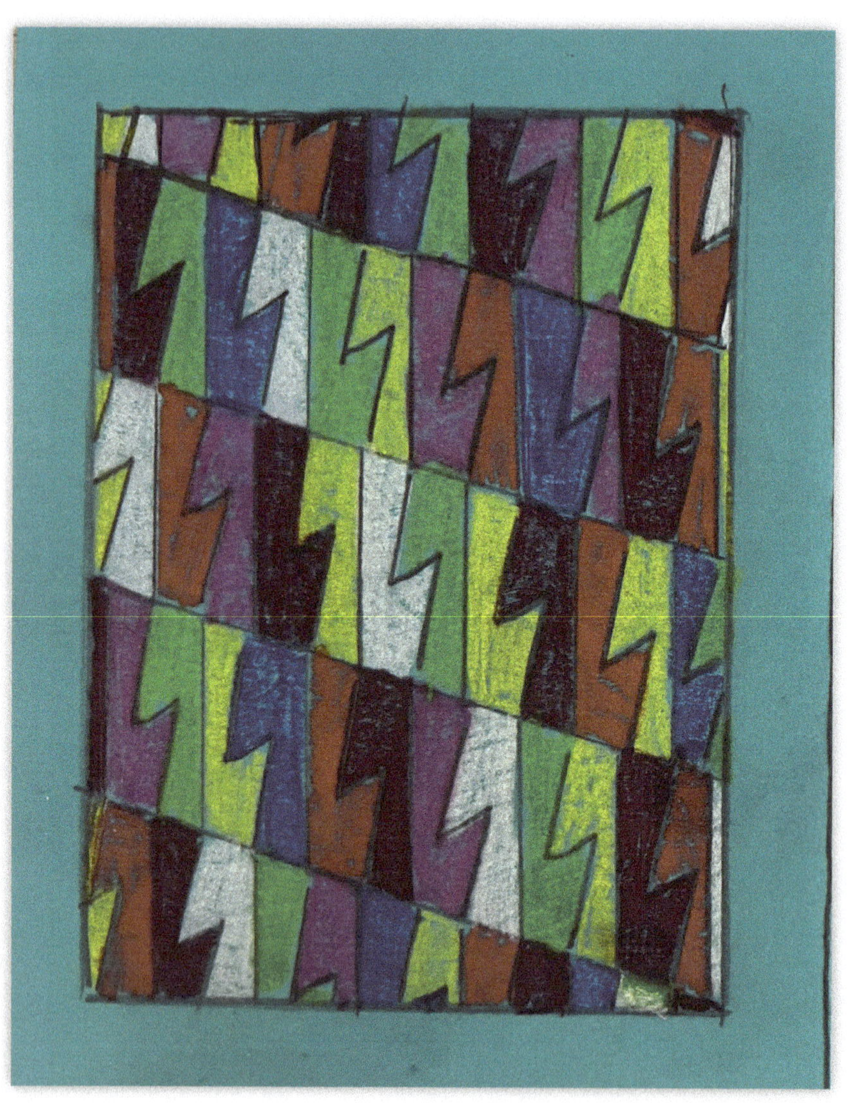

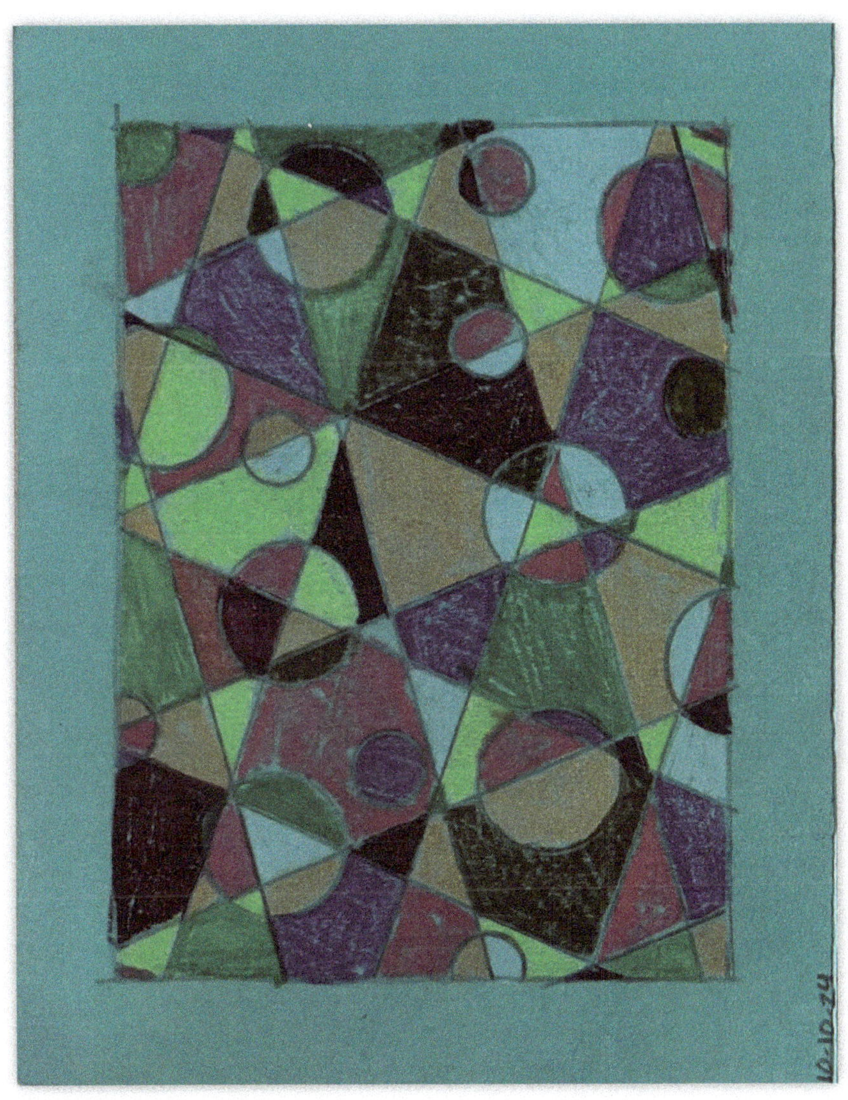
10.10.24

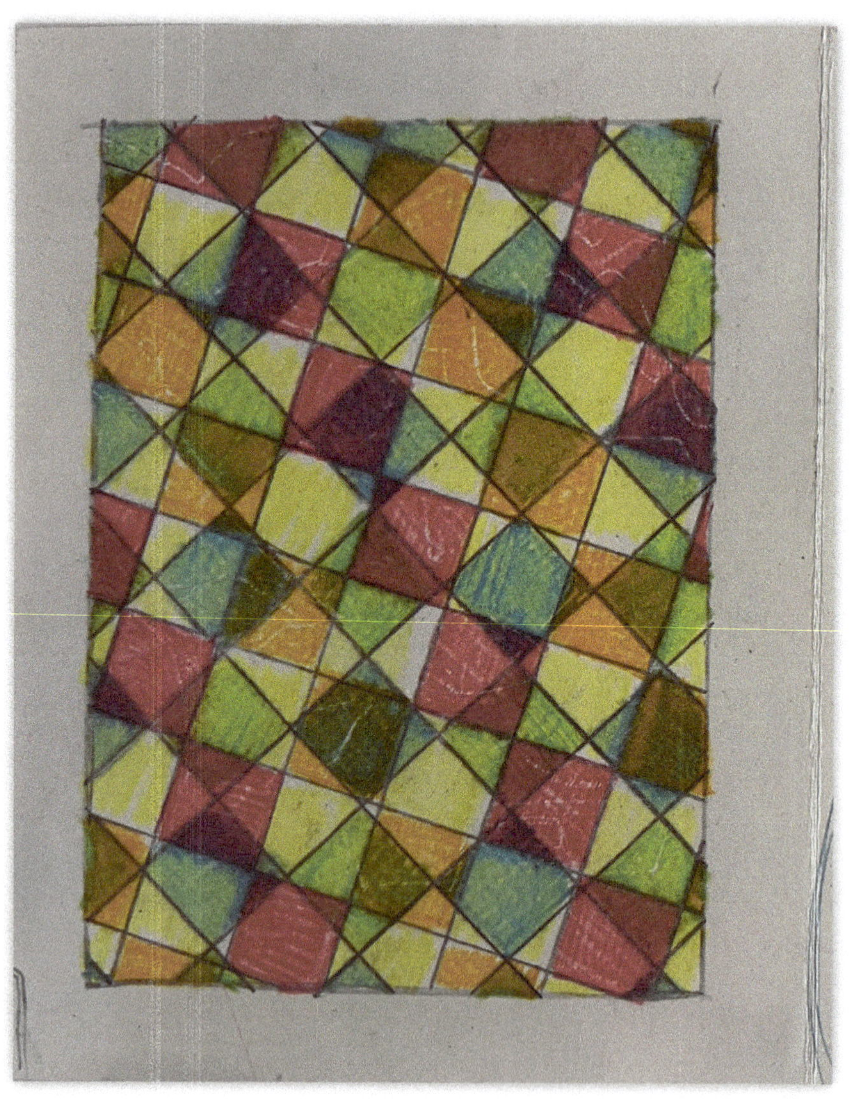

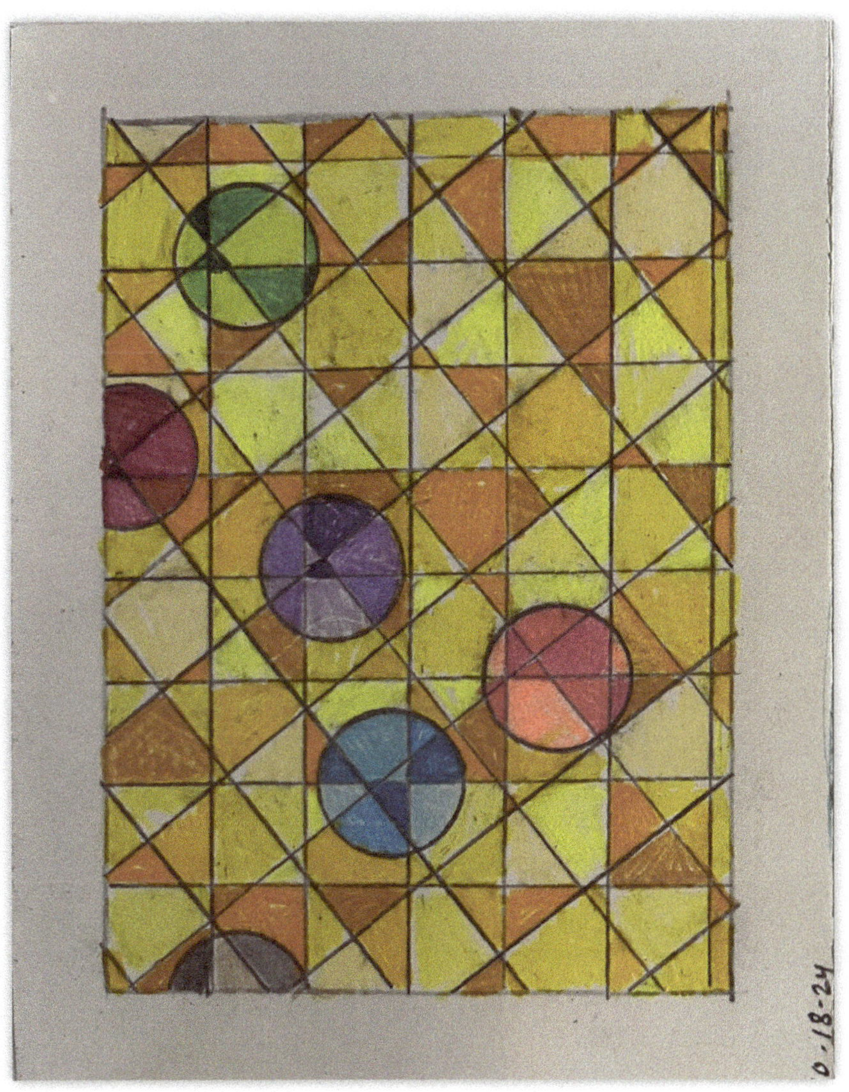

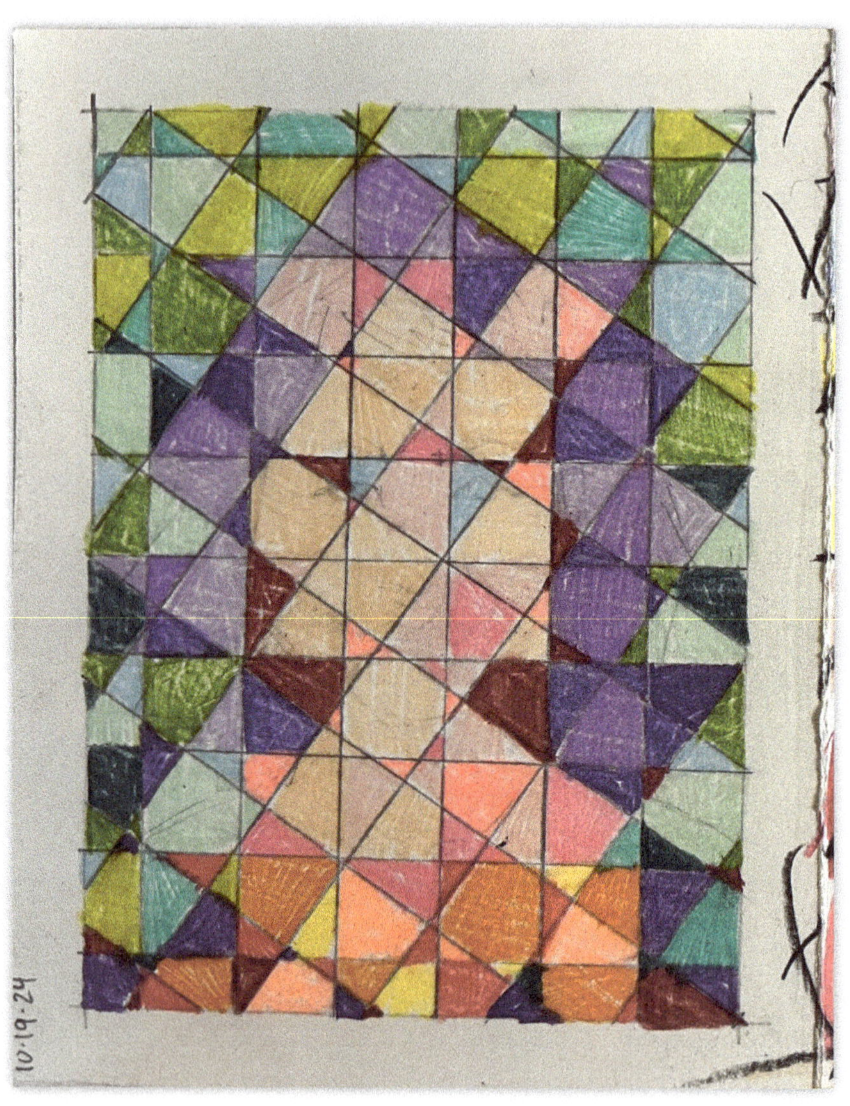

10·19·24

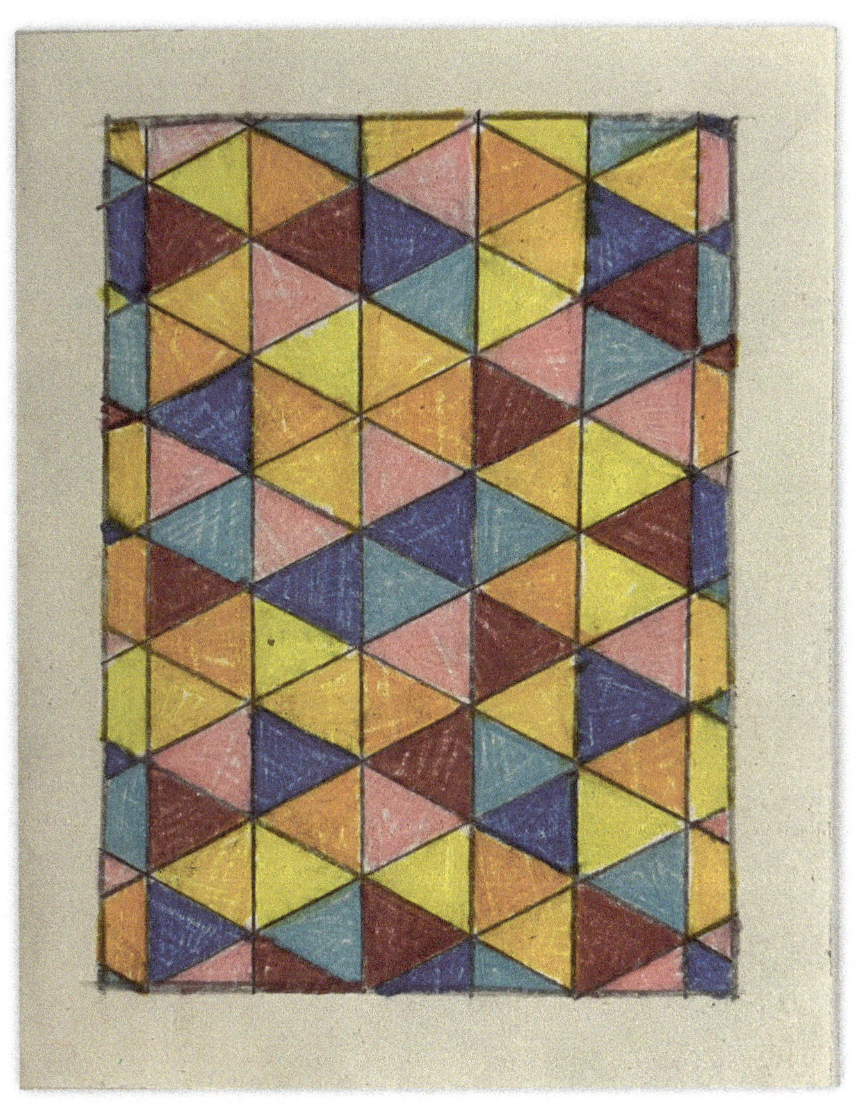

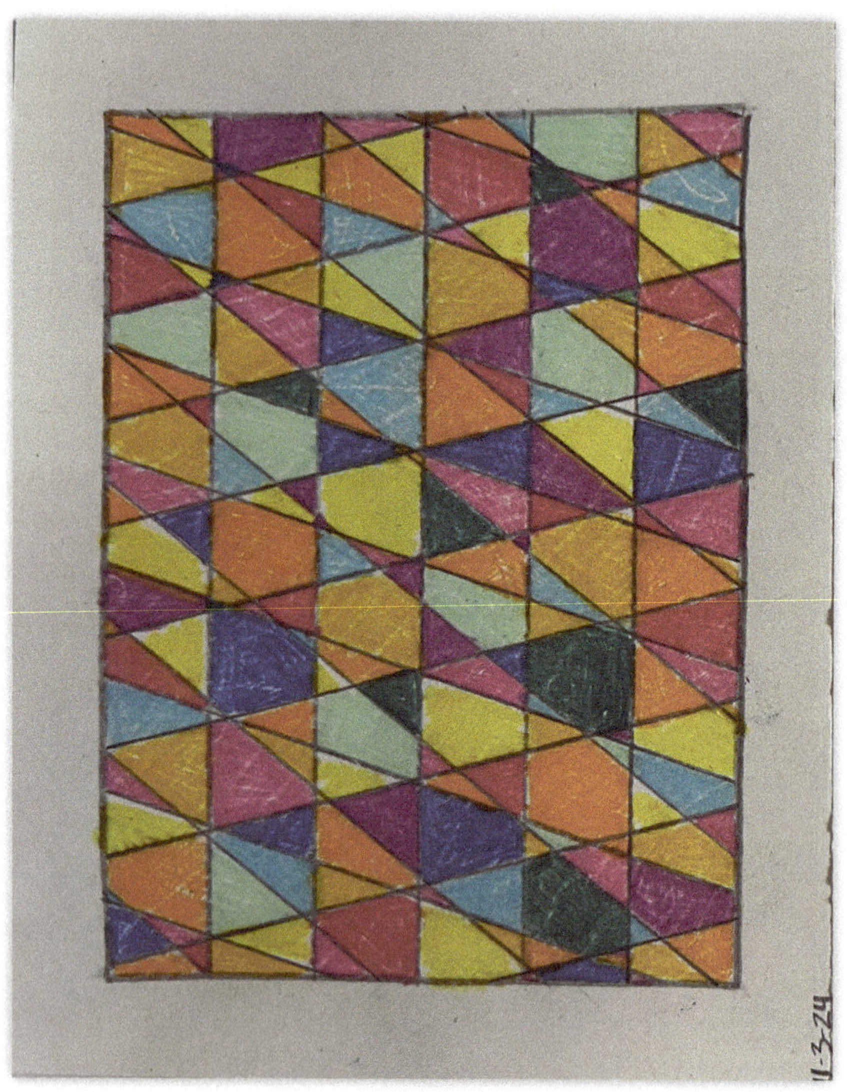

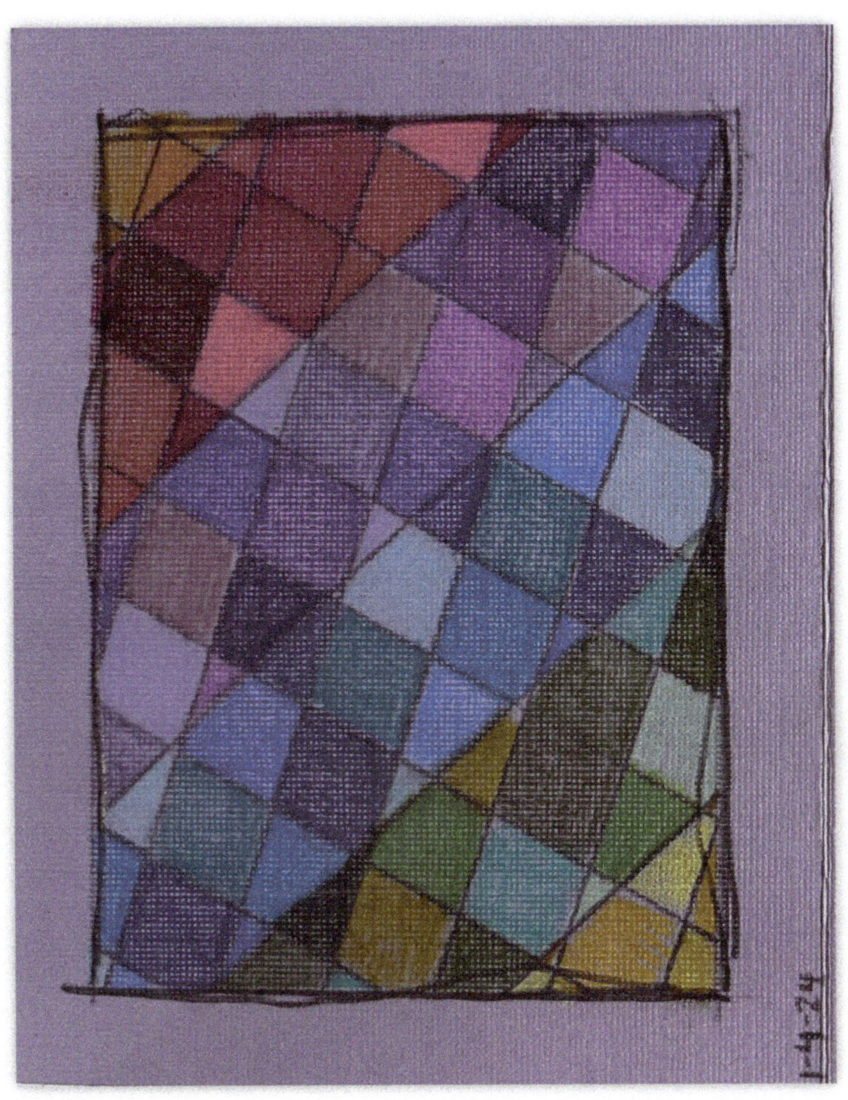

149

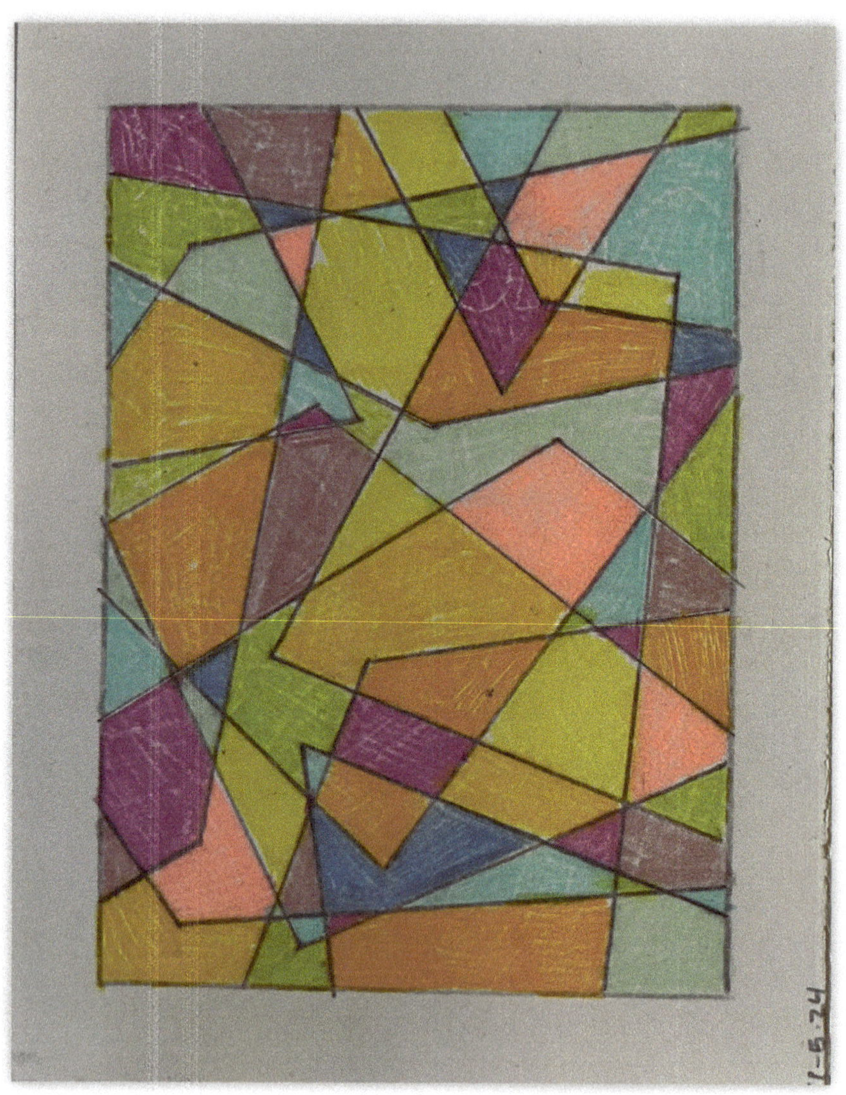

1-5.74

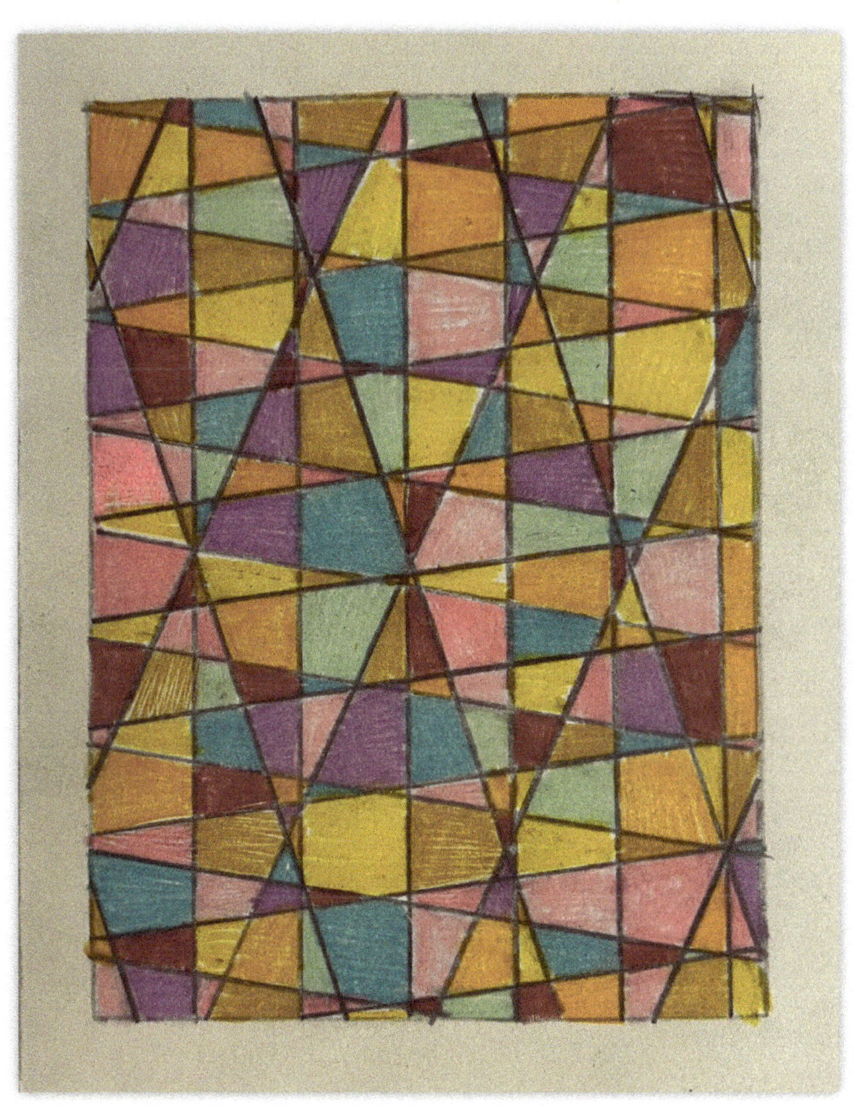

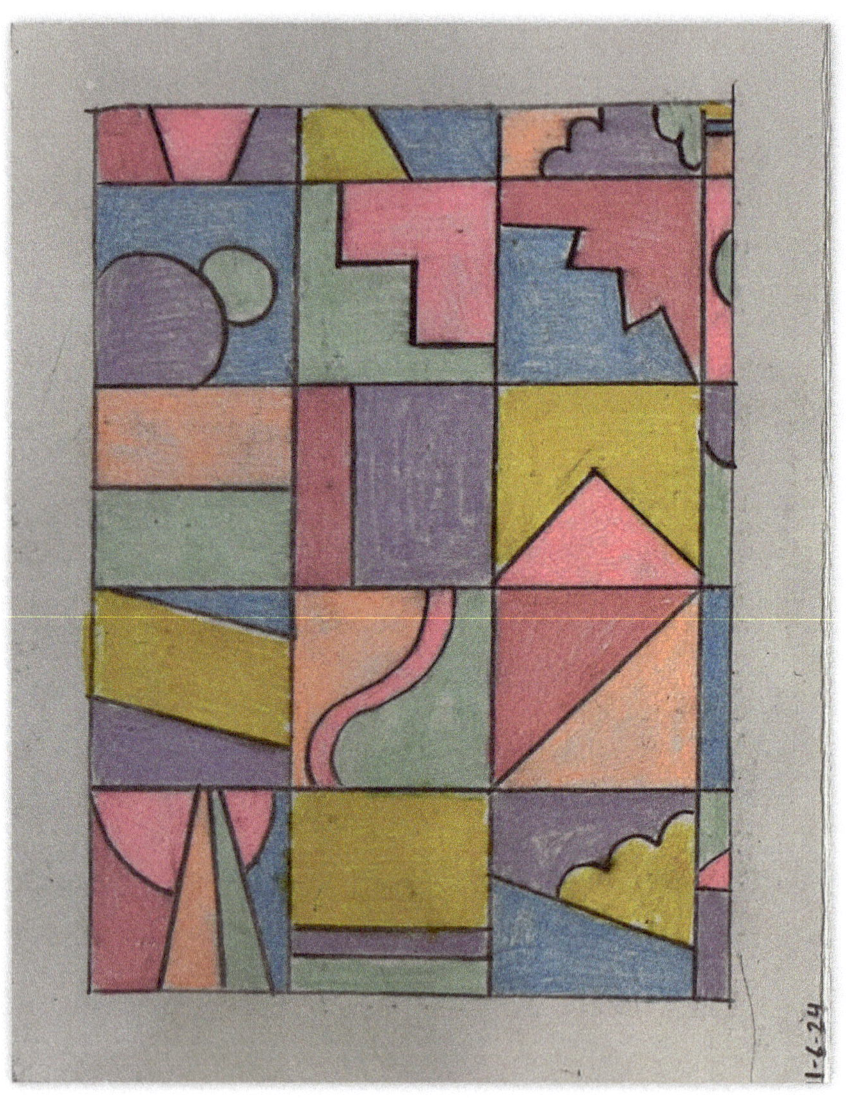
11-6-24

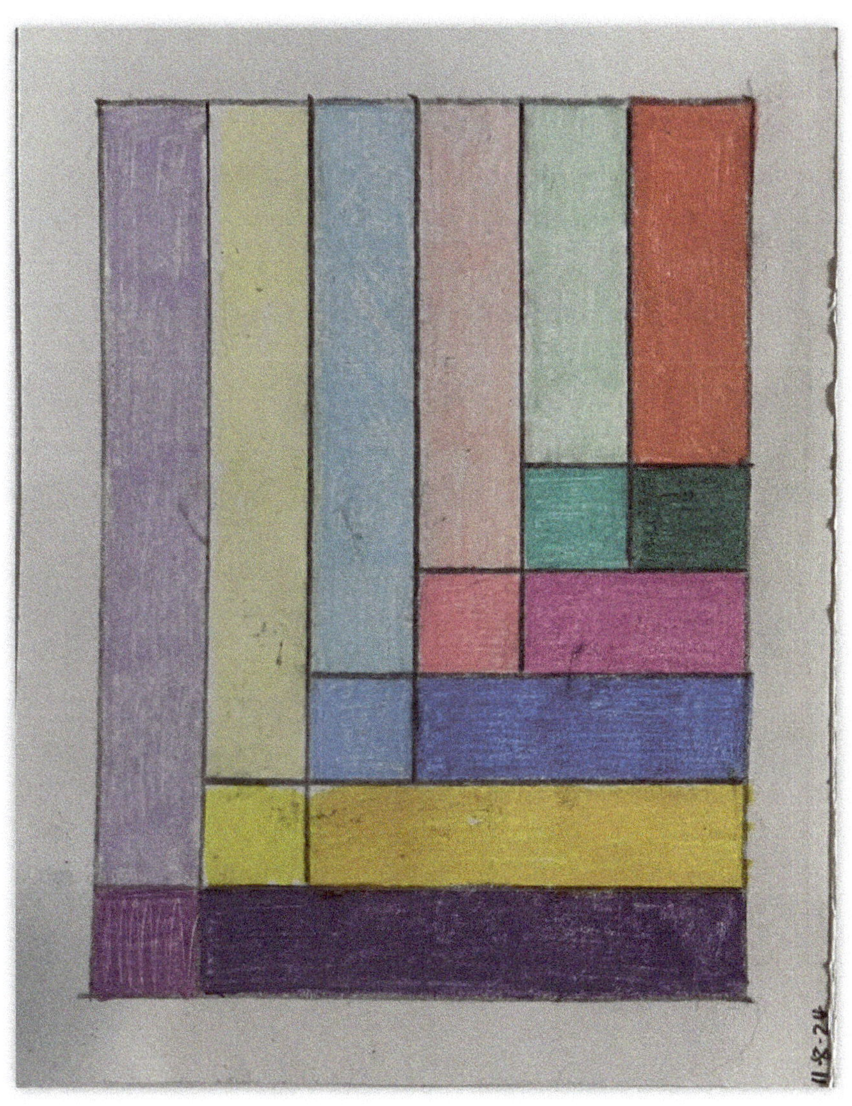

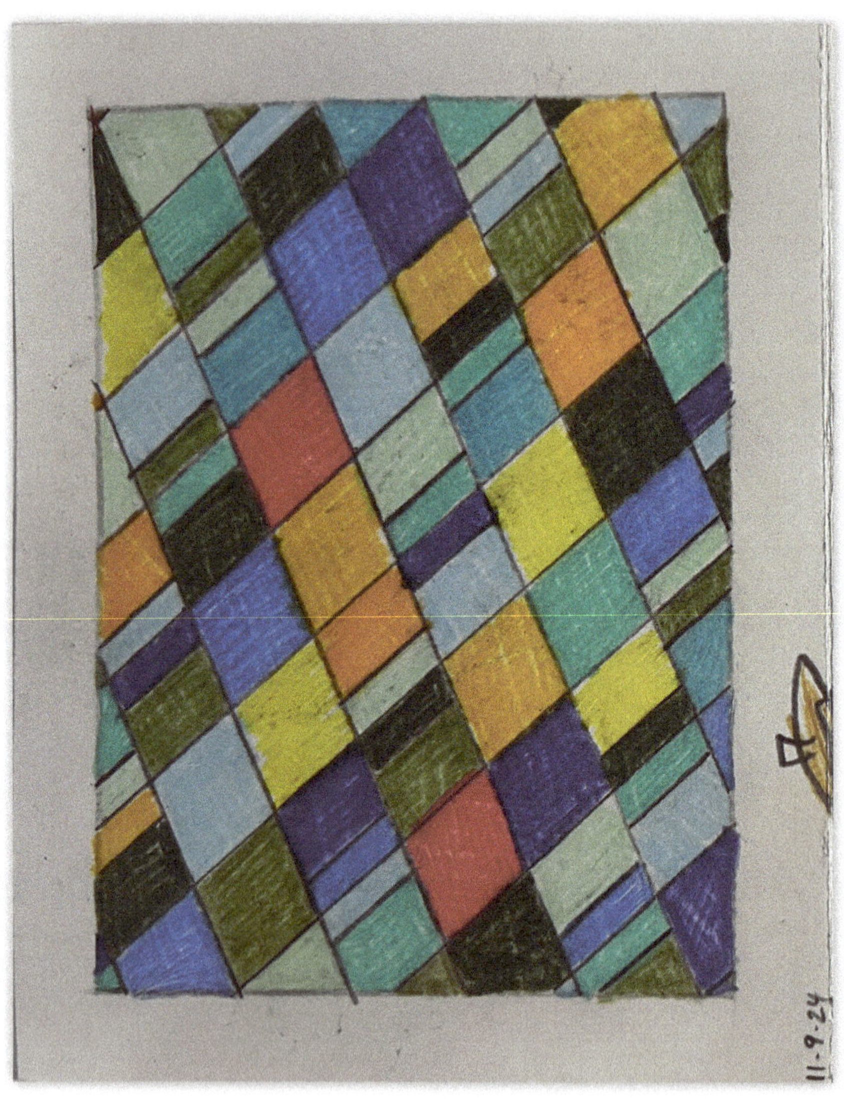

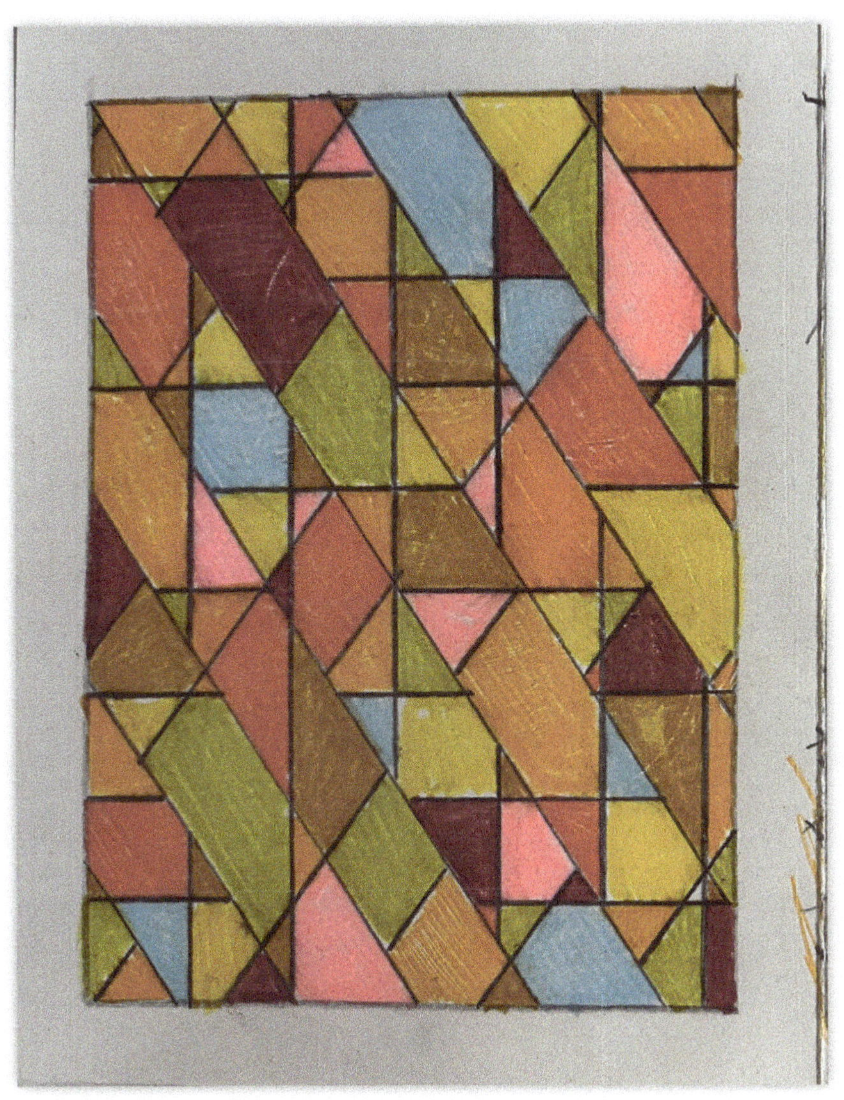

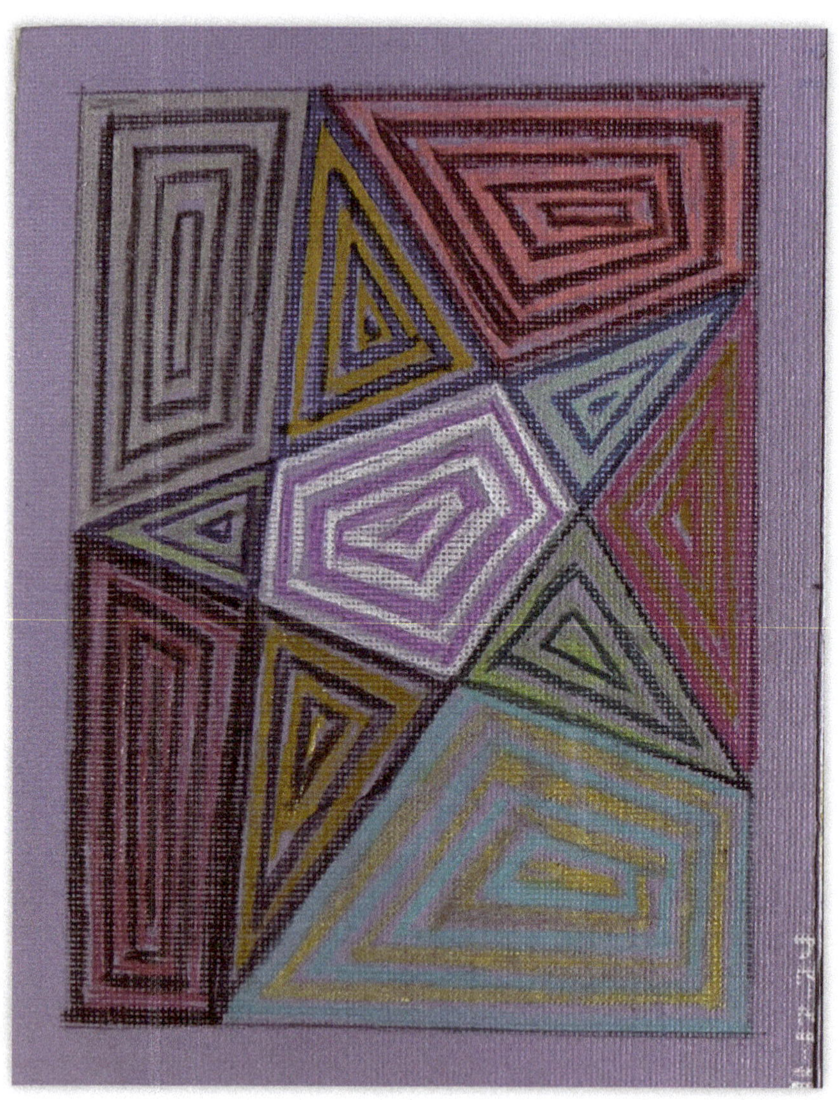

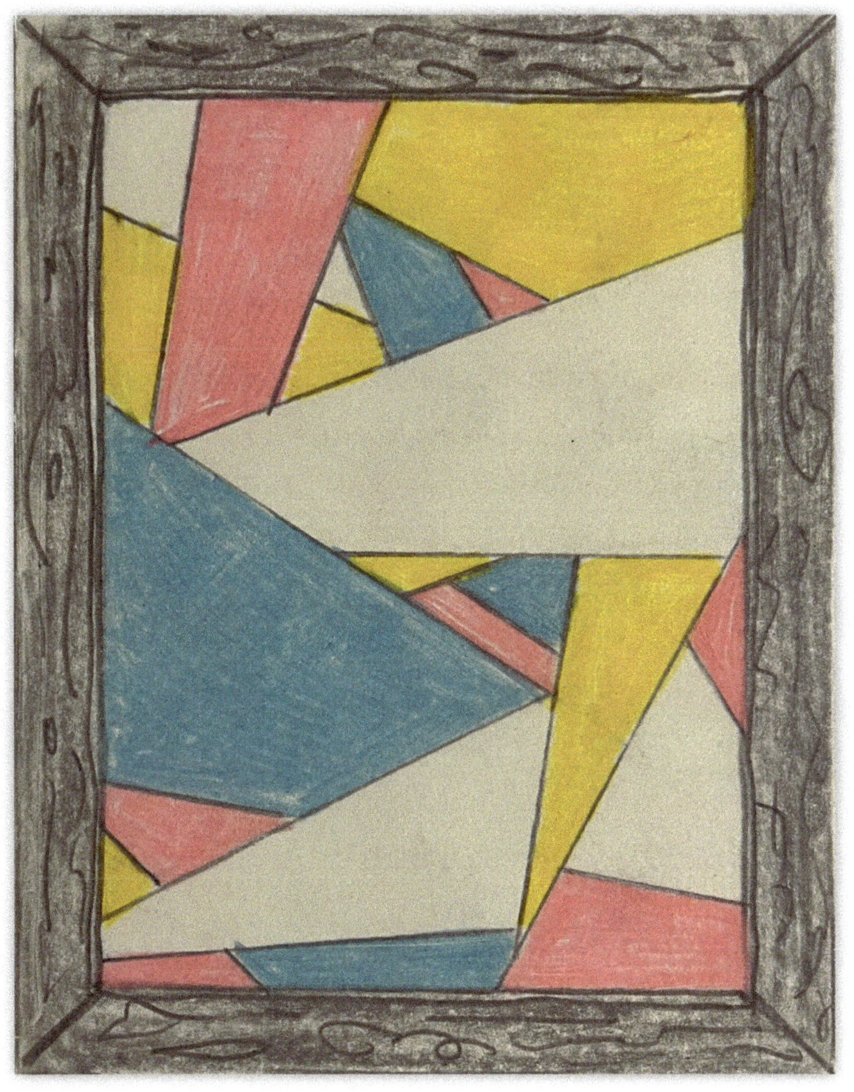

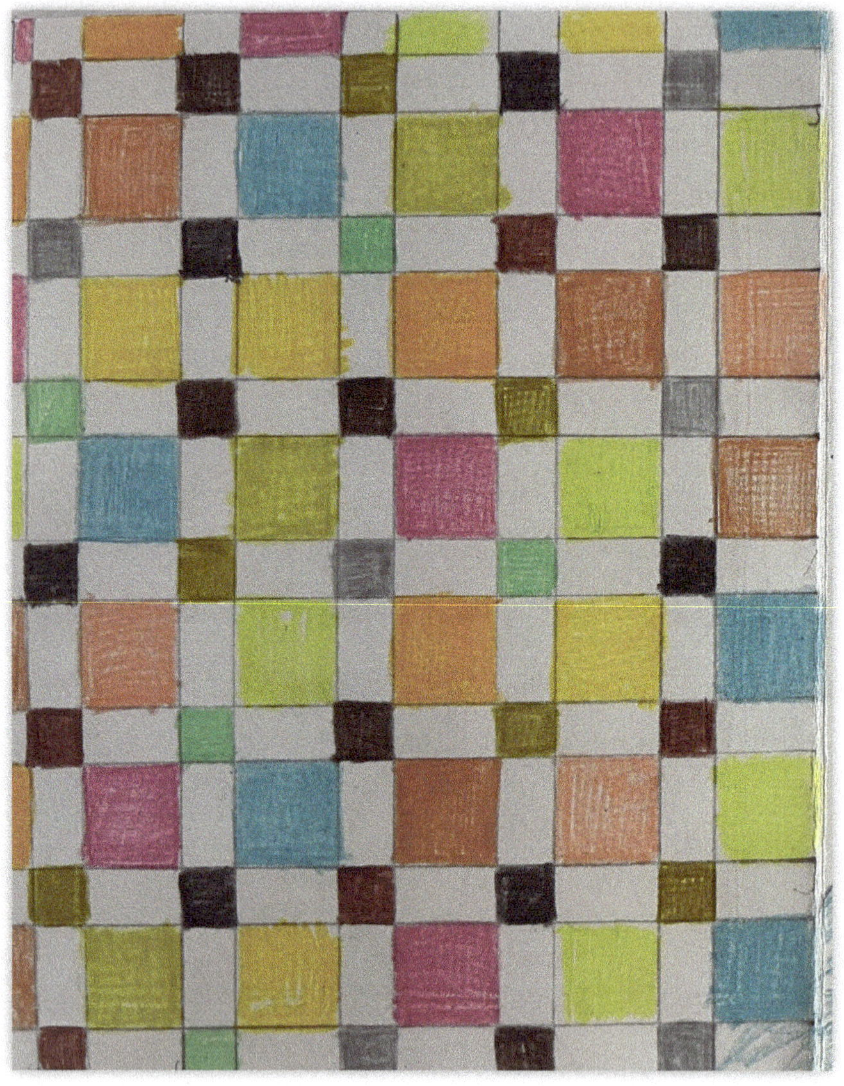

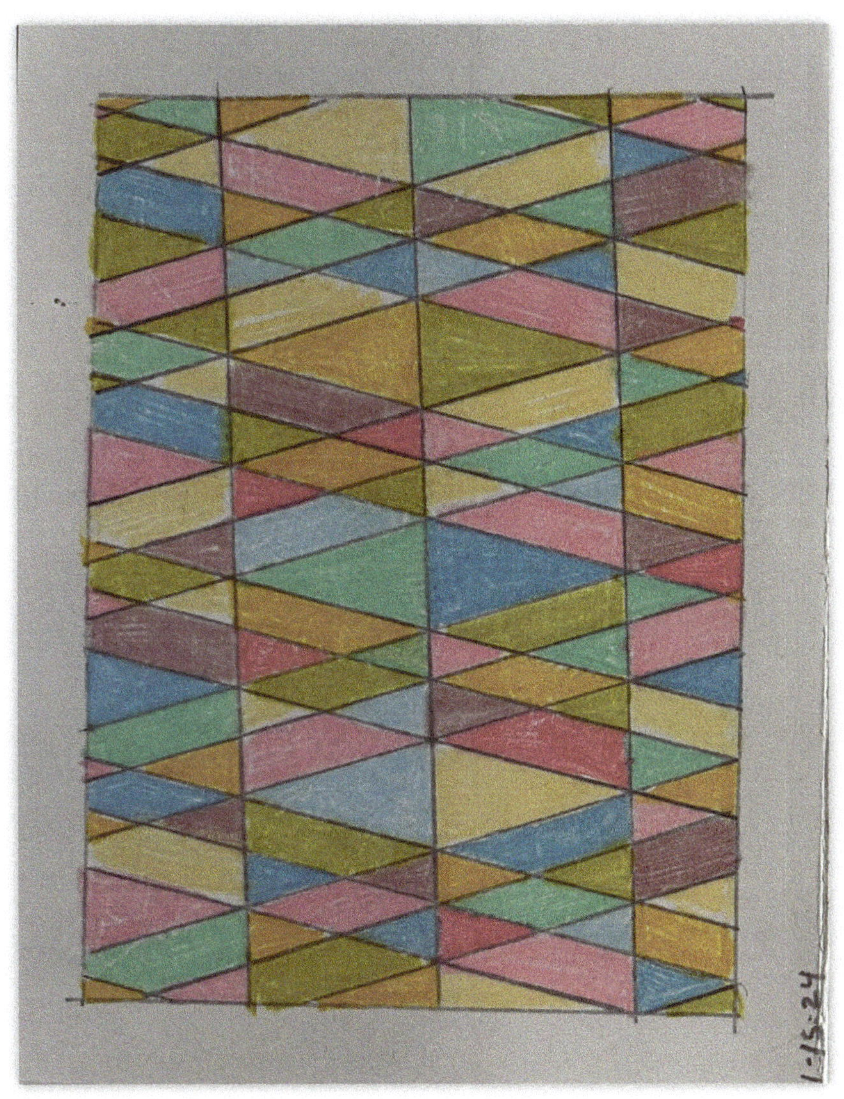
1-15-24

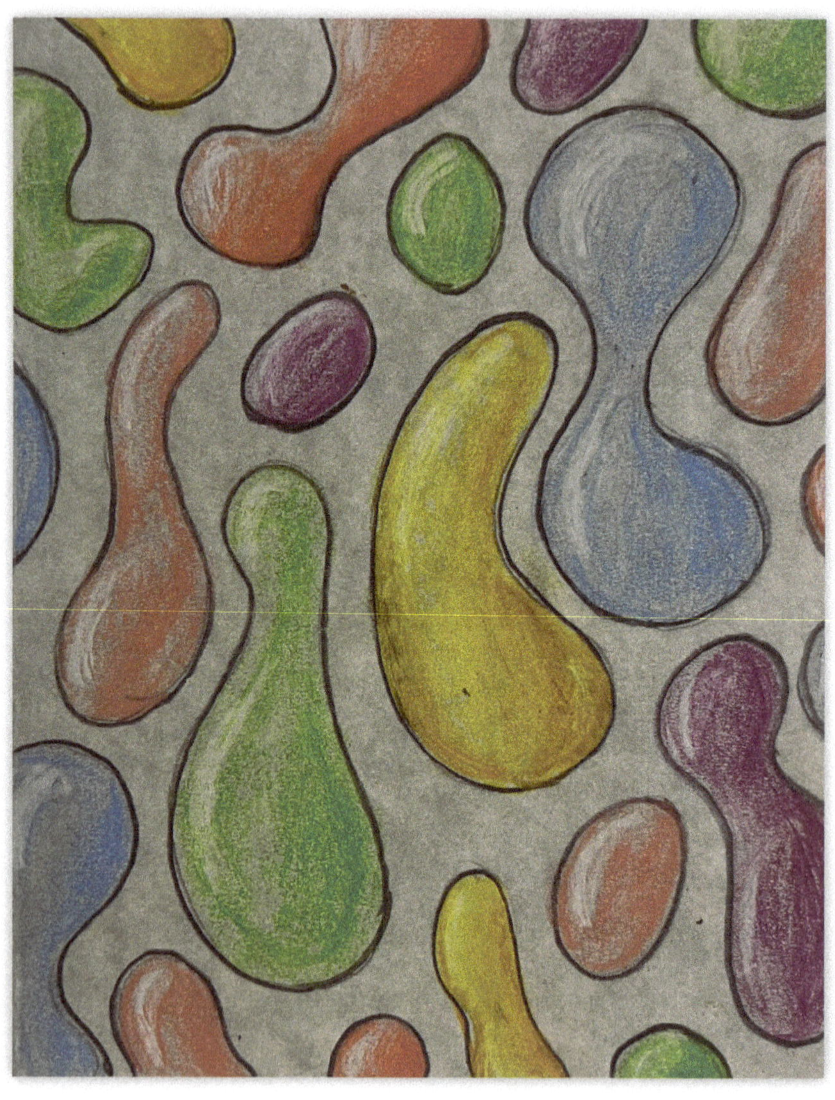

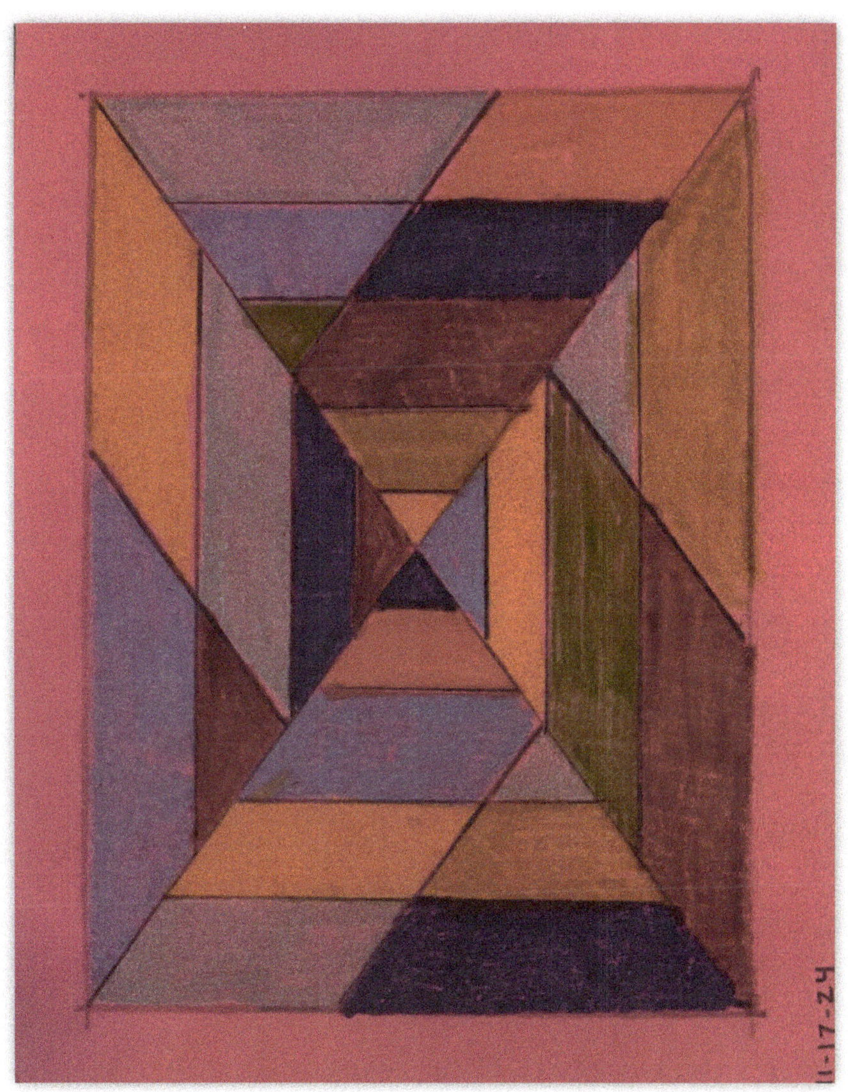
11-17-24

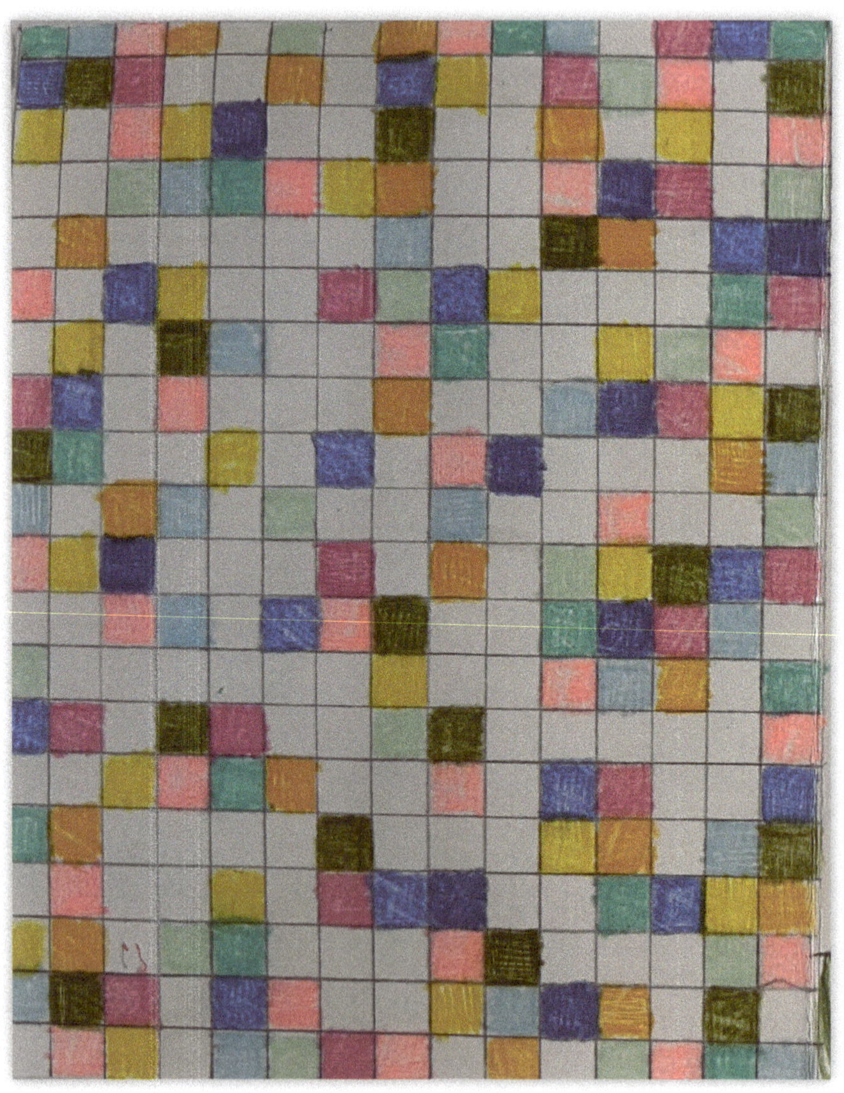

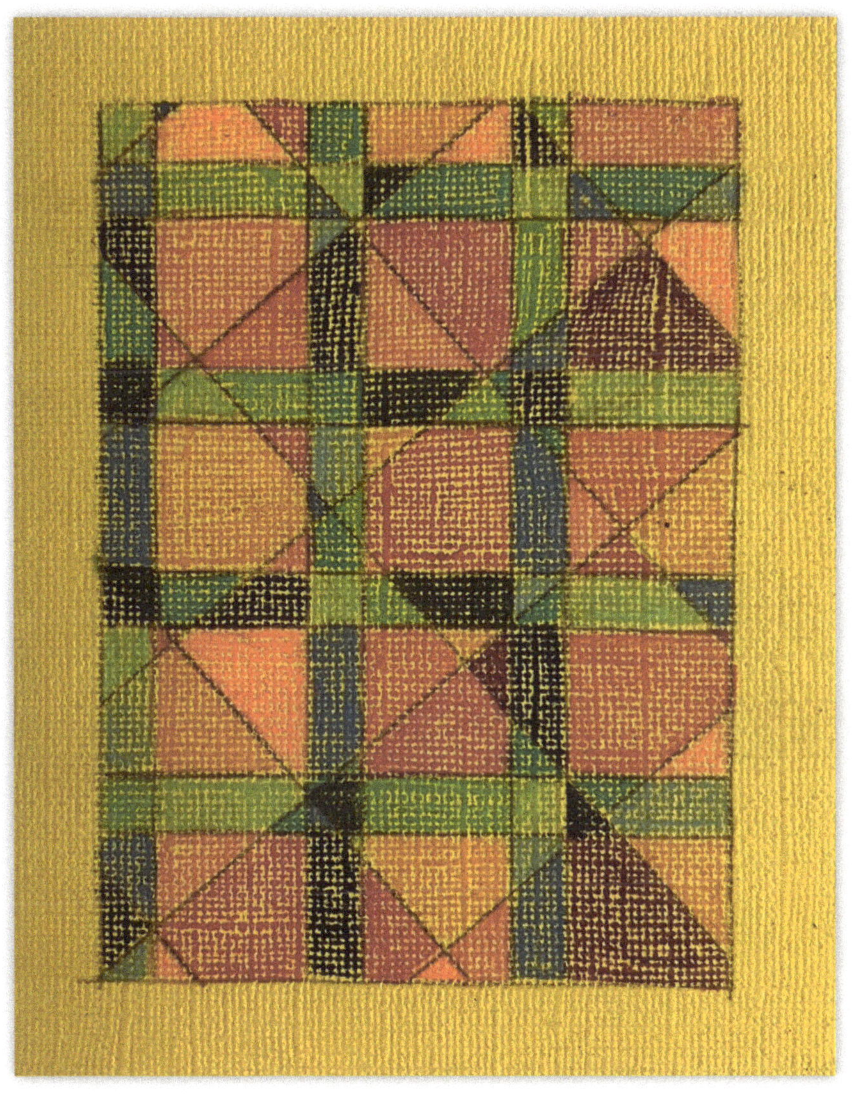

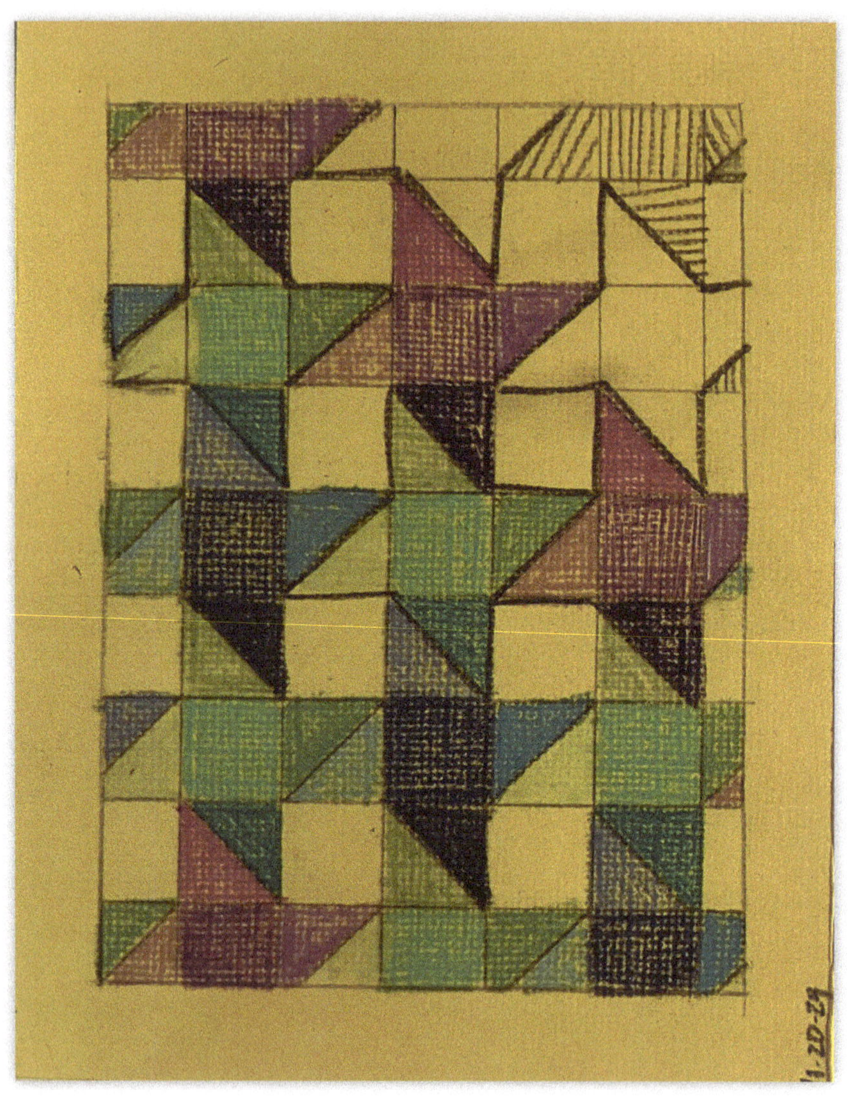

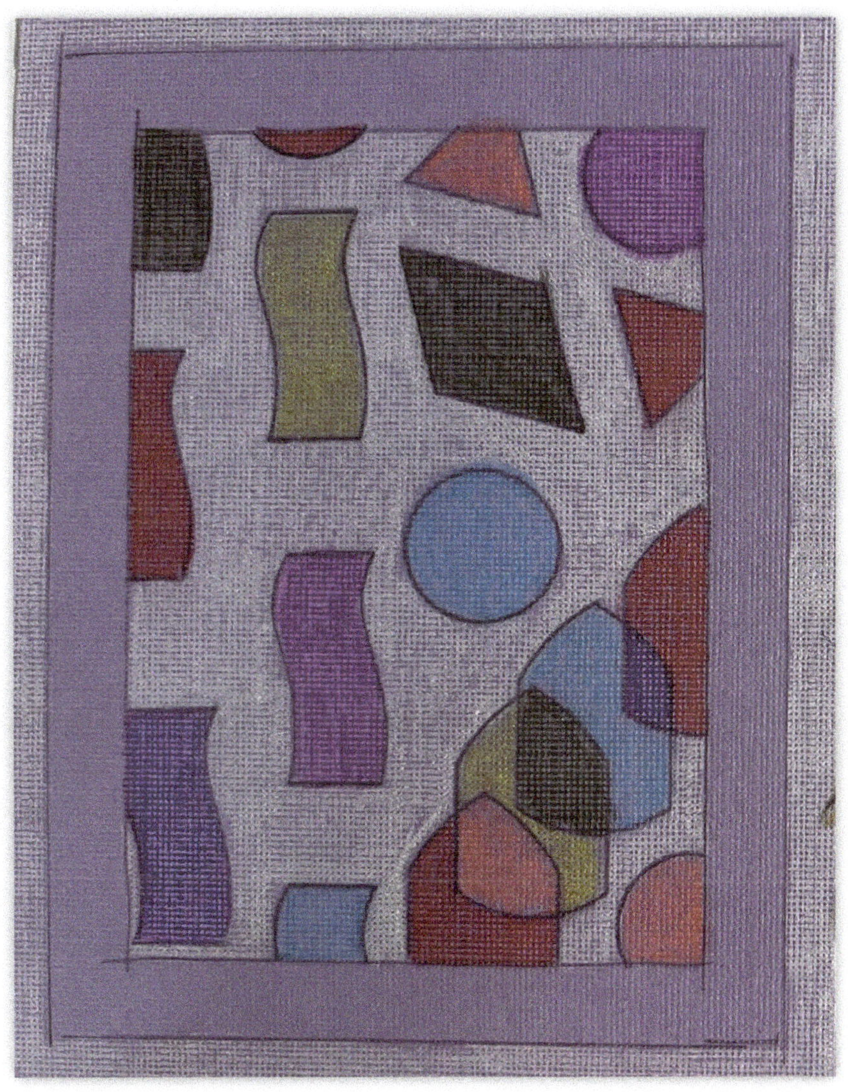

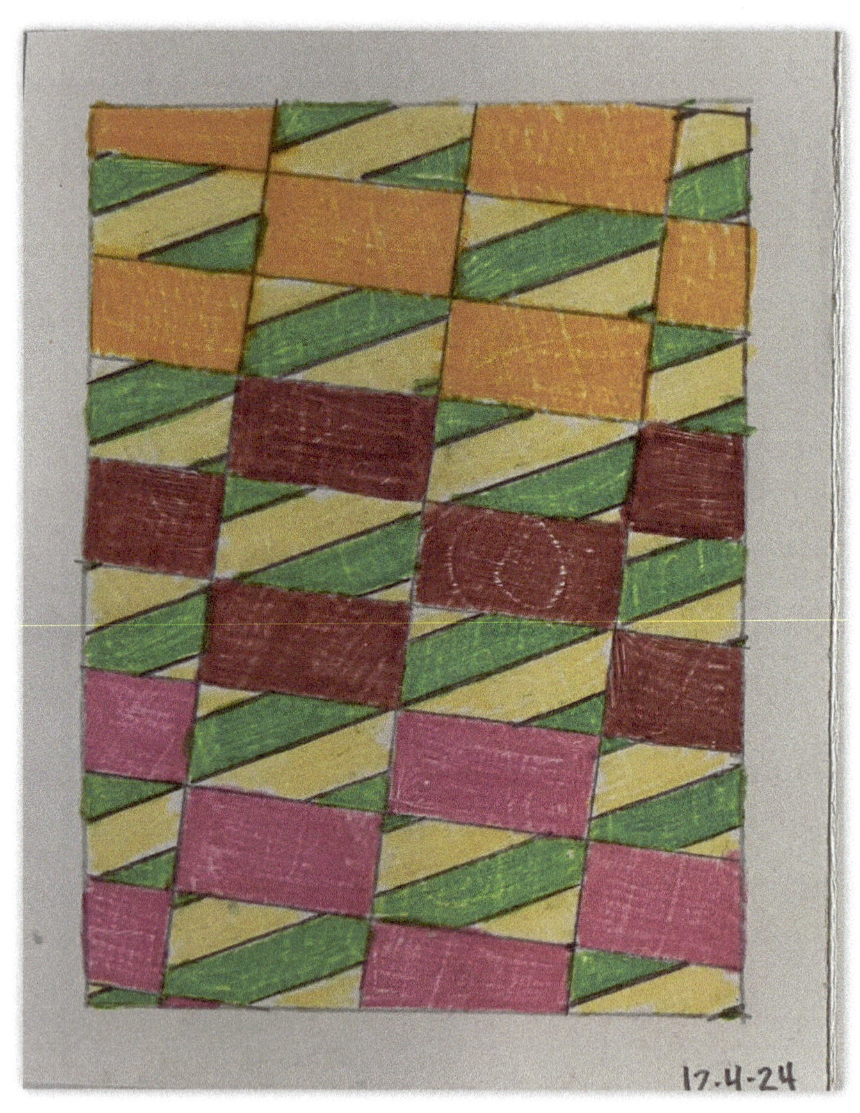

17.4.24

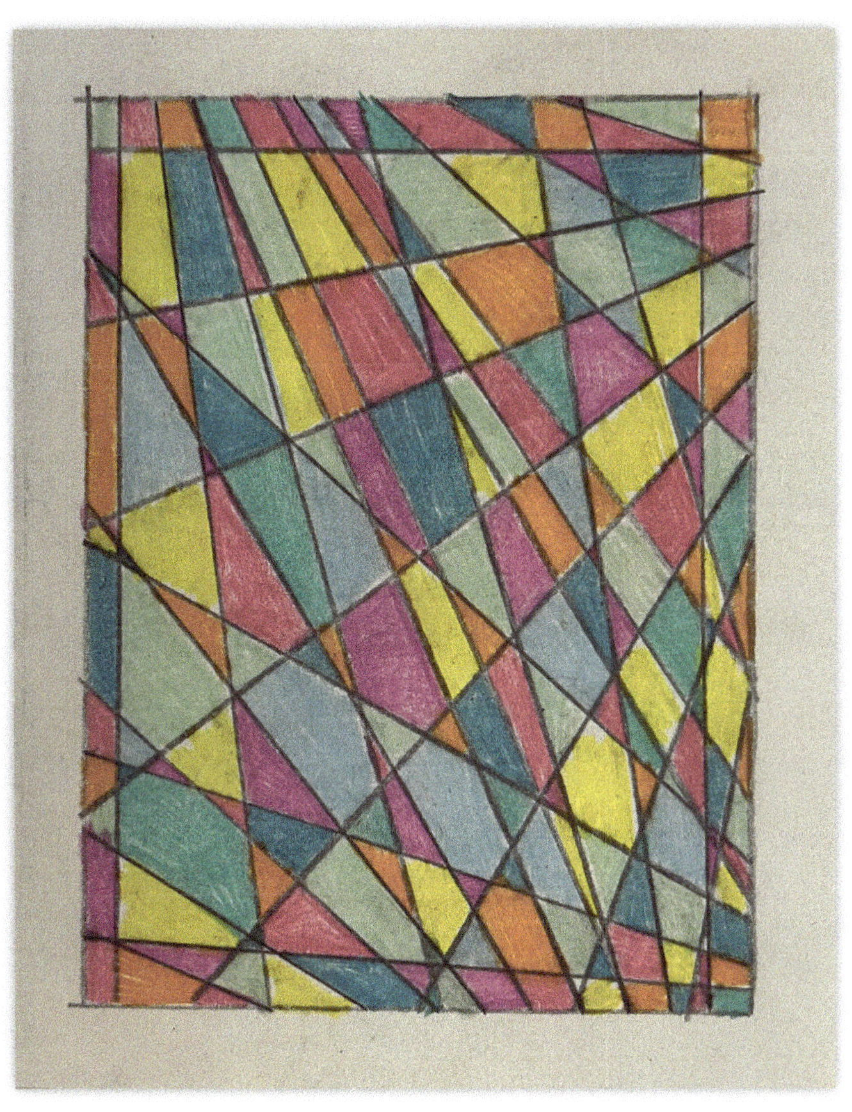

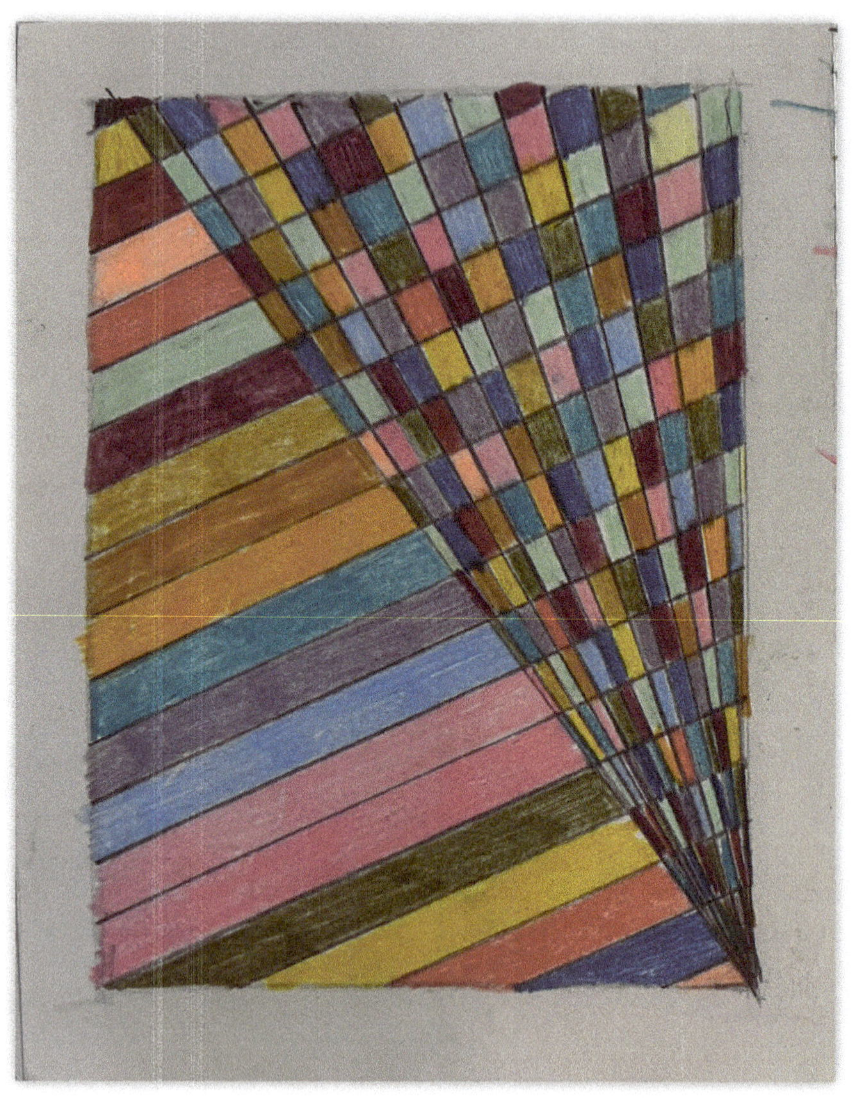

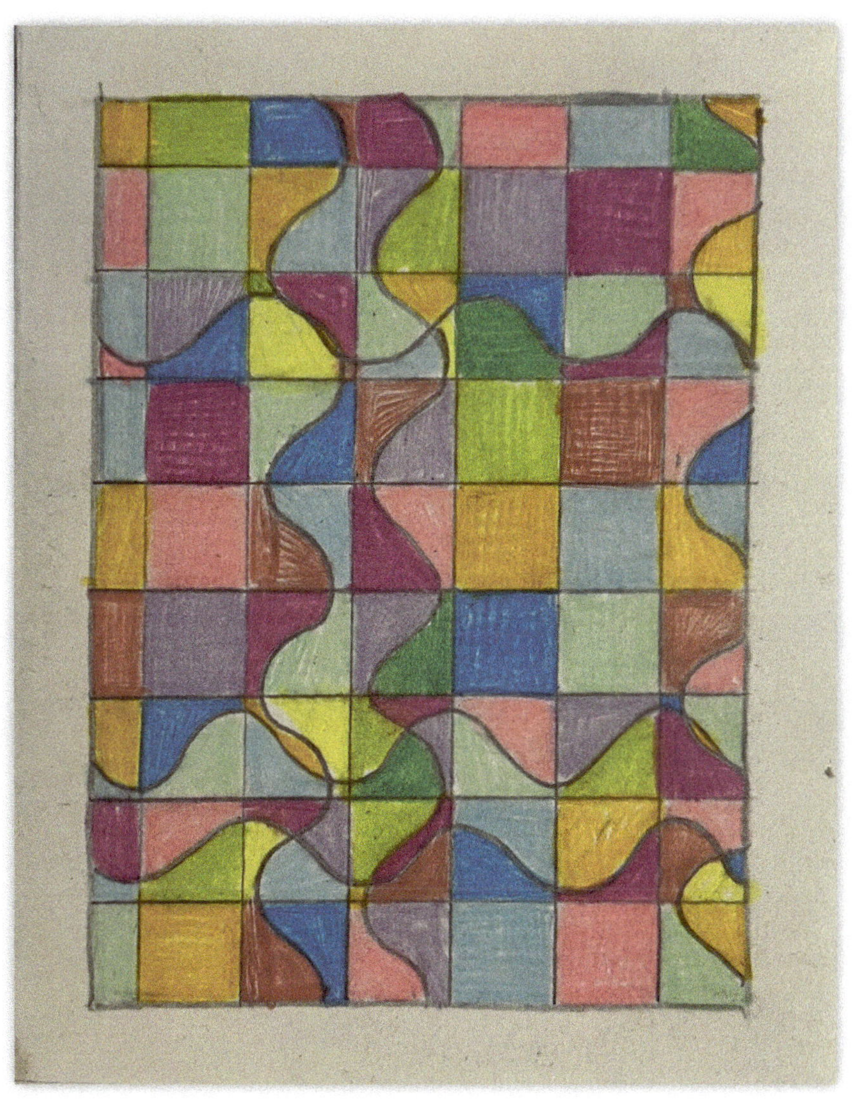

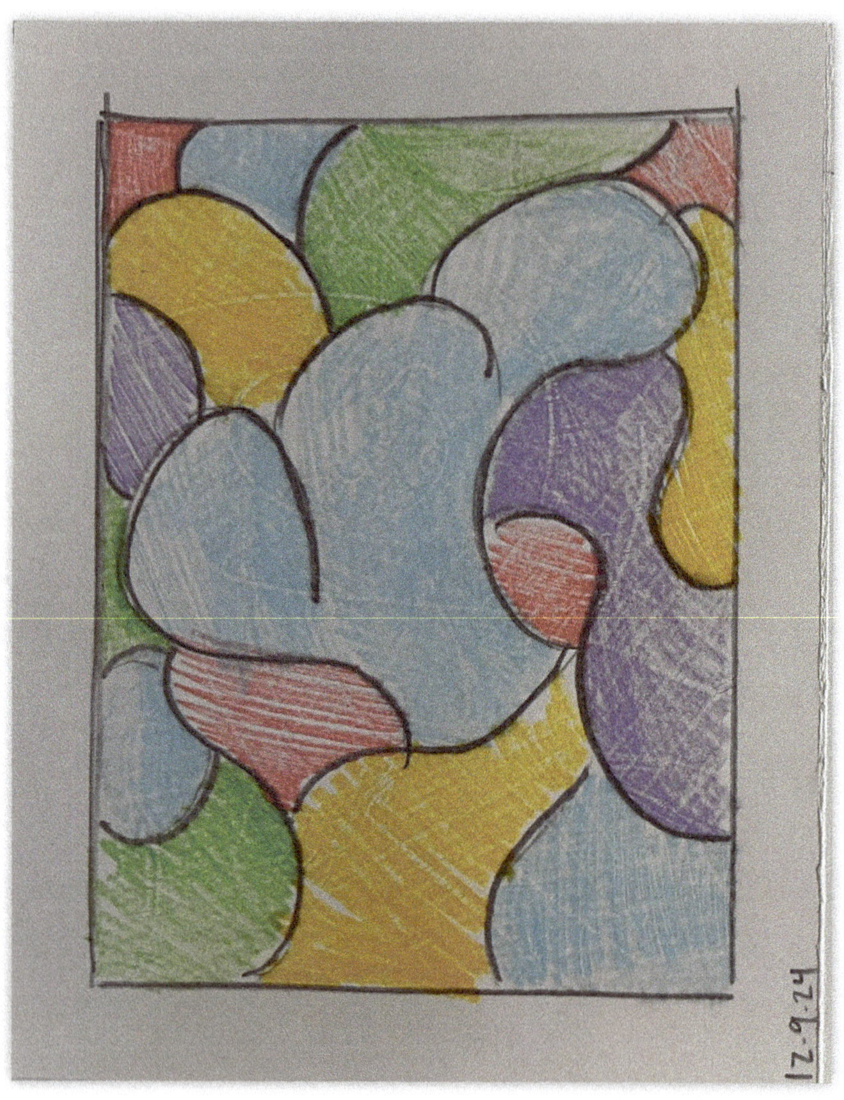

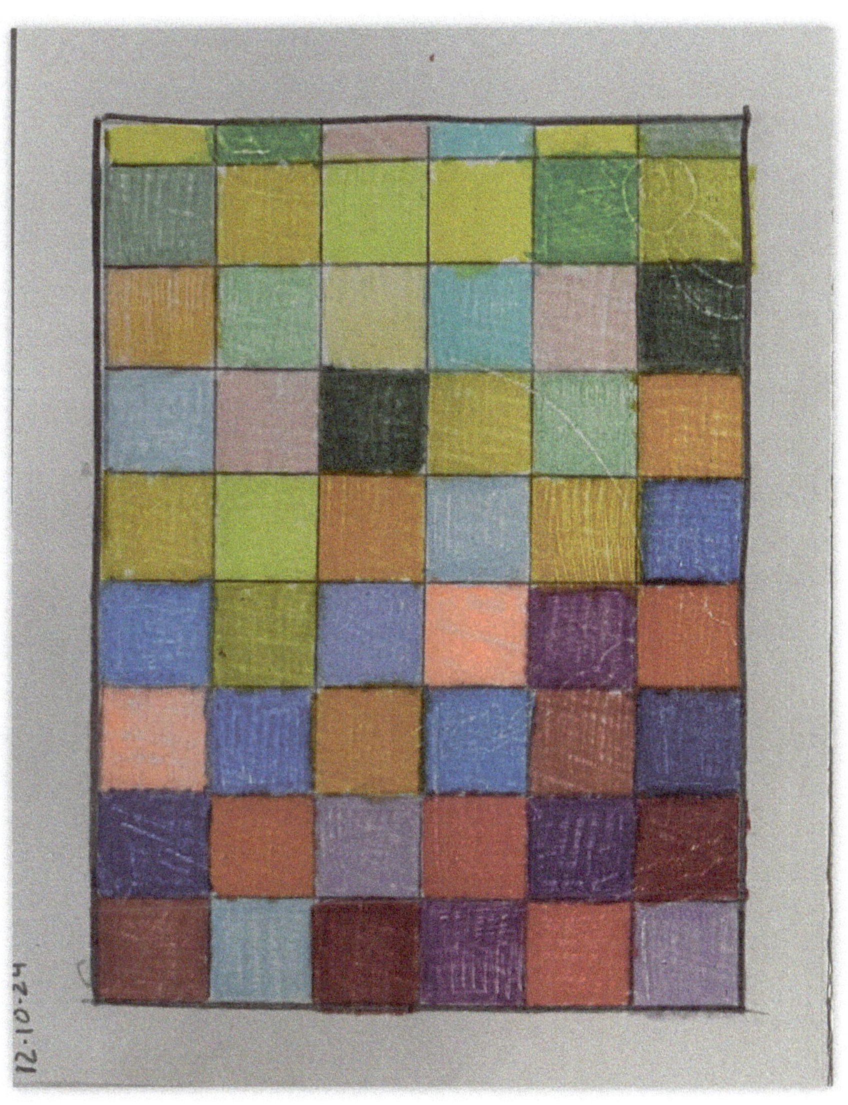

12.10.24

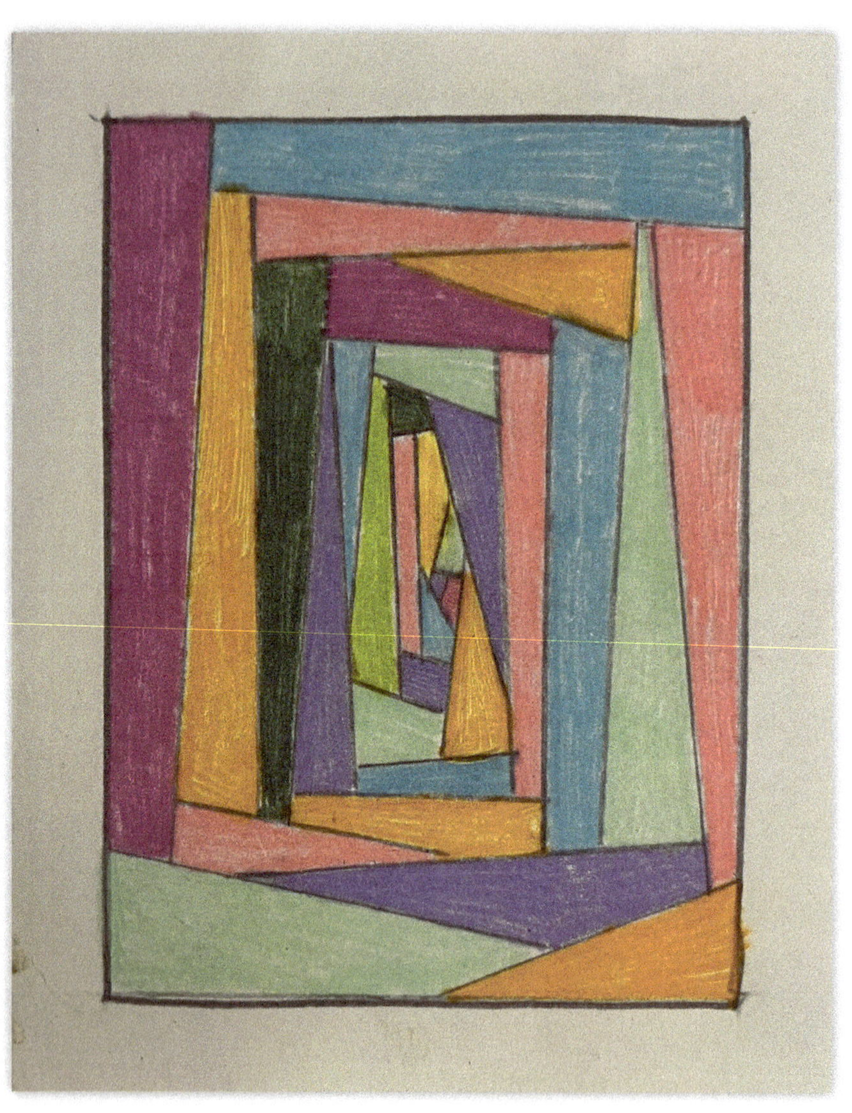

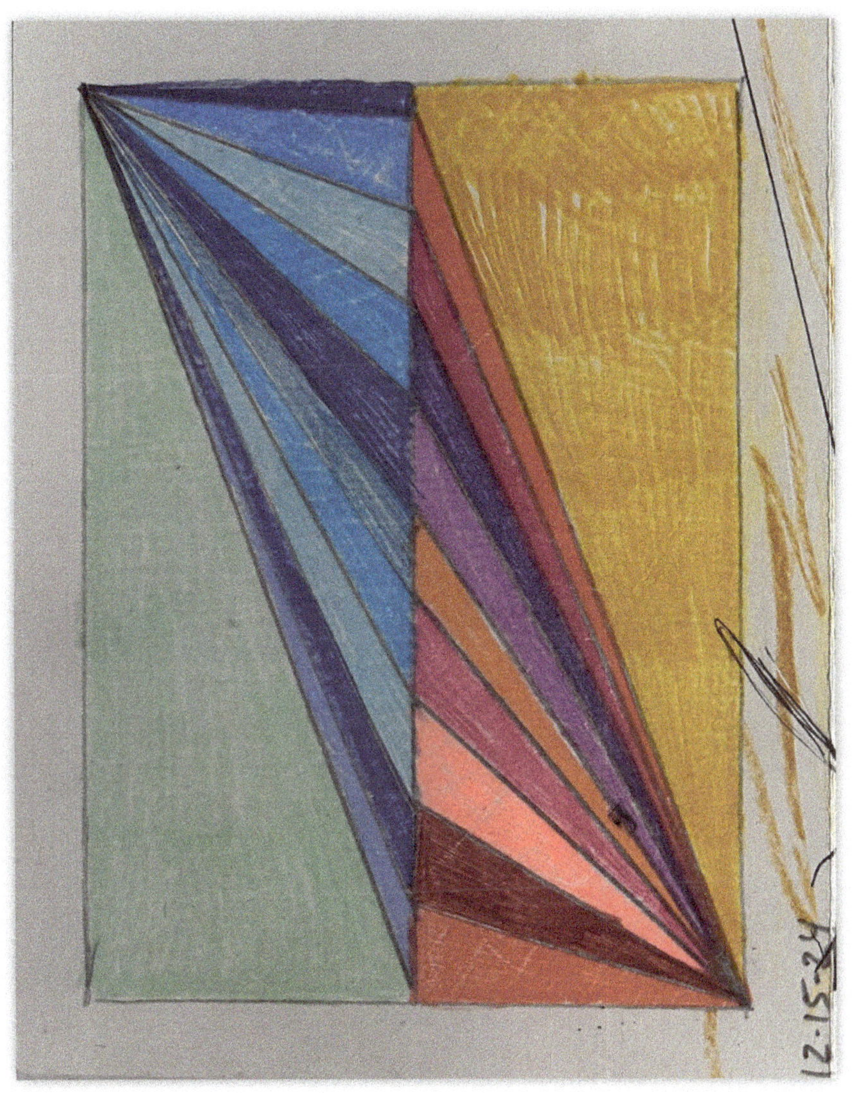

12-15-24

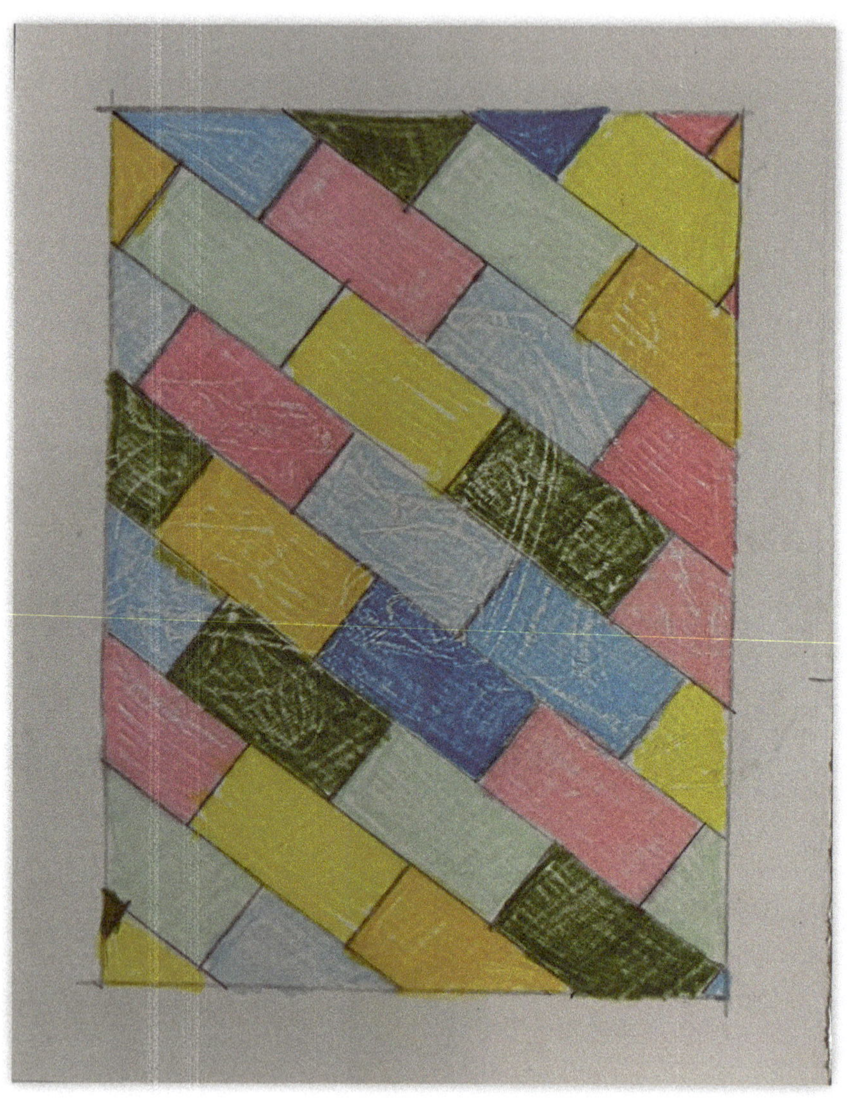

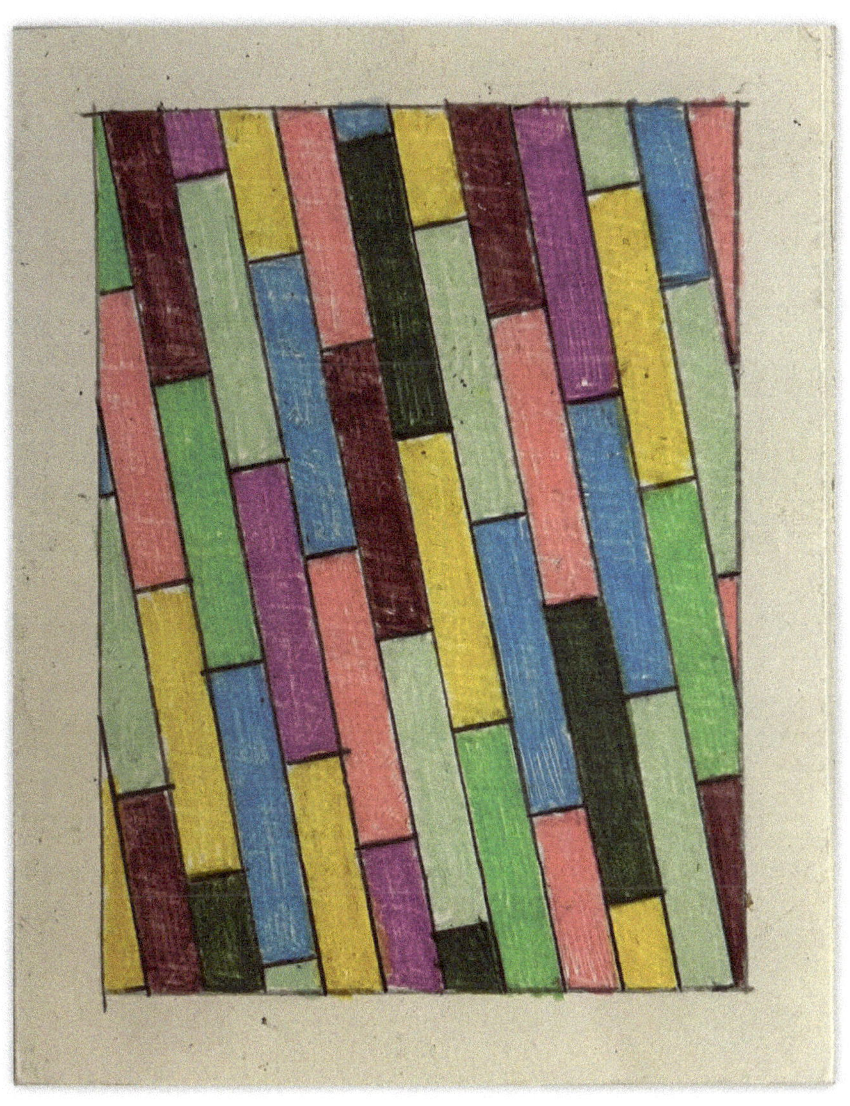

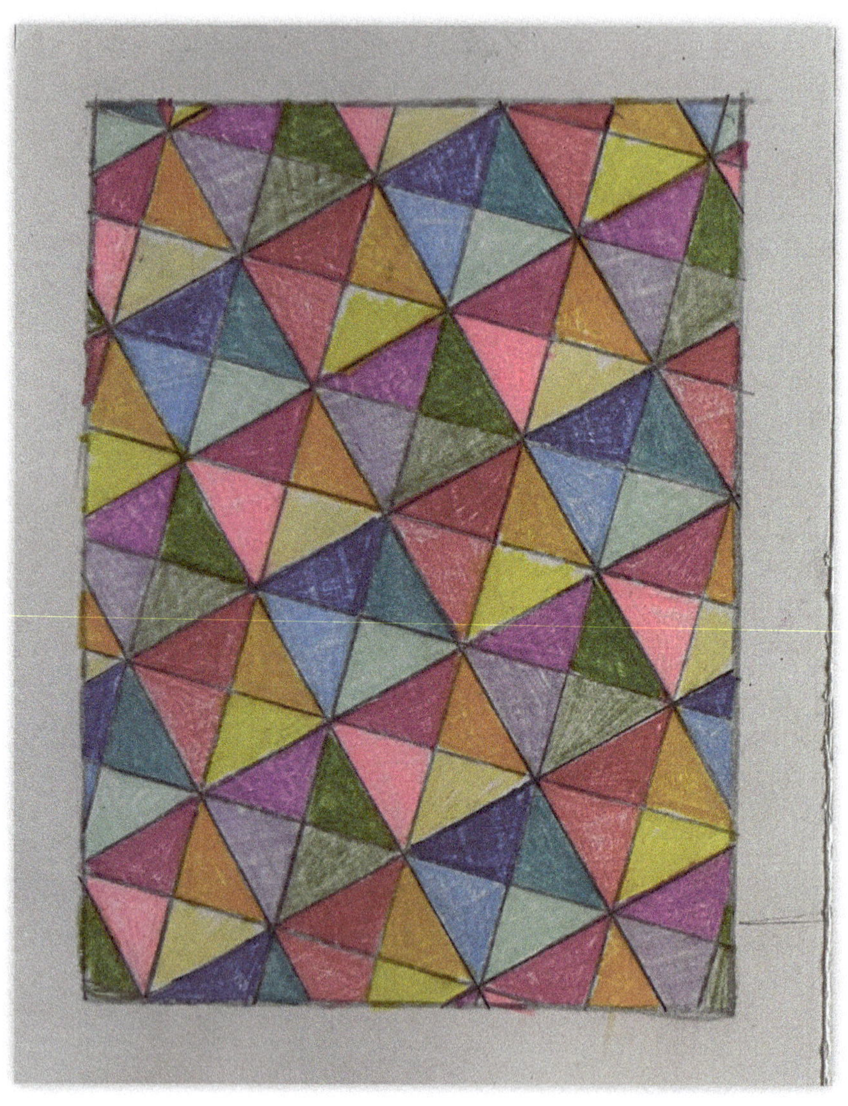

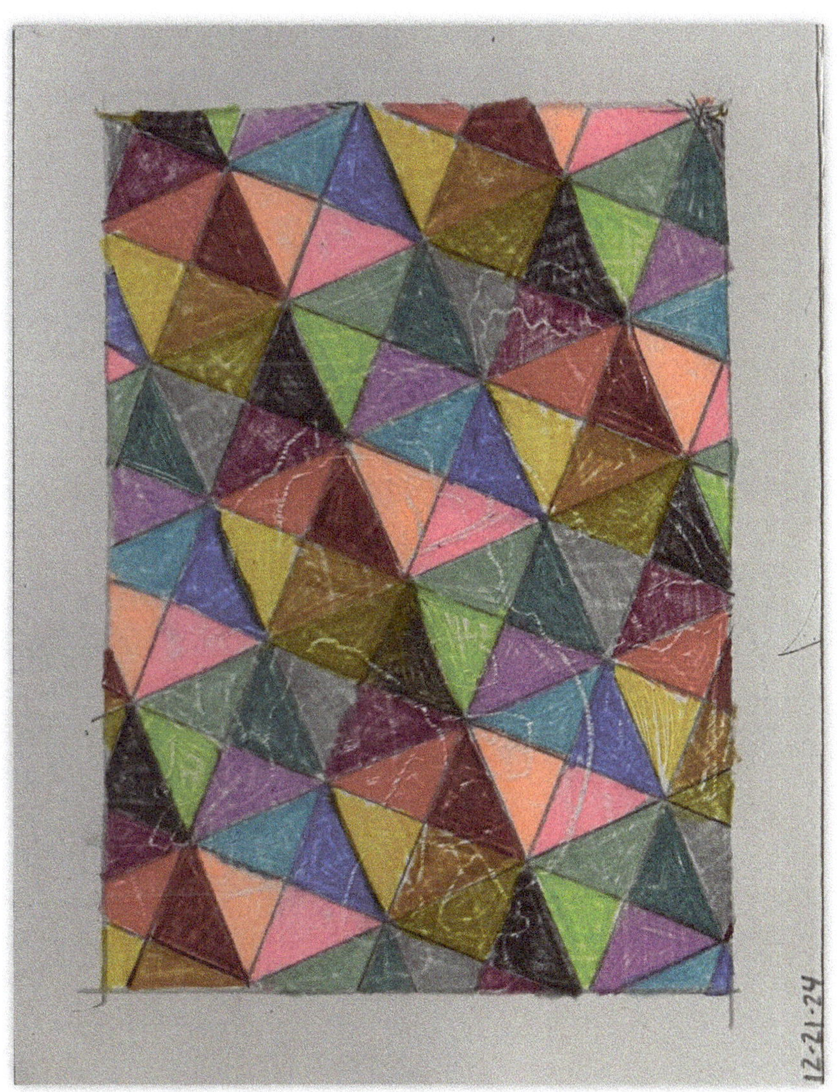

12-21-24

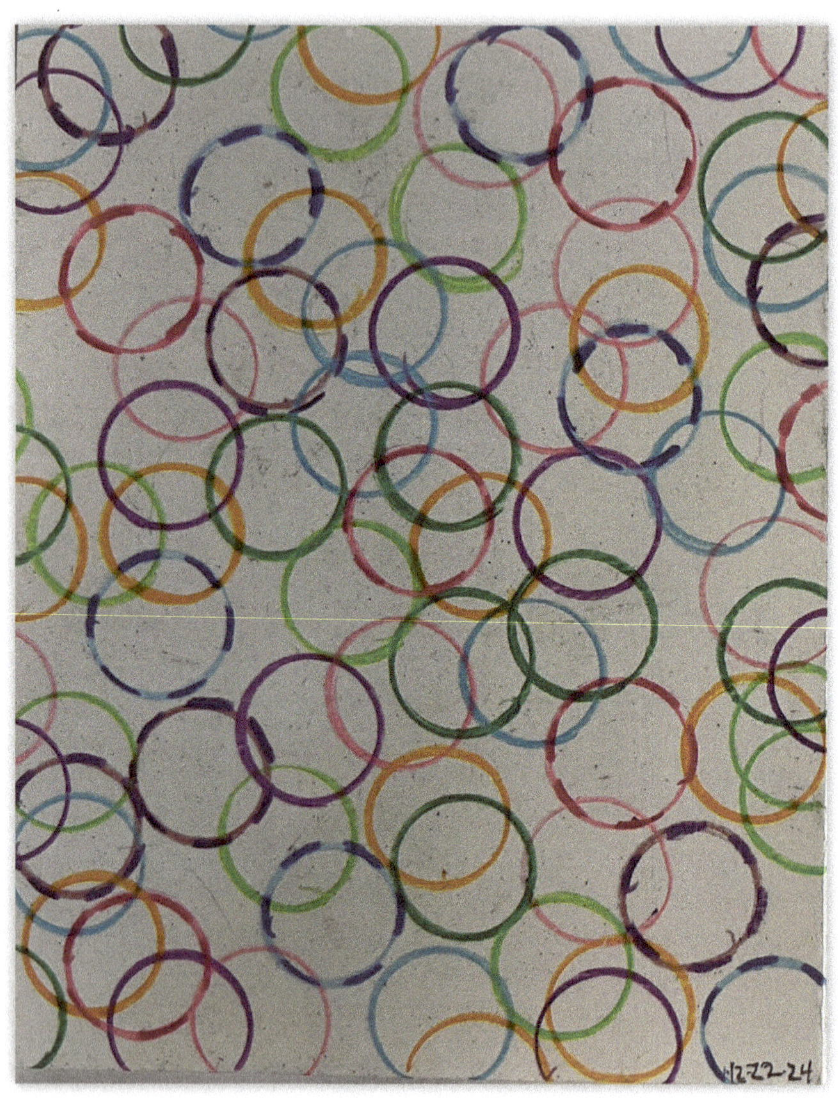

4-22-24

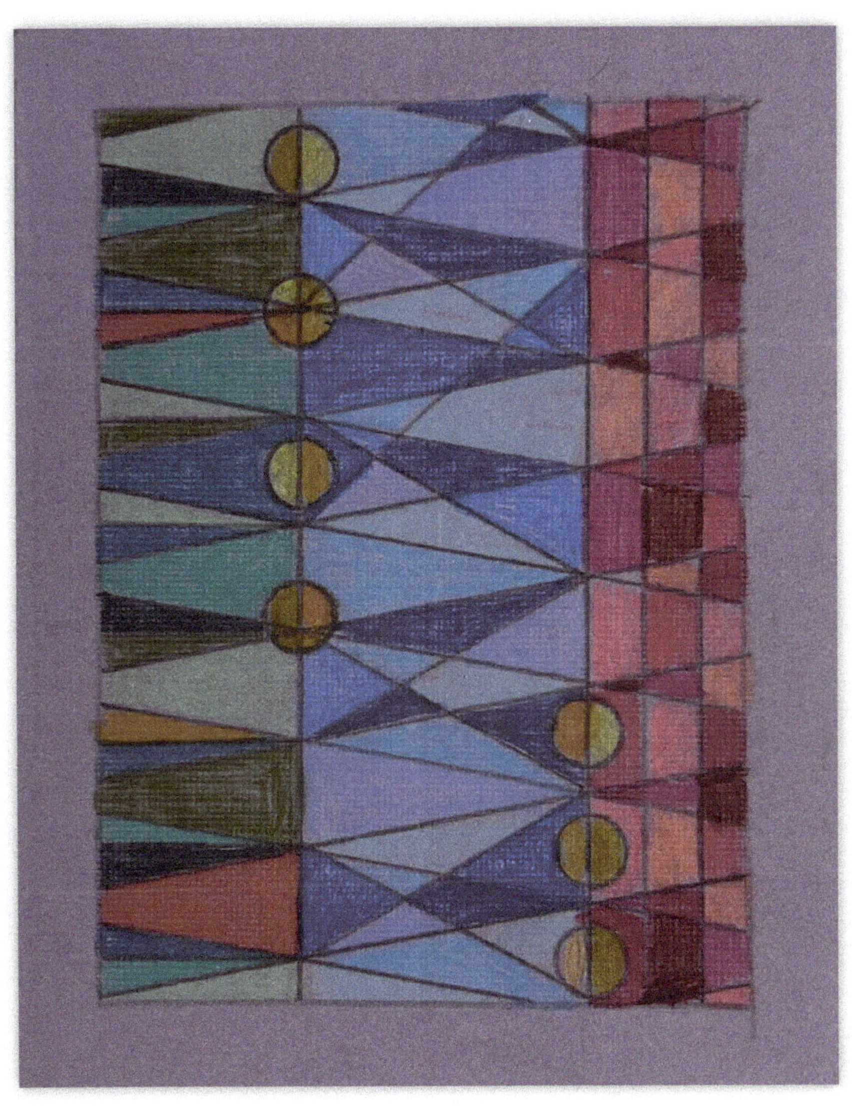

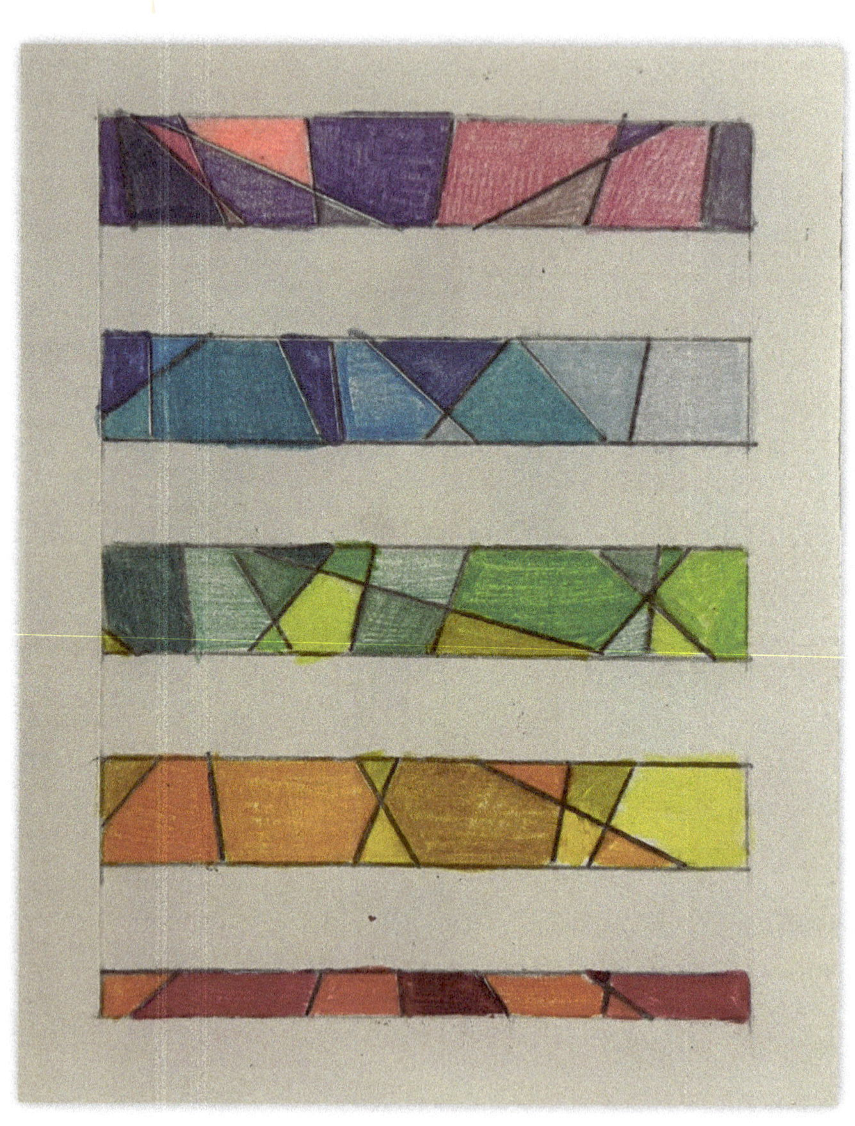

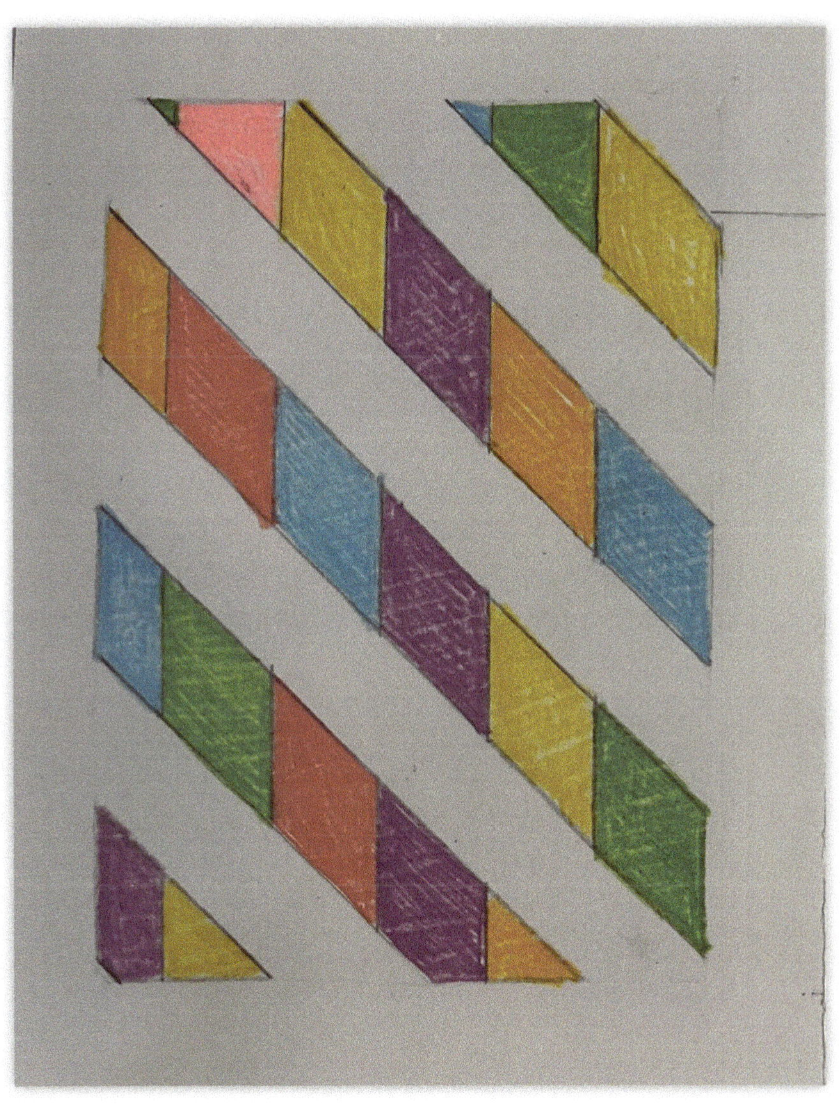

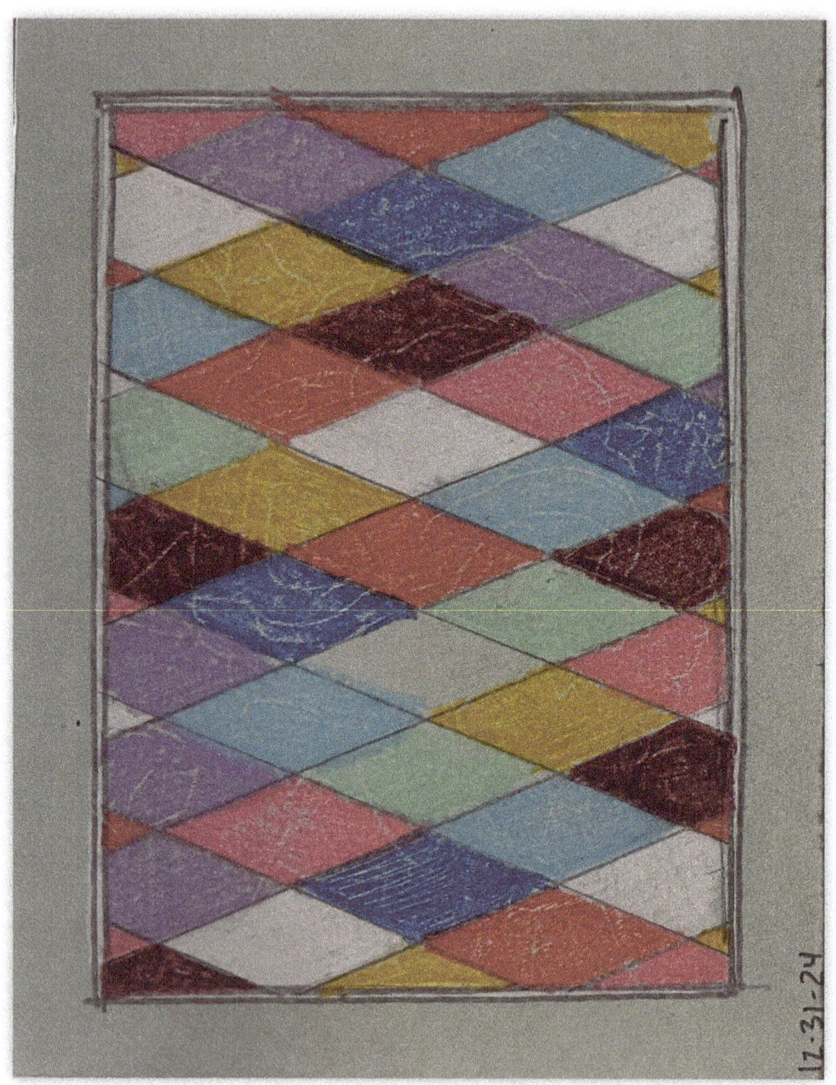

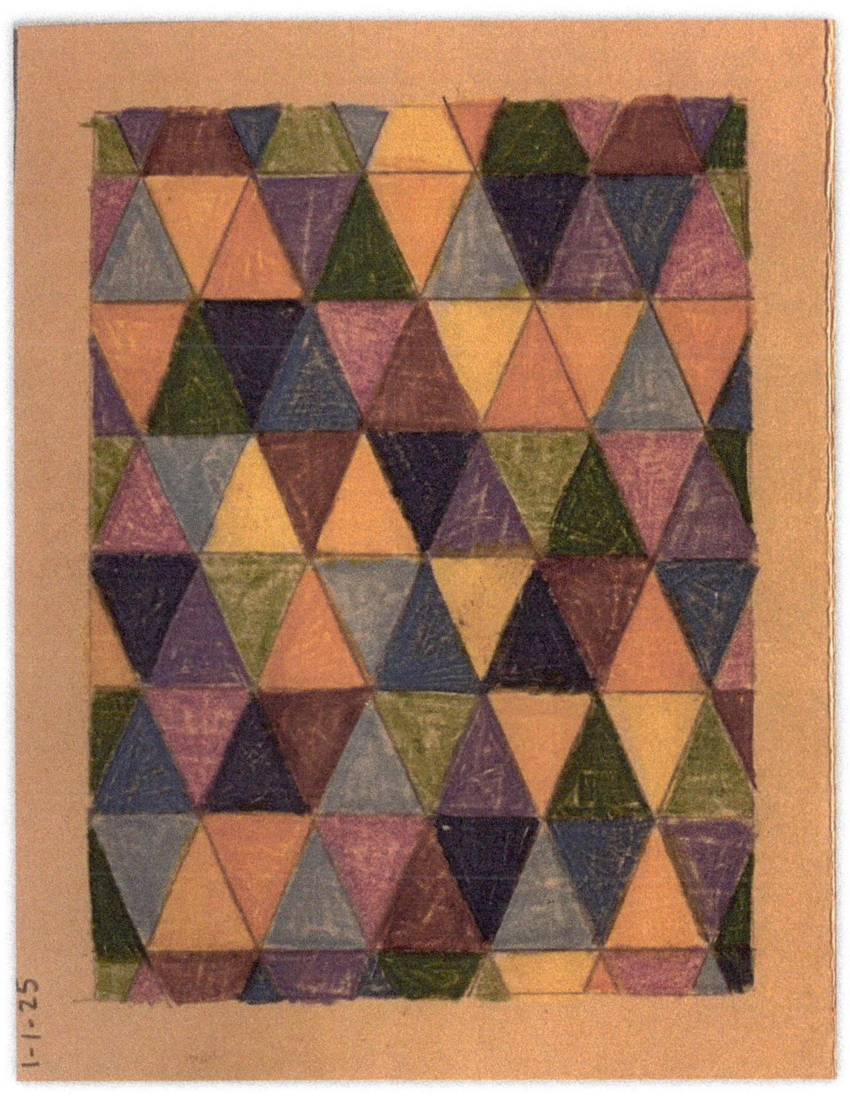

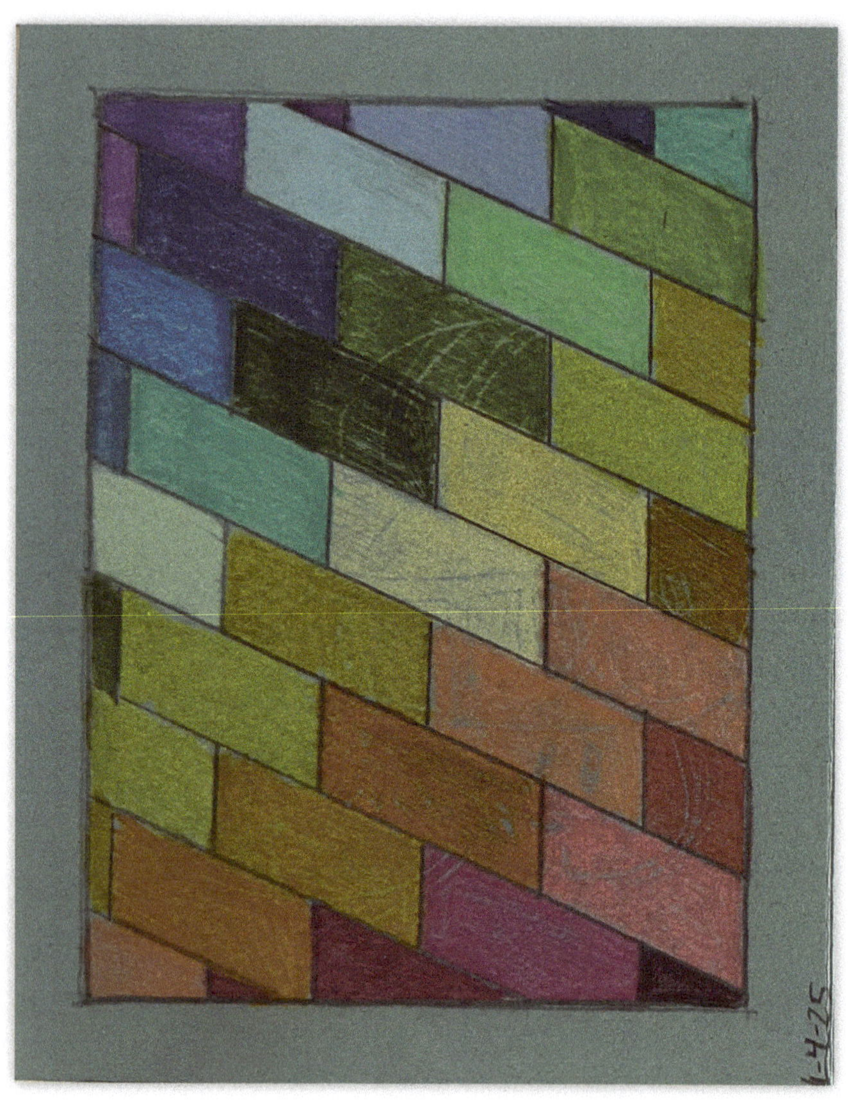

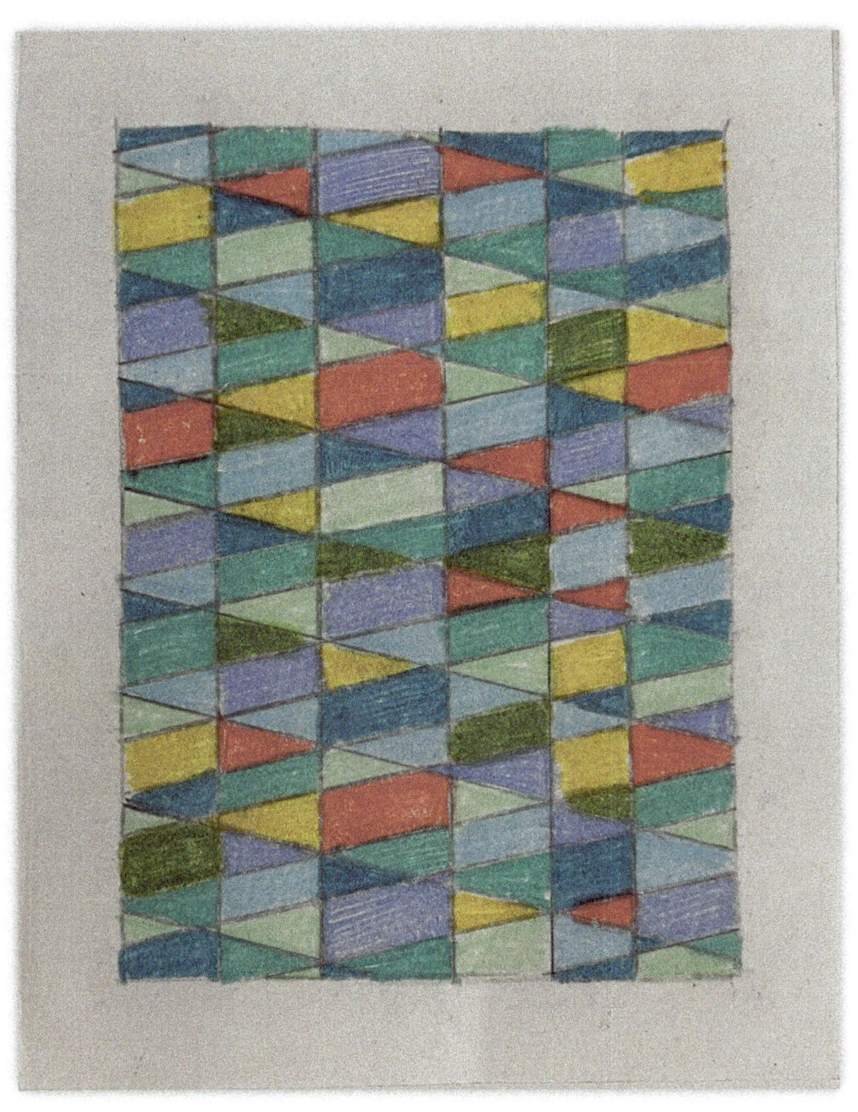

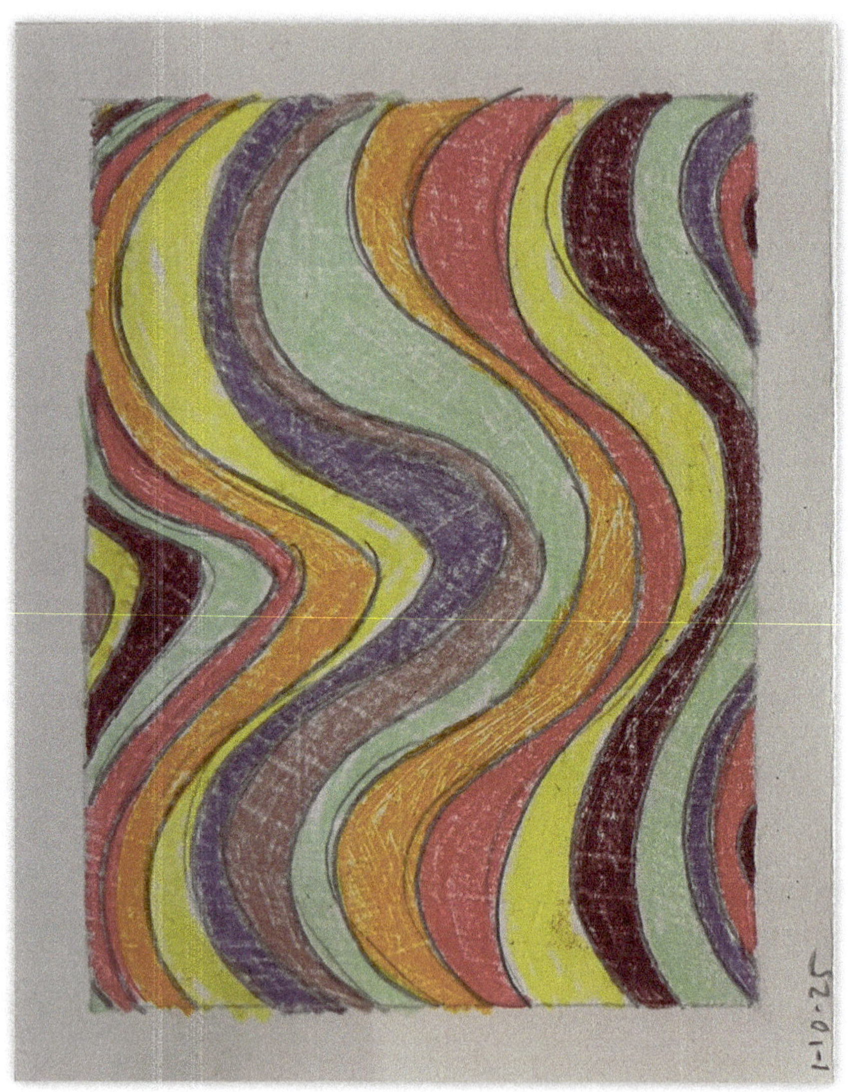

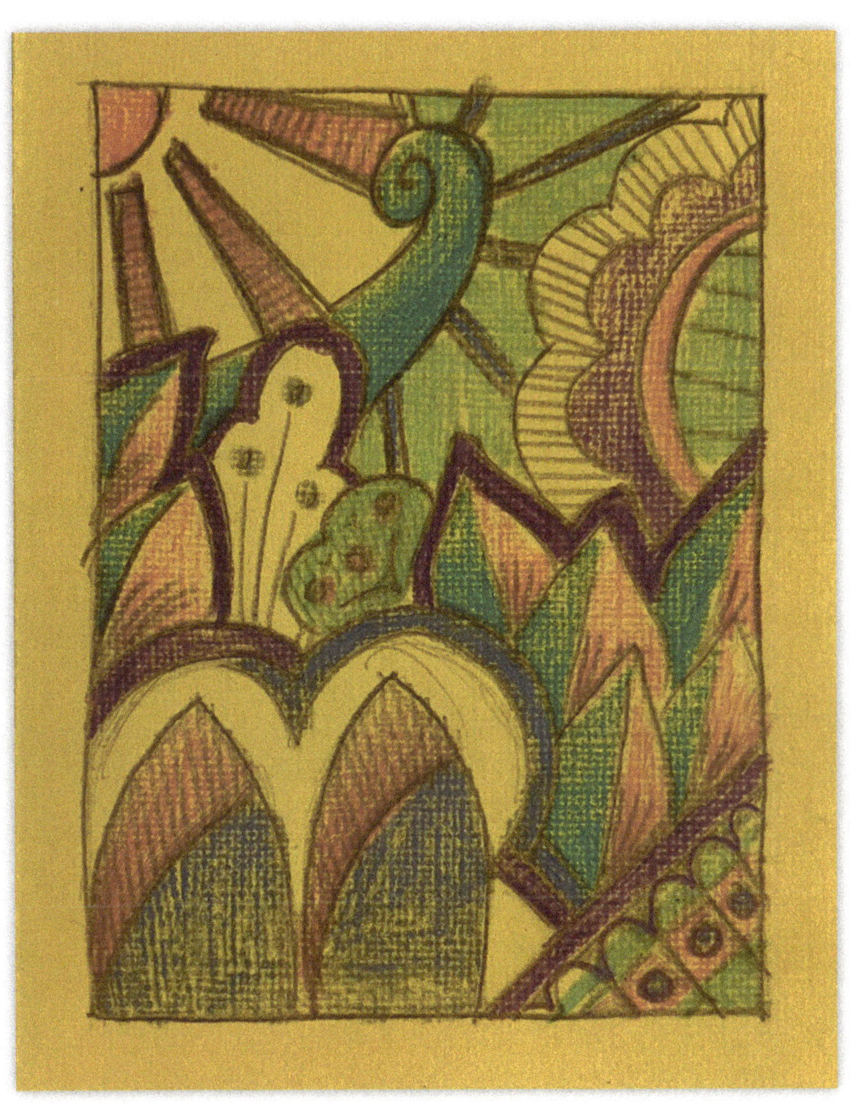

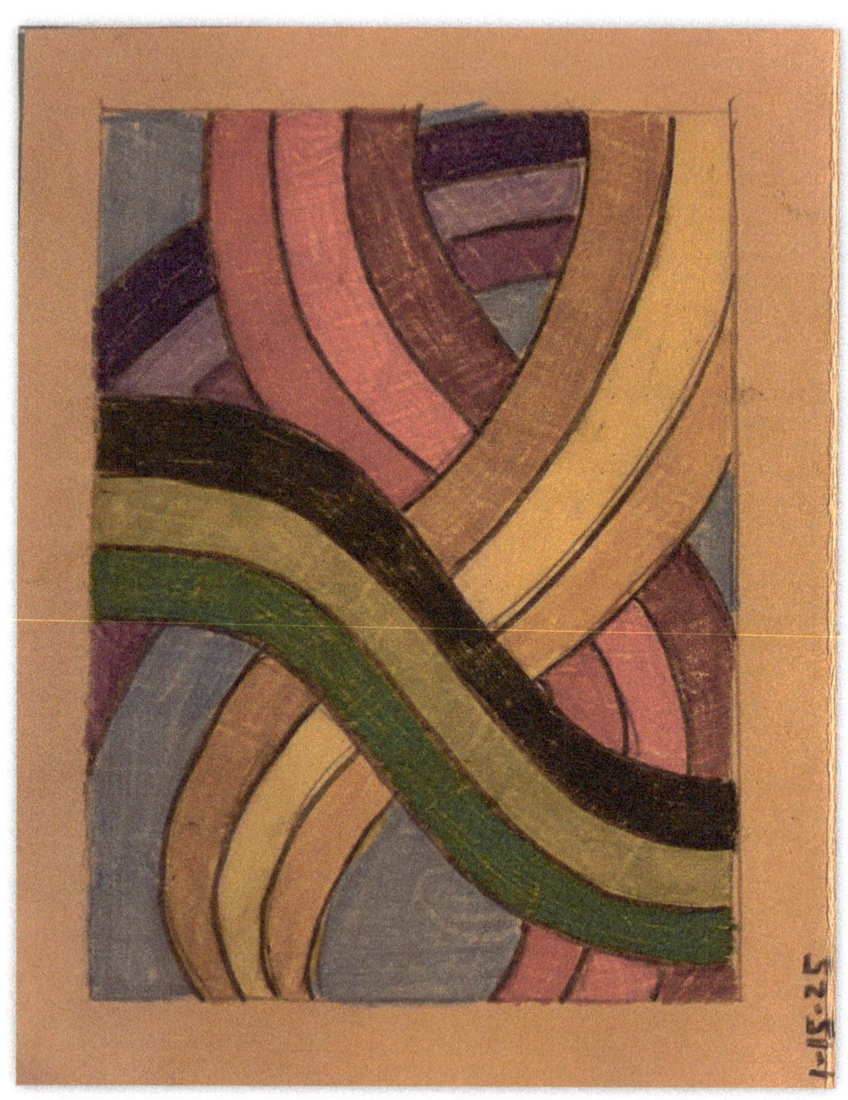

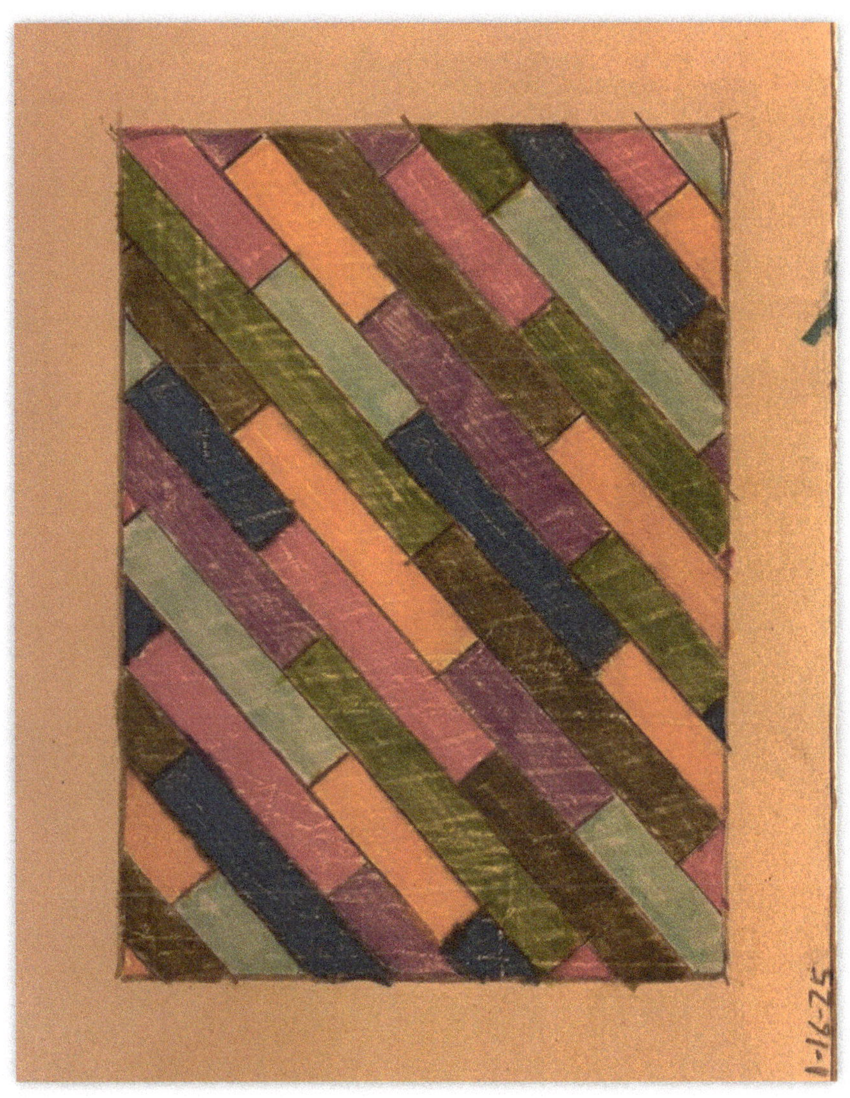

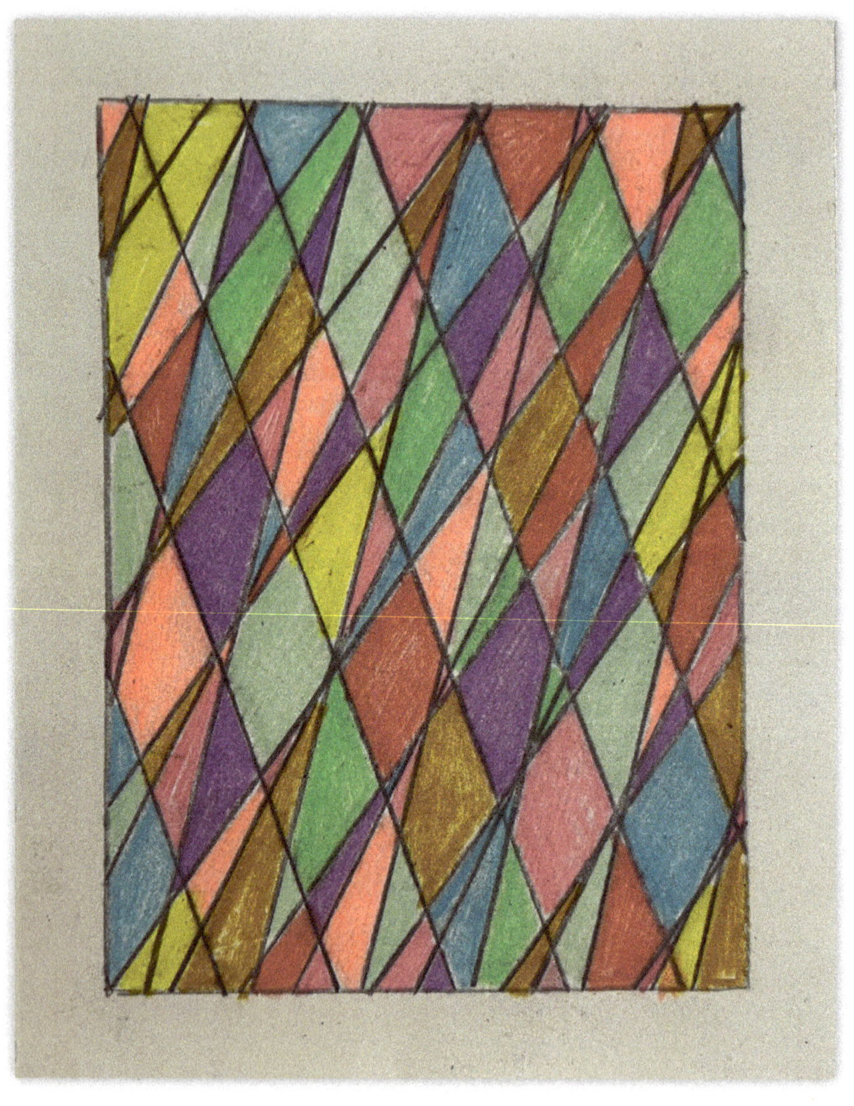

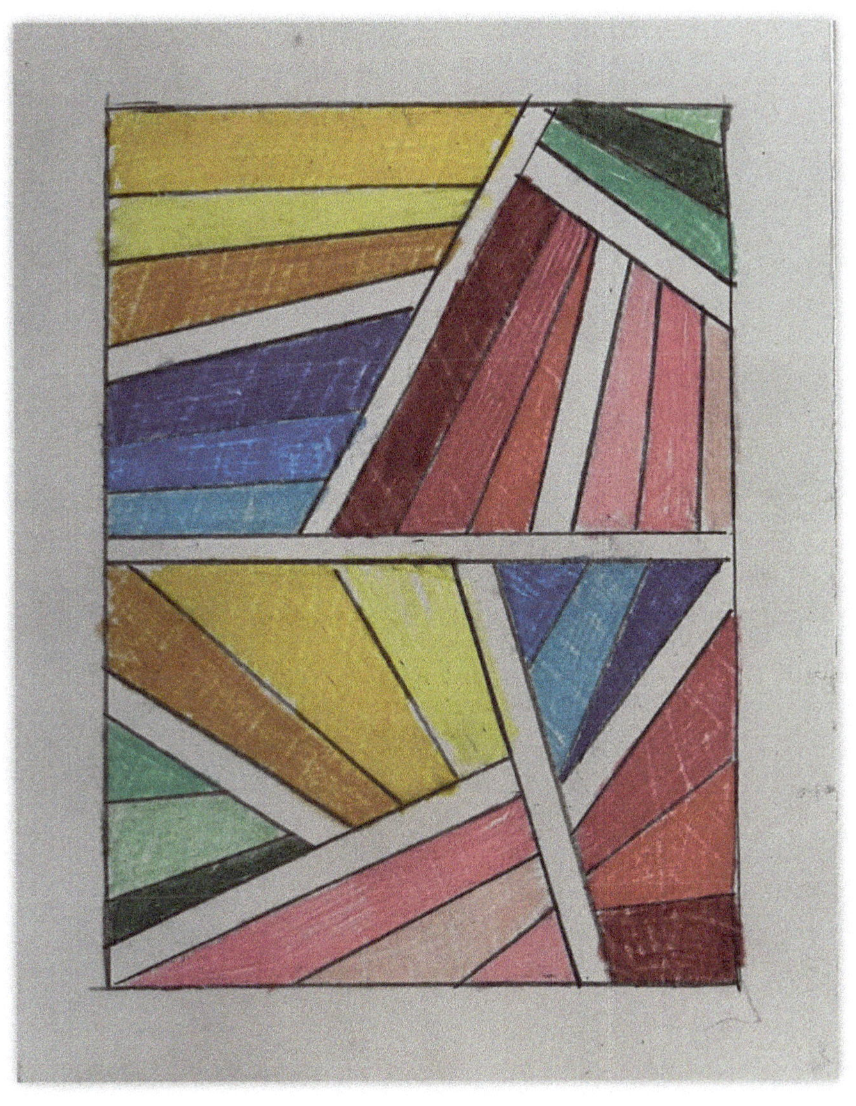

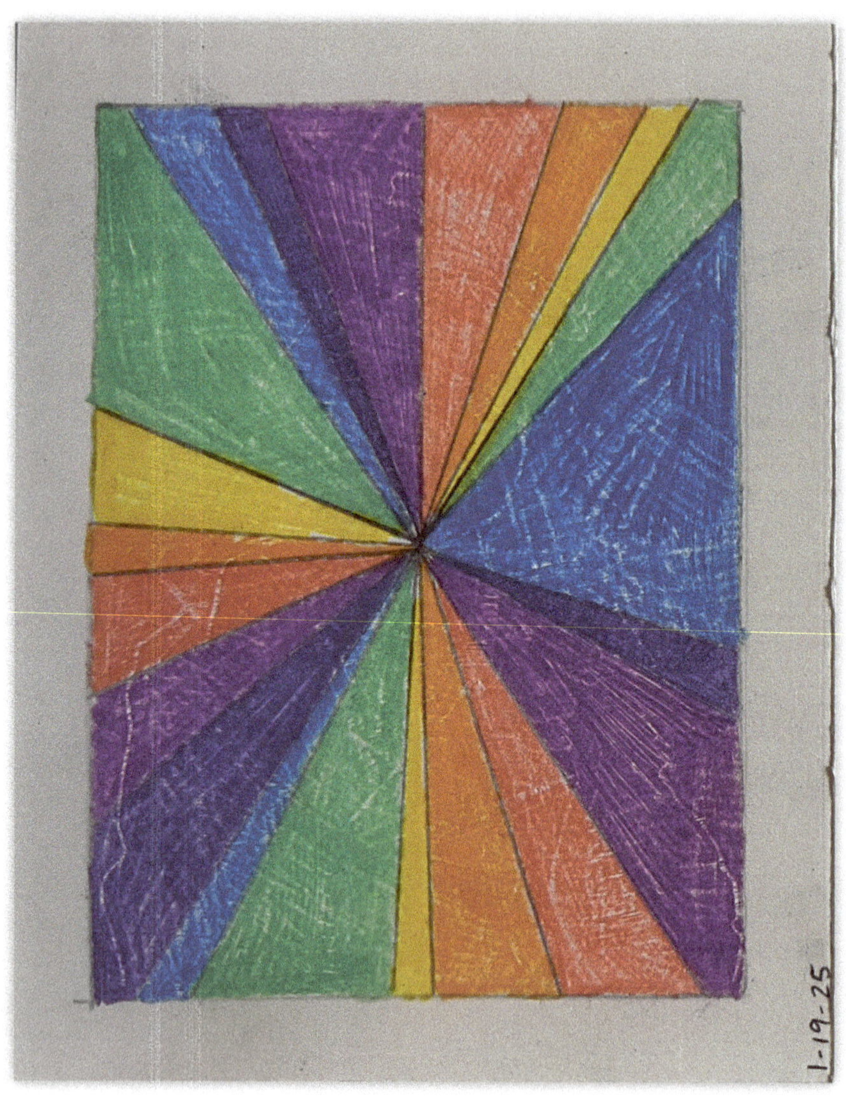

1-19-25

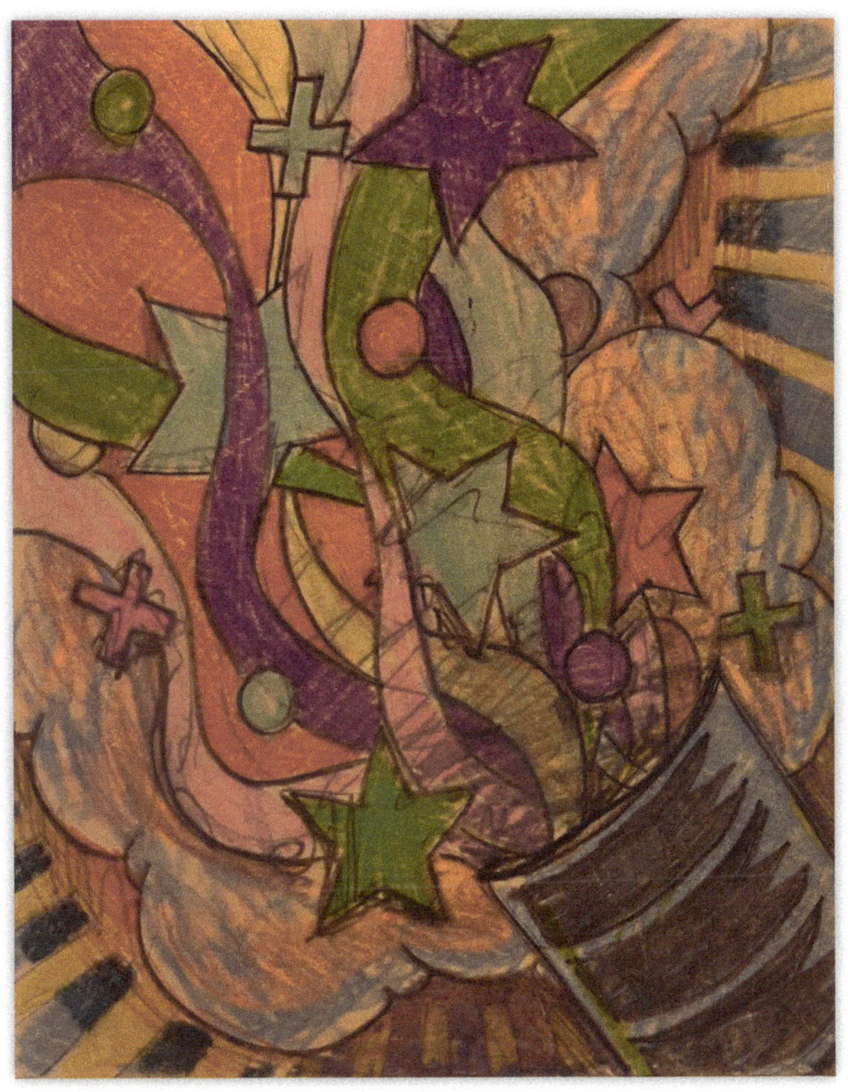

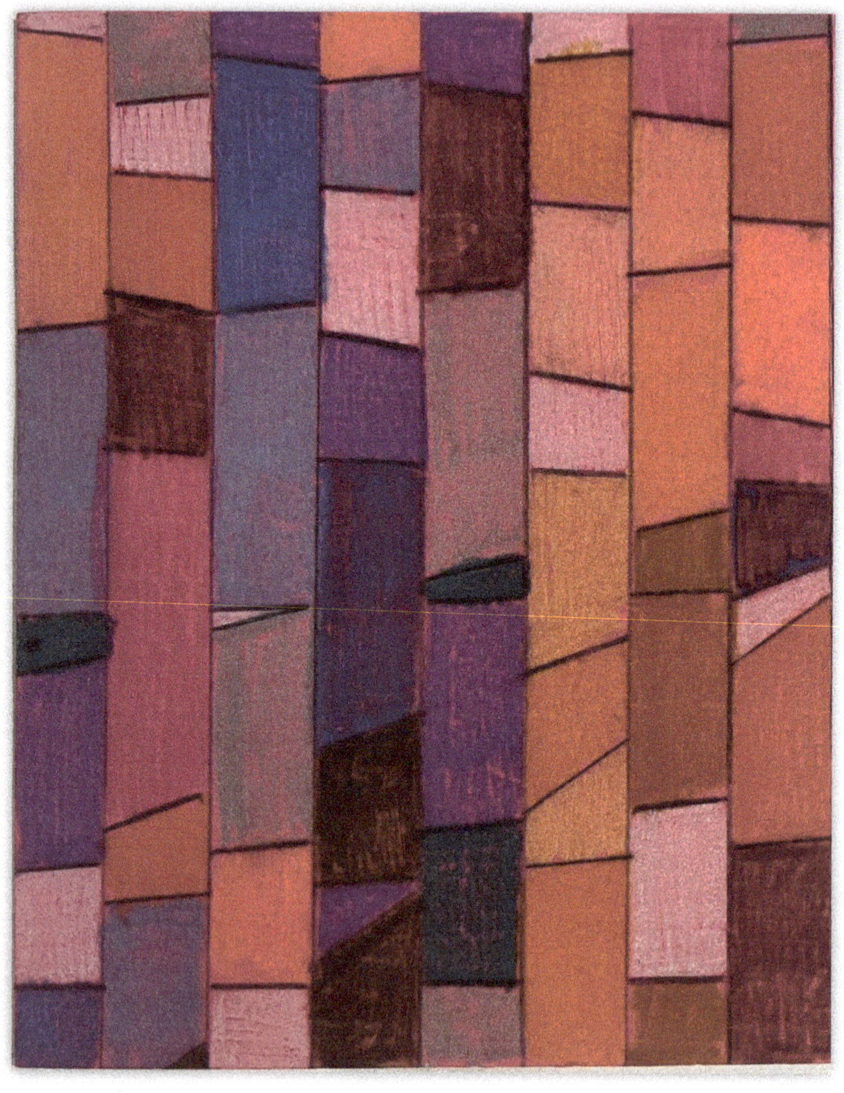

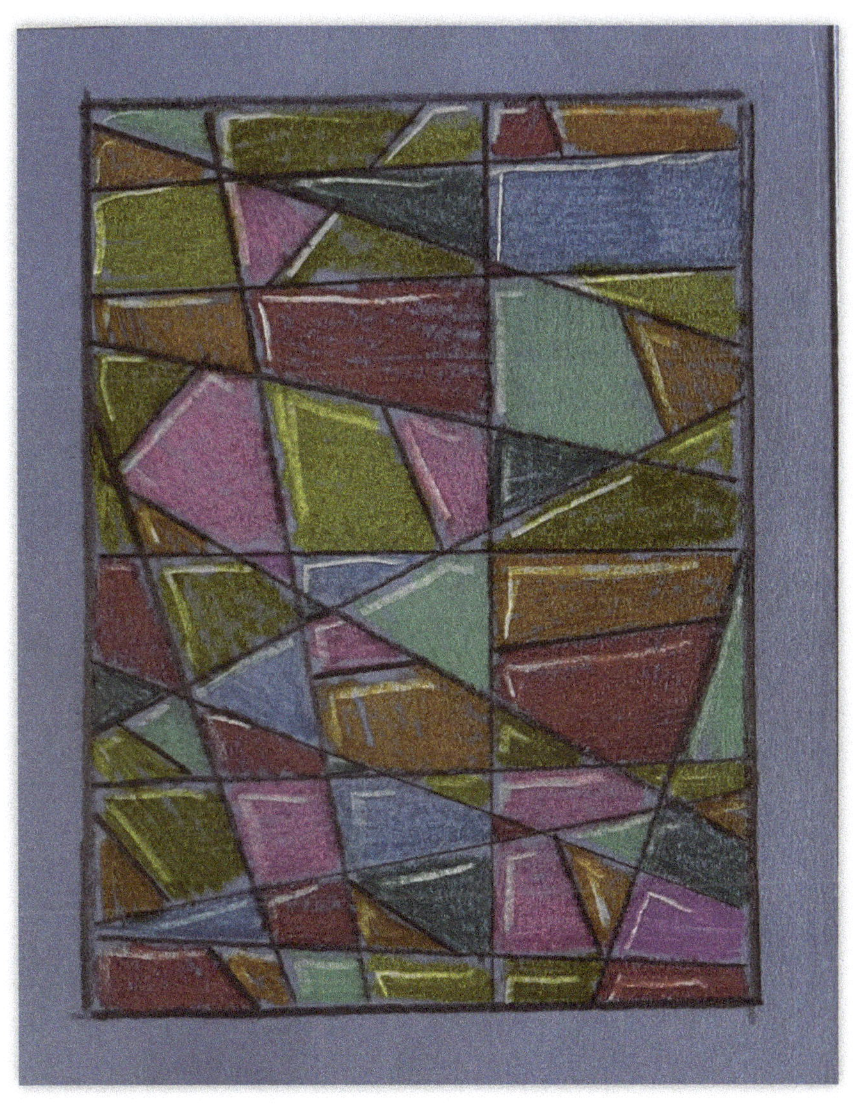

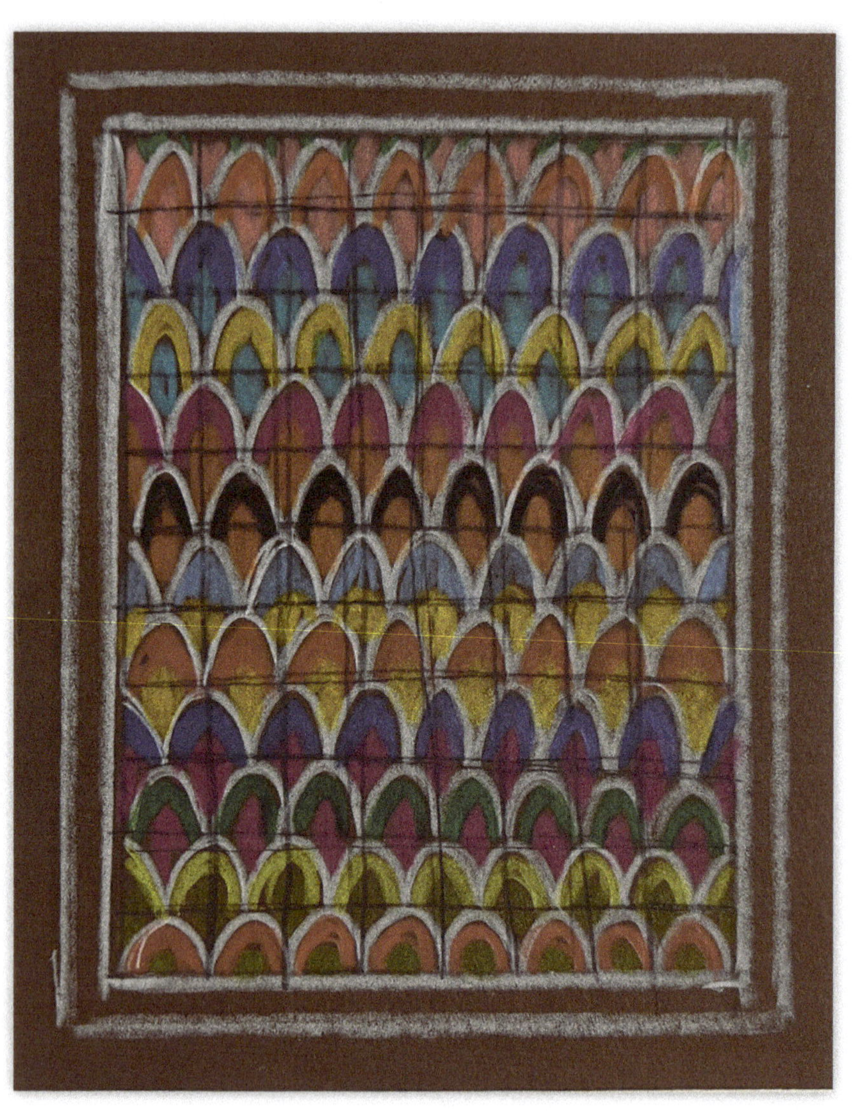

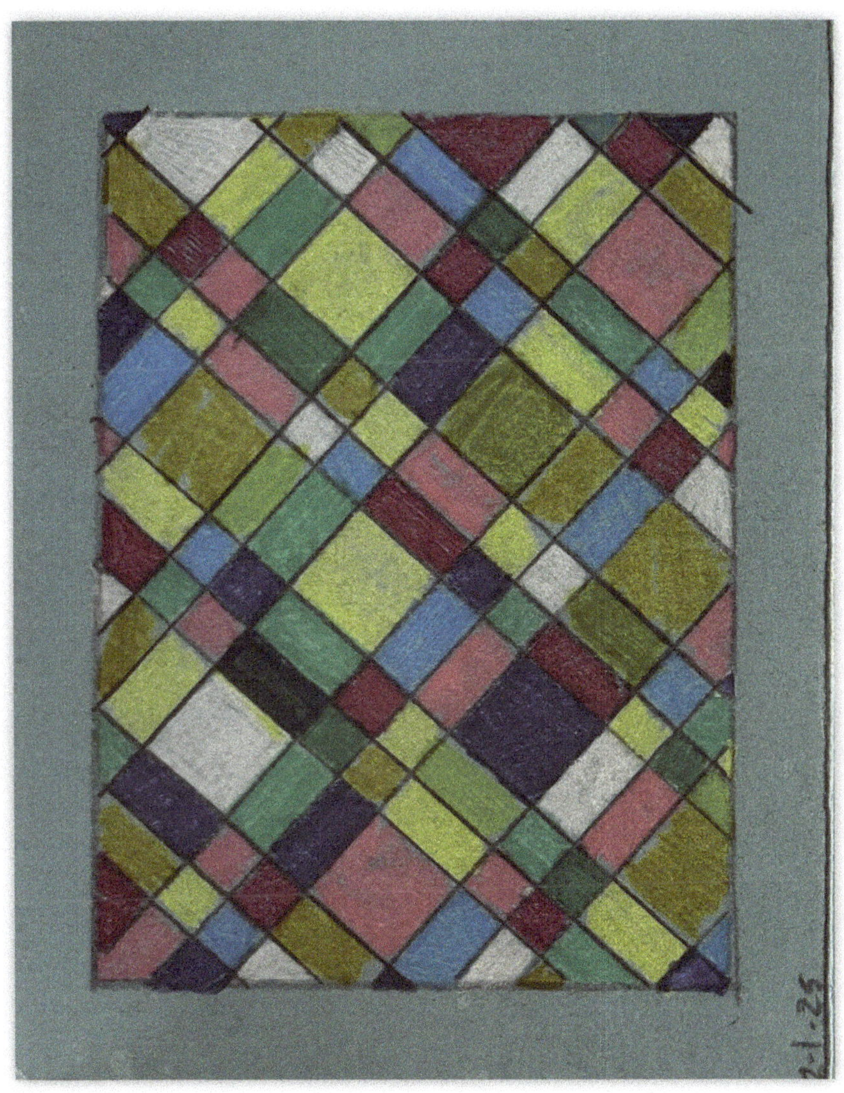

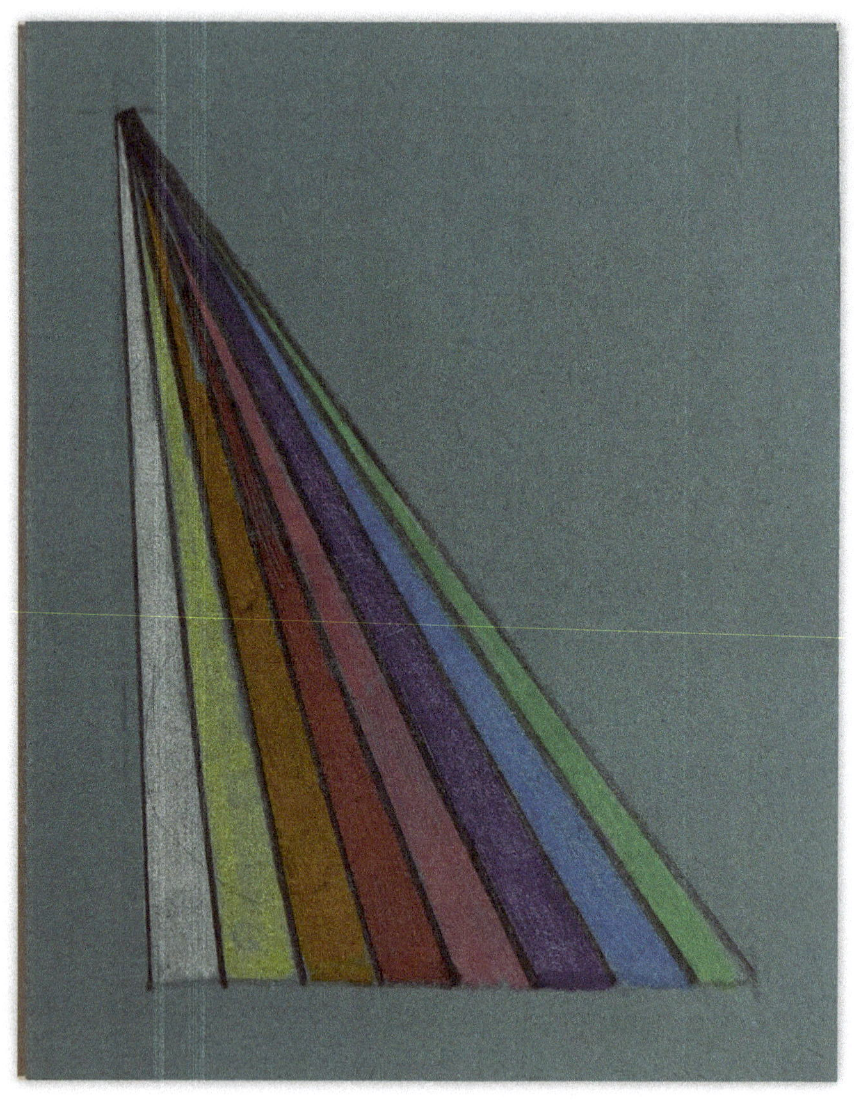

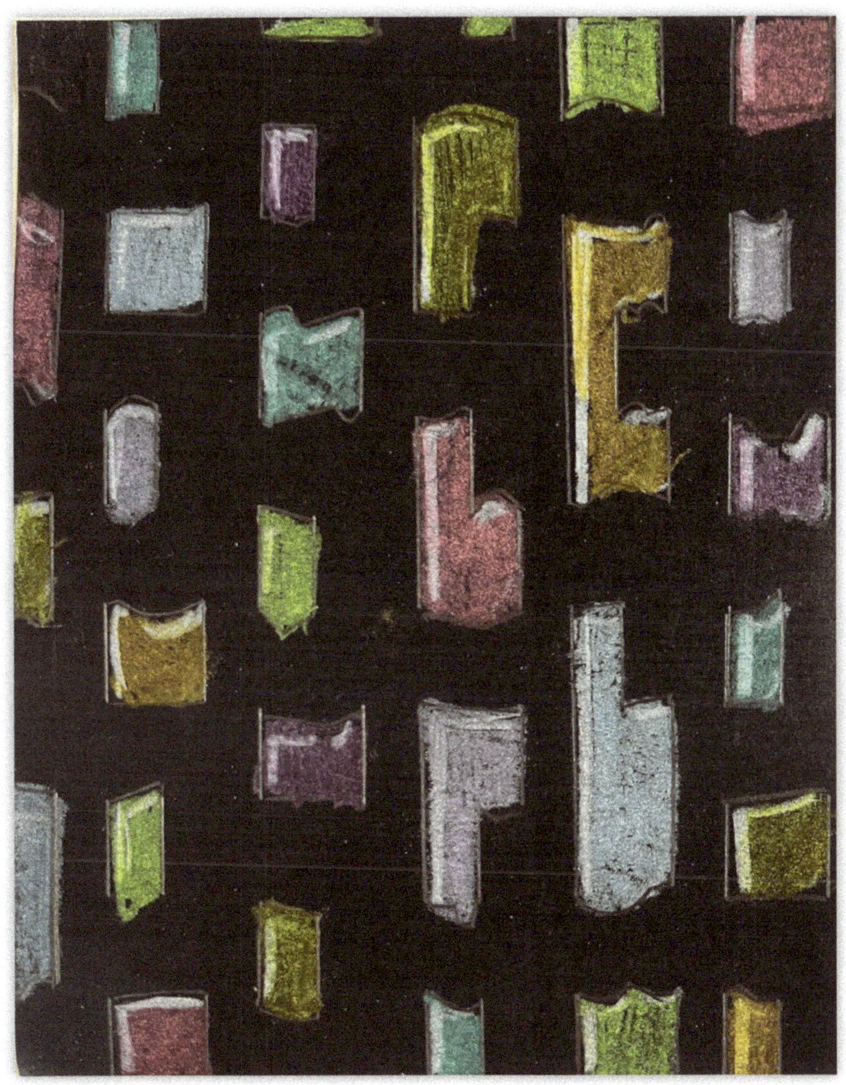

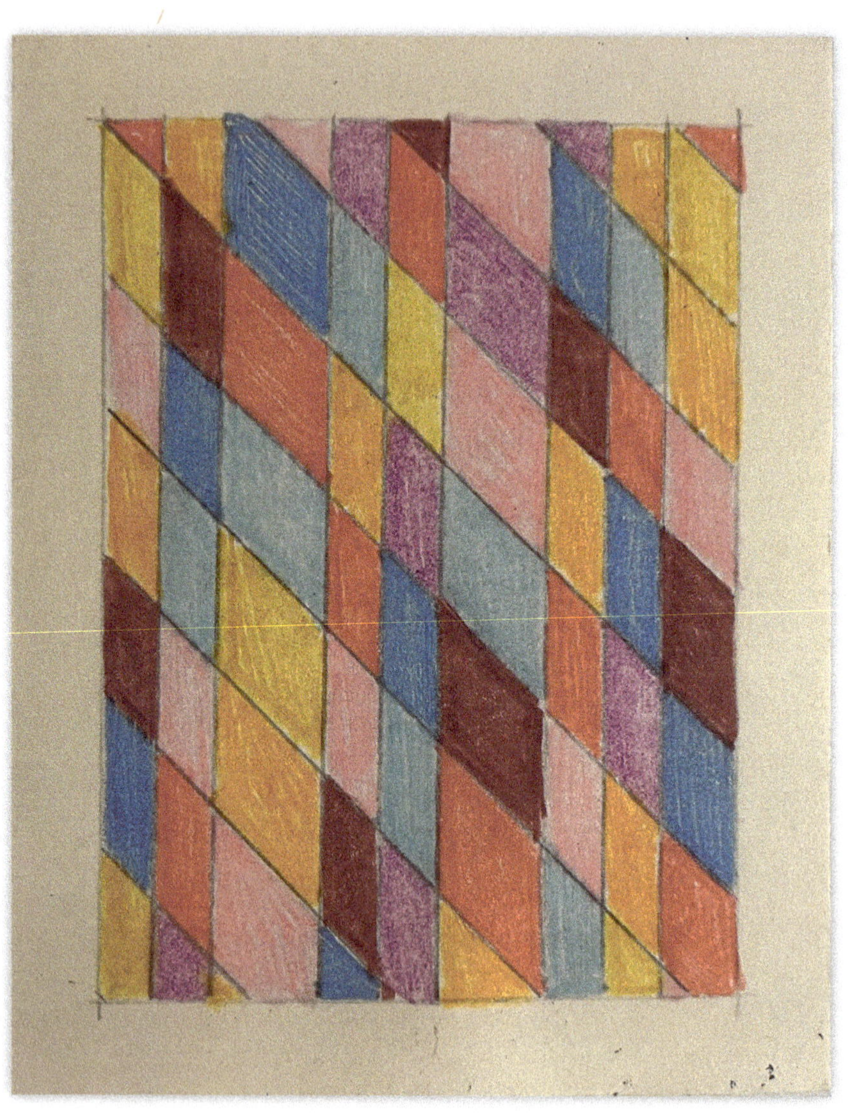

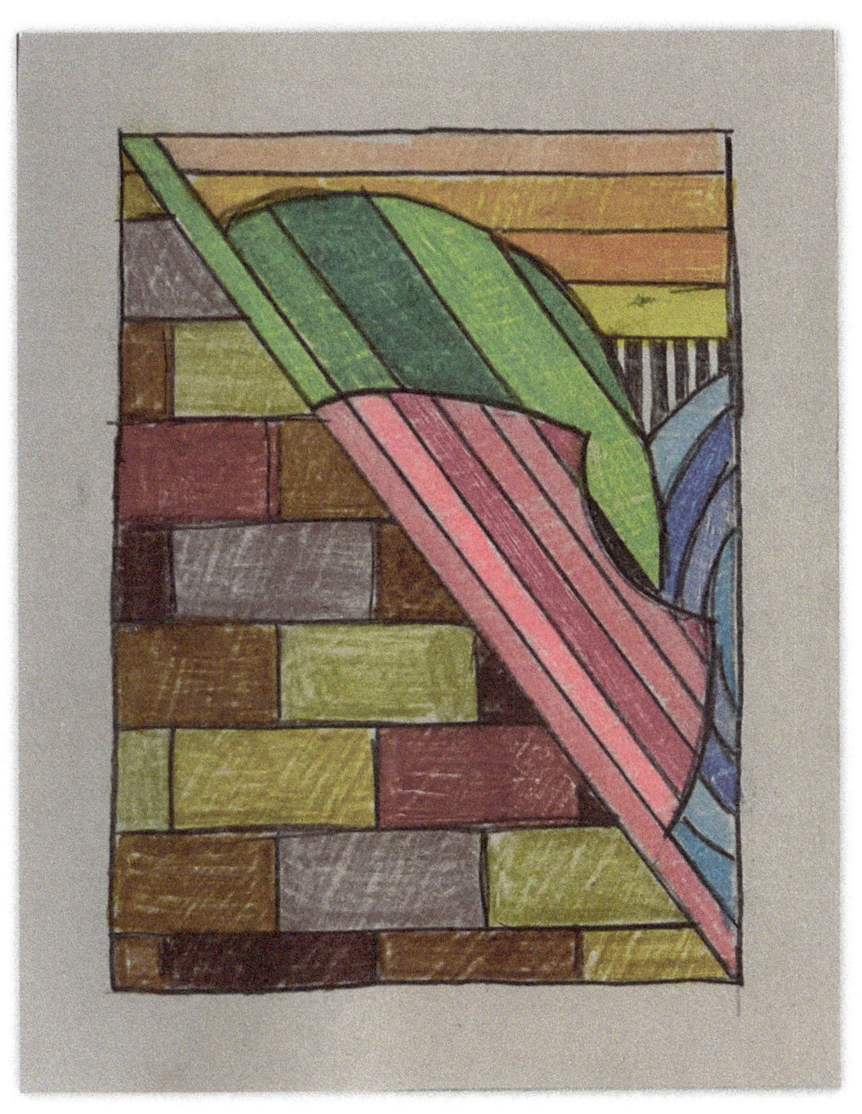

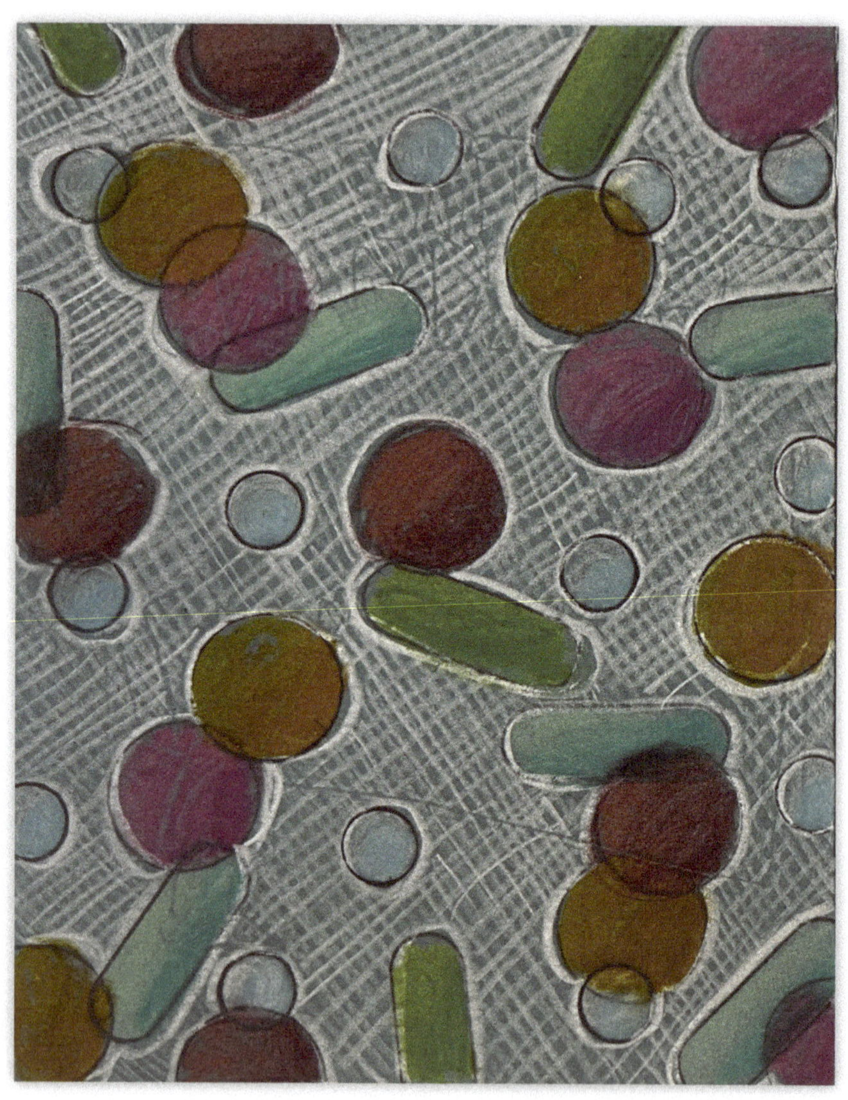

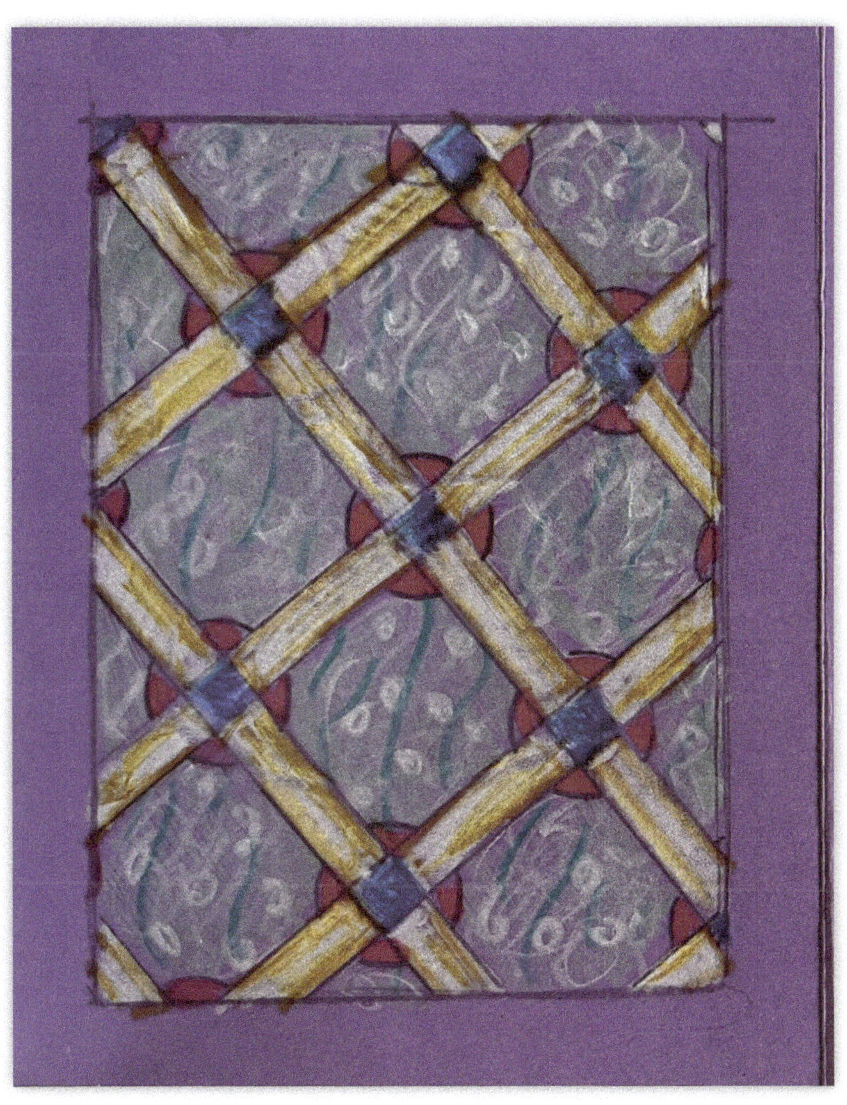

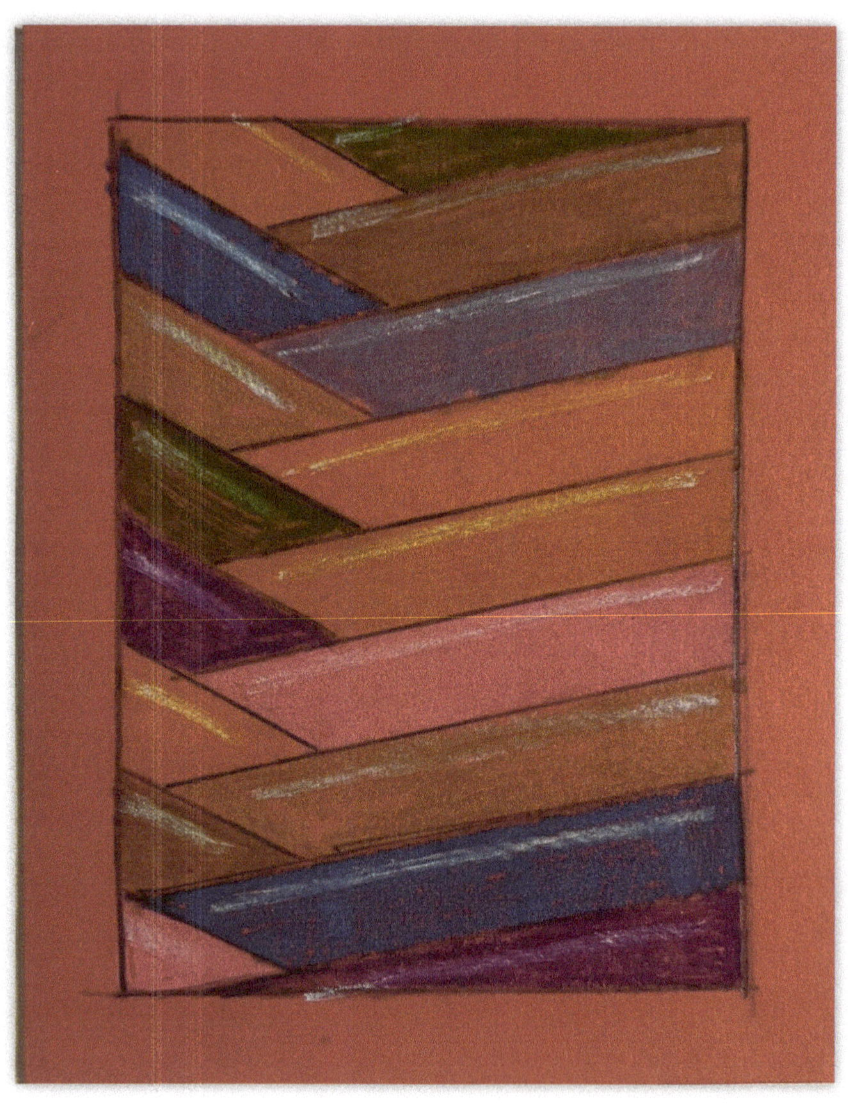

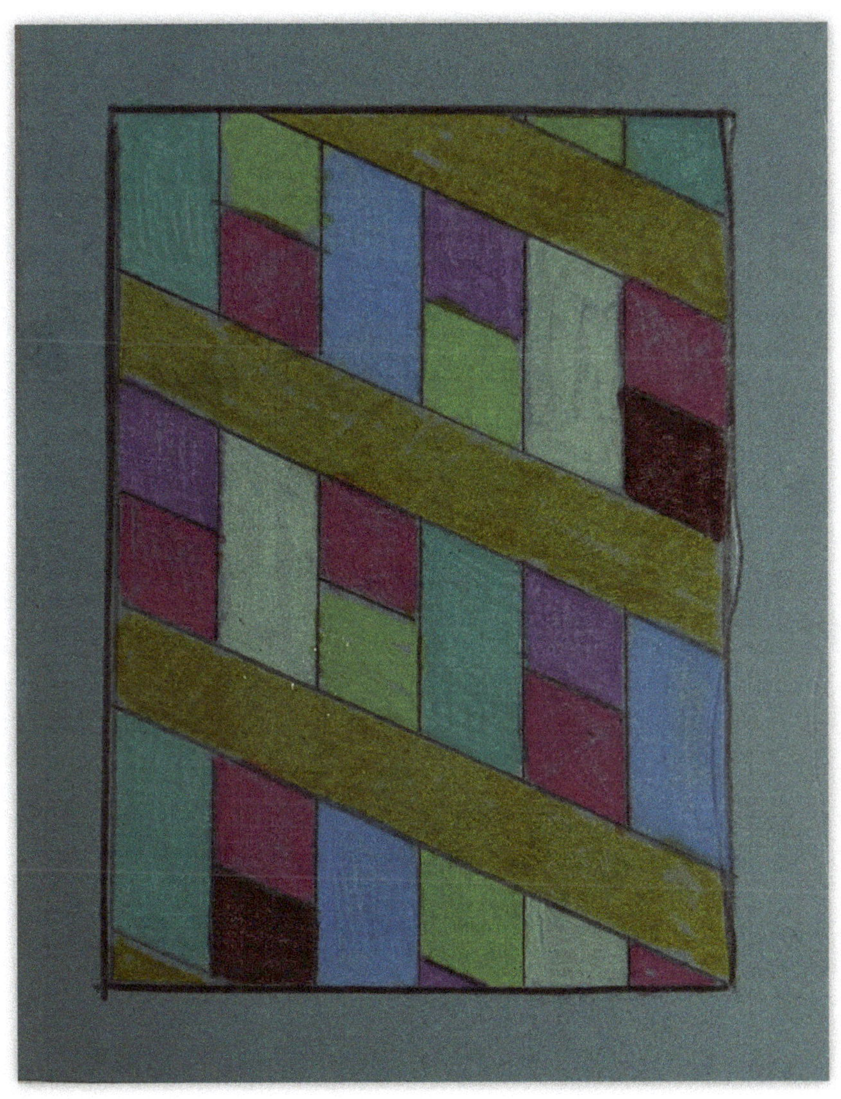

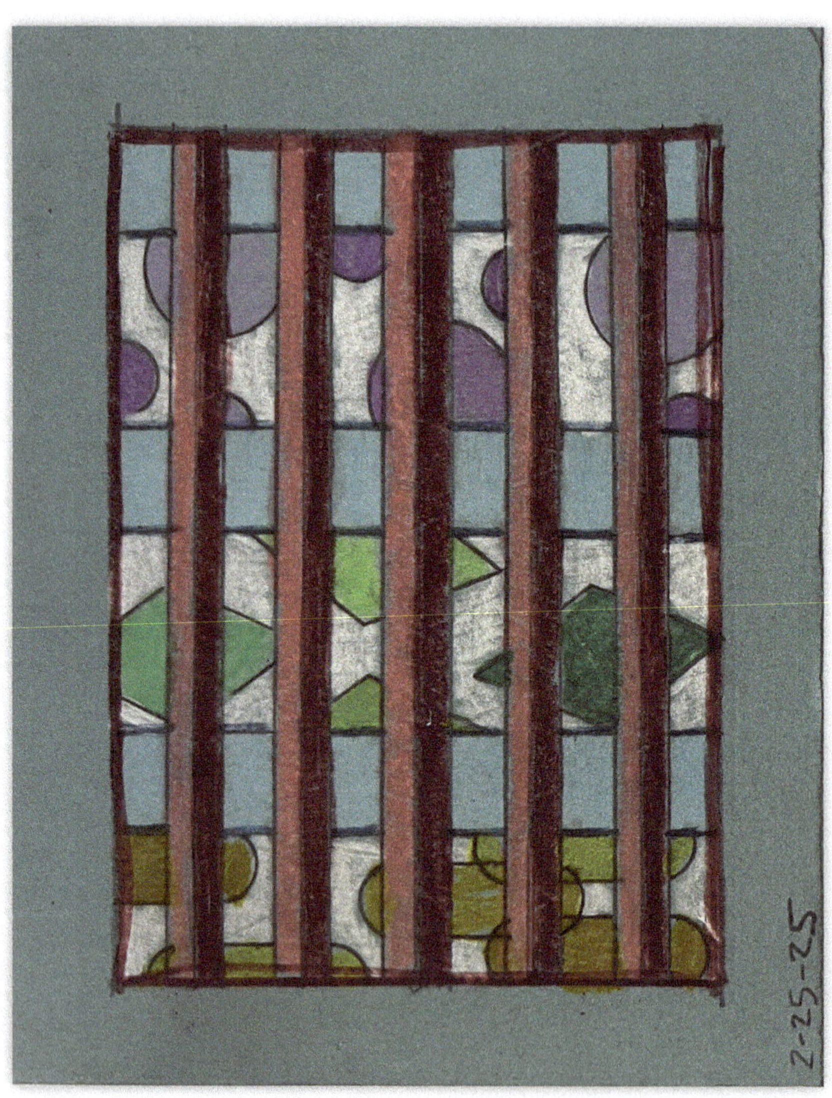

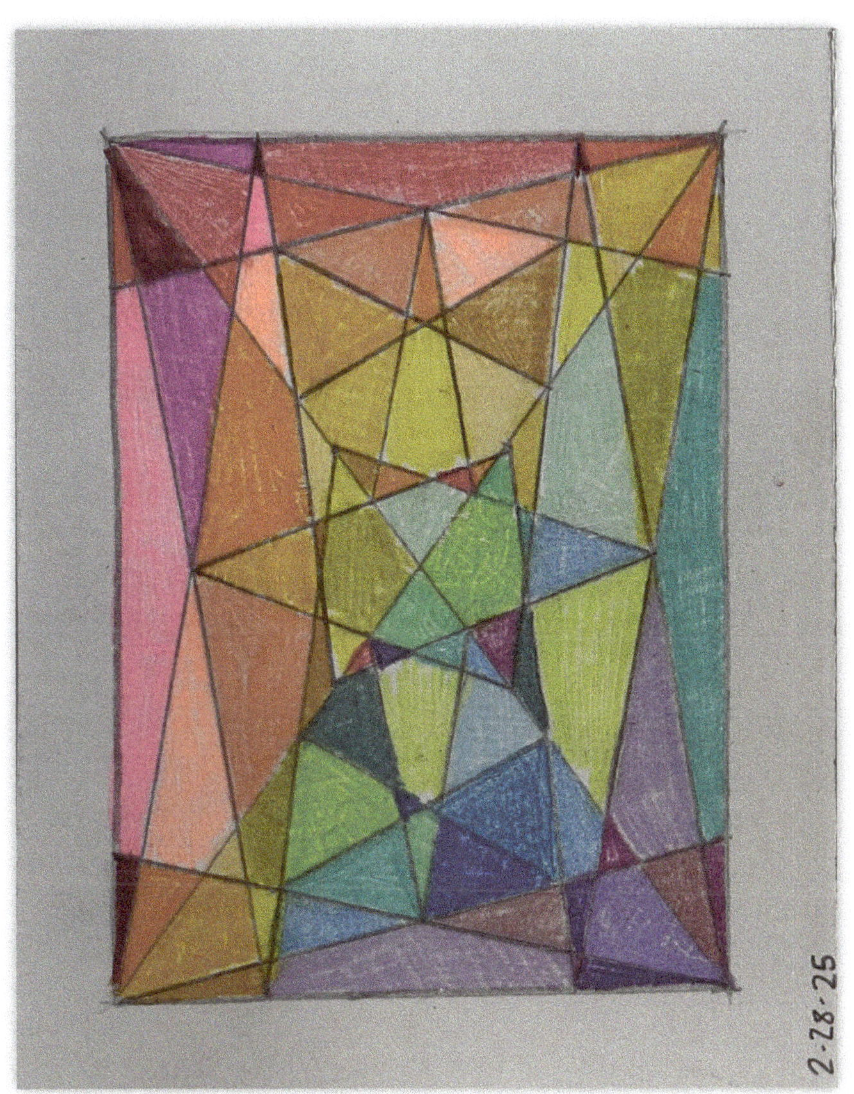

2-28-25

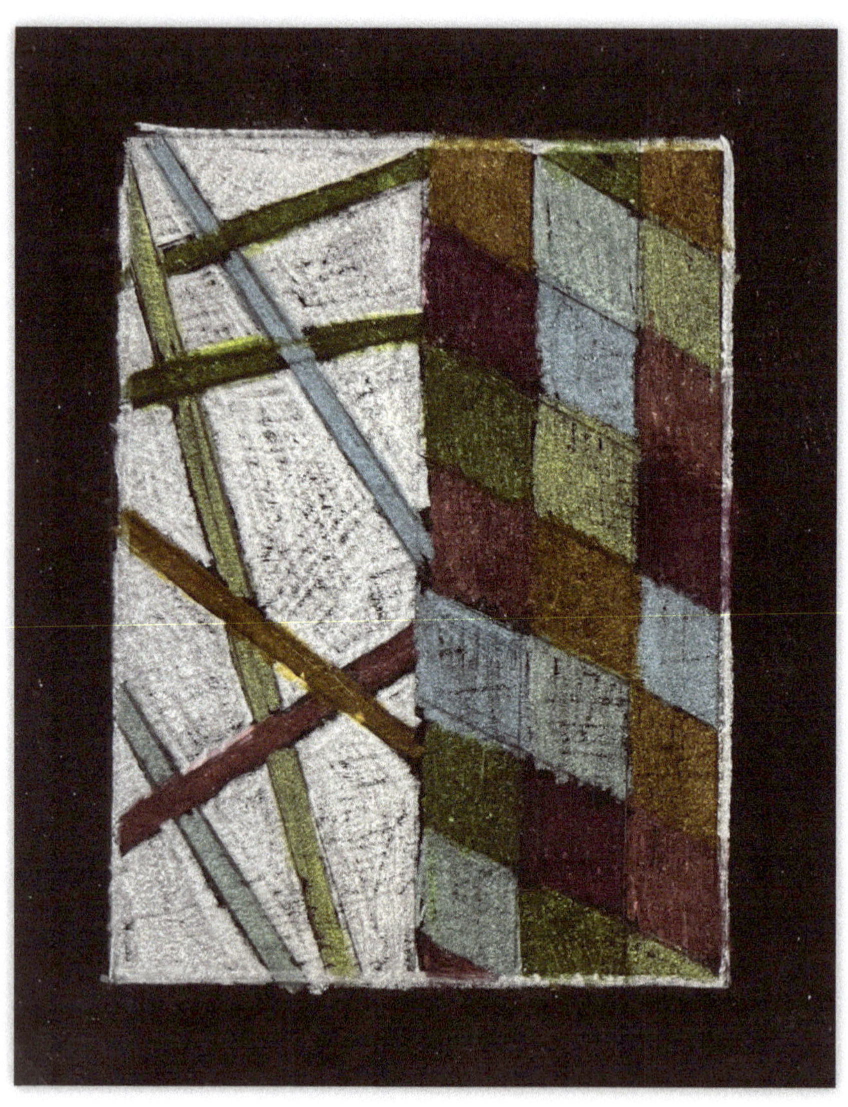

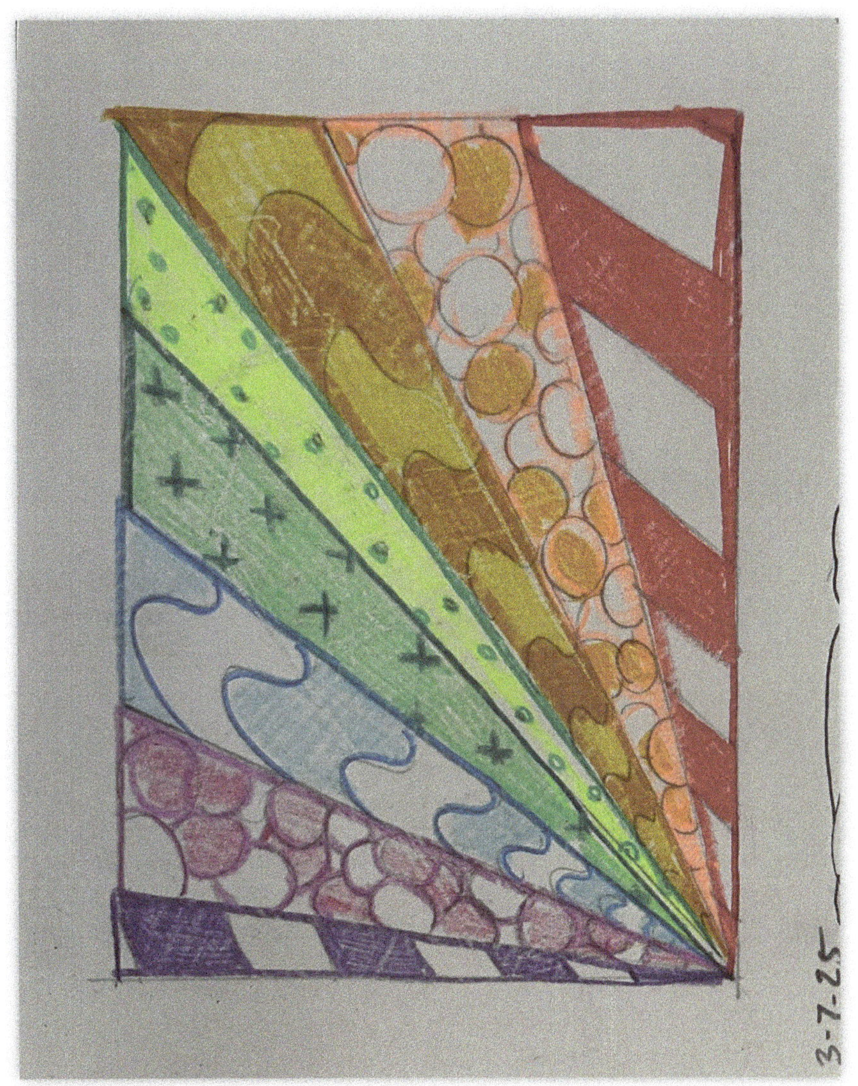

3-7-25

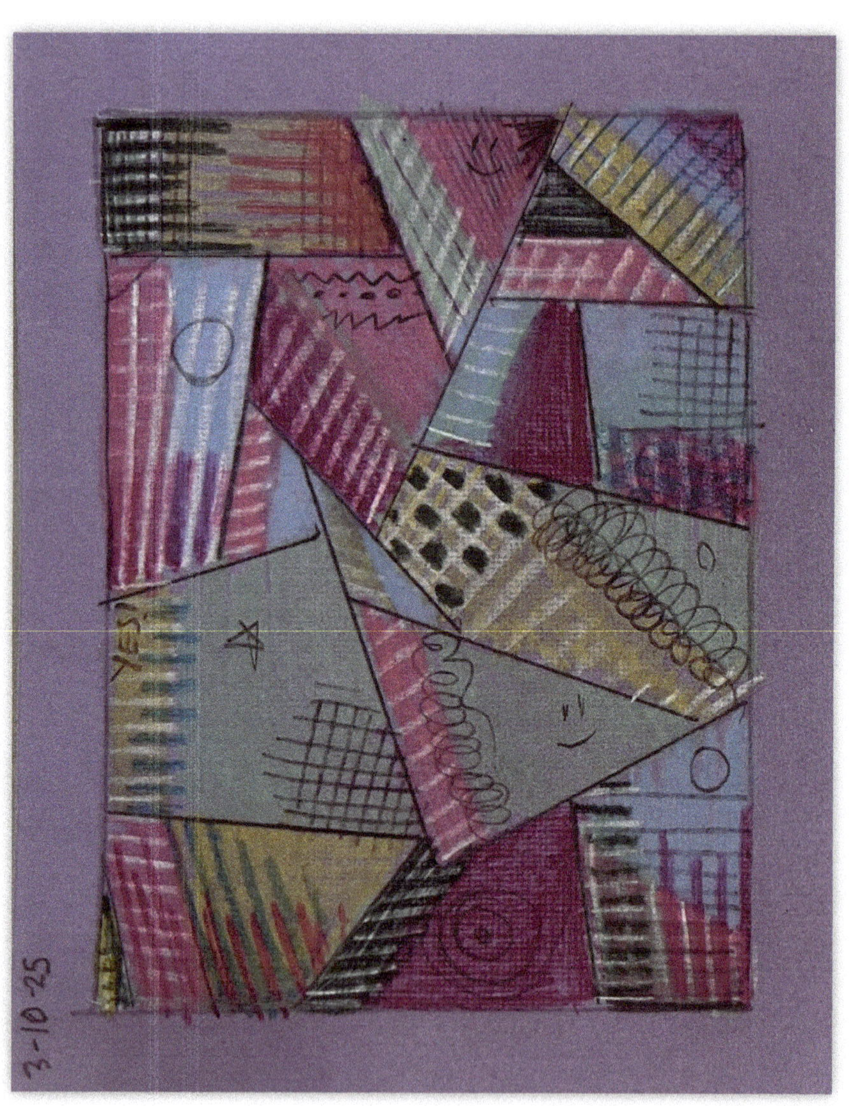

3-10-25

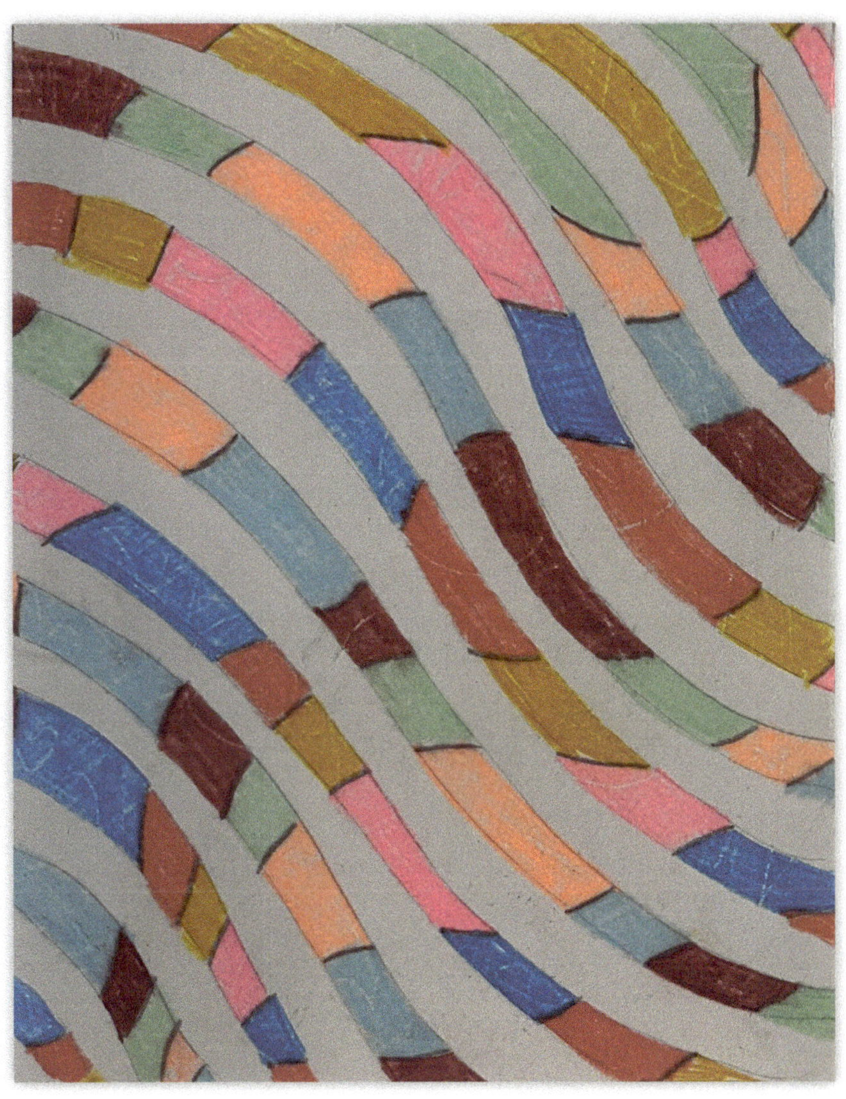

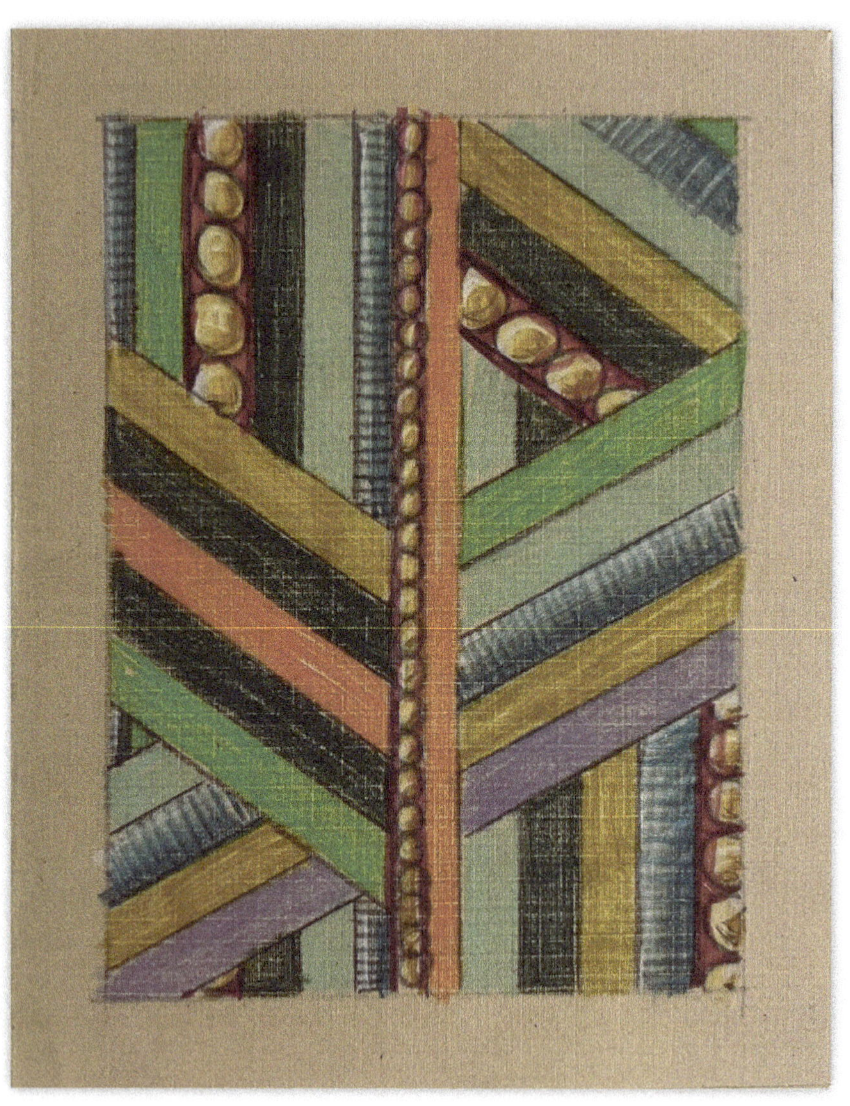

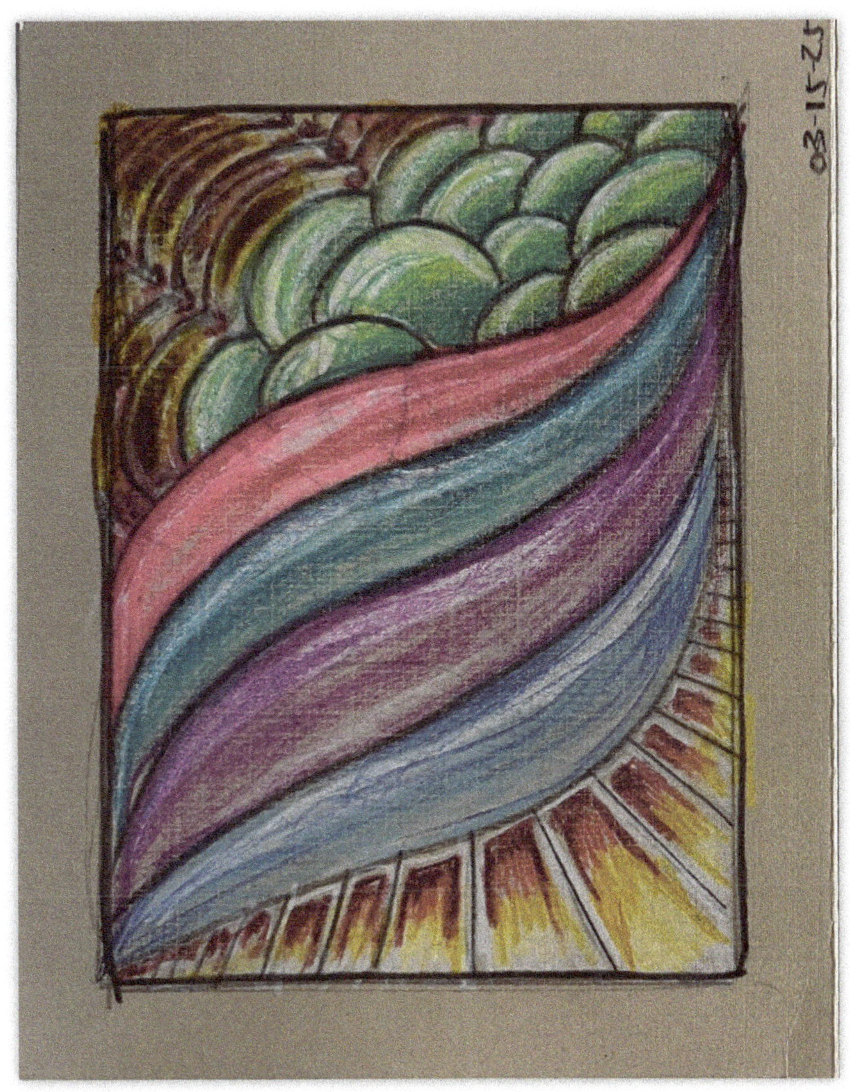

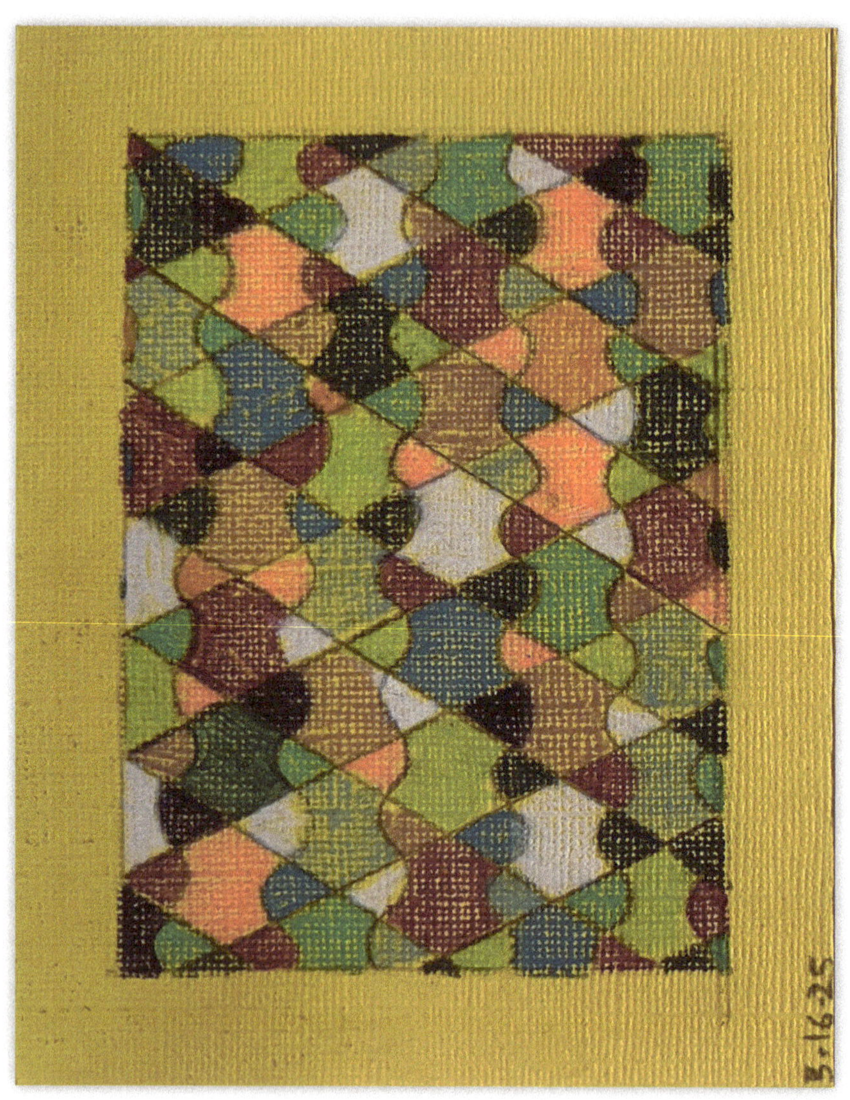

5.16.25

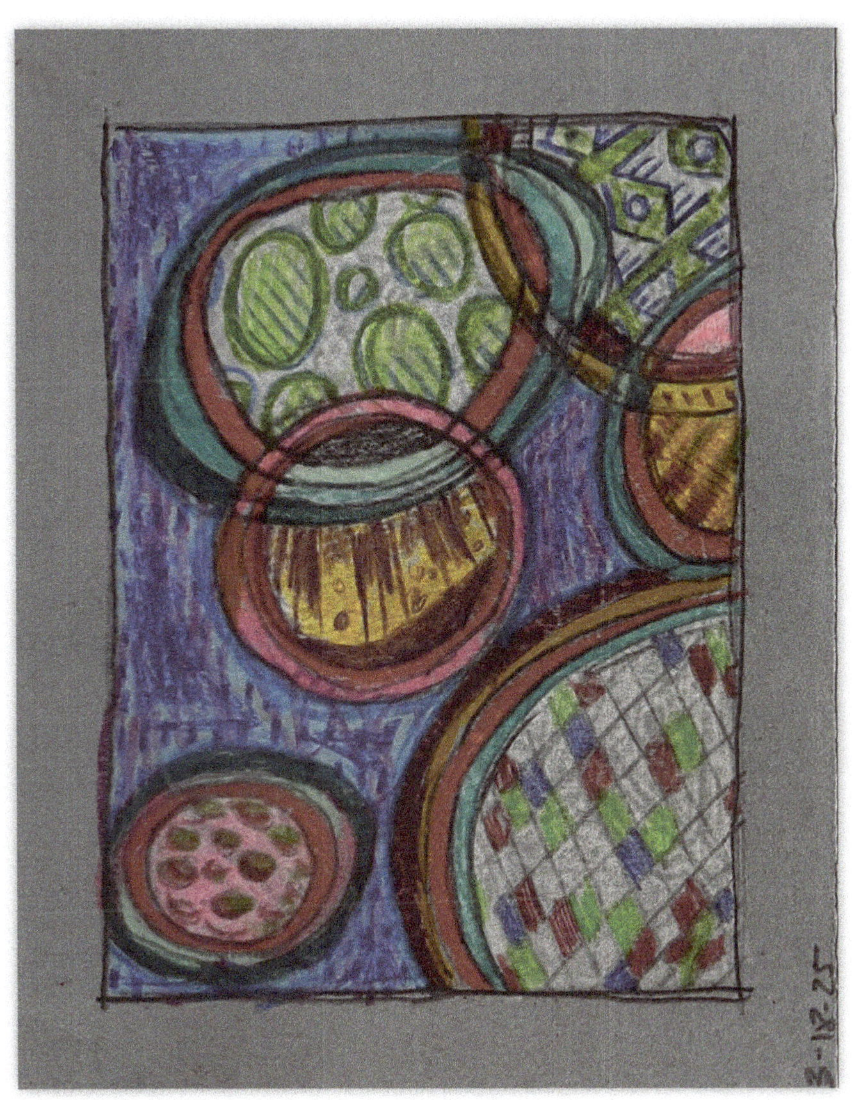

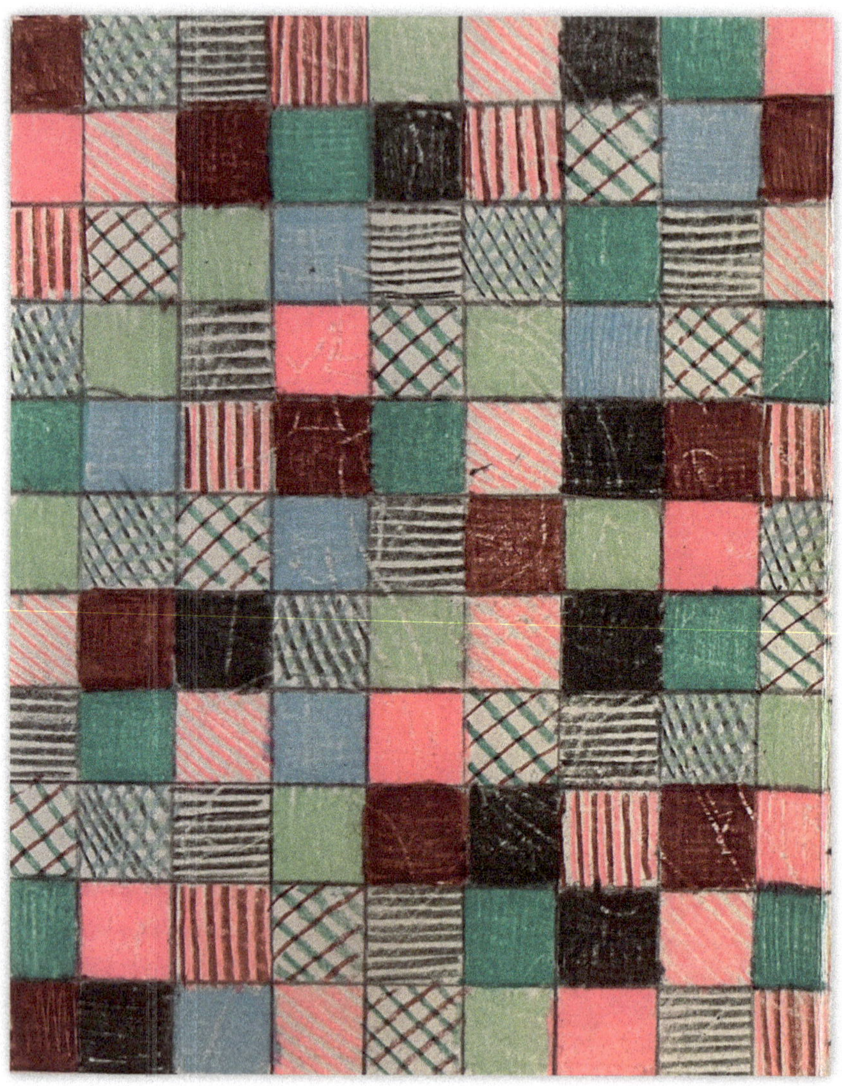

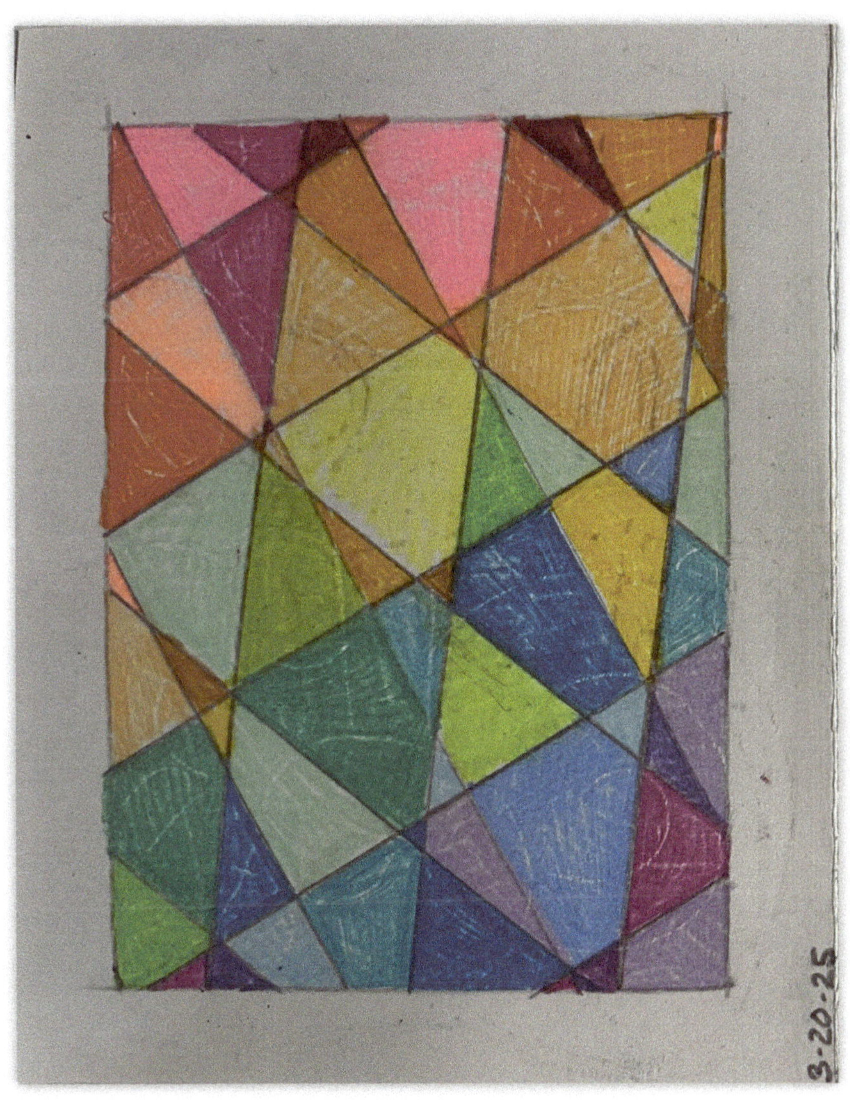
3-20-25

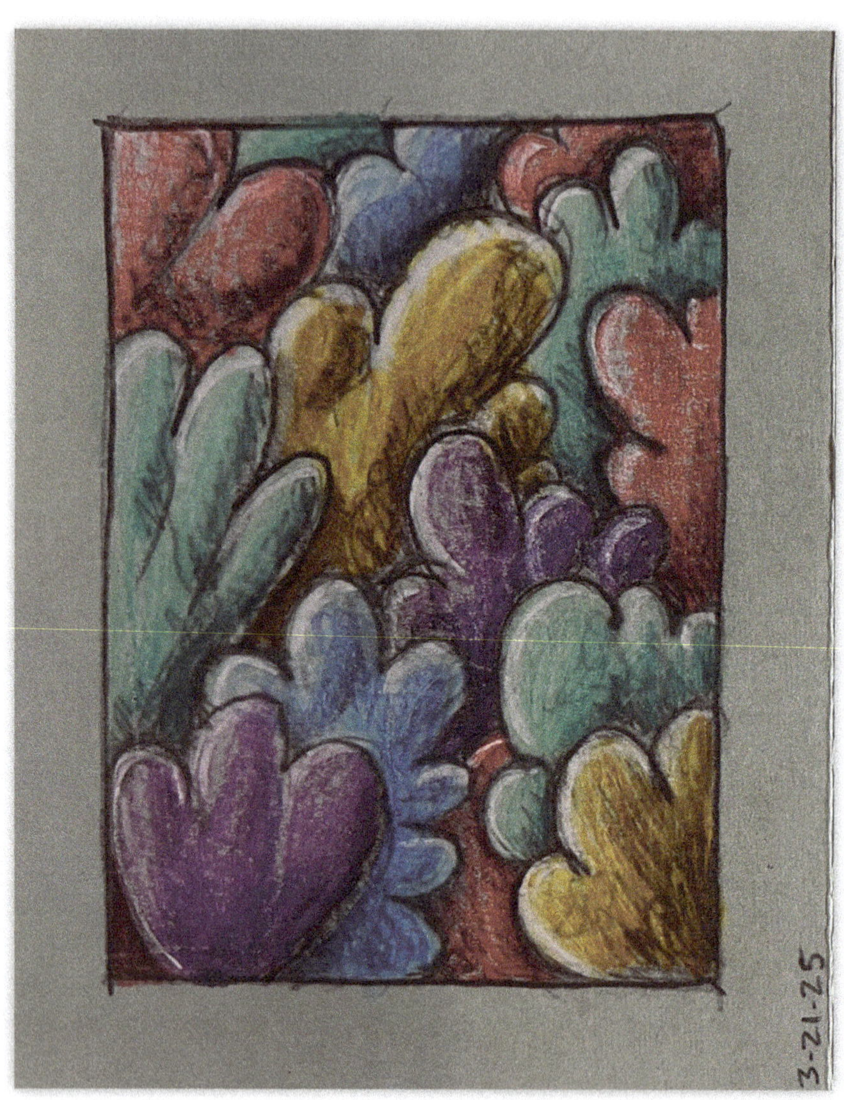

3-21-25

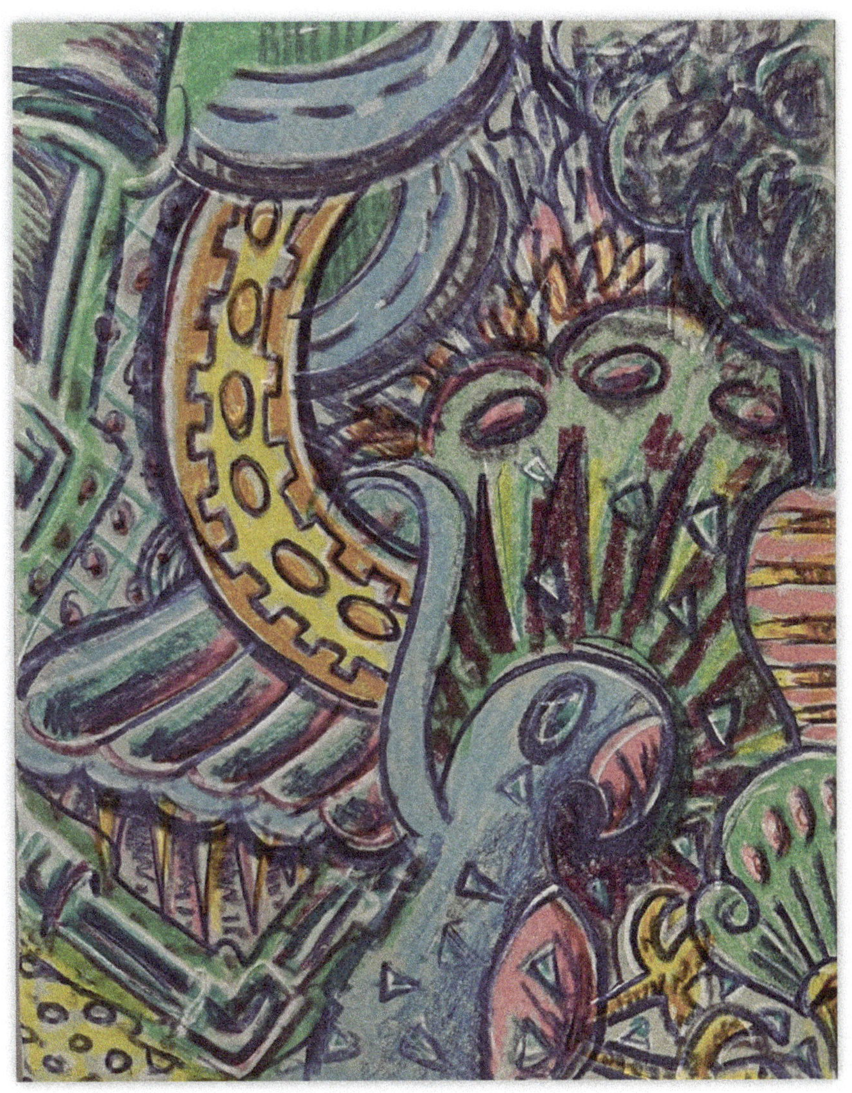

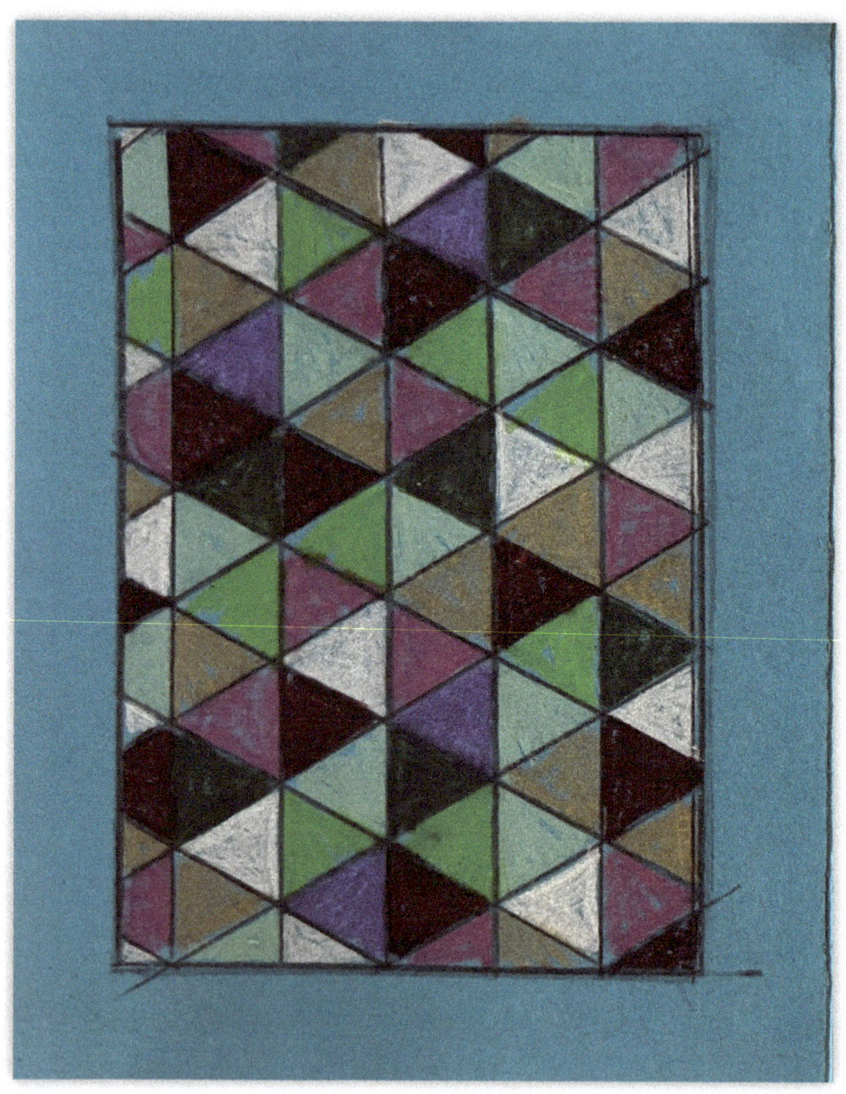

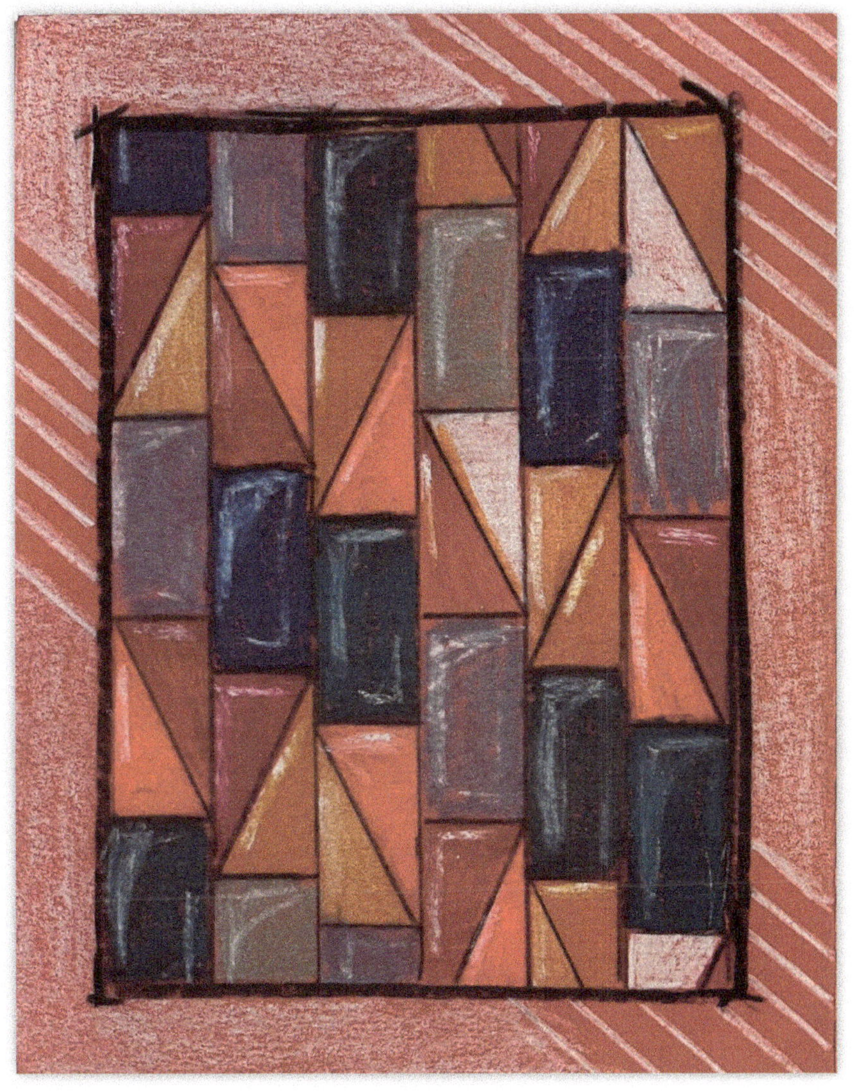

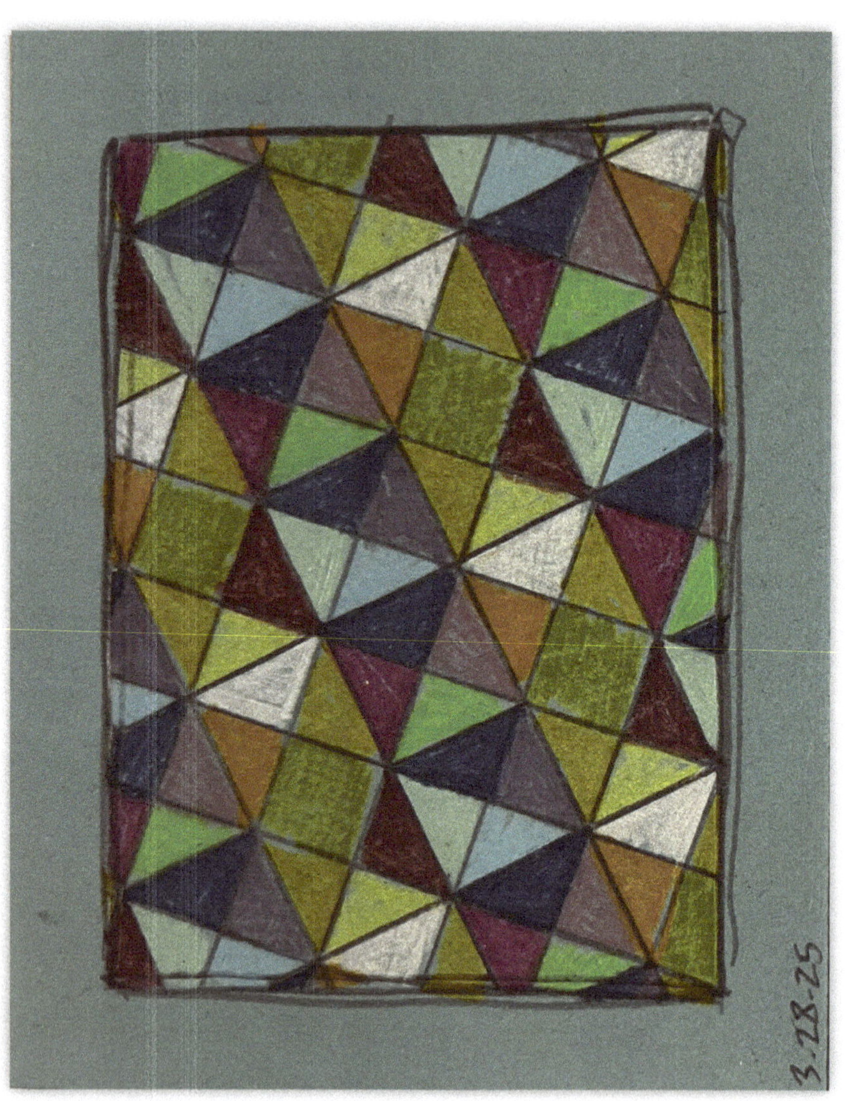

3.28.25

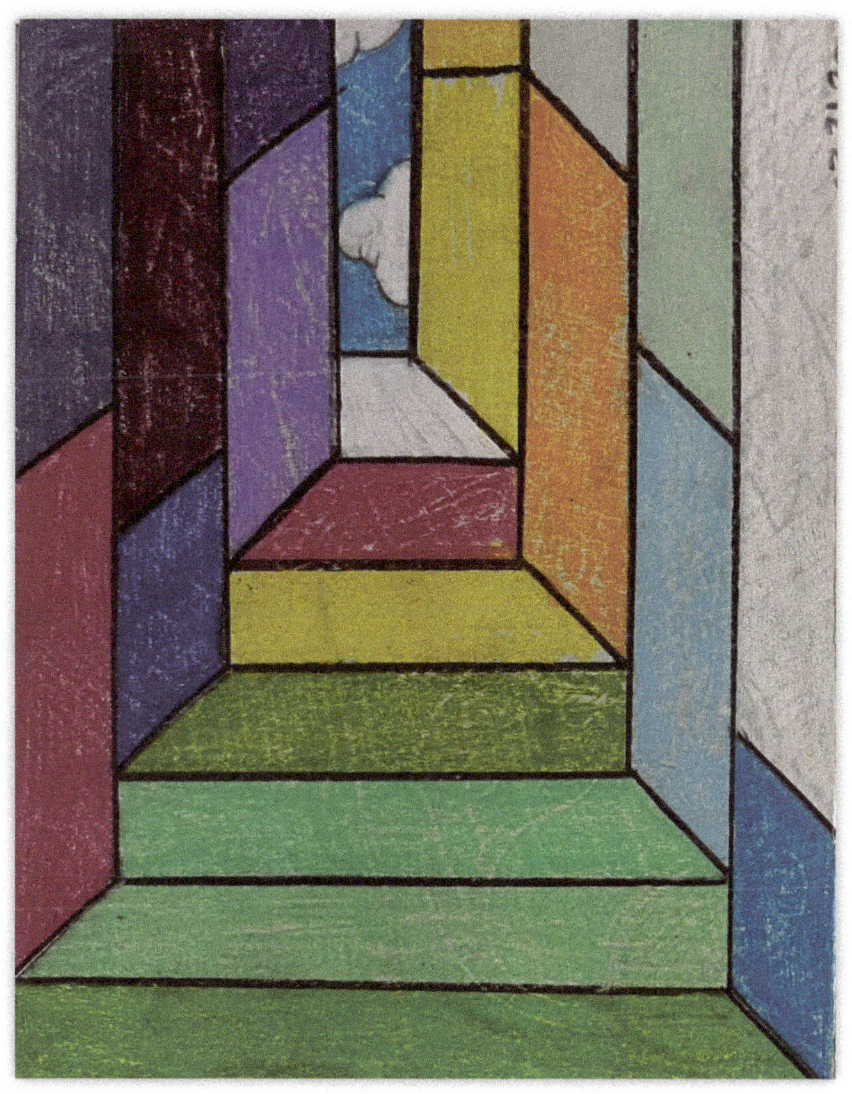

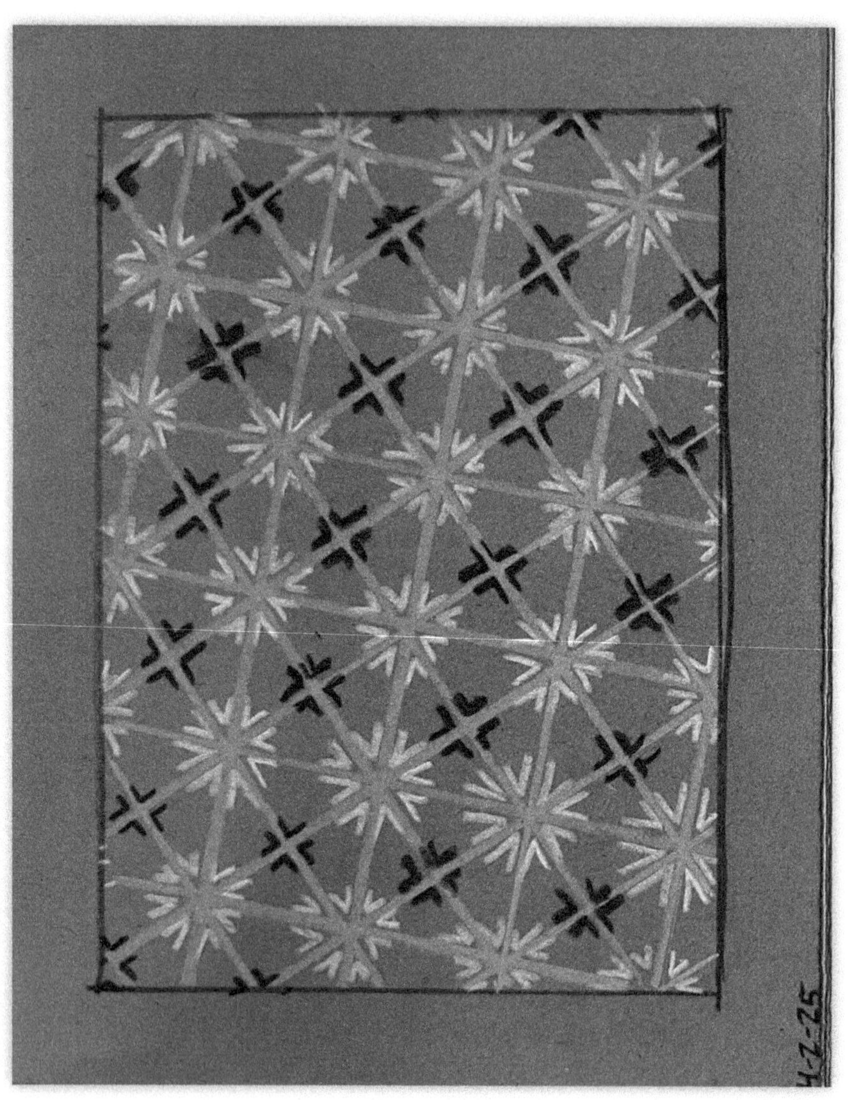

4-7-25

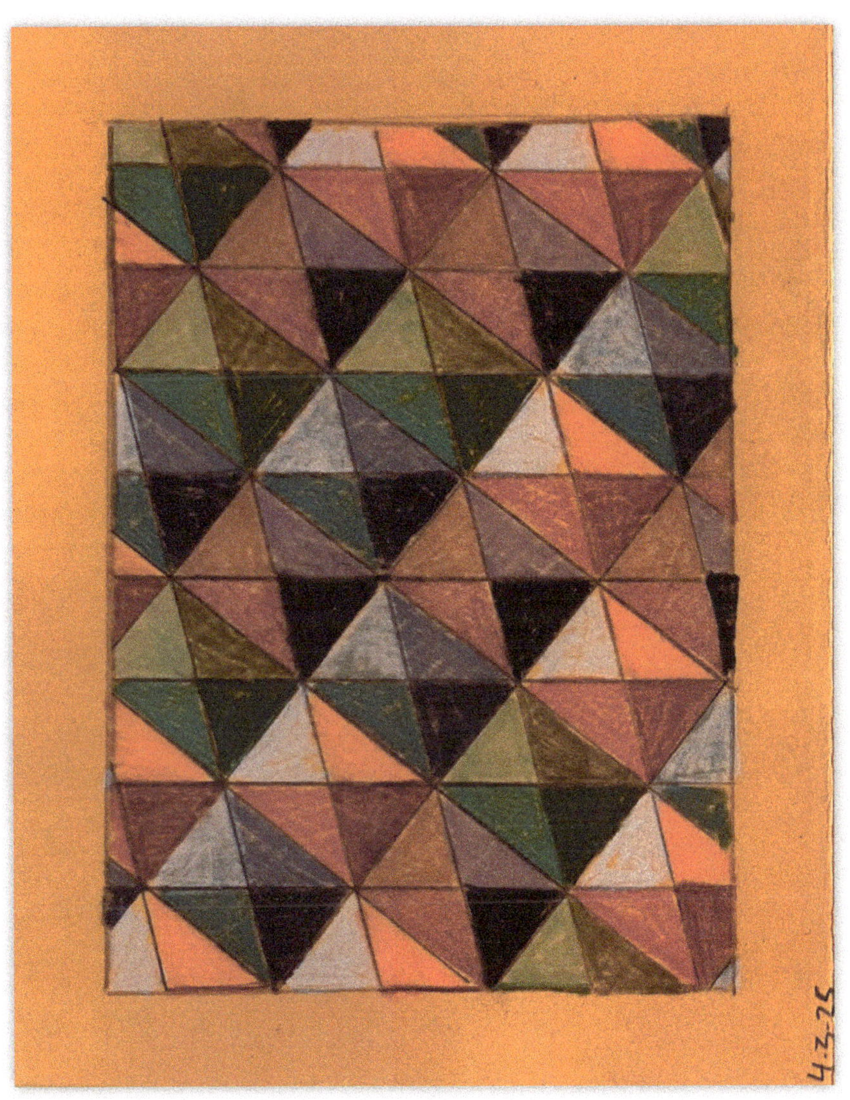

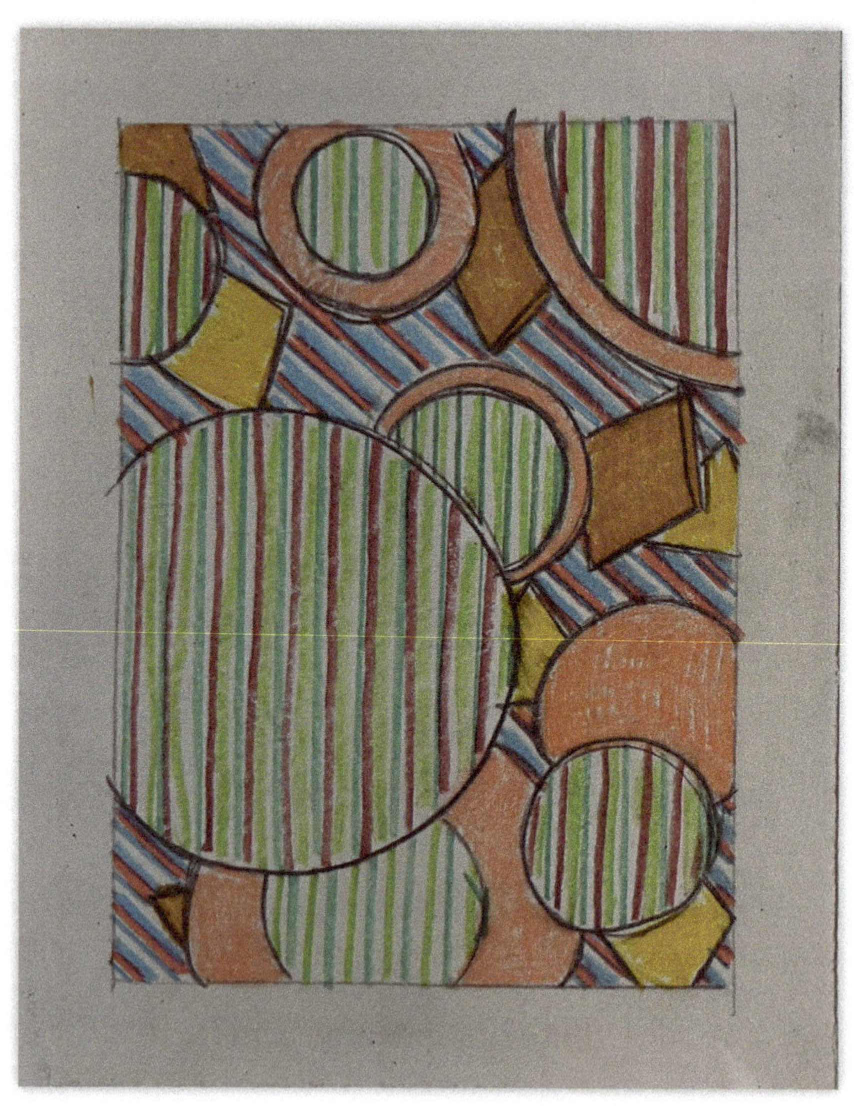

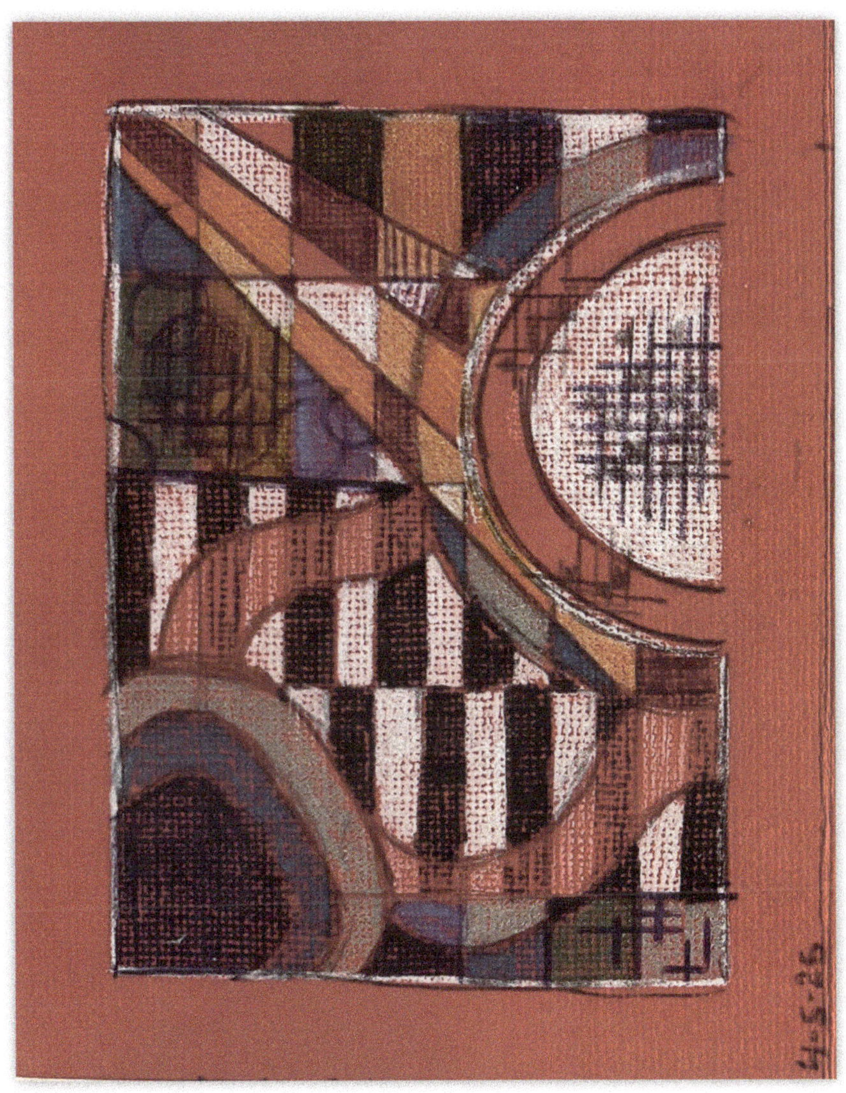

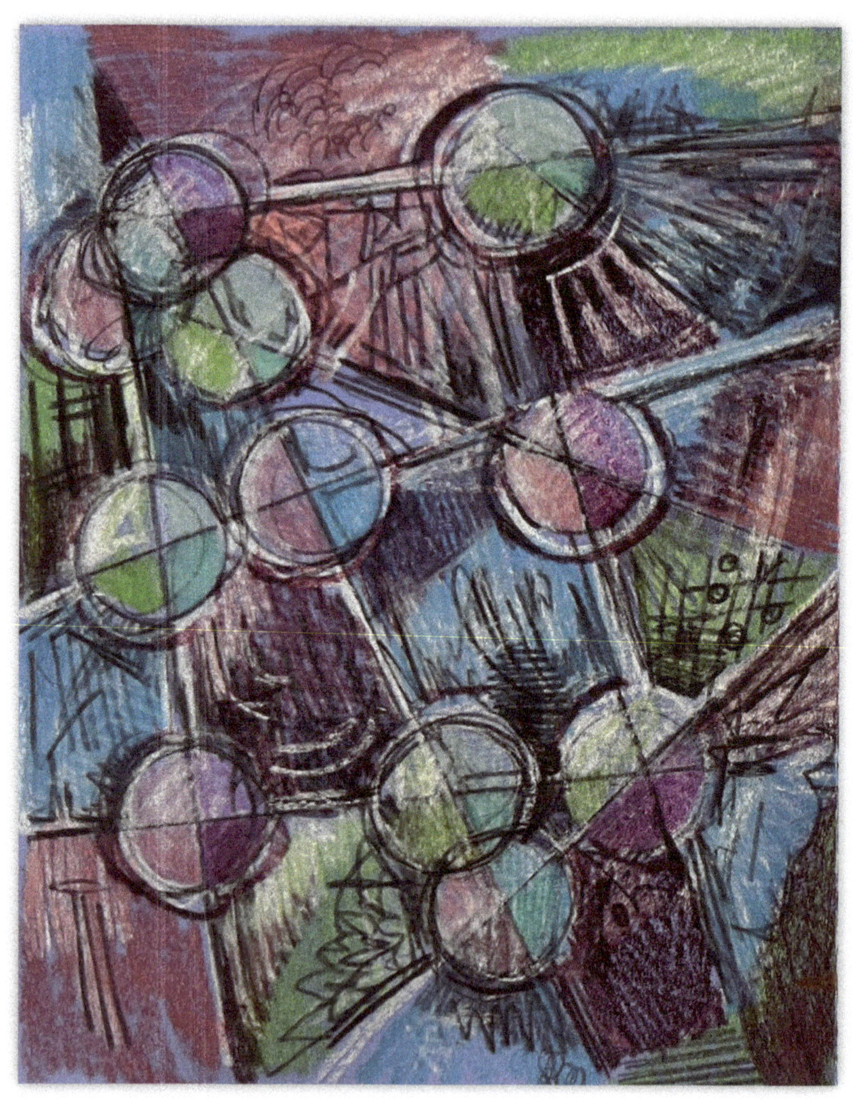

ACKNOWLEDGMENTS

Thank you first to Leana and Illy. You both make me feel like the luckiest man on earth. Thank you to Susie and Randall Moore, Carolyn and Ron Mooradian, Matty Bloom and David Klausner, Lisa Baldwin and Jack Christman, The Steeles, The Campbells.

Thank you to my beta readers who are also my friends:
Autumn Bettinger, Joel De Gan, Adam Oyster-Sands.

Thank you for your friendship and encouragement to Greg Foulkes, Morgan Oyster-Sands, Timur Nowrouz, Gabby and Cloe Merlet, Alex Behr, Matthew Dickman, Cameron and Phi, Jeff Davis RIP, Cody Ross, Matt Riggle, Nathan Holman, Riley Morris, Bri and Sean Reiley, Erin and Taylor Clarke, Dario LaPoma, everyone at JuiceLand, especially the Rodgers, the Turners and Matt Shook, Nettie Tisso, Dylan Stagner, Adam Burden, Trevor Kniffin, Nick Hill, Amanda May, Justin Wilson, the God's Place crew from way back in the day, Kate Jenkins and her family. Naaman and Rodges' and Hayes', Oh my. Thank you to all my friends in DFW and Austin who fill my mind and heart often. We're all growing up, aren't we?

Thank you to Michelle Gutman at Up Up Books, Ali Shaw at Bold Books. Olivia Hammerman at Indigo Consulting, John at Steel Toe Books, everyone I worked with at Picture Frame Press, Jim Ether, Walter O. Beaton, Anne and Miles Johnson, everyone at Sidestreet Arts Gallery, everyone at The Green Microgym on Belmont especially Dan, Jonathan, Doug, and Caitlin. Hmmm, who else? Oh, Friendly Monster Press ...can't forget them.

Thank You, person reading this, for picking up my book, spending time with it, and presumably making me some money along the way.

Thank you, truly, to the ones who keep me believing in tomorrow.

REFERENCES & ALLUSIONS

More information about James Gurney can be found at jamesgurney.com

The lyric I paraphrased in Part Three of "Daily" is from the song "I'll Be Your Man" by The Elected, which you should go listen to.

Jones, Owen. The Grammar of Ornament. 1856. DK Publishing, 2001.

ABOUT THE ARTIST

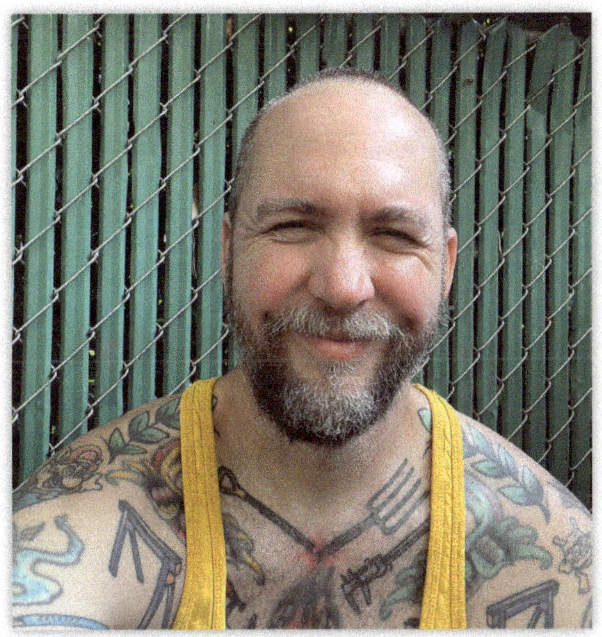

Scott Cannon lives with his partner and daughter in the evergreen city of Portland, OR. He draws, paints, does woodworking, plays piano, writes short fiction and poetry, and publishes whatever he feels like with his friends. He has an alarming amount of tools, Legos, storage containers and horizontal surfaces. Sometimes he goes to the gym.

www.ingramcontent.com/pod-product-compliance
Lightning Source LLC
Chambersburg PA
CBHW050025040726
47599CB00015B/1539